THE CELTIC UNCONSCIOUS

THE
CELTIC
UNCONSCIOUS

Joyce and Scottish Culture

RICHARD BARLOW

University of Notre Dame Press
Notre Dame, Indiana

University of Notre Dame Press
Notre Dame, Indiana 46556
www.undpress.nd.edu

Published in the United States of America

Library of Congress Cataloging-in-Publication Data

Names: Barlow, Richard, 1983– author.
Title: The Celtic unconscious : Joyce and Scottish culture / Richard Barlow.
Description: Notre Dame : University of Notre Dame Press, 2017. |
Includes bibliographical references and index.
Identifiers: LCCN 2016049591 (print) | LCCN 2017005365 (ebook) |
ISBN 9780268101015 (hardback) | ISBN 0268101019 (hardcover) |
ISBN 9780268101039 (pdf) | ISBN 9780268101046 (epub)
Subjects: LCSH: Joyce, James, 1882-1941—Criticism and interpretation. |
English literature—Scottish authors—Influence. | Ireland—In literature. |
Scotland—In literature. | BISAC: LITERARY CRITICISM /
European / English, Irish, Scottish, Welsh.
Classification: LCC PR6019.O9 Z5256816   2017 (print) |
LCC PR6019.O9 (ebook) |
DDC 823/.912—dc23
LC record available at https://lccn.loc.gov/2016049591

Dialogue. 1980. Lilac Doorway U.S.A. Time: Spring.

She: (laying aside a copy of *How to Get Rid of Parasites*) I have been thinking.
What *was* the name of that family that was always in trouble over there in Europia?

He: (seizes jug) You're asking me.

She: The man had a wall eye, I think. Was it Wallenstein?

He: (replaces jug) Jucious!

She: Jucious! That was the name. I knew it had something to do with Scotland.

—James Joyce,

from a letter to Eugene Jolas, 1940; *LI*, 417

CONTENTS

ACKNOWLEDGMENTS

A version of the first chapter appeared as "Crotthers: Joyce's Scots Fellow in *Ulysses*," *Notes and Queries* 57, no. 2 (2010): 230–33. A short version of chapter 2 appeared as "'Hume Sweet Hume': Skepticism, Idealism, and Burial in *Finnegans Wake*," *Philosophy and Literature* 38, no. 1 (2014): 266–75. Chapters 3 and 4 contain sections which appeared in "The 'united states of Scotia Picta': Scottish Literature and History in *Finnegans Wake*," *James Joyce Quarterly* 48, no. 2 (2011): 305–18. A version of chapter 5 appeared as "James Macpherson in *Finnegans Wake*," *Founder to Shore: Cross-Currents in Irish and Scottish Studies*, ed. S. Alcobia-Murphy et al. (Aberdeen: Research Institute of Irish and Scottish Studies, 2011), 33–42. An early version of chapter 5 appeared in "Joyce's Burns Night," *Papers on Joyce* no. 17/18 (2011/2012): 279–311. Part of the conclusion appeared as "What Might James Joyce Have Made of 21st-century Scottish Independence?," *Guardian*, January 31, 2014. I'm grateful to the editors of these publications.

Special thanks to Brian Caraher for his supervision and support during my time at Queen's University Belfast and to Stephen Little and everyone at University of Notre Dame Press. I'd also like to express my gratitude to Willy Maley for all his help over the last few years. Thanks to Niall Whelehan and Nicholas Allen for helpful advice on the manuscript. In the Joyce and Irish studies community my appreciation goes to John McCourt, Michael McAteer, David Dwan, Paul Fagan, and Laura Pelaschiar. Thanks also to Neil Murphy, C. J. Wee Wan-Ling, and Terence Dawson at the Division of English, Nanyang Technological University. I am grateful to QUB and NTU for funding different stages of this project, to Nicole Ong for proofreading the manuscript, and to Bob Banning for copyediting and valuable suggestions. I'd also like to thank the anonymous readers who read my manuscript for University of Notre Dame Press. My friends and family in Aberdeen, Edinburgh, Limerick, Galway, London, and Singapore have put up with a lot of talk about Joyce over the years, so thanks to them. Above all, I would like to express my deepest thanks to Guinevere for her many years of help, encouragement, and support. This book would not have been written without her help.

This is dedicated to Niamh and Clodagh.

A lion beag is bheagan, mar a dh' ith an cat an t-iasg.

ABBREVIATIONS

CP	Joyce, James. *Collected Poems*. New York: Viking Press, 1957.
CSD	Robinson, Mairi, ed. *Concise Scots Dictionary*. Edinburgh: Polygon at Edinburgh, 1999.
CW	Joyce, James. *The Critical Writings of James Joyce*. Edited by Ellsworth Mason and Richard Ellmann. New York: Viking Press, 1959.
D	Joyce, James. *Dubliners*. London: Penguin, 2000.
FW	Joyce, James. *Finnegans Wake*. New York: Viking Press, 1939. Citations are made in the standard fashion, i.e., page number followed by line number.
JJI	Ellmann, Richard. *James Joyce*. New York: Oxford University Press, 1959.
JJII	Ellmann, Richard. *James Joyce*. Rev. ed. New York: Oxford University Press, 1982.
LI, LII, LIII	Joyce, James. *Letters of James Joyce*. Vol. I, edited by Stuart Gilbert. New York: Viking Press, 1957. Vols. II and III, edited by Richard Ellmann. New York: Viking Press, 1966.
OCPW	Joyce, James. *Occasional, Critical, and Political Writings*. Edited by Kevin Barry. Oxford: Oxford University Press, 2000.
OED	Online edition of the *Oxford English Dictionary*.
P	Joyce, James. *A Portrait of the Artist as a Young Man*. London: Penguin, 2000.
PE	Joyce, James. *Poems and Exiles*. London: Penguin, 1992.
U	Joyce, James. *Ulysses*. Edited by Hans Walter Gabler. Corrected text. New York: Random House, 1986. Citations are made in the normal way: episode number followed by line number.

Introduction

Joyce, Celticism, and Scotography

Over the past few decades the critical conception of James Joyce as a detached, apolitical, and denationalized writer has been abandoned. Works such as Emer Nolan's *James Joyce and Nationalism* (1995), Vincent Cheng's *Joyce, Race, and Empire* (1995), Trevor Williams's *Reading Joyce Politically* (1997), and Andrew Gibson's *Joyce's Revenge* (2002) have placed Joyce's work firmly within political contexts and into the vexed debates of postcolonial discourses. According to Leonard Orr, "it will surprise most readers to note how recent the concept of a political Joyce is. . . . Critics of the 1950s through 1970s treated Joyce as either entirely disinterested in politics or having only a superficial understanding [of] matters outside of literature and aesthetics" (Orr, 1). Furthermore, Joyce's specific cultural and historical context—his background in late nineteenth- / early twentieth-century Ireland—has been given much greater attention. Gregory Castle has commented that "Joyce's Irishness, when it is not subordinated to considerations of style and narrative, frustrates those critics who wish to read his work in the context of an Anglo-European tradition of modernism that eschews the local in favor of a pan-historical universalism" (*Modernism*, 208).

Naturally, as part of this relatively new presentation of Joyce as a writer engaged with the themes of imperialism, colonialism, and Irish history, a great deal of attention has been paid—in theory—to Joyce's commentary on Britain. Unfortunately, what this has almost always meant in practice is the production of work on Joyce and England. See for example the absence of any real deconstruction of the term Britain in Andrew Gibson and Len Platt's *Joyce, Ireland, Britain* (2006). As a result of this critical neglect, a crucial area of Joyce studies has been left totally underdeveloped, namely the matter of Joyce and Scotland. And as Willy Maley points out, "the separateness of Scotland from the rest of Britain has, along with its affinities with Ireland, been rendered invisible in much history and criticism" ("Kilt by Kelt," 202). This is despite the fact that, for example, "Ireland . . . was a lordship of the English crown from the twelfth to the sixteenth centuries while Scotland enjoyed relative autonomy" (203). Maley argues that "any critique of the British state has to be thoroughgoing. It cannot stop at 1800, or at Ireland" (203).

Why is a consideration of Joyce and Scotland important for an understanding of modern(ist) literature? There are two main reasons. First, the work of writers such as James Hogg, David Hume, and Robert Louis Stevenson provided Joyce with the means with which to create what I call a de-Anglicized unconscious in *Finnegans Wake*. The double consciousness and radical interiority of *Finnegans Wake* is partly based on Scottish (and therefore, for Joyce, "Celtic") precedents. As any student of Irish literature or modernism knows, Ireland and her history are near obsessions in Joyce's texts. So, a second reason to consider the relationship between Joyce and Scotland is that in order to gain a comprehensive overview of Joyce's commentary on Irish history it is necessary to view all of the separate political and cultural relationships at work in the Atlantic archipelago—including the vital Irish-Scottish connection—rather than concentrating narrowly on the singular English/Irish colonial interface. As the historian J. G. A. Pocock has noted, "'British history' itself has in the past denoted nothing much more than 'English history' with occasional transitory additions" (Pocock, 77). However, the convenient, simplistic, and incorrect conflation or interchanging of the terms "Britain" and "England" in Joyce studies (see, for one example in a general myriad, Nolan, *Nationalism*, 215–16) is not conducive to a thorough understanding of the representations of Ireland's past that underpin *Ulysses* and *Finnegans Wake*. As Maley has written, "Cyclopean Joyceans holding to a singular vision of Ireland and Panoptic Joyceans wishing to cut him loose from any national moorings are ill-equipped to discern divisions within British identity. Joyce, on the other hand, is famously adept at seeing double" ("Kilt by Kelt," 203). In line with developments in the study of "British" history such as Pocock's treatment of an archipelagic "plural history" (29) and developments in politics such as the advent of Scottish Devolution in 1999, the Scottish Independence Referendum of 2014, or the 2016 EU "Brexit" crisis, the time is ripe for a "devolved" and unpacked reading of Joyce and Scottish culture. As Pocock argues, "there was, and still is, no 'British history' in the sense of the self-authenticated history of a self-perpetuating polity or culture. The term must be used to denote a multiplicity of histories, written by or (more probably) written about a multiplicity of kingdoms and other provinces" (75).[1]

The critical discussion of Joyce and Scotland is relatively unheard of. Maley's groundbreaking essay on Joyce and Scotland, a piece by Scott W. Klein examining Walter Scott's influence on *A Portrait of the Artist as a Young Man*, and Anne Marie D'Arcy's article in *The Review of English Studies* on the two-headed octopus of *Ulysses* are the very small number of available attempts at discussing the Scottish aspects of Joyce's work. As Maley points out, a silence on the topic of Joyce and Scotland has been part of a larger problem: "Those engaged in Irish studies appear reluctant to enter into dialogue, or 'proximity talks,' with Scotland, and for good historical reasons, for their own standpoints depend upon an unproblematized Anglo-Irish relationship and a safe and smooth passage between 'English' and 'British' paradigms. The significant works on Ireland in recent years have largely ignored the impact and influence of Scotland" ("Kilt by Kelt," 203–4).[2] Maley wrote his essay in the late '90s. Since then, the larger issue of a lack of critical material bringing Scotland into the Irish studies equation has been addressed to some extent by the inauguration of a combined Irish and Scottish studies field. The cooperation of Queen's University Belfast, Trinity College Dublin, and the Research Institute of Irish and Scottish Studies at the University of Aberdeen has resulted in the production of a great deal of work on the area Maley delineated in his essay. But with regard to the particular scotoma of Joyce and Scotland, there have been precious few developments.

The "unproblematized Anglo-Irish relationship" Maley describes is well demonstrated by the volume *Joyce, Ireland, Britain*, which, regrettably, hardly bothers to mention Scotland at all. None of the essays in this volume actually address the issue of Joyce's views on Ireland's relationships with the various countries and cultures found across the Irish Sea. The supposed aim of the collection of essays is described in the foreword: "Joyce is placed in four widening circles: as an English writer, as an Anglo-Irish writer, as a European, and as a citizen of the world. The first of these is not a misprint: part of this book's genius is to refocus critical attention on Joyce's affinities with English culture" (Knowles, vii). Certainly Joyce was influenced by English culture, but that hardly makes him an English writer or a "British Irishman" (Gibson and Platt, 47). Furthermore, his decision not to avail of an Irish passport after the establishment of the Free State does not mean that he did not consider himself an Irishman: "He may have been a British subject, but he was scarcely a patriotic one" (A. Gibson, *James Joyce*, 107). With regard to culture, how could any writer growing up under the British Empire avoid English culture? In *Ulysses*, as Andrew Gibson has demonstrated in *Joyce's Revenge*, English culture is very often "defaced" or purposefully contaminated (182). Furthermore, the case for "affinities" can also be overstated. For example, and as I shall discuss later, it is remarkable how uninterested Joyce is in English philosophy. And as he remarked to Arthur Power, "It is my revolt against the English conventions, literary and otherwise, that is the main source of my talent" (quoted in Golden, 429). See also the following: "I cannot express myself in English without enclosing myself in a tradition" (*JJII*, 397); "I have little or nothing to learn from English novelists" (*LII*, 186); and "To me . . . an Irish safety pin is more important than an English epic" (*JJII*, 423). Joyce is also reported to have described English novels as "terribly boring" (*JJII*, 233) and English literature as "pompous and hypocritical" (*CW*, 212). [3]

In any case, the foreword of *Joyce, Ireland, Britain* does not really apply to the content of the essays. The introduction to the volume promises to address the "complications of British-Irish" politics:

> Complication is partly what emerges from this collection as a whole. In this respect, it does something to mirror what have traditionally been and still are (at times forbidding) ramifications and complications of British-Irish politics. *Joyce, Ireland, Britain* is centrally shaped by the notion that to think of Joyce in relation to Ireland

also requires that we think of him in relation to Britain, not least because Ireland as Joyce knew it for most of his life was still in some degree a part of Britain. These relations are nothing if not intricate, nuanced, ambivalent, even byzantine. The subject is explicitly treated in only one section of the book, "British-Irish politics"—the others are "Joyce and English Culture" and "Joyce, the Local, and the Global"—but the political theme is never far from the surface. (Gibson and Platt, 20)

Of course, Gibson and Platt are correct to assert that we must think of Joyce in relation to Britain as well as to Ireland while also embracing "complications" (Gibson and Platt, 20). However, in many ways, the volume avoids intricacies. In the book's introduction Britain and Ireland are described as "two different constituencies" (Gibson and Platt, 23). That is a stunning oversimplification, especially appearing as it does in a book that claims to be dealing in complications. In relation to Scotland, the writers of *Joyce, Ireland, Britain* have kept to the "unproblematized" position Maley has described, largely equating Britain with England. Joyce's texts outline much more complicated relationships involving the various societies and cultures of the Atlantic archipelago rather than narrowly focusing on connections between English politics and culture and their counterparts in Ireland. Scotland's distinctness (its long and separate pre-Union history; its detached religious, legal, and education systems; its particular philosophical and cultural traditions; its different languages; its own interactions with other European nations) is totally overlooked in *Joyce, Ireland, Britain*. I suggest it would be advantageous for Joyce's students to consider Britain as a multination state consisting of distinct nations—in line with modern historians such as Pocock—rather than as one indivisible entity or "constituency" à la Gibson and Platt. Moreover, all of these nations have had different and complicated historical relationships with Ireland. In other words, Joyceans should start treating Britain as a multination state rather than as a nation-state. Throughout his work, in his fiction and his nonfiction, Joyce himself approaches Scotland, England, and Wales as distinct entities.[4] This work will be operating in the same manner since it will be a more appropriate method for dealing with the "complications" of Joyce's texts.

There are few countries in the world where the Irish have had such a long-standing impact as in Scotland. Since Joyce's massive, all-encompassing text *Finnegans Wake* is so concerned with Irish history, it follows that Scotland would have a significant presence in the work, that the work would demonstrate a "caledosian capacity" (*FW*, 187.07). Commenting on Joyce's *supposed* lack of engagement with Scottish issues and on the work of Willy Maley, Edna Longley has written: "On the one hand, Joyce is perfectly entitled to 'overlook Scotland.' On the other hand, when 'Irish nationalist critics' also overlook Scotland, or notice it selectively, it is precisely owing to Presbyterian Scotland's complicity in 'plantation and partition.' It is because 'Scotland and Ulster' lurks in 'Scotland and Ireland'" (Longley, 157).

No, Joyce is categorically *not* entitled to overlook Scotland. Not if he wants to create an in-depth and comprehensive vision of Irish culture and history in *Finnegans Wake*, an assignment that is evidently a crucial part of the overall enterprise. As Pocock writes, "no nation's history can be understood without that of its interaction with other histories" (Pocock, 94–95). So how can we hope to understand fully Joyce's view of Irish history if we fail to grasp his representations of Ireland's inter-actions with the histories of other nations? As for negligence in "Irish nationalist critics" towards Scotland, Scottish involvement in the "partition and plantation" in the north of Ireland is more—not less—of a reason to consider Scotland when engaged in Irish studies (especially the study of *Finnegans Wake*, a text composed in the years following the partition of Ireland). In short, the new "Irish," more local readings of Joyce cannot function properly and completely without a clear understanding of all of Ireland's historical relationships and their place in his work. However, a consideration of Joyce and Scotland can also form an important and unique bridge between readings of Joyce as Irishman and Joyce as cosmopolitan European modernist. This is because, on the one hand, Scottish history is so closely intertwined with Irish history, while on the other, Scottish culture provides important influences on Joyce's avant-garde literary innovations.

Paradoxes abound in Joyce's engagements with Scotland. For example, Joyce's attacks on early twentieth-century notions of racial purity can be illustrated through references to a shared Irish/Scottish past of repeated migrations and population mixing. However, Joyce also appeals to a shared "Celtic spirit" in his lecture "Ireland: Island of Saints and Sages" and is happy to categorize Ireland as a "Celtic" nation despite it being an "immense woven fabric" in terms of race (*OCPW*, 118). In a chapter entitled "Joyce, Colonialism, and Nationalism" Marjorie Howes has stated that "[Joyce's] works offer many different ideas about what kinds of community or collectivity might exist or be possible. Most of them involve the Irish, or some portion of them, but they rarely coincide neatly with the borders of the whole island or of the twenty-six counties of the Irish Free State. Here again, Joyce is most interested in an Irish nation characterized by global connections and internal divisions" (266). Joyce's tracing of the "global connections" of the Irish in *Finnegans Wake* inevitably leads him to Scotland. Furthermore, in Scottish history—namely the Ulster Plantation—he locates important sources of Ireland's "internal divisions." Thomas Hofheinz notes that "Joyce, in his lifetime, participated in a vast immigration from Ireland to many different countries" and asks, "How could [Joyce] avoid mapping Ireland onto the world, or the other way around?" (Hofheinz, 187). Joyce's charting of Scottish/Irish connections is a vital illustration of this "mapping" of Ireland onto the world and the world onto Ireland. Scottish history provides one of the earliest example of the Irish existing as a community not "coinciding neatly with the borders of the whole island." Especially in his final two works, Joyce follows the wake-like patterns created by successive journeys of Irish and Scottish seafarers.

As we shall see, this complicates our understanding of Joyce as an anti-imperialist writer somewhat, since he includes Ireland in his sometimes rather neutral and ambivalent critique of empire building and overseas conquest. And while Joyce does probe constructed racial or national identities in *Finnegans Wake*, at other points in his career he clearly buys into essentialist notions of the Celt and the Anglo-Saxon. As Nabokov once remarked, "Joyce is sometimes crude in the way he accumulates and stresses so-called racial traits" (Nabokov, *Lectures on Literature*, 287). In "Realism and Idealism in English Literature" (1912) a Scottish figure is linked by Joyce to the visionary Celt, distant from the more practical Anglo-Saxon in terms of genetics or "blood" (*OCPW*, 185). Parts of "The Centenary of Charles Dickens" (1912), with its talk of "spirit" and "blood" (*OCPW*, 185), now appear like notions that derive from the era of Ernest Renan and Matthew Arnold rather than from the pen of a supposedly completely progressive and unprejudiced modern writer.

So, the current view of Joyce as the epitome of a modern "liberal broadmindedness" as questioned by Emer Nolan (Nolan, *Nationalism*, 52) is also tested by a consideration of Joyce's views on Scotland and its contrasts with England (as well as its "familial" links with Ireland). If Joyce totally gives up these ideas by the time he composes *Finnegans Wake*, it represents something of a volte-face. If not, it poses a problem for critics such as Len Platt who read Joyce as a radical dismantler of ideas of national or racial cohesion. Even if Joyce seeks to dismantle ideas of racial types, there still remain—at least—important elements of "culturalism" in his works. As Nolan suggests, that Joyce rejects ideas of racial purity does not mean that he does not have an interest in racial "identity" (see Nolan, *Nationalism*, 148). I hope to demonstrate that these quasi-Arnoldian cultural conceptions stay with Joyce throughout his career and influence the very concept and style of *Finnegans Wake*. Joyce remains—and will remain forever—a writer of the early-to-mid-twentieth century.

It is difficult to navigate by stormy issues such as migration and the nation in modern literature without in some way confronting the treacherous waters of postcolonialism. So, how do we approach the delicate issues of Joyce as postcolonial writer and of Scotland as a potentially postcolonial or semicolonial society? In *Reading Joyce Politically*, Trevor Williams has discussed the problematic issue of Joyce's insecure status as colonial or postcolonial author: "It is still difficult to visualize Joyce, the giant of modernism, the genius, the law unto himself, as a colonial or a postcolonial writer . . . partly because Joyce is white and partly (an old problem) because Ireland is so close to the British metropolis that it is difficult for non-Irish to see it as 'different.'" (Williams, 119). For strikingly similar reasons, many critics have been unwilling to stamp Scotland's "postcolonial passport" due to its incorporation into the British state and its closeness to "the British metropolis" (Maley, "Kilt by Kelt," 207). In the postcolonial manual *The Empire Writes Back*, Ashcroft, Griffiths, and Tiffin discuss the banishment of Ireland, Wales, and Scotland from the postcolonial studies territory: "While it is possible to argue that these societies were the first victims of English expansion, their subsequent complicity in the British imperial enterprise makes it difficult for colonized peoples outside Britain to accept their identity as post-colonial" (33).[5] For both Joyce and Scotland then, proximity to a domi-nating culture is given as a reason for their exclusion from postcolonial discourse. The writer and the nation, respectively, are both considered not sufficiently marginal; they are too central to be accepted as postcolo-nial "subjects."

However, as we shall see, much of Joyce's interest in Scottish litera-ture and philosophy stems from his attempt to create a kind of Celtic consciousness (or unconscious, to be more specific) as a cultural response to what he saw as an overwhelmingly materialist English civilization. Scottish writing and history is drawn into Joyce's powerful response to British imperialism in *Ulysses* and *Finnegans Wake*, through a kind of ethno-philosophical aesthetic that seeks to undermine colonial values. Furthermore, attention paid by Joyce to racial or psychological doubling points towards another type of postcolonial legacy, that of cultural and psychic division. So, regardless of whether or not we can consider Joyce a "true" postcolonial writer or Scotland a "valid" postcolonial society, Joyce's work displays all the classic hallmarks of postcolonial literature—obsessions with language, "hybridity," power struggles, and so on—while persistently raiding Scottish culture in order to create a response to, or diagnosis of, a colonial legacy. For Attridge and Howes, it is best to adopt a "semicolonial" template, which they describe as "a complex and am-bivalent set of attitudes, not reducible to a simple anticolonialism but very far from expressing approval of the colonial organizations and meth-ods under which Ireland had suffered during a long history of oppres-sion" (Attridge and Howes, 3).[6]

Despite being informed by postcolonial theory and discourse, this text is more concerned with viewing Irish and Scottish historical con-nections in terms of processes of ongoing seaborne exchange in a time frame that includes, but is more extensive than that of, the British Em-pire. Such a model can consider the relationship between Ireland and Scotland as an evolving pattern of contacts connected by industry, poli-tics, culture, and migrations rather than as discrete components of a Celtic "periphery," "fringe," or "margin" to an English "center." As Ray Ryan has noted, "the need now is for more alternative analyses and com-parisons, histories and causalities, than can be produced under a single

methodology like postcolonialism or a single notion like identity"
(10–11). Reading the Scottish aspects of Joyce's work complicates and
undermines the standard historical and critical British (read English)/
Irish binary relationship as exemplified in texts such as *Joyce, Ireland,
Britain* by stressing not only Joyce's awareness that the term Britain is
not synonymous with England, but that Ireland and Scotland have had
their own distinct relationship and attendant processes of cultural and
social exchange. Considering Joyce's extensive work on Scotland will also
challenge the standard "colonial-postcolonial" binary system in accordance with current critical developments. This type of reading will be in
line with "recent work in Irish studies [which] tends to problematize bi-
narity by focusing on contradictory, multiple and fluid historical conditions and social spaces" (Castle, "Post-colonialism," 100). Furthermore,
this approach allows us to explore Joyce's unique vision of Celtic identity,
one based less on Irish Literary Revival–type concerns of "authentic"
folklore, primitive vitality, and linguistic or cultural "purity" and more on
an idiosyncratically Joycean concept of a shared philosophical culture of
skepticism and idealism. Admittedly, it is a strange state of affairs where
the most modern of modernists draws heavily from eighteenth-century
philosophy. However, much of literary modernism is decidedly backward
looking.

Joyce's various representations of Scottish culture and history desta-
bilize the traditional binary representation of Ireland and Britain as two
detached, contrasting, and homogenous entities, an enterprise that is
part of his overall project aiming to undermine the traditional structures
and categories that exerted such an influence on the imaginations of his
peers: "The complexity of the Joycean cultural critique was its refusal to
inhabit the binaries of Celtic or Saxon, Catholic or Protestant, modern
or traditional, national or cosmopolitan, English or Irish—the binaries
that so transfixed his contemporaries (and later commentators). Yeats,
for example, reversed the value systems of Celtic/Saxon, traditional/
modern, but still left the binaries intact. Joyce rejected the categories, instead seeking to dismantle the binary system itself" (Whelan, 66–67). I
would suggest that instead of rejecting the categories, Joyce finds new
ways of deploying them and for new ends. However, as Megan Quigley
rightly points out, "historical dynamics make taking a post-colonial approach to Irish literature necessary. That said, they must always be care-

fully weighted against other historical factors . . . which stretch beyond any simple Ireland/England, colonized/colonizer binary" (172). We will see the extent to which Joyce reinvents the classic nineteenth-century Celtic/Saxon binary and how he investigates and blurs the binary relationships of Ireland and England by bringing Scotland into the equation. Sometimes Joyce replaces one set of oppositions with another less obvious pairing, or places a binary set within another to produce a kind of *mise en abime* structure. The net effect is a constant clashing of identities and language where no origin or resolution can be found. However, the very incertitude this confusion creates, the disordered and enigmatic universe these patterns are set into, is, I will argue, a representation of Joyce's summing up of Celtic culture.

Although the standard binary systems of postcolonialism—center and periphery, colonizer and colonized—are steered clear of here, close attention is paid to Joyce's use of contrast and duality in relation to Ireland and Scotland (and to the Celt and the Anglo-Saxon). For this study G. Gregory Smith's concept of the "Caledonian Antisyzygy"— his theory that Scottish literature is marked by the coming together of contraries—is adopted. This idea can be profitably applied to much of Joyce's work, especially *Finnegans Wake*, where Joyce creates what may be termed a "Hibernian Antisyzygy" in order to reflect both the pre- and post-partition internal divisions of Ireland and to register a type of Celtic "spirit." On the whole, however, it is wise to bear in mind Thomas Hofheinz's caution that "an obsession with axiomatics often reveals a temptation to reduce Joyce's texts to data accessible through theoretical programs" (Hofheinz, 54). If ideas can be communicated without extra complications, then Occam's Razor should be applied. *Finnegans Wake* is complicated enough as it is.

Joyce's final and most ambitious work provides a far more advanced and nuanced sense of Scotland's identity and role in Irish history than has previously been supposed. Maley, in his essay "'Kilt by Kelt Shell Kithagain with Kinagain': Joyce and Scotland," discusses a small selection of Scottish "interludes and interpolations" (209), including a few words from *Finnegans Wake*, before offering this tentative conclusion:

My own impression, tinged with sadness, is that Joyce appears to have shared the prejudice of those Irish of the time who assumed that all Scots were incorrigibly Protestant, Conservative, and Unionist. Certainly, in Arthur Balfour they had a prime example of that type. In *Finnegans Wake* a reference to a "scotobrit sash" reminds readers that the origins of Orangeism and its continuing influence in the North of Ireland have a distinct Scottish dimension (387.5). Other histories, other possibilities, remain hidden. (216)[7]

It is certainly true that *Finnegans Wake* records the Scottish dimension to the origins of Orangeism with the reference that Maley quotes here. However, the present study explores some of the previously neglected "other possibilities" Maley alludes to. The aim here is to shed some light upon an area that has so far languished in obscurity, putting forward alternative ways of interpreting Joyce's views on Scotland and highlighting where Joyce engages with Scotland's radical poetic traditions, its history of resistance to English rule or Unionism, its strong cultural links with Ireland (especially in terms of language, mythology, and philosophy), and its various cultural similarities.

The idea that Scotland and Ireland possess clear likenesses is hardly novel: J. G. A. Pocock has described the formation of a "Celtic, oceanic and extra-European world" to the west of England during the period of consolidation of the Scottish kingdom (31). Of course, the Celtic world here is "extra-European" since "the Roman empire . . . [did] not effectively penetrate to all the oceanic or Atlantic regions of the archipelago, and the second-largest island [was] not directly affected by Roman government" (30). In subsequent chapters we shall examine the attention Joyce pays to the "oceanic" nature of this "extra-European world." Cullen and Smout have pointed to the numerous parallels between Ireland and Scotland: "Even on the most superficial examination, it [is] clear that both countries have been profoundly affected by a similar geography, by a Celtic heritage, and by a history of close political and economic links with England" (v). Ray Ryan has elaborated this theme: "The empirical and cultural bases for the Scottish comparison are easily listed: Scotland and Ireland both have Gaelic and English linguistic tradition (with Scots a third dimension in Scotland), a Catholic and Protestant sectarian conflict, urbanized centres, and benighted rural hinterlands; and linked to this last point, the creation of a mystique of Irishness and Scottishness traceable to these depopulated zones" (10).

Given these factors, it should not be surprising that Joyce often uses Scotland as a point of comparison for Ireland. Disagreeing strongly with Maley that Joyce held a prejudiced view of Scotland, this study shows that Joyce used Scotland as a symbol of the convergence of a number of contrasting tendencies in *Finnegans Wake*, such as the division of individual and national psyches into divergent yet mirrored elements and the formation of countries through the amalgamation of separate peoples. Scotland is drawn into an exploration of the national configuration of Ireland and vice versa. In the text, the twins Shem and Shaun—who in turn are connected to Irish and Scottish tribes and who, at one point, appear as HCE stares at his own reflection in a mirror—represent this simultaneous contrast and connection. This focus on internal division must, of course, be read in the historical context of postpartition Ireland, a schism which Joyce links to Scottish involvement in the Plantation of Ulster. Scotland often functions as a mirror image of Ireland, with a certain "invertedness" (*FW*, 522.31) serving to highlight both the underlying connections of the two countries and their "reversed" features. What this means in practice is that representations of Scotland as a combination of imperial aggressor and victim often also applies to Ireland in a two-way critique. However, this connection of Scotland with inner psychic division operates in tandem with an idealist vision based on Joyce's conception of a "'Celtic" form of philosophy that is at a remove the external world but which "contains" history. This Celtic unconscious is a response to what Joyce saw as an essentially materialist Anglo-Saxon culture. All of this can easily be reconciled with the central aim of Joyce's artistic project. As Seamus Deane has declared, "An act of writing which will replace all earlier acts; which will make history into culture by making it the material of consciousness—this extraordinary ambition is at the heart of Joyce's enterprise" (*Celtic*, 97).[8]

As I have suggested, Scotland looms large in Joyce's work due to its critically important historical links with Ireland and because of the strong influence of Scottish literature on his texts. However, Joyce's interest in Scotland also stems from the incidents and connections of his own life. In fact, Joyce had a number of Scottish relatives, and this association began at one point to influence his rather ostentatious fashion sense. In 1930, Joyce developed a certain fondness for tartan clothing and became interested in the Scottish Murray clan: "On 5 October he writes to the wife of Herbert Gorman, enclosing a letter from someone he alludes to as his 'Scotch cousin.' On 22 October he writes to her again, this time asking whether she might be able to find him a plaid tie, patterned after the Murray tartan. Mrs Gorman duly obliged. . . . One of the ties can be seen in the well-known photograph (monochrome, unfortunately) taken of Joyce with Augustus John" (V. Deane et al., 6. See cover image).[9] Following this letter, Joyce then writes again to Gorman of "that highly treasonable Stuart tie" (*LIII*, 206), highlighting "the Jacobite loyalties of some of the Murrays" (D'Arcy, 10).

Joyce's mother's maiden name was Murray, and Joyce must have felt that this gave him a family "tie" with Scotland as well as with Jacobitism, since Murray is a Scottish as well as an Irish name.[10] Joyce must have developed a sense of kinship towards the Murray clan in general (a feeling not shared by his father).[11] His sporting of tartan apparel, a dandy-like display of cultural identification and personal connection with Scotland, is certainly not the kind of thing someone with an antipathy towards the country would be likely to consider, although the idea that Joyce resented Scotland has previously been suggested (see Maley, "Kilt by Kelt," 216). It would be far-fetched to describe Joyce as ever feeling "half Scotch" (*FW*, 487.15) (although Ezra Pound did once describe him as a "dour Aberdeen minister" [*JJII*, 510]). However, this affiliation-flaunting tartan fashion show goes some way to proving that Joyce cannot have held a total aversion towards Scotland as has previously been suggested. Furthermore, Scotland was also the very first foreign country the eventual exile Joyce ever visited, the first port of call in Joyce's life of European travel.

Joyce's maiden venture outside of Ireland was a sea voyage with his father to Glasgow in 1894 when he was twelve years old. The original plan was to make it as far as Edinburgh, but the intrepid Dubliners quickly ran into difficulties. John Wyse Jackson has described the background of the journey and the trip itself, which perhaps descended into a pub-crawl:

> In June news came that Jim had vindicated his father's boasts about him to FR Conmee and had been awarded £22 for himself and £12.4s.od for the College in the 1894 Preparatory Grade Intermediate Examination. The money was paid to John but he passed it on

to Jim, who promptly began to spend it, even taking his parents out to dinner at an expensive restaurant. It was probably this windfall and the goodwill it engendered between them that prompted John to invite Jim to accompany him on a summer trip to Scotland (perhaps, as "The Dead" seems to hint, for the wedding or funeral of one of the Malinses). John did not have to pay for the sea crossing: as a seafaring man who knew the language since his Queenstown days, he had made friends with some of the personnel of the shipping companies when he was a collector in the North Dock Ward and persuaded the captain of one of the Duke Line steamers to allow them an unused berth up the Irish Sea. Jim with his winnings could help to subsidise food, entertainment and somewhere to stay. . . . As Stanislaus remembered, they went first to Glasgow, then a city with a greater claim than Dublin to be the second city of the Empire: its industrial vigour unlike anything to be found in Dublin. James Joyce's notes for *Stephen Hero*, however, strongly suggest that a visit to Edinburgh featured in the lost chapters of that book—the existing parts of which are firmly rooted in fact. Depressingly, it poured with rain, which likely forced them to spend much of their time sheltering in city gin palaces. (Jackson and Costello, 185–86)[12]

It is unfortunate that so little is known about Joyce's trip to Scotland. Equally unfortunate is that the latter chapters of *Stephen Hero* (the abandoned novel later reworked as *A Portrait of the Artist as a Young Man*), which probably featured a trip to Edinburgh, have not survived. Scotland provided Joyce's first taste of a physical escape from Ireland. Later its literary culture would provide a different type of withdrawal.

It should be of little surprise then, given this biographical background, that Joyce goes on to study the effects of sea crossings between Ireland and Scotland, having in all probability gained insights into the large-scale Irish emigration to the Scotland of this period through this trip. His early passage from Dublin must have given Joyce a vivid sense of the proximity of the two countries, of how the Irish Sea acts as a corridor for migration, and of the inevitable links that the sea had brought about. Joyce goes on to use maritime imagery to highlight in his work the unavoidable historical clashes and connections the sea link between Ireland and Scotland has created.

The themes of sea and distant family connections—together with aspects of Scottish culture—gather mainly in Joyce's work in the polysemic, polylingual, allusion-heavy murk of his final text, *Finnegans Wake*. Joyce's slightly belated attention to Scotland means that we are not given an immediately clear view of his observations on Scottish issues since matters will always be partially hidden in the infamous Wakean obscurity. However, this point is revealing in itself, since it is when Joyce attempts to describe mental interiority in a sustained way that Scottish culture becomes heavily involved in his work. Most of the material relating to Scotland in *Ulysses* is scarcely any more straightforward or transparent than that in *Finnegans Wake*, however, appearing as it does in the more challenging sections of the work such as "Oxen of the Sun" and "Circe." Why is it that, in general, Scotland is most present in "late Joyce"? What is it about *Finnegans Wake* in particular that requires Joyce to borrow lines of poetry from Macpherson and Burns and to discuss ethnic groups from ancient Scottish history?

Well, as Colin MacCabe has suggested, "*Finnegans Wake*, with its sustained dismemberment of the English language and literary heritage, is perhaps best understood in relation to the struggle against imperialism" (MacCabe, "*Finnegans*," 4). This assault is a continuation and elaboration of a feature of *Ulysses* which Andrew Gibson has called Joyce's "Celtic revenge" (*Joyce's Revenge*, 1). But aside from its assault on novelistic conventions and linguistic "purity," how is this struggle actually enacted? I want to argue that the *methodology* of *Finnegans Wake* is an application of what Joyce saw as a specifically Celtic form of skeptical idealism, an inner, alternative world of possibilities as opposed to the actualities of Anglo-Saxon materialist civilization. Scottish literature and philosophy provided Joyce with valuable material in this late, peak modernist, anti-imperialist, anti-materialist phase of his career where "the English language and literary heritage" are most enthusiastically assailed. The complications of Joyce's response to Scotland's own role in imperialism will be addressed in due course.

In his 1901 letter to Henrik Ibsen, Joyce writes of his interest in the Norwegian playwright's "battles": "not the obvious material battles but those that were fought and won behind your forehead" (*LI*, 52). Despite the bodily nature of much of his work, the mind is always the site of the real battles in Joyce's output, whether in the struggle with paternal authority in *A Portrait of the Artist as a Young Man*—"But he'll beat you here, said the little old man, tapping his forehead and raising his glass to drain it" (*P*, 101)—or in the case of a more specific reaction to the imperial (and clerical) presence in the "Circe" episode of *Ulysses*: "(*he taps his brow*) But in here it is I must kill the priest and the king" (*U*, 15.4436–37). In other words, the British Empire (and the Catholic Church) must be overcome in the mind. Similarly, Joyce preferred the wily Odysseus to a host of Homeric hard men. Declan Kiberd has written of the main characters of *Ulysses* that "each . . . is driven back into his or her head as a consequence of frustration and defeat in the outer world. . . . [It is a] defensive tactic of the marginalized" (Kiberd, "Postcolonial Modernism?," 279).[13] As Stephen famously declares in the "Nestor" chapter of *Ulysses*, "History . . . is a nightmare from which I am trying to awake" (*U*, 2.377). Seamus Heaney claimed that Joyce attempted to "marginalise the imperium which had marginalised him by replacing the Anglocentric Protestant tradition with a newly forged apparatus of Homeric correspondences, Dantesque scholasticism and a more or less Mediterranean, European, classically endorsed worldview" (Heaney, 199). In *Ulysses*, perhaps. In *Finnegans Wake*, however, Humean idealism and a more or less Celtic, skeptical worldview prevails. For Kimberly Devlin "the Wakean dreamer shares with Joyce's earlier characters the desire to escape from a mundane, transient, and imperfect world" (*Wandering*, 65).[14]

Sheldon Brivic has linked the attempt to distill the thought of humanity into a singular consciousness in Joyce to the plight of Ireland: "To construct the human mind through his own is a goal Stephen Dedalus announces, referring to the mind of man in the singular: 'to forge in the smithy of my soul the uncreated conscience of my race' . . . This consciousness, however, is not something that has never existed, but something that has been uncreated by denial, by the unfairness of history, and by the fallen world—factors that Stephen sees most directly in Ireland" (Brivic, "Mind Factory," 8). By *Finnegans Wake*, the mind and its attendant language becomes the only available refuge since it is—in keeping with the idealist philosophy that Joyce becomes increasingly attracted to—all we really have access to. Furthermore, the third chapter of the present study demonstrates that a major preoccupation of *Finnegans*

Wake is the connection between the (sleeping) individual mind and the nation, the "imagined community" of the "little brittle magic nation, dim of mind" (*FW*, 565.29–30). See also "hiberniating" (*FW*, 316.15–16).

The terms Celtic and "unconscious" should be clarified at this point. Joyce uses the word Celtic in a very loose and atypical fashion. Rather than using the term to define a strict linguistic or cultural community or the members (or descendants) of an ancient European race or culture, he uses it simply to denote the non-English nations and inhabitants of the Atlantic Archipelago, regardless of period, place, or language. For example, the modern, lowland, non-Gaelic speaking Scot David Hume is described as Celtic (see Joyce's notes for *Exiles* [*PE*, 353]). Furthermore, Joyce writes in the present tense of the "five Celtic nations" (*OCPW*, 124) despite there being no modern nation that could be considered purely Celtic in terms of everyday language, let alone through "Celtic blood" (*OCPW*, 115).[15] As Joyce writes in "Ireland: Island of Saints and Sages," "What race or language . . . can nowadays claim to be pure?" (*OCPW*, 118). However, this does not stop Joyce from using the term, even when discussing modern cultural matters. Furthermore, Ireland and Scotland are both considered "Celtic" by Joyce despite their mixed linguistic and racial compositions. Likewise, Anglo-Saxon is used as a code word for English, despite the corresponding complications. Instead of addressing issues pertaining to the entire "Celtic world" (*OCPW*, 124) here, I will focus specifically on Scotland and Ireland, as Joyce is particularly interested in the historical and cultural links between these two nations and because Joyce's work creates important connections between Irish and Scottish cultures.

The unconscious is, of course, an area of great significance in psychoanalysis and in literary theory. This area has been approached in diverse ways by thinkers such as Freud, Jung, Lacan, Deleuze, Jameson, Agamben, and many others. Joyce's aversion to Freud is well known: "In biographical terms, at least, Joyce's manifest hostility to Freud and all things 'freudful' (*FW*, 411.35–36) can hardly be disputed" (Thurston, "Scotographia," 407).[16] However, I would argue that the works of Freud and Joyce do at least share a vision of the unconscious as intrinsic, as opposed to thinkers such as Lacan for whom it is extrinsic.[17] As we shall see, Joyce also shares with Freud an interest in doubles and split psyches. Regarding Jung, the "Swiss Tweedledum who is not to be confused with the Viennese Tweedledee, Dr Freud" (*LI*, 166), Luke Thurston has noted that "our interest in Jung as a reader of Joyce is always supplemented and complicated by our knowledge of his role in Joyce's life: primarily, as a psychiatrist who briefly (and unsuccessfully) undertook the clinical treatment of Joyce's daughter Lucia" ("Scotographia," 407). According to Jean Kimball, "both Jung and Joyce, contemporaries in an age that discovered and validated the role of unconscious motivations in human behavior, . . . were engaged in a lifelong investigation of what goes into the making of a personality" (139).[18]

Freud's great reinterpreter Jacques Lacan argued that the unconscious is structured like a language and is extrinsic to the individual: "I say somewhere that *the unconscious is the discourse of the Other*. Now, the discourse of the Other that is to be realized, that of the unconscious, is not beyond the closure, it is *outside*" (*Fundamental Concepts*, 131). For Lacan, truth is not found in the ego; it is elsewhere. This "locus of the Other," part of the "Symbolic Order," resides—structured—in intersubjective, sociolinguistic relations (such as the relationship between the analyst and the "analysand"): "What is being unfolded there is articulated like a discourse, whose syntax Freud sought to define for those bits that come to us in privileged moments, in dreams, in slips of the tongue or pen, in flashes of wit" (*Ecrits*, 193). According to Benvenuto and Kennedy, "in Lacan's view, the unconscious is the language or form through which . . . knowledge (savoir) about truth is always and exclusively represented" (167).[19] It has been suggested that Joyce anticipates Lacan in his treatment of myth:

> Writing . . . became for Joyce a sort of linguistic psychoanalysis of the repressed poetics of mythology. In the *Wake* he proposes to "psoakoonaloose" (*FW* 522.34) the multi-voiced unconscious of myth, to trace the original sin of the World back to its fall from univocal meaning into a medley of different languages. . . . By composing a language that discloses [an] unconscious "law of the jungerl" (*FW* 268.n3), Joyce dismantles the conventional notion of meaning as transparent representation of some mental intention. Against this representational model, the Joycean text shows, some fifty years

before Lacan and the poststructuralists, how myth is: 1) structured like the unconscious and 2) operates according to a complex logic that allows for at least "two thinks at a time" (*FW* 583.07). (Kearney, 183)

Commenting on the *Wake*, Giorgio Agamben brings a fairly Lacanian reading of the unconscious to bear: "Lucidity consists precisely in having understood that the flux of consciousness has no other reality than that of the 'monologue'—to be exact, that of language. Thus in *Finnegans Wake*, the interior monologue can give way to a mythical absolutism of language beyond any 'lived experience' or any prior psychic reality" (*Infancy and History*, 54–55). For Agamben, the "territory of the unconscious, in its mechanisms as in its structures, wholly coincides with that of the symbolic and the improper. The emblematic project, which dissociates every form from its signified, now becomes the hidden writing of the unconscious" (*Stanzas*, 145).

For Deleuze—like Joyce, a reader of Hume[20]—the unconscious is involved in his criticism of the Cartesian cogito as a way of eliminating doubt: "Perhaps Cogito is the name which has no sense and no object other than the power of reiteration in indefinite regress (I think that I think that I think . . .). Every proposition of consciousness implies an unconscious of pure thought which constitutes the sphere of sense in which there is infinite regress" (*Difference and Repetition*, 203). As Adrian Parr writes, "Deleuze holds that no thought is free of sensation. The cogito cannot be self-evident, because sensation always extends to a multiplicity of further conditions and causes" (52). So, the unconscious is, for Deleuze, a place of endless repetitions and reiterations generated by the "propositions" of consciousness and linked to sensory experience.

To shift from psychoanalysis and epistemology to Marxist theory, Fredric Jameson claims that texts are the only access we have to certain master-narratives, an "unconscious" which is ever-present in our cultural environment: "The Real itself necessarily passes through its prior textualisation, its narrativisation in the political unconscious" (Jameson, *Political Unconscious*, 20). In connection with this, narratives are "socially symbolic acts" that resolve certain contradictions in society. Applying Jameson's thesis to the *Wake* is difficult since it is not a straightforward "narrative." However, perhaps we can see this text as a resolution to the nightmare of (Irish) history, symbolically containing the history of the world: "If Ireland could not be herself, then, by way of compensation, the world would become Ireland" (S. Deane, "Joyce the Irishman," 50). Furthermore, Joyce's work suggests—in a rather Jamesonian fashion—that cultures are determined by historical circumstances. For example, as I shall discuss later, he implies that the imperial and capitalist past of England has led to its culture being "almost entirely a materialist civilization" (*OCPW*, 125). On the other hand, the Celtic nations are seen as being possessed of a more idealist culture (this is despite the varying degrees of involvement of the Celtic countries in the British Empire). Declan Kiberd has described Ireland as "England's Unconscious": "Victorian imperialists attributed to the Irish all those emotions and impulses which a harsh mercantile code had led them to suppress in themselves" (*Inventing Ireland*, 29–30).

Rather than being employed here in any of these "classic" senses (although informed by Deane's usage), "unconscious" is used here in a perhaps more straightforwardly Joycean application of the term, relating to the "dead to the world" "dreamer" of *Finnegans Wake*. My claim is that Joyce's use of sleep as a "setting" for the *Wake* functions as an illustration of his general conception that we as individuals are limited to the internal functions of the mind, caught in a Humean—and therefore, for Joyce, a Celtic—void of interiority and doubt. Thus the Celtic mind contains all of the world and its history as a form of compensation or revenge.[21] The unconscious dreamer presents a view of *consciousness itself*, one based on a Humean foundation. As Joyce said of his own work, "the thought is always simple" (*JJII*, 476).

Upon completing *Finnegans Wake*, Joyce announced that "the war between England and me is over, and I am the conqueror" (*JJII*, 693). In *Finnegans Wake*, Joyce seeks a liberation from what he earlier saw as the "materialism" of the "Anglo-Saxon civilization": "I confess that I do not see what good it does to fulminate against English tyranny while the tyranny of Rome still holds the dwelling place of the soul. Neither do I see the use in bitter invectives against England, the despoiler, or in contempt for the vast Anglo-Saxon civilization, even if it is almost entirely a materialist civilization" (*OCPW*, 125). In the original Italian of his Trieste lecture this passage reads, "Non vedo che cosa giovano gli invettivi acerbic coutro l'Inghilterra spogliatrice, il disprezzo della vasta civiltà anglo-sassone, sebbene questa sia quasi del tutto una civiltà materiale" (*OCPW*, 259). Perhaps a more accurate translation of the phrase "civiltà materiale" than the one given in the *Occasional, Critical, and Political Writings* translation would be "materialistic civilization." In any case, it is clear that Joyce sees the materialist/materialistic "Anglo-Saxon civilization" as being fundamentally opposed to the "Celtic spirit" (*OCPW*, 124), which, as I will argue in the following chapters, is always related in Joyce to incertitude and interiority. Joyce's comments on the supposed materialism of the Anglo-Saxon world are made at an early stage in his career, in his piece from 1907 entitled "Ireland, Island of Saints and Sages." John McCourt describes Joyce's nationalism as peaking in 1907 (see McCourt, "Multiple," 130). However, there is a striking resemblance between these early ideas and the nature of his later project *Finnegans Wake*.

According to Len Platt, the *Wake* "insists on constructing England in materialist and 'Anglo-Saxon' terms, usually from a mock critical perspective" (*Joyce, Race*, 44). Can we be so sure Joyce is writing from this ironic stance, given his earlier comments?[22] I would suggest that, although Joyce does not "fulminate" against the "Anglo-Saxon civilization," his work does respond to it in a number of subtle and fascinating ways. This can partly be attributed to Joyce's thirst for what Andrew Gibson has termed "Celtic Revenge" against the civilization which had oppressed Ireland for centuries, partly to Joyce's aim of developing a literature that could reflect his view of human existence as permanently suspended in doubt, and partly to his desire to place his work into what he regarded as a tradition of Celtic literature and philosophy (while simultaneously renewing and transforming that culture).

Joyce's response to the certainties of modern rational discourse also needs to be seen in the wider context of variegated modernist-era reactions against scientific materialism: "Already in the nineteenth century, the rise of scientific and technical education had been opposed by the institution of Catholic universities in many European countries.... Opposition to materialism and modern science also found expression in the mushroom growth of movements such as spiritualism, occultism, theosophy, religious transcendentalism and vitalism around the turn of the century" (Parrinder, 17).[23] Forms of both nationalism and modernism can also be read as responses to the dominance of scientific, technical, commercial, and materialist culture. As Terry Eagleton has remarked, "The modernist sensibility . . . is not of course synonymous with *modernity*. On the contrary, it is in one sense its sworn enemy, hostile to that stately march of secular reason which was precisely, for many a nineteenth-century Irish nationalist, where a soulless Britain had washed up. . . . Modernism is among other things a last-ditch resistance to mass commodity culture" (*Heathcliff*, 280).

The identification of modern English culture with materialism is not limited to Irish writers. Virginia Woolf shared Joyce's view of a materialist and realist tendency in English letters:

> In "Modern Novels"—an essay first published a few months after the armistice, demanding new priorities for fiction—it is significant that Virginia Woolf chooses the term "spiritual" to describe one of the emerging writers whose work she recommends, James Joyce. . . . Psychology, mentioned on the next page of her essay, might have offered a term more obviously appropriate in defining the quality she most admires in Joyce's work. . . . Labeling Joyce . . . highlights preferences for Joyce "in contrast to those whom we have called materialists"—principally an older generation of novelists, including Arnold Bennett, John Galsworthy and H. G. Wells. . . . In her view, the work of [the] older generation was covertly complicit with advancing materialism on the level of style, through its meticulously descriptive concentration on an external, everyday, material world. (Stevenson, *Great War*, 218)

Ironically, Woolf lifts Joyce's techniques in *Ulysses* for her own novels—some of the central texts of English modernism—without realizing that those techniques developed partly as a response against English culture.[24]

To understand Joyce's conception of the contemplative Celt standing in opposition to the practical, rational, "dour" Anglo-Saxon, let us consider the following passages from his lecture "Realism and Idealism in English Literature," in which he discusses the "prosaic realism" of Daniel Defoe, "the father of the English novel" (*OCPW*, 167, 164). First, here is a description of Defoe's character Robinson Crusoe as the Anglo-Saxon and proto-Imperialist par excellence:

The account of the shipwrecked sailor who lived for four years on a lonely island reveals, perhaps as no other book in all English literature does, the cautious and heroic instinct of the rational being and the prophecy of the empire. . . . All the Anglo-Saxon soul is in Crusoe: virile independence, unthinking cruelty, persistance, slow yet effective intelligence, sexual apathy, practical and well-balanced religiosity, calculating dourness. Whoever re-reads this simple and moving book in the light of subsequent history cannot but be taken by its prophetic spell. (*OCPW*, 174)

Crusoe, despite his "calculating dourness," is defined by "subsequent history" as the nonspiritual and practical colonist, a harbinger of empire, the conquering master of the exterior world of territory and matter (by extension, the British Empire itself must be rational, practical, and dour). The Celt is positioned as the antithesis of this. Here is Joyce—in a section foreshadowing the Celtic visions of *Finnegans Wake*—on Defoe's *Duncan Campbell*, a story "which must have been the result of a sojourn in the Scottish Highlands or islands" (*OCPW*, 171): "Seated at the bedside of a boy visionary, gazing at his raised head, noting his fresh complexion, Defoe is the realist in the presence of the unknown; it is the experience of the man who struggles and conquers in the presence of a dream which he fears may fool him; he is, finally, the Anglo-Saxon in the presence of the Celt" (*OCPW*, 171).[25] The "realist" Anglo-Saxon carries out scientific analysis of the boy. In doing so he is working in line with a Baconian, materialist method. Indeed, Karl Marx himself saw the birthplace of Bacon as the "mother country" of scientific and philosophical materialism (154). The passage on *Duncan Campbell* suggests a slight Marxist tendency in Joyce since he also associates philosophical materialism—which he elsewhere denounces as "fatuous" (*OCPW*, 179)—with English culture. But the industrial, commercial, mercantile, middle-class values of the empire so detested by the Irish Revivalists are also seen by Joyce as the antithesis of the "Celtic spirit" in "Ireland: Island of Saints and Sages" and are parodied throughout *Ulysses*, particularly in the extreme materialism and scientism of the "Ithaca" chapter. Scotland is somehow excluded from Joyce's diagnosis of imperial materialism and commercial soullessness, despite the industrial importance of cities like Glasgow.

Whether we read Joyce's use of the term "civiltà materiale" as more focused on materialist science (faith in reason, observation) materialist or realist literature, or on a materialistic culture of commodities and commerce, either way the Anglo-Saxon is associated with the exterior world, in the study and control of matter, while the Celt is concerned with—or perhaps is imprisoned in or has retreated into—the mind, the "tenebrosity of the interior" (*U*, 14.380). This feature of Joyce's work can be seen as early as *Dubliners*, in the meeting in "A Little Cloud" of Little Chandler (Irishman) and Ignatius Gallagher (Irishman now based in London) in a Dublin bar: "In national terms this meeting in Corless's seems, from the Irish viewpoint, to be the classical one of Ireland, Land of Saints and Sages, with the commercial giant Britannia; in individual terms, it suggests a meeting between the typical Celt who values art, religion, and the life of contemplation with the crass, materialistic Sassenach" (Herring, 58).

For Joyce, here is where the dividing line between the Celt and the Anglo-Saxon runs: the Anglo-Saxon seeks control and understanding of the exterior world while the Celt, as we shall see, is associated with interiority and incertitude. Recent studies such as Vincent Cheng's *Joyce, Race, and Empire* have continued to attempt to construct what Emer Nolan described in 1995 as the supposed "liberal broadmindedness" of Joyce, despite "*Ulysses*'s allegorical incarnation of Englishness and Irish Protestantism in the figures of Haines and Deasy [which] must surely raise problems for any [such] account" (*Nationalism*, 52). How can we read Joyce as an enlightened, progressive modernist while at the same time recognizing the culturalist streak in his work? As Nolan rightly points out with reference to Irish identity, "Joyce's refusal of any notion of 'purity of descent' . . . does not apparently deter him from analysing and describing this 'compound'—but none the less identifiable—quality of 'Irishness'" (148). Joyce is perfectly happy to write of the "fabric" of the Irish nation while also addressing its "soul" (*OCPW*, 118, 125). In other words, for Joyce, the nonhomogenous nature of a people does not mean that they cannot possess certain unifying characteristics. The characteristics Joyce associated with Celtic civilization are emphasized in *Finnegans Wake* at the expense of those he associated with Anglo-Saxon civilization.

Furthermore, I wish to extend the debate on Joyce's analysis of a compound Irishness to include Scotland. After all, if this "compound" depends to some extent on foreign influx into Ireland, could we not consider Irish emigration part of a complementary, external amalgam? Joyce's work stresses time and again the links between Ireland and Scotland while forming a new type of Celtic interior identity, a modernist version of "the idealist other-world" that, for writers such as Yeats, "the Celt had come to inhabit" (Chapman, 103). To utilize Joyce's own phrasing in "'Realism and Idealism in English Literature," *Finnegans Wake* is a "dream" which may "fool" readers, causing them to struggle in the "presence of the unknown." Or, the obscured, purposefully difficult language of the text is "the non-Irish speaking Irish author's way of being unintelligible to the British" (Eagleton, *Heathcliff*, 268). In other words, it is Joyce's way of making his language attain the condition of his namesake Myles Joyce's defense in "Ireland at the Bar."[26] The linguistic possibilities and difficulties of the *Wake* also, of course, have the effect of barring readers from certainty with regard to plot and character.

While there is little or no suggestion of a belief in racial purity in Joyce, there is a real examination of racial and national identities or "souls," however elusive or constructed these may be. As Seamus Deane writes, "Joyce is as willing as Pearse to speak of Ireland's soul, to speak of the nation as a spiritual entity, and to conceive of her plight as one in which something ethereal has been overwhelmed by something base" (*Celtic*, 96). James Fairhall: "Pearse and his fellow rebels . . . felt a sense of moral superiority toward England, toward what they perceived as middle-class English materialism and hypocrisy" (*History*, 181).[27] Furthermore, Joyce's work comes close to a type of nationalist declaration of inner independence since "nationalism's claim for state power is generally posited on spiritual *difference* from (and superiority to) imperial or Western culture" (Nolan, "State of the Art," 78–79). As Nolan points out, nationalism frequently prizes "the private, spiritual, or inner realm—this anticolonial version of civil society" (79).

In Joyce's final text the modernist "inward turn" seems less a Woolfean atomic recording than a response to Ireland's past. Here the avant-garde and the anticolonial aspects of modernism converge: "History . . . must be countered by fiction" (S. Deane, *Celtic*, 93). I want to argue here that, despite the fragmentary and illusive nature of Celtic identity in *Finnegans Wake*, Joyce still, to some extent, clung to his earlier impressions of two opposed races (or at the very least cultures), never quite totally freeing himself from these essentialized, quasi-Arnoldian conceptions (hence the "Celtic" of the present text's title—the complications of this term will be returned to throughout). Joyce's early comments above even display some of the hallmarks of nineteenth-century English notions of the Celt as summarized here by Len Platt:

> Firstly, the English intelligentsia used the idea of the Celt to delineate a romantic but wild and often "primitive" Irish identity. A key text here was Matthew Arnold's *The Study of Celtic Literature*, which identified the "Celtic Irish" in traditionally racist terms as "undisciplinable, anarchical and turbulent by nature," "ineffectual in politics" and "poor, slovenly and half barbarous," but which also detected an eloquence and delicacy in Celtic literature indicative of an ardent aspiration "after life, light and emotion, to be expansive, adventurous and gay." According to Arnold, this instinct for "spontaneity" and "imagination" stood in stark contrast to the materialism of Victorian England. . . . Revivalist cultural historiography exploited Arnold's concerns about the materialism of modern England to develop a thoroughly racialised "Anglophobia." One of the key features distinguishing the national identity, in both Protestant and Catholic versions of Irish cultural nationalism, was its Celtic "spirituality," which was positioned against the materialist, aggressively assimilative Anglo-Saxon or Roman-Briton. Irish revivalism also appropriated Arnold's conception of the Hellenistic antidote to modern (i.e. English) materialism. (*Joyce, Race*, 43)

According to Arnold, "the skilful and resolute appliance of means to ends which is needed to make progress in material civilization, and also to form powerful states, is just what the Celt has least turn for" (*Study of Celtic Literature*, 89). While he rejects the notion that the Celt is "anarchic" or "turbulent," Joyce's version of a Celtic "imagination" or "visionary" tendency in opposition to Anglo-Saxon materialism has its antecedents in this English racial discourse. However, instead of the typical Revival concepts of Irish or Celtic spirituality, racial purity, or heroism deployed by Yeats and others as a response to materialism, Joyce prefers to abandon materialism altogether through recourse to what he regards as specifically Celtic forms of modern philosophy, namely skepticism and idealism. As Gregory Castle has made clear, "Joyce refused the mystic essentialism that underwrote Yeats's Revivalist aesthetics": "Yeats's mystical view of the Irish folk tradition, developed partly in response to Matthew Arnold's imperialist Celticism, was grounded in what Yeats called 'our "natural magic" [which] is but the religion of the world, the ancient worship of Nature and that troubled ecstasy before her, that certainty of all beautiful places being haunted, which it brought into men's minds'" (Castle, *Modernism*, 174). Yeats takes up Arnold's binary system only to reverse its values. Joyce also adopts this system but modifies it in order to add a philosophical component and to suspend or cloud the value system in uncertainty. Celts are often seen as "visionary" in Joyce's fiction, but this is not necessarily a positive estimation, and *Finnegans Wake* as a title is, in one very important sense, an exhortation.

Throughout Joyce's career his interest in philosophy is almost totally in "Celtic" (David Hume, George Berkeley) or continental European (Thomas Aquinas, Giordano Bruno, Giambattista Vico) thought—he has hardly a word to say about, for example, Francis Bacon or Thomas Hobbes. As I shall discuss later, Joyce believed that Hume and Berkeley belonged to a specifically "Celtic" school of philosophy, along with Henri Bergson and Arthur Balfour. We might see this as a fairly idiosyncratic grouping and one that is not particularly Celtic, but, as George Cinclair Gibson has pointed out, a "symptom of Joyce's borderline 'madness' was his amazing proclivity to make outlandish correspondences, connections, and associations between apparently unrelated things" (G. Gibson, 20).

Through the extreme modernist aesthetic of interiority and incertitude inspired by Hume and others and applied in *Finnegans Wake*, Joyce presents an imaginative realm in total opposition to the external world of materialism. In this textual oblivion two main characteristics of Joyce's fiction converge—his audacious formal innovation and his program of literary decolonization. As Robichaud comments, "the competing claims of nationalism and modernism need not . . . be seen as mutually exclusive": "Joyce's centrality in the modernist canon, upheld by both aesthetic and political readings of his fiction, has obscured his role as a peripheral writer of the English-language novel and his continual exploration of the meaning of nationality. It is possible, however, to transform our understanding of Joyce as a cosmopolitan writer by recognizing that such sophistication is directed *against* the Englishness of the novel in English, a strategy that enacts its linguistic deterritorialization" ("Narrative," 185–86).[28] Of course, this strategy shares aims with a Revival movement that we have come to see as alien to the supposedly indifferent, apolitical, cosmopolitan modernist Joyce.[29]

As Richard Begam points out, "Joyce is not unsympathetic to the larger goal of the Revival—establishing a genuinely Irish culture—but . . . he is hostile to the specific means it employed" (194).[30] I would argue that in order to establish a vision of this "genuine" culture Joyce involves other "aligned" societies (that Joyce believed Scotland and Ireland to be fundamentally linked will be demonstrated in the following chapters) and radically different means from that of the Revival. As Platt rightly points out, "it was extremely unlikely, given Joyce's representations of Celticism in the pre-*Wake* fictions, that the *Wake* would authorise any conventional support of Celticism as a romantic ideology" (Platt, *Joyce, Race*, 46). However, he does authorize an unconventional, nonromantic, and highly original version of Celticism.

It is through the Humean, de-Anglicized night of *Finnegans Wake* that the Anglo-Saxon materialism and the "Englishness" of the novel as a format finally disappear. Like the dream of the boy visionary of *Duncan Campbell*, the *Wake* is an "unknown," a state of inner exile from a world dominated by a threatening materialist civilization. For Joyce, this is a quintessentially Celtic procedure that connects to a larger attachment to obscurity in the "Celtic world": "This fundamental tendency to obscure and thus conceal, is quintessentially Celtic. The very word *Celt* (etymologically associated with *ceilt*, 'an act of concealment') is derived from an ancient expression meaning 'the hidden people' because of this Celtic proclivity to conceal their lore and their rituals by means of oral tradition and obscure language. . . . The *Wake*'s obscurity, perhaps its most striking quality, is also one of its most profoundly Celtic characteristics" (G. Gibson, 226). As I will demonstrate in the subsequent chapters, Joyce's representations of Scottish and Irish history are almost always linked to dreams and the unconscious, to literature based on the workings of inner life. Indeed, Scotland is rarely mentioned in Joyce's work before *Finnegans Wake*. This constant linkage suggests that, for Joyce, the brain and its functions is the only place in which the Celtic "spirit" can—albeit temporarily—prevail. As Margot Norris states, "In the enduring struggle between the individual's anarchic psyche and the

laws that make civilization possible, the psyche is momentarily triumphant only in the dream" (44). Or, as Sheldon Brivic puts it, "To transform the world into art, one must withdraw from it and promote spirit
at the expense of matter" (*Joyce between Freud and Jung*, 202).[31] However,
"the success of the modernist artist in creating what virtually amounts
to a parallel universe paradoxically produces anxiety about the insecurity
and the baselessness of this very world . . . the ineffectualness and
impotency of merely imagined solutions to political problems" (Nolan,
Nationalism, 160).

Such a "parallel universe" functions as an equivalent in *Finnegans
Wake* of the disappearing materiality of the city in *Ulysses*, which has been
read as a strategy of subaltern utopian imagination:

> Reading modern works, critics tend to consider the unsaid a nega-
> tive entity: the secret the text pushes into its unconscious. This is
> appropriate for texts that bolster existing hegemonic powers. When,
> however, a subaltern text is in question, then the unsaid may exist as
> the unarticulated possibility of a utopia. By refusing to map out in
> the novel the full cityscape of colonial might, with its monuments
> on the one hand and its degrading effects, the slums it has created,
> on the other . . . *Ulysses* leaves these spaces as imaginatively blank
> cityspaces that might therefore be filled with some other hopeful
> version of governance, of community and of the features that would
> memorialize it. (Duffy, "Disappearing Dublin," 54–56)

At the same time, this imaginative conception of a national or racial
psyche removed from the material world avoids a standard "crude, and
crudely spatial, conception of the nation" (Howes, 61). This creation of
a "parallel universe" is part of what Michael Mays has described as a type
of "negation" of colonial culture:

> Unlike *Ulysses*, which has been read as an excessive extreme or ter-
> minal point in the historical development of the (essentially Realist)
> novel, *Finnegans Wake* doesn't make any sense in those terms. Rather,
> its very strangeness needs to be seen as a form akin to what Homi
> Bhabha has called "the language of colonial nonsense," the non-
> sense of a cultural incommensurability which manifests itself in

negation, in a procedure whereby "the impossibility of naming the difference of colonial culture alienates, in its very form of articulation, the colonialist cultural ideals of progress, piety, rationality and order." (21)

The representation of a sleeping mind in *Finnegans Wake*, with all the distortions, strangeness, or "non-sense" that that entails or allows, can be thought of as a deliberate form of alienation, a manifestation of difference from the "colonialist cultural ideas," especially "rationality" and "order." In the chapters that follow, I want to show just how much this "psyche" of alienation and strangeness in Joyce's postcolonial ethno-philosophical text is connected to Scottish literature and philosophy and, by extension, to a broader "Celtic" culture.

This is why a focus on Joyce's engagements with the theories of David Hume is so important, because the basis of the "parallel universe" of *Finnegans Wake* is achieved through what Joyce reads as a unified "Celtic" philosophy, a combination of skepticism and idealism. This "ontology" becomes an alternative to imperialism, since it focuses on an exploration of the inner world at the expense of the material world. As MacCabe suggests, *Finnegans Wake* is Joyce's answer to English culture in terms of the novel's assault on the English language, but it is also a "mental" riposte to Joyce's conception of the struggling, conquering, martial, commercial Anglo-Saxon "spirit." Robert Burns—though he has been appropriated by Orange Order lodges and is linked in *Finnegans Wake* to British imperialism through close association with the Ulster Scots—is also brought into Joyce's anti-imperialist campaign. Allusions to James Macpherson—which will be discussed in relation to the theories of Ernest Renan and Matthew Arnold—function as a reminder of the linked cultural heritages of Ireland and Scotland as well as a commentary on the "constructedness" of texts, dreams, and nations. The copied nature of Macpherson's work fits Joyce's vision of a "copied" or "constructed" consciousness at a remove from reality.

———

We begin our examination of Joyce and Scotland by looking at the "Oxen of the Sun" episode of *Ulysses*, which includes a Scottish character named

J. Crotthers, and the first chapter of this book provides a new explication of the unusual name of that character. Through this process we can develop a fresh conception of how Joyce viewed Scotland in his works predating *Finnegans Wake*. The name Crotthers can be read as a hidden presentation of the maritime links between Scotland and Ireland—and of the resulting mixed nature of both nations—chosen specifically by Joyce in order to reflect this idea. The Crotthers character foreshadows Joyce's later work on mixture and duality in relation to Scotland while appearing in a section of *Ulysses* in which the possibility of accessing a verifiable truth is questioned. From this skepticism we move, in chapter 2, into the "Incertitude" (*FW*, 178.32) of *Finnegans Wake*, studying Joyce's references to the philosopher and historian David Hume. This chapter will trace how Joyce associates Hume's work with endings, viewing Hume's mixture of skepticism and idealism as the conclusion of a certain branch of philosophy. The chapter will also describe how *Finnegans Wake* functions as a space of Celtic interiority though the application of Hume's thought. Taken together, these opening chapters form the basis for our exploration of the Scottish culture in *Finnegans Wake*.

An examination of how Joyce utilizes the works of Robert Louis Stevenson and James Hogg as a way of working with the idea of split identity or divided consciousness in *Finnegans Wake* forms the nexus of the third chapter, entitled "Celtic Antisyzygy." Here we see the two main subjects of the opening introductory chapters converge—interiority is now linked with duality and mental division. Having looked at how Joyce creates a vision of Scottish and Irish hybridity in *Ulysses* and how this links to a kind of evasive attitude to history and having established the connections between Scotland and (a) idealism and skepticism and (b) duality in the *Wake*, we can then, in chapter 4, bring these themes together by examining a textual motif Joyce bases on early Scottish history, on the merging of the Picts and the Scots. We will also study how Joyce contrasts Irish colonialism in ancient Scotland to the Scottish hand in the divisions of modern Ireland. This section also comments on national or racial mixing and discusses these ancient tribes with reference to the rival twin figures of the *Wake*, Shem and Shaun.

We can then move on to see how these ideas are applied to two major Scottish authors. Chapters 5 and 6 are case studies on Joyce and two Scottish poets. Chapter 5 will look at how Joyce considers the after-

effects of Irish civilization in Scotland in combination with a consideration of James Macpherson's place in the *Wake*. Chapter 6 looks at the
"reverse" of this—the Scottish presence in the north of Ireland—in conjunction with a study of Joyce's use of the poetry and songs of Robert
Burns. The final chapter studies how Joyce uses Burns's work to explore
the Scottish presence in Ulster—an inversion of the pattern of the previous chapter—while paradoxically enlisting Burns in his act of literary
decolonization.

Through a discussion Joyce's use of Scots characters, his adaptations
of Scottish culture—prose, poetry, and philosophy—as well as his references to the history of "Alba" (*FW*, 463.24) a comprehensive overview
of Joyce's substantial and varied engagements with Scotland will take
shape. Since Joyce's ideas are often obscured or disguised by language,
a philological-type approach will often be needed. The central argument of this study is that in *Finnegans Wake* Joyce creates a Celtic void
of interiority and idealism removed from history while marked by division and recurrence: a "Celtic unconscious."

In III.i of *Finnegans Wake*, the authoritarian figure Shaun is being
interrogated by "the Four," a group of old men who represent the Irish
provinces, the writers of the Gospels, and the authors of the *Annals of the
Kingdom of Ireland*. In response to a question regarding Shaun having
"painted our town a wearing greenridinghued" (*FW*, 411.24), a phrase
that relates to the nationalist practice of painting red postboxes green in
preindependence Ireland, Shaun replies with reference to contrasting
terms of darkness and light such as "lampsleeve" (*FW*, 411.26), "shy of
light" (*FW*, 411.27), and "The gloom hath rays" (*FW*, 411.27–28). This
interest in light and dark continues onto the next page: "But it is grandiose by my ways of thinking from the prophecies. New worlds for all!
And they were scotographically arranged for gentlemen only by a scrip-
chewer in whofoundland who finds he is a relative. And it was with my
extravert davy. Like glue. Be through. Moyhard's daynoight, tomthumb.
Phwum! (*FW*, 412.1–6).[32] Here "scotographically" (Grk. σκότος/*skotos*,
"darkness"; γράφω/*graphō*, "I write") refers to an alternative name for
radiography, the practice of using radioactive materials rather than light
in order to create images.

The term Scotography might serve as a description of focus of the
present study, since we are considering Joyce's use of Scottish literature,

and because this subject has been hidden in darkness until now, a blind spot in Joyce studies and Irish studies. To add to the sense of obscurity, the vast majority of Joyce's commentary on Scotland is found in the depths of *Finnegans Wake*, while Scottish culture is employed to create that obscure universe. Scotland, for Joyce, is on the one hand a site of ancient Irish colonization and expansion and on the other the origin of settlers into Ireland, and is thus both a Celtic relative and an accomplice in modern British imperialism. Joyce saw Scotland and Ireland as existing in a symbiotic and cyclical relationship, one that produces dual identities and cultures in each nation. Joyce signals this concept through patterns based on the mergings and schisms of Hibernian/Caledonian history, through allusion to Scottish texts concerned with internal partitions, and through his constant linkage of Scottish writing to his construction of the unconscious void of *Finnegans Wake*.

Joyce associates Scotland with different types of duality: through its dual identity as a Celtic relation of Ireland and as part of the British imperial dominating society, through its amalgamated nature as a nation founded upon an absorption of Irish immigrants, and through its literature exploring themes relating to split personality and doppelgängers. Regarding Scotland as closely linked to Ireland, Joyce saw the two nations existing in an almost mutualistic relationship, with Scotland not encompassing one set of values but being divided and composed of contrasting elements, in keeping with the trends of *Finnegans Wake*. This presentation fits the "truth-dismantling" (Thurston, *Problem*, 111) atmosphere of the *Wake*, while the inversions and repetitions of their shared histories provide a sense that history is a nonteleological or nonprogressive process. This text will endeavor to show that, rather than identifying Scotland with the "Protestant, Conservative and Unionist" (Maley, "Kilt by Kelt," 216) traditions that have previously been discussed in connection with his thoughts on Scotland, Joyce uses Scotland as a symbol of the convergence of opposites in *Finnegans Wake* while drawing upon Scottish culture to form the text's "inner exile." Though he sees Ireland and Scotland as almost inverted entities, he also views them as linked through processes of seaborne exchange, through a shared mythology, and through a philosophical preoccupation with skepticism and idealism.

Reviewing the texts of Andrew Gibson, in which Gibson presents Joyce as working "towards a liberation from the colonial power and its culture" and "[taking] his revenge on them" (*Joyce's Revenge*, 13), John McCourt writes:

> For Gibson's Joyce, the will to freedom and to justice is read exclusively in terms of Ireland's attempts to gain political freedom and justice from British colonization. It might more usefully be suggested that, while this is certainly an important and indeed a central concern of *Ulysses*, to limit the book only to this idea or to suggest that it is the dominating intention is to provincialize Joyce's work and to ignore its larger reach and ambition. This is not to call for a return to a non-political Joyce, to the Joyce of Ezra Pound or even Richard Ellmann—quite the contrary. It is to say that Joyce, while concerned with the English-Irish knot, did everything in his literary power not to remain caught up in it, Mangan-like, and his works offer considerable tools for its untying. (Review, 890)

In the following pages I do not wish to suggest that Joyce's work is limited to a specific response to colonialism or imperialism; that would indeed provincialize his output. Joyce's range of interests, subject matters, techniques, and insights is vast, perhaps unparalleled in literature. However, Joyce's responses to Ireland's past and his reaction to the empire are central themes of his oeuvre. Furthermore, a discussion of Joyce and Scotland—while relating to those central themes—might help us understand Joyce's attempts to untie that "English-Irish knot" somewhat, since such a discussion will entail his consideration of Irish culture and history in different contexts. It could also offer ways of thinking about how Joyce sought "not to remain caught up in" that knot (and the extent to which he is successful). Such an enterprise will also involve some of his other concerns. In Joyce's Scotography we can see some of his important late artistic preoccupations develop: his conceptions of art and of dream, his views on the formation and character of nations, his representations of individual and national psyches. The aim here, to borrow a phrase from the above section of the *Wake*, is to develop new "ways of thinking."

ONE

Crotthers

A "Scots fellow" in *Ulysses*

Scottish culture is utilized in Joyce's work to create the inhumed and divided Celtic consciousness of *Finnegans Wake*'s "dreamer." However, Joyce's later portrayal of a Celtic unconscious removed from the external world of materiality—and of constant cyclical maritime exchange between Ireland and Scotland—is preceded by some preliminary moments in his earlier texts. Most of Joyce's pre–*Finnegans Wake* (1939) engagements with Scottish matters appear in the latter half of *Ulysses* (1922). In the fourteenth chapter of *Ulysses*, "Oxen of the Sun," Joyce creates a character that is emblematic of maritime crossings and ties between Ireland and Scotland. An understanding of Joyce's early vision of the two countries as historically interlinked will aid our examination of his later work. Here the focus is on the crossings and genetic mixings of the two countries. Before we consider Irish and Scottish subjects in tandem, we must look at the ways in which Joyce links the two nations in order to understand the mixtures and connections permanently linking the two countries. This is first achieved in a sustained way in *Ulysses*, particularly in the "Oxen of the Sun" episode. However, on a number of important occasions Scotland and Scottish culture are evoked in the short stories of Joyce's first work, *Dubliners* (1914). These instances form the embryo of Joyce's Scottish theme at the onset of its development.

The novelist and poet Walter Scott is rather unromantically involved in the unsettling story "An Encounter," when a lecherous old man asks a group of boys if they have read any of Scott's works. According to James P. Degnan, the man's liking for Scott is in keeping with the corrupted nature of his character: "From the narrator's point of view, the pervert is 'well spoken' and 'well read,' though the pervert's taste in literature, in keeping with his character, is apparently for a kind of decadent romanticism" (Degnan, 92). Then in "Araby," a copy of Scott's novel *The Abbot* is left behind—by a priest—in a pile of "old useless papers" (*D*, 21).[1] In *A Portrait of the Artist as a Young Man* the "captain" announces that Scott "writes something lovely" (*P*, 247), although this is perhaps not an opinion that Stephen Dedalus or James Joyce shares (although Joyce memorized sections of "The Lady of the Lake" in his later years). This early use of the texts of Walter Scott as thematic devices is, like those useless papers, largely disposed of as Joyce's career develops. During the story "Grace," we are told that one of Mrs Kernan's sons works "in a draper's shop in Glasgow" (*D*, 155), reflecting the economic pull of the west of Scotland for Irish workers in early years of the twentieth century. Mrs Kernan is likely putting a positive spin on her son's employment, however, draping over a more mundane job in the burgeoning Scottish textiles sector: "Irish immigration from 1851, assessable from the census returns, shows movement to Glasgow from virtually all counties of Ireland . . . in association with the textile industries" (Fraser and Maver, 150).[2] While Mrs Kernan's account of an Irish émigré's life in Scotland seems slightly unreliable, the final story of *Dubliners* sets alarm bells ringing.

In "The Dead," after the coquettish Celtic Revival enthusiast Miss Ivors teasingly whispers the insult "West Briton" (*D*, 188, 190) into Gabriel Conroy's ear and rebukes him for not visiting the west of Ireland or practicing the Irish language, a flustered Gabriel makes a swift exit from the scene of his embarrassment:

> When the lancers were over Gabriel went away to a remote corner of the room where Freddy Malins' mother was sitting. She was a stout feeble old woman with white hair. Her voice had a catch in it like her son's and she stuttered slightly. She had been told that Freddy had come and that he was nearly all right. Gabriel asked her

whether she had had a good crossing. She lived with her married daughter in Glasgow and came to Dublin on a visit once a year. She answered placidly that she had had a beautiful crossing and that the captain had been most attentive to her. She spoke also of the beautiful house her daughter kept in Glasgow, and of all the nice friends they had there. (*D*, 190–91)

The vivacious Miss Ivors, connected with the supposedly more "authentic" west of Ireland, is deliberately contrasted with the "feeble" white-haired Mrs Malins—who is herself associated with Scotland.[3] Mrs Malins continues, unbidden, to ramble on about Scotland later in "The Dead": "While she was threading her way back across the room Mrs Malins, without adverting to the interruption, went on to tell Gabriel what beautiful places there were in Scotland and beautiful scenery. Her son-in-law brought them every year to the lakes and they used to go fishing. Her son-in-law was a splendid fisher. One day he caught a fish, a beautiful big big fish, and the man in the hotel boiled it for their dinner" (*D*, 192).[4] Mrs Malins's descriptions of her new life are simply too positive and idyllic to be a realistic account of an Irish immigrant's experience of life in early twentieth-century Glasgow. There is an unspoken, avoided gnomon at work here. As R. F. Foster has noted, "The Irish found prejudice to contend with [in Scotland]; anti-Irishness and anti-Catholicism took a special colouration where Presbyterian values saw the very existence of destitute Irish Catholics as an outrage. . . . Catholics remained a disadvantaged minority there until the 1920s" (*Modern Ireland*, 368). Such prejudice is perhaps best exemplified in the Church of Scotland's notorious 1923 report *The Menace of the Irish Race to Our Scottish Nationality*.[5]

The emphasis on catching in the two sections—Mrs Malins's voice has a "catch" in it, and we are told that her son-in-law once "caught a fish, a beautiful big big fish"—is noteworthy. Economic forces are reeling in migrants from Ireland to Scotland. But there is an undeclared negative "catch" to their emigration. Mrs Malins's near manic repetition of the word "beautiful"—"beautiful house," "beautiful crossing," "beautiful scenery," "beautiful places," "beautiful big big fish"—suggests that she is trying desperately to impress Gabriel, and the catch in her voice hints at a certain restrained emotion caused by her reflection on this situation.

Is she trying to convince herself or Gabriel of the happiness of her new life? And what are we to make of the strange reference to Scotland's "lakes"? Anyone with even a passing knowledge of Scottish geography and language would know that a "lake" is referred to in Scotland by the Gaelic word *loch*.[6] A visit "every year" to the countryside would certainly have provided Mrs Malins with the relevant information here. Has Mrs Malins really seen anything of Scotland outside of the deprived areas of Glasgow?

Mrs Malins is inventing or embellishing the details of her life in Scotland to impress Gabriel and to avoid confronting a harsher or more mundane situation. This is a typically Joycean diagnosis of something contributing to the paralysis of Dublin—a failure to confront or communicate reality. One of the themes of "The Dead" is the unsuccessful or botched message; think of Gabriel's anxieties concerning his Christmas toast, for example: "His whole speech was a mistake from first to last, an utter failure" (*D*, 179). In Mrs Malins's case however, speech communicates perfectly. But what is communicated is the exact *reverse* of what Mrs Malins had intended. Her strained and agitated attempt to construct a heavenly alternative reality—an imaginary escape comparable to the mirage of Buenos Aires in "Eveline"—only serves to raise doubts and to communicate uncertainties (it is often useful to maintain a suspicious, distrustful attitude to the speech of Joyce's characters). Even the ominous "mal" of her name suggests something corrupt or incorrect, ill or *malign* (although the Malinses were a real family known to the Joyces). At this early stage in Joyce's career Scotland is associated with escape, although the reports created of it are essentially imagined and veiled in doubts (puzzles and enigmas recur *Dubliners*—remember the doubts surrounding Father Flynn in "The Sisters," for example). Throughout *Finnegans Wake* Scotland is again associated with migrations, and with incertitude.

Uncomfortable with what Connacht and the west of Ireland represents, Gabriel is reluctant to join Miss Ivors in an excursion that will take her in the opposite direction from Mrs Malins. When asked if his wife is from Connacht, Gabriel attempts to reduce her connection by saying only that "her people" (*D*, 189) are from there. Gabriel's regular cycling trips to Belgium, Germany, and France represent only temporary escape from a country he professes to be sick of. Meanwhile, the elderly and feeble Mrs Malins portrays another potential escape-route for Dubliners such as Gabriel, a more traditional passage east to the industries of Scotland, but this portrayal is highly unconvincing and evokes containment and decay. In contrast to the slight taint of death emanating from Mrs Malins and her inane babble, Miss Ivors and her planned trip west to the Aran Islands is associated with youth, vigor, and passion. There is even a suggestion of sexual tension or chemistry between Gabriel and the confusing "girl or woman" (*D*, 191) Miss Ivors, with her flirtatious whisperings and the suggestive "warm grasp" of her hand (*D*, 189). During a dance Gabriel is "surprised to feel his hand firmly pressed" (*D*, 190). Of course, the presentation of Miss Ivors as an embodiment of youthful ardor—erotic attraction even—and western Irish "authenticity" foreshadows Gretta Conroy's story of her doomed young Galway love Michael Furey. Joyce acknowledges the romantic power of nationalistic aspiration and the west of Ireland alongside the stale, mundane alternative of eastern economic emigration. Dublin, the city of paralysis and endless circular wanderings (illustrated by the humorous story of Johnny the Horse), exists as a crossroads between these two spheres and the different options they offer.

So, in Joyce's fictional works preceding *Ulysses*, Scotland is presented as a source of "decadent" romantic fiction and as a potential economic escape-route. It offers an idealized leisure resort for characters such as Mrs Malins, although we clearly do not receive honest appraisals of the situation of the Irish who, like Mrs Malins, have migrated to Scotland. Instead these appraisals offer—in keeping with Scott's decadent romanticism—an idealized and corrupted vision of these emigrants' new home across the Irish Sea. In *Dubliners* it is the Irish who are relocating in Scotland, a common historical occurrence after the catastrophic potato famine of the mid-nineteenth century.[7] In "Oxen of the Sun"—the fourteenth chapter of *Ulysses*—Joyce presents a Scottish character named J. Crotthers who has made the opposite journey.[8]

Crotthers is one of a group of rowdy young students who are spending the evening carousing at the Holles Street maternity hospital in Dublin.[9] Mr Leopold Bloom also arrives at the hospital in order to check on the health and progress of one Mrs Purefoy, who has been in labor for three long days. Crotthers makes a further brief appearance in the subsequent hallucinatory chapter, "Circe," where he is one of a number of doctors who perform an examination of Bloom. Problematically, in "Oxen of the Sun" the characters and their actions are overshadowed by the shifting styles in which the text is written. The chapter was designed by Joyce to demonstrate (and satirize) the development of English language prose, and Joyce links this progression to the gestation of the embryo in the womb. We are not presented with as "clear" a view of the character as we are of, for example, the Englishman Haines, who first appears in the "Telemachus" chapter, long before Joyce's stylistic experiments take hold of *Ulysses*. Furthermore, there is not much in the way of action in this chapter, and so Crotthers does very little other than drink and make speeches. However, as we shall see, the fact that a Scotsman appears as "reality" begins to disappear is telling in itself.

Significantly, Crotthers is not presented as an outsider in the chapter; he has obviously been fully integrated into the company of the young men. Near the beginning of the chapter there is a partly ironic description of the place of medicine in Celtic society: "It is not why therefore we shall wonder if, as the best historians relate, among the Celts, who nothing that was not in its nature admirable admired, the art of medicine shall have been highly honoured" (*U*, 14.33–35). According to Marilyn French, "The second part of the prelude, describing the reverence for motherhood and the excellent medical facilities of the Celts, has . . . grim humor in light of the poverty and starvation seen by Joyce" (174).

Crotthers, representing another Celtic country, is clearly at home with the clique of medical students, part of a "fellowship" (*U*, 14.187) rather than an outsider like the "Sassenach" Haines (*U*, 1.232). Crotthers takes particular pleasure in sexual repartee, telling bawdy stories to accompany the drinking. In other words, he behaves pretty much like many other young male students on a night out. His manner, his quasi-insider status, and his popularity can be contrasted to situations of some other non-Dubliners of the book. He is harmless enough compared to the patronizing English cultural tourist and amateur ethnographer Haines, who reappears in the chapter. As Vincent Cheng has pointed out, "Stephen . . . see[s] in Deasy (as he had seen in Haines) 'The seas ruler'" (Cheng, *Joyce, Race, and Empire*, 165). The Ulsterman Deasy and the Englishman Haines are associated by Stephen with the dominant power, with imperialism. In contrast to the English soldiers of "Circe," Crotthers is not an authority figure or representative of imperial power and violence. Furthermore, Crotthers does not assault anyone (unlike Private

Carr) or discharge a firearm (unlike Haines). As Emer Nolan has noted, the "allegorical incarnation of Englishness" in the figure of Haines provides a problem for those who would read Joyce as the epitome of "liberal broadmindedness" (Nolan, *Nationalism*, 52). Is Crotthers an allegorical incarnation of Scottishness? If so, how does this allegory function?

Paradoxically, one of the most noticeable things about Crotthers is the extent to which he blends in; he does not stand out like Carr, Compton, or Haines. For example, if we compare the following two sections of "Oxen," we see that while Crotthers is presented fairly neutrally (despite the style of Richard Brinsley Sheridan coloring the section), Haines is cast as a horrific and disturbing pantomime villain, associated with ethnography and an evasive attitude towards history:

> I must acquaint you, said Mr Crotthers, clapping on the table so as to evoke a resonant comment of emphasis, old Glory Allelujurum was round again today, an elderly man with dundrearies, preferring through his nose a request to have word of Wilhelmina, my life, as he calls her. I bade him hold himself in readiness for that the event would burst anon. 'Slife, I'll be round with you. I cannot but extol the virile potency of the old bucko that could still knock another child out of her. (*U*, 14.886–93)

> The secret panel beside the chimney slid back and in the recess appeared—Haines! Which of us did not feel his flesh creep! He had a portfolio of Celtic literature in one hand, in the other a phial marked *Poison*. Surprise, horror, loathing were depicted on all the faces while he eyed them with a ghostly grin. I anticipated some such reception, he began with an eldritch laugh, for which, it seems, history is to blame. (*U*, 14.1011–16)

The passage above featuring Crotthers fits in with the general themes of the chapter, with its focus on "virile potency" and his insensitive acclaim for the production of "another child," but substituting the name of Crotthers for another of the medical students would cause minimal disruption to the text. In other words, almost any of the characters of "Oxen of the Sun" could have been given these lines; there is nothing particularly Crotthers-esque about them. Crotthers is handed no phial marked *Poison*, he has no ghostly grin or eldritch laugh (although these features relate to some extent to the Gothic style of the particular section of "Oxen" in which Haines appears. (See Kenner, *Ulysses*, 122). His script has nothing as memorable as Haines's infamous "It seems history is to blame" (*U*, 1.649).[10] So, what *is* of interest about Crotthers? A consideration of the name itself in connection with a small number of clues may be the only way of gaining any useful knowledge of this character, since his "personality" is so inconspicuous.

Both Willy Maley and Claire Culleton have offered some possible explanations for Joyce's use of the name "Crotthers." As Culleton has highlighted, onomastics—the study of proper names and their origins—is of critical importance to the study of Joyce and his texts: "Joyce's fiction resounds with onomastic consequence, not only teeming with what many readers see as his nominal play but fertile with indications of the importance of names and naming. Engaged and fascinated with names, Joyce inscribed in his works his onomastic curiosity, and an examination of the names, their functions, their origins, their pluralities, and their exploitable suggestiveness remains essential to our understanding of Joyce and his writings" (7). Coupled with this interest in names is the fact that in Joyce's work "rebuses abound" (33). As Stephen announces in "Eumaeus," "Sounds are impostures . . . like names" (*U*, 16.362–63). The name Crotthers is an imposture in the sense that there are hidden messages within it while its surface is deceptive. Before we turn to some new "functions" and "pluralities" of Crotthers's name, let us consider how Maley and Culleton have considered the "exploitable suggestiveness" of this "nomen." For Maley, the name has decidedly negative connotations:

> The name is an odd one, suggesting "rotters" (Caledonian rotters perhaps). It may be that Joyce is playing with the name of one of George Russell's intellectual adversaries, the "wild professional Scot," and apocalyptic visionary, S. Liddell MacGregor Mathers (Gifford, ed., *Ulysses Annotated*, 173). The word "crott," according to the *OED*, means "dung" or "dirt," while "crottle" is Scots Gaelic for "a species of lichen used in dyeing," which would chime with "Mat." The fact that Crotthers is described as "a little fume of a fellow" suggests that Joyce may have had this etymology in mind. . . . The description of Crotthers "at the foot of the table in his striking

Highland garb, his face glowing from the briny airs of the Mull of
Galloway," is hardly complimentary. ("Kilt by Kelt," 214)

As will be elaborated later, this description of Crotthers as "a little fume
of a fellow" most probably relates to Crotthers's heavy drinking, and
since almost every character in the chapter is drunk, though not complimentary, it is hardly a damning indictment.[11] Maley is certainly correct
to point to the oddness of Crotthers's name, however. In her work *Names
and Naming in Joyce*, Culleton provides some alternative associations for
this strange name and notes some other information provided about
Crotthers:

> Crotthers—undeniably a Scottish student, as he is called a num-
> ber of times in the chapter—is identified as "one from Alba Longa,
> one Crotthers." While the Alba reference at once connects Crot-
> thers with Scotland (*Alba* being the Gaelic name for Scotland), the
> Alba Longa reference connects him as well with the ancient Roman
> city of Latium, and not unequivocally with the Scottish. Moreover,
> since Latium is the birthplace of famed twins Romulus and Remus,
> the Alba Longa reference suggests a duality on the part of Crot-
> thers; and given Joyce's interest in twins, and the evidence of his
> extensive knowledge of the mythology of twins in *Finnegans Wake*,
> Crotthers' birthplace is important to our understanding of his line-
> age, if, indeed, the reader is meant to recall Rome's antagonistic
> twins. . . . Notwithstanding these complications, the name *Crotthers*
> is not a Roman name, either; it is a variant of the Scottish name
> *Carruthers*, "from the lands of Carruthers in the parish of Midlebie
> Dumfriesshire, in local speech pronounced Cridders." . . . Crotthers,
> as the name appears in *Ulysses* with its uncharacteristic double t's,
> seems like an Irishman's bungled phonetic attempt to reproduce the
> common, local *Cridders* pronunciation. The name *Crotthers* alone,
> then, has an implied heritage, an affected heritage, and an unspoken,
> hidden, and true heritage. By proclaiming to be Scottish, indeed, by
> dressing like one in Highland garb. . . . Crotthers can fool all but
> the genealogists. . . . Yet names are rarely to be trusted in *Ulysses*, as
> they are often "impostures," functioning like sounds to trigger false

associations, false allegiances, and false correspondences (Crotthers sounds more dignified than *Cridders*, for instance). (58–60)

Culleton's comments on the name are based on Crotthers's connection to "Alba Longa" and the actual history of the name. However, these lines of inquiry do not take into account any other information about the character himself. Her comment on the possible duality of Crotthers is important though, since it ties with frequent, near constant connections between duality and Scotland in Joyce's later work. Also of interest is her focus on twins. As we shall see in the subsequent chapters, Joyce's allusions to the Picts and the Scots play with the idea of Scotland and Ireland as uncanny, inverted, "twin" nations.

Based on the other details Joyce gives us about this character and taking into account that names in Joyce often function as "supplemental allusions" or "shorthand" for "the full context" (Culleton, 12), an alternative and suggestive reading of the name Crotthers presents itself. Three main subjects or themes Crotthers is associated with in "Oxen of the Sun" and "Circe" are Scotland (of course), the sea or maritime imagery, and drunkenness. As Culleton points out, Crotthers is twice described as being from "Alba Longa" (*U*, 14.191, 233); he is also named as "a Scots fellow" (*U*, 14.506), as well as "the Scotch student" (*U*, 14.738), "the Scotchman" (*U*, 14.1207–8) and "the Caledonian envoy" (*U*, 14.988–89). A considerable amount of Scots language also appears in "Oxen of the Sun." Either Crotthers's intoxicated condition leads him to exaggerate his Scottishness for comic effect or his friends are attempting to sound Scottish and use Scots vocabulary in order to "make a feck of him" (or a mixture of the two). In any case, Scots appears in the episode due to the presence of Crotthers in such sentences as "Dinna forget the cowslips for hersel" (*U*, 14.1522–23), "Hoots, mon, a wee drap to pree" (*U*, 14.1532), "Aweel, ye maun e'en gang yer gates" (*U*, 14.1538), and "D'ye ken bare socks?" (*U*, 14.1548). The phrase "wee drap to pree" alludes to Robert Burns's song "Willie Brew'd a Peck o' Maut," and the chorus of this song is echoed at the end of the "Oxen of the Sun" episode: "We are nae fou. We're nae tha fou. Au reservoir, mossoo. Tanks you" (*U*, 14.1505–6); "We're nae tha fou. The Leith police dismisseth us" (*U*, 14.1565). The work of Robert Burns is also alluded to in another section of "Oxen of the Sun" that uses Scots language: "Collar the leather, youngun. Roun wi the nappy. Here, Jock braw Hielentman's your barley-bree. Lang may your lum reek and your kailpot boil!" (*U*, 14.1489–91). The allusion is to a section of "Love and Liberty: A Cantata" as well as to the popular Scottish expression "Lang may your lum reek and your kailpot boil."[12]

Crotthers's face is described, as Maley points out above, as "glowing from the briny airs of the Mull of Galloway" (*U*, 14.1205–6), one of a number of occasions where the Scotsman is linked to the sea. This "glow" probably has more to do with Crotthers's heavy alcohol intake than any "briny airs." Nevertheless, a maritime connection is established by Joyce with the use of this word. The word "briny" relates to the saltiness of the sea ("brine" is, of course, water saturated with salt) and, according to the *OED*, can be used as a colloquial or jocular term for the sea itself. There is also a slight suggestion of the word "salinity" or "saline" in the use of the word "salient" (*U*, 14.740) in connection with Crotthers. Crotthers is also described as being "blond as tow" (*U*, 14.739), tow being flax fiber used to make rope.[13] However, tow can also mean "a rope used for towing, a tow-line" and can function as a verb, "the action of towing or fact of being towed" (*OED*), tying Crotthers to shipping terminology. His designation as "Caledonian envoy" stresses the sense of him as a traveler, one sent on a voyage of some kind. Also, since he is reportedly from "Alba Longa," he perhaps shares the fate of the population of that town in being exiled (at least temporarily) (Davies, 151).

In "Oxen of the Sun" Crotthers is, like his medical student companions, steaming drunk. This is hardly surprising, since when he is focused on in the text he is either being poured a drink or requesting more drink. Ian MacArthur has gone as far as suggesting that Crotthers's qualification "(Disc. Bacc.)" (*U*, 14.1257) stands for "disciple of Bacchus" (530), which would further highlight his connection with intoxication.[14] The phrase "Roun wi the nappy" (*U*, 14.1489) is a traditional Scottish request for a drink refill but is amusingly fitting in the environs of a maternity hospital. A further description of Crotthers also highlights his drunken state:

Here the listener who was none other than the Scotch student, a little fume of a fellow, blond as tow, congratulated in the liveliest fashion with the young gentlemen and, interrupting the narrative at a salient point, having desired his visavis with a polite beck to have the obligingness to pass him a flagon of cordial waters at the same time by a questioning poise of the head (a whole century of polite breeding had not achieved so nice a gesture) to which was united an equivalent but contrary balance of the bottle asked the narrator as plainly as was ever done in words if he might treat him with a cup of it. (*U*, 14.738–46)

This euphemistic description converts an inebriated Scottish student unable to keep his head up into a "polite" gentleman who desires to drink "cordial waters" and whose slumped, drunken posture is a "questioning poise of the head." The focus on "poise" and "balance" is rather comical given the circumstances. Furthermore, Crotthers is positioned "at the foot of the table" (*U*, 14.1204). This phrase is slightly ambiguous, since "foot" can mean "the lowest part or bottom of an eminence, or any object in an erect or sloping position, as a wall, ladder, staircase, etc.," or "the lower (usually projecting) part of an object, which serves to support it; the base" (*OED*). Rather than being at the table's end, Crotthers, due to the drunken difficulties he was having with his balance earlier, may have slumped to the floor. If this is the case, the scene could hardly be less "gallant" (*U*, 14.1203). This would also make the phrase "the land he stood for" (*U*, 14.989–90) heavily ironic, since one thing Crotthers cannot do is stand. Again, the "reality" of the situation is divorced from its textual representation.

How then does the convergence of the themes of maritime- or travel-related imagery, Scottishness, and drunkenness explain Crotthers's name? In order to understand this, we must turn our attention to the very last paragraph containing Scots speech in the chapter. As Crotthers departs, perhaps to find some female company for the evening, he manages to emit the following Wakean mixture of song, poetry, tongue twisters, and involuntary diaphragm contractions: "Your attention! We're nae tha fou. The Leith police dismisseth us. The least tholice. Ware hawks for the chap puking. Unwell in his abominable regions. Yooka. Night. Mona, my thrue love. Yook. Mona, my own love. Ook" (*U*, 14.1565–68). That this is Crotthers speaking is made clear by the Scots terms "fou" for drunk and "nae" for not. Again, drunkenness is apparent as Crotthers hiccups repeatedly: "Yooka," "Yook," "Ook." He also attempts a traditional tongue twister connected with drunkenness: "The Leith Police dismisseth us" (Leith being the port of Edinburgh, a further maritime and Scottish connection).[15] Crotthers is having great difficulty articulating anything clearly, and despite his protestations, he is totally "fou." Hence he lisps "least tholice" instead of "Leith Police," slurs "thrue" for "true" when attempting to sing the line "Mona, My Own Love" and garbles "abdominal" as "abominable."[16]

It is this drunken verbal confusion or distortion and lack of clear articulation that can help explain Joyce's selection of the name Crotthers for this Scottish character. As Culleton has noted, "Joyce often used sounds and words that smacked of something else, incorporating into his works items that by design were redolent and allusive" (22). The three main features of Crotthers's character are the fact that he is from Scotland, that he is associated with the sea, and that he is drunk and therefore begins slurring and lisping his speech. These factors can explain the choice of the name Crotthers, a proto-Wakean word distortion from Joyce in which a sibilant is replaced by a fricative and which is an example of his "nominal play" (7).[17] The word "crossers" is drunkenly articulated—by the text itself—as "Crotthers."

A similar switch between an *s* sound and a *th* sound can be seen with the change from Leith to "least" in the text. Crotthers himself also replaces the *p* of "police" with *th* to form "tholice," and a similar process results in "thrue" for "true" (*U*, 14.1567). Crotthers's speech problems are also apparent in the "Circe" chapter, where, ostensibly, Bloom is examined by a succession of medical students including Mulligan, Dixon, and Costello. The medical examination is of Crotthers himself as well as Bloom, or, to use Freudian terminology, Crotthers is "projecting" his own problems onto Bloom. Crotthers comments of a "patient" that "Salivation is insufficient" (*U*, 15.1793–94). Of course, technical difficulties in saliva production have been known to be caused by heavy drinking and have often led to lisping and slurring. The late hour and the large amounts of alcohol taken have begun to affect the language of the text itself. In other words, Joyce adapts and distorts particular words in order to reflect the scene or situation or for certain thematic purposes. This activity, where names are created to suit the mood or activity of the chapter and to develop themes, is possible only in the more outré chapters of *Ulysses*, such as "Oxen of the Sun" and "Circe," but is commonplace throughout *Finnegans Wake*, where the names of the various figures are constantly transforming.

"Crotthers," a drunken, thick-tongued version of "crossers," ties in with the maritime-related imagery of the words "briny," "tow," and "Mull of Galloway" in relating to sea travel (the place name Galloway contains the Celtic root "gal," indicating that it is a place of the Gaels [see Davies, 87–88], linking Crotthers to the wider Gaelic world). The choice of the Mull of Galloway as the place associated with Crotthers can also be explained by its position as one of the closest locations in Scotland from which to cross to Ireland, along with the Mull of Kintyre. It is the southernmost point in Scotland, and Ireland is visible across the North Channel from this location (depending on the weather). Clearly Joyce is working with the concept of the sea linking Scotland and Ireland here, deliberately choosing to associate the washed-up Crotthers with an area in Scotland so close to Ireland, an ideal place from which to *cross*. Joyce was certainly aware by the time of the composition of the *Wake* that the formation of the Scottish nation began with the crossing and arrival of an Irish group known to the Romans as the "Scoti" and their cross-fertilization with the indigenous Picts; his notes from Stephen Gwynn's *History of Ireland* on this topic can be found in *Finnegans Wake* notebook VI.B.6.[18] Joyce also took notes from J. M. Flood's *Ireland: Its Saints and Scholars* (1917) and Benedict Fitzpatrick's *Ireland and the Making of Great Britain* (1922), both of which feature material on the Irish influence on ancient Scotland.

Since the Middle Irish for harp is *crott*, Crotthers's name also contains the emblematic musical instrument of Ireland (see also "Two Gallants"), thus sounding the hidden Irishness of Crotthers and "the land he stood for" (*U*, 14.989–90).[19] As Willy Maley observes in "'Kilt by Kelt Shell Kithagain with Kinagain': Joyce and Scotland," Joyce also plays with the theme of crossers or crossings between Scotland and Ireland in "The Dead." Maley is correct to draw attention to the importance of the imagery of crossing here—as well as in the crossings of the dancers at Mrs Morkan's Christmas party—but this concerns the historical crossings and recrossings of peoples between Ireland and Scotland, as well as a disguised "double-cross" as he has suggested ("Kilt by Kelt," 211). We can see the brief, sketchy beginning of Joyce's treatment of Irish-Scottish crossings in "The Dead" with the figure of Mrs Malins, a further development in the character of Crotthers in "Oxen of the Sun," and—the fullest elaboration—in the shadowy world of *Finnegans Wake*, the principal subject of the present study.

One further gloss we can apply to the word "crossers" in relation to Crotthers is that of a mixed breed, since to cross can mean to mix or breed two different animals or plants together to produce something new. Crotthers is linked in the text to "breeding" (*U*, 14.743), and his banter is almost exclusively limited to discussions on procreation. Meanwhile the chapter itself is set in a maternity hospital, a space obviously suggestive of fertilization and reproduction, and the linguistic and stylistic experimentalism of "Oxen" foreshadows the hybridized language and verbal metamorphoses of *Finnegans Wake*. Scots and Scottish culture appear in "Oxen" and the *Wake* partly because Joyce thought of Scotland as an example of Irish transformation through cross-fertilization or "hybridity." The concept of hybridity, "a kind of fluid, catch-all counter-hegemonic means of reaffirming identity over and against essentializing discourses of ethnicity or nationalism" (Syrotinski, 27), was first developed by Homi Bhabha:

> In *The Location of Culture* (1994) . . . Bhabha creates a series of concepts that seek to undermine the simple polarization of the world into self and other. Bhabha's writing emphasizes the *hybridity* of cultures, which on one level simply refers to the mixed-ness, or even "impurity" of cultures—so long as we don't imagine that any culture is really *pure*. This term refers to an original mixed-ness within every form of identity. In the case of cultural identity, hybridity refers to the fact that cultures are not discrete phenomena; instead, they are always in contact with one another, and this contact leads to cultural mixed-ness. (Huddard, 6–7)

Bhabha's observation that "the margin of hybridity . . . resists the binary opposition of racial and cultural groups . . . as homogenous polarized political consciousnesses" (Bhabha, 296) is pertinent here. Joyce's work on Scotland is a key component of his efforts to resist concepts of homogeneity, or polarized opposition through a vision of "mixedness." Strangely, paradoxically even, these attempts rely to some extent on the binary system of the twins Shaun and Shem in *Finnegans Wake*. This binary system of the brother figures—which represents, among other things, the racial or historical links between Scotland and Ireland—works in an almost deconstructive fashion to show how identities or cultures are never quite pure, self-contained, or static, that there is always a destabilizing element of the "Other" operating within the "self." Joyce uses this system to envisage a structural relationship whereby Ireland exists *within* Scotland and vice versa just as Shem and Shaun can never be fully separated or isolated. Furthermore, this vision of hybridity works alongside—and in spite of—an overall representation of the nature and character of Celtic culture. As was mentioned in the introduction, that Joyce denies the notion of racial or national purity does not mean that he does not have an interest in racial or national "identity" (see Nolan, *Nationalism*, 148).

The commentary on Alba Longa by the Scottish anthropologist James Frazer (i.e., from the other Alba)—likely one of Joyce's sources for information on this area of pre-Roman history—concludes that the kings of the settlement "acted as public rain-makers, wringing showers from the dark sky by their enchantments whenever the parched earth cried out for the refreshing moisture" (Frazer, 119). They did so through fertility rituals, by "pretending to make thunder and lightning" (Frazer, 118–19).[20] Fittingly, "Oxen of the Sun" is based on pregnancy/childbirth and takes place during a thunderstorm (presented in a seventeenth-century diarist style): ". . . this evening after sundown, the wind sitting in the west, biggish swollen clouds to be seen as the night increased and the weatherwise poring up at them and some sheet lightnings at first and after, past ten of the clock, one great stroke with a long thunder" (*U*, 14.483–87). So, the appearance of a talismanic envoy from Alba Longa acts as another link to ancient fertility customs. Indeed, the quasi-Bacchic festivities of "Oxen" resemble some kind of sympathetic magic ritual in which quenching thirsts will somehow bring about rain and fertility. The episode begins with a Celtic *deisil* or "Deshil" (*U*, 14.1) and as John Gordon has commented, "'Oxen of the Sun' persistently encourages us to reflect on the extent to which the heart has affinities with ancestral codes" ("Obeying the Boss," 245).

Interestingly, considering the maternity hospital setting of "Oxen" and the birth of a baby boy, much of Frazer's discussion of Alba Longa is concerned with female succession rules:

Now it is very remarkable that though the first king of Rome, Romulus, is said to have been descended from the royal house of Alba, in which the kingship is represented as hereditary in the male line, not one of the Roman kings was immediately succeeded by his son on the throne. Yet several left sons or grandsons behind them. On the other hand, one of them was descended from a former king through his mother, not through his father, and three of the kings, namely Tatius, the elder Tarquin, and Servius Tullius, were succeeded by their sons-in-law, who were all either foreigners or of foreign descent. This suggests that the right to the kingship was transmitted in the female line, and was actually exercised by foreigners who married the royal princesses. (122) [21]

Frazer's discussion provides another context for the questions of maternity and paternity in *Ulysses*: "Mrs. Purefoy's annual producing of a child develops *The Golden Bough*'s implications concerning the parodic nature of the recurrent and the cyclical" (Vickery, *Literary Impact*, 389). According to Stuart Gilbert's *Ulysses* "schema," the symbol for this episode of the text is "mothers" (Gilbert, *Ulysses*, 288). Furthermore, Gilbert has the "colour" of "Oxen'" as white, which in Latin is *albus*, a near match for *alba* (288). In "Circe," "DR CROTTHERS" points out that a patient's urine is "albuminoid" (*U*, 15.1792–93). Since "albumen" is the white of an egg, the patient (Bloom) is linked to female fertility, part of his presentation as the new "womanly man" (*U*, 15.1799).[22] However, albuminoid urine is slightly surprising given Crotthers's heavy drinking, since low albumin levels are generally associated with liver disease (See Longmore et al., 700).

In *Joyce's Revenge*, Andrew Gibson discusses the function of the fertility theme of "Oxen" in relation to Irish cultural traditions: "The poetic affirmation of fertility had been traditional in Irish culture. For Yeats and others, the theme had its origins in fertility rituals. But it is its political inflection that is most important: as Murray Pittock has demonstrated, from at least the seventeenth century onwards, the fertility theme was never simply literal. It also had an allegorical significance relative to the fortunes of the nation, national prosperity, and national renewal" (156). The young men at the National Maternity Hospital on Dublin's Holles Street are nationalists but not of a type interested in "a singular, unitary, national identity" (178). Instead, *Ulysses*—through the techniques, themes, and characters of "Oxen"—promotes "antagonisms, contradictions, social differences, cultural hybridity" (178–79). The antisectarian move of including the (probable) Protestant Crotthers at a Catholic hospital functions—alongside the "adulterated" (178) nature of the "Oxen" episode—as an exemplary vision of a more fertile, hybrid, nonsectarian Ireland.

The fertile crossings of the Irish and the Scots have spawned "hybreds" (*FW*, 152.16) or mixed populations in both countries, something Joyce would have become aware of at an early age. As was mentioned in the introduction, very little is known about Joyce's ferry trip to Glasgow made with his father in 1894, the occasion of his first departure from Ireland. However, it is highly likely that it would have brought him into contact with the results of waves of emigration, the mass movement of Irish labor-seekers into western Scotland in the late nineteenth century and early twentieth century. Indeed, given the very high numbers of Irish immigrating to Glasgow and environs in this period, it would have been difficult to avoid coming into contact with Irish workers. This "upsurge in immigration from Ireland after the Great Famine" was due to "the employment opportunities in Scottish industry" and contributed to a marked increase in Scottish population during the Industrial Revolution (Devine, *Nation*, 252). As R. F. Foster has noted, "By 1851, 6.7 per cent of the entire Scottish population was Irish-born, a percentage that rose to over 18 per cent in Dundee and Glasgow" (*Modern Ireland*, 368). Indeed, Glasgow's rise to commercial prominence in the eighteenth and nineteenth centuries owed to its links with Ireland and the wider Atlantic economy (see Devine, *Nation*, xx).

Subsequent chapters of this text will look at how Joyce develops the idea of amalgamated or "crossed" Scottish/Irish populations in *Finnegans Wake* with reference to the historical foundation of Scotland, which was itself the result of the mixing of "Irish" and "Scottish" peoples. However, in *Finnegans Wake* Joyce uses this mixing to create a divided mental state based upon pretexts from Scottish literature. The character Crotthers can be seen as a forerunner to the presence of Scottish/Irish mixing in *Finnegans Wake* and to the exploration of divided identity. Crotthers's name appears in this reading as representative of Joyce's view of the crossbreedings of Scottish and Irish histories, a disguised and small-scale hint towards a subject he would expand on in his later work. This vision of a fluid "contact zone" (Cheng, *Joyce, Race, and Empire*, 217) between Ireland and Scotland undermines the standard, simplified British/Irish conceptual framework as represented by the "two different constituencies" (Gibson and Platt, 23) of recent work in Joyce studies such as *Joyce, Ireland, Britain*. Moreover, Joyce's attention to the essentially mixed ethnic nature of Scotland is part of his attack on the idea of racial or national "static essences" (see Cheng, *Joyce, Race, and Empire*, 53). This replacement of "static essences" with marine fluidity and mixing is present both in the figure of Crotthers and in Joyce's construction of his Pictish/Scottish "nodal" system.

What kinds of international relations were brought about by these connections? Did Joyce regard the North Channel as creating, if not entirely friendly, then at least productive contacts between Scotland and Ireland? If so, the "cordial waters" (*U*, 14.742) in "Oxen" can be read not only as referring to alcoholic drink and to the convivial spirits it instills but also as Joyce's comment on how the sea links between the two countries have the capacity to create useful relationships across the water. Certainly the relationships Crotthers has formed in Dublin are "cordial." The phrase could also be an ironic, sarcastic, or bitter statement on the historical traumas Ireland has suffered at the hands of seaborne raiders or colonists from Scotland, including the invasion of Edward Bruce in 1315 and the later arrival of Protestant settlers during the seventeenth century. The word "cordial" also contains "cord," as in a length of rope, which "ties" in with the imagery of linkage, also present in the use of the word "tow" in association with Crotthers. Joyce conveys the idea that the waters between Ireland and Scotland, rather than dividing the two countries and "the Celts" generally (*U*, 14.34), act as a length of rope or cord tethering them together. The phrase "cordial waters" also links to the overarching theme of the chapter—embryological development—relating to the umbilical cord and to the amniotic fluid of the womb. Fittingly enough, a character associated with the sea is found in a chapter also concerned with both alcoholic and amniotic fluids.

"Oxen of the Sun" is concerned not only with "the Celts" (*U*, 14.34) but with the course of European civilization. John Gordon has included Crotthers in a discussion of the ending of the episode, with reference to the histories of Europe and Christianity:

Civilization, sick of its past, turns in a "romantic" gesture to local dialects and literatures, willfully forgetting the great root and branch of its inheritance. . . . Here the last few apocalyptic pages are characterized by an influx of Irish, Scottish ("Carlyle," Crotthers), American (Dowie), and other dialects from the extreme borders of Western civilization, along with various references to "injuns," "coons," "sheenies," "Rooshians," "Jappies," and so forth. It becomes, in the strictest meaning of the word, provincial. Civilization has "evolved" from Rome to the provinces, from Latin into a multitude of dialects, from communal memory and veneration into a collection of private memories, from Roman classicism into provincial romanticism, from Catholicism into Protestantism. ("Multiple Journeys," 165–66)[23]

So, Crotthers is part of this move towards the "extreme borders'" of civilization in "the very last islands of Europe" (*OCPW*, 124–25) and a move towards Protestantism. He is a representative of the western limits of Europe and of one of the most Protestant countries on the continent (though adherence to organized religion has been on the wane in Scotland for decades). In these two senses, Scotland—and also because the Roman Empire never fully extended its control beyond the Antonine Wall—is perhaps the most obviously "removed" location in Europe from Rome.

For Gordon, the last pages of "Oxen" are "apocalyptic," and, tellingly, Scotland is associated with "doom" elsewhere in Joyce's writings.[24] In the "Lestrygonians" and "Circe" episodes of *Ulysses*, the end of the world takes the form of a bizarre two-headed octopus with a "Scotch accent." For Anne Marie D'Arcy the octopus represents the creeping influence of Freemasonry in Ireland.[25] However, since the octopus is "twoheaded," it is perhaps "in two minds" itself as to what it represents. The enigmatic mollusk image fits in with other Scottish and maritime linkages elsewhere in Joyce's writing—as well as with the end of the world in a geographical sense—while the phrase "end of the world" itself echoes Stephen Dedalus's thoughts as he walks along Sandymount Stand (another liminal maritime area) in the earlier "Proteus" episode: "world without end" (see *U*, 2.203–4; 3.27–28). Stephen associates the final line of the Gloria Patri with his conclusion that the external world does not depend on his perception of it. Stephen's musings—which here conflate spatial, temporal, and theological aspects—invert the earlier proclamation of his boss Deasy that "All human history moves towards one great goal, the manifestation of God" (*U*, 2.380–81). Stephen's reversal here suggests a skepticism that there is an ultimate "end" or "goal" for humanity. As David Sidorsky notes with reference to *Finnegans Wake*, "Joyce negates any suggestion of teleology or ends in history" (305).[26] However, Stephen's thoughts also contrast with the idealist notion that nothing exists outside of our minds, or that only mental representations exist, that our inner world is the only genuine reality. An alternative sense of the phrase "end of the world" in *Ulysses* is the idealist position that, in a sense, the world "ends" when we are not perceiving it. The image of the octopus is perhaps a trap, leading us to interpret it as symbolizing some insidious threat but actually meaning something quite different, namely the "Scotch" state of "being in two minds" (a link to hesitation, skepticism) and at the "end of the world'" (a link to idealism). Joyce's interest in Scottish skepticism and idealism will be explored in subsequent chapters.

A more literal doom is associated with Scotland in Joyce's lectures. In a discussion on Irish affairs as part of his lecture "Ireland: Island of Saints and Sages," which was presented at the Università Popolare in Trieste in 1907, Joyce speculates on the fate of Ireland and of the greater "Celtic world":

> Is this country destined some day to resume its ancient position as the Hellas of the north? Is the Celtic spirit, like the Slavic one (which it resembles in many respects), destined in the future to enrich the consciousness of civilization with new discoveries and institutions? Or is the Celtic world, the five Celtic nations, pressed by a stronger race to the edge of the continent—to the very last islands of Europe—doomed, after centuries of struggle, finally to fall headlong into the ocean? (*OCPW*, 124–25)[27]

A further reason Crotthers appears in the "Oxen of the Sun" chapter is—as Gordon gestures towards—as a representative of the "extreme borders of Western civilization," part of a trend towards the "provincial" within the chapter. But, strangely enough, since Crotthers hails from "Alba

Longa" he represents both the beginnings of Western civilization in Latium, the precursor to Rome, and also some of its furthest geographical or cultural reaches through the Gaelic word for Scotland. Thus Crotthers functions as the sort of paradoxical coincidence of historical opposites which, for David Sidorsky, signals a denial of historical progress (see Sidorsky, 303–4), and the character can be read as emblematic of what Terry Eagleton reads as a modernist tension between the contemporary and the archaic (See *Heathcliff*, 278–79). Furthermore, Crotthers also fits in with the shift from Catholicism to Protestantism that Gordon mentions:

> The presence of the Scotsman Crotthers among the students may well be significant. From the mid-eighteenth century onwards, the Rotunda maternity hospital had always specified Protestant staff and management. So, too, the founders of the National Maternity Hospital declared that "the management of the hospital be exclusively Catholic." The masters, doctors, resident pupils, nurses, and all intern servants and assistants were Catholic, the only exception being students. In a piece of historical realism that is also a gesture of resistance to sectarianism, Joyce emphasizes the mixed character of the group. (Gibson, *Revenge*, 166)

As well as a shift from east to west and from Catholicism to Protestantism (a further connection to the disguised "cross" in Crotthers's name), Crotthers's appearance in *Ulysses* also intentionally coincides with an increasing skepticism in the text.

Richard Ellmann sees Crotthers's fellow Scot David Hume as being the main influence behind this progression, and, according to Jeri Johnson, Hume's writing style serves as one of the sources for Joyce's portrayal of literary "gestation."[28] According to Ellmann, "The dominant mood from the *Wandering Rocks* through *Circe* is scepticism, Bloom's day but also, for the nine hours from three to midnight, Hume's day" (*Liffey*, 96). So, the appearance of the Scotsman Crotthers aligns with the increasingly Humean, skeptical influence in *Ulysses* that culminates in the hallucinatory drama of "Circe," a chapter that involves "the colonization of the Dublin unconscious" (Gibson, *Revenge*, 183) and that is itself "the unconscious of the text" (McGee, *Paperspace*, 116). In these chapters, the external world of matter and phenomena becomes more uncertain and removed, prefiguring the overwhelming incertitude of *Finnegans Wake*, where Joyce develops his literary skepticism and idealism to its logical conclusion.[29] Furthermore, the various styles and final linguistic tangle of the embryonic "Oxen of the Sun" episode serve to suggest that reality itself cannot be replicated by writing: "If coition leading to conception and birth is seen ambivalently, literary expression is shown to be inadequate to confer certitude, incapable of rendering ultimate reality. In the end, reality itself is undercut. . . . The terrible fact that truth is not Truth, or that many bits of truth add up not to a final great knowledge but to a final great confusion and incertitude, need not be underlined" (French, 176, 179). Elsewhere, French claims that "incertitude" and "relativity" are the "central problem[s] of the novel" and that "the latter half of the book clamorously reminds us how difficult it is to be sure what is real" (112, 118). In a similar vein, Colin MacCabe has written that in "the finale of "The Oxen of the Sun" . . . there is no longer any extra-discursive criterion of truth" (*Revolution*, 127). Literature becomes "a covering and an artificial obstruction of the real, a contraception" (McGee, *Paperspace*, 112). The first appearance of the Scotsman Crotthers coincides with a "Scottish school" (*OCPW*, 157) form of skepticism towards our chances of reaching "certitude": "The narrator flips through his deck of styles tauntingly: he knows we want, not truth, but certitude. He, or the author behind him, also knows that such is not a gift he can honestly confer on us" (French, 184). Joyce once offered help with *Ulysses* to his friend Frank Budgen in the following terms: "If I can throw any obscurity on the subject let me know" (*LIII*, 261).

Crotthers is not seen as a representation of imperial or colonial power in the way in which the Englishman Haines and the Ulsterman Deasy are. Neither is he seen as a victim of oppression, though we could describe him as being presented as a member of a minority culture, since his speech marks him as being non-English and therefore from outside of the center of the dominant culture. Crotthers first appears in a chapter in which the blurring of styles and languages acts as a precursor to the more radical linguistic strategies of the *Wake*. As Jacob Korg notes of the *Wake*, "Hybrids . . . imply resistance to linguistic authority" (64). Since the linguistic hybridity of the *Wake* can be read as an assault on English literary and cultural standards or as a "struggle against imperialism"

(MacCabe, "*Finnegans*," 4), the hybridity or fertility—including the figure Crotthers and the attendant Scots language—of "Oxen" can be read
as an earlier phase of this development. Furthermore, the shifting styles
of "Oxen," which deny our attempts to reach a stable truth, form an
antechamber to the abyss of incertitude that is *Finnegans Wake.*

Crotthers also exists as a "semicolonial" hybrid combination of the
dominated and the dominating. As a Scot, Crotthers hails from a country that was one of the first to experience English domination. He is also
a representative of a nation that had become absorbed into the British
state and is therefore part of the dominant society controlling Ireland in
the early twentieth century. We can read Crotthers not only as symbolizing the mixed ethnicities of Ireland and Scotland—a representation
that undermines the essentialized racial, cultural, and national discourses
of the late nineteenth and early twentieth centuries—but also as a figure
alluding to the nature of Scotland as a colonial intersection, a cross between "Celtic counterpart and British adjutant" (Maley, "Kilt by Kelt,"
201). The recurring associations between Scotland and duality in Joyce's
works can be read as a commentary on Scotland's dual links to Ireland as
Gaelic or Celtic "sister" (*PE*, 109) and imperial subordinate.

It is relatively unusual for Joyce to "typecast, to speak of someone as
representative of a nation" (Maley, "Kilt by Kelt," 213). However, rather
than appearing as a crude and reductive "stage Scotchman" embodying
a vision of a singular, static, and homogenous nation, Crotthers embodies relations, connections, and processes, and he appears in an episode
in which little is fixed or stable or certain. This presentation of a character that represents a type of "intercourse" or umbilical link between
two countries is an apt feature of "Oxen of the Sun," since part of the
focus of the chapter is on fertility, gestation, and birth. Furthermore, as
Culleton has highlighted, Crotthers is associated with duality, through
the reference to "Alba Longa." This duality is at base an Irish/Scottish
connection—as suggested by the reference to the Mull of Galloway—as
well as an overt connection to ancient Latium. In the following chapters
we shall see how Joyce adapts this vision of Celtic connections to create
the divided mind-set of *Finnegans Wake.* Joyce performs this through
the adaptation of Scottish literary techniques and through the application of what he saw as a specifically Celtic strain of philosophy. Willy
Maley uses his discussion of Crotthers to justify his feeling that Joyce

had a negative view towards Scotland and Scottish people. However, if we read the name Crotthers as emblematic of historical connections between Ireland and Scotland and as a connection to the Humean sections of *Ulysses* and to the total incertitude of *Finnegans Wake* rather than as a character associated with "dirt" (Maley, "Kilt by Kelt," 214), then we can begin to reappraise Joyce's attitudes to Scotland and begin to understand how Scotland functions in his texts.

TWO

Exhuming the Enlightenment

Edinburgh, Hume, *Ulysses*, and the *Wake*

Now that the links between Scotland and Ireland in works previous to *Finnegans Wake* have been established, we can go on to consider the role of Scottish culture in the *Wake* itself. The creation of a Celtic space of incertitude and interiority will be discussed here in connection with the theories of the Scottish Enlightenment philosopher and Edinburgh native David Hume. Along with the likes of Amsterdam, Budapest, Copenhagen, New York, Rio de Janeiro, and Vienna, Edinburgh is one of the cities which Joyce uses as reference points on which to map out the *Haveth Childers Everywhere* fragment of "Work in Progress" (*JJII*, 628). As a result, an array of Edinburgh landmarks may be viewed in the text of *Finnegans Wake*. For example, "Rest and Be Thankful," an old route over the city's Corstorphine Hill, is diverted into a minor description of sleeping and dreaming in the phrase "Rest and bethinkful" (*FW*, 543.13), and the hill of Arthur's Seat looms over the text as "arthruseat" (*FW*, 577.28). There are also allusions to the Morningside and Echobank cemeteries on page 543. Joyce may have seen some of these sights himself. As was discussed earlier, Joyce most likely visited Edinburgh in 1894 (see Jackson and Costello, 185–86). And as we shall see in the next chapter, there are numerous allusions in the *Wake* to James Hogg's *Private Memoirs and Confessions of a Justified Sinner*, which is largely set in "odinburgh" (*FW*, 487.9–10).

Edinburgh figures largely in *Finnegans Wake* through its intellectual achievements, specifically through various products and thinkers of the Scottish Enlightenment, the eighteenth-century period of extraordinary philosophical and scientific progress that gave the world the works and achievements of figures such as Adam Smith (whose *Wealth of Nations* [1776] is referred to in the *Wake* as the "culminwillth of natures" [*FW*, 593.12]), Francis Hutcheson, Thomas Reid, James Hutton, Dugald Stewart, Adam Ferguson, Joseph Black, and David Hume. In addition to the literary accomplishments of Burns, Scott, Hogg, and others during this period, the installation of Hugh Blair, supporter of Macpherson's *Ossian*, as first Regius Professor of Rhetoric and Belles-Lettres at the University of Edinburgh in 1762 can be considered the beginning of the modern form of literary studies (see R. Crawford, *The Scottish Invention of English Literature*). According to the subtitle of a history of the era by Arthur Herman, the achievements of this period amount to "the Scots' invention of the modern world" (see subtitle of Herman, *The Scottish Enlightenment*). Herman points out the importance of Scotland's advanced education system in creating the conditions necessary for the Enlightenment. For Fredric Jameson this era is a candidate for the starting point of modernity itself, since it is the moment when "Adam Smith and others make the emergence of capitalism an unavoidable narrative option" (*Modernity*, 31). However, like the work of James Macpherson, the efforts of the Scottish Enlightenment can be seen as a concerted reaction to political events in Scotland, an attempt to restore some pride to a nation that had lost its crown in 1603 and its parliament in 1707.

It is an irony that *Finnegans Wake*, Joyce's "lingerous longerous book of the dark" (*FW*, 251.24), should interact so extensively with a movement dedicated to illumination. However, this is indeed the case. As is well known, Joyce consulted the famous eleventh edition of the *Encyclopaedia Britannica* frequently during the composition of *Finnegans Wake*, exploring it for words or phrases or ideas that could be deposited into his text. The information about Edinburgh that Joyce uses in *Finnegans Wake* comes via this source. The *Encyclopaedia Britannica* is a legacy of the Scottish Enlightenment. It was first edited by William Smellie, a carousing companion of Robert Burns, its initial edition produced between 1768 and 1771 in Edinburgh. Len Platt has discussed Joyce's use of the *Encyclopaedia Britannica* and how the *Wake* and the encyclopedia stand in opposition to each other in terms of their approaches to knowledge and certainty:

> The eleventh edition, from which Joyce worked, describes how the project was designed as a "digest of general information," its purpose being nothing less than to "give reasoned discussions on all the great questions of practical or speculative interest." The *Wake*, positioned very differently at the tail end of the modern age, is far from a digest, but it reflects back on the encyclopedic tradition in fascinating ways. To put it simply, *Finnegans Wake* is a text that has apparently swallowed or "digested" vast amounts of information only to return it in ways that seem outside all reasoned discussion. . . . In the ambitious and characteristically modern approach it takes to a universal and democratizing epistemology, the *Encyclopedia Britannica* stands as the antithesis of the *Wake*. . . . The *EB* is a text that achieves certainty in areas where the *Wake* "fails," performing in ways the *Wake* simply cannot. For this reason, it plays a precise part in framing what it is that the *Wake* articulates against—the knowledge the world claims to have of itself. ("Unfallable encycling," 107)

While the *Encyclopaedia Britannica* "achieves certainty," according to Platt, *Finnegans Wake* purposefully promotes obscurity, uncertainty, and doubt. For Joyce, somewhat paradoxically, these are specifically Celtic qualities. Indeed, as Seamus Deane has pointed out, attempts by a reader to come to terms with the difficulty of Joyce's texts function as a kind of reminder of our limitations as readers: "The switching back and forth from one order or kind of knowledge to another, and the discovery that knowledge is useful only to a limited and formal degree, never in a substantial, historical sense, leaves the reader in the curious position of realizing that the kind of research which these books demand is itself parodied by the way in which its discoveries are shown to lead nowhere" (*Celtic*, 104). However, aside from the *Encyclopaedia Britannica*, other aspects of the Scottish Enlightenment—particularly the skeptical philosophy of David Hume—strongly resemble the pervasive atmosphere of incertitude in the *Wake*. The *Encyclopaedia Britannica* and the works of Hume grew out of a culture in which human reason was considered to be of the utmost importance (and which led to the scientific materialism of Joyce's age). However, Hume's philosophy—as opposed to the optimism of the *Encyclopaedia Britannica* and the general confidence of the Enlightenment—demonstrates how reasoning leads only to increased skepticism regarding what we can actually know. As Robert J. Fogelin notes, "For Hume, things get worse the more we reason" (228). As Hume himself writes in the *Natural History of Religion*, "Doubt, uncertainty, suspence of judgement appear the only result of our most accurate scrutiny" (*Dialogues*, 185).

In *Finnegans Wake* Joyce refers to the work of a number of writers associated with the period of the Scottish Enlightenment and its aftermath. In fact, most of the cast of Scottish writers Joyce ropes into *Finnegans Wake* were born in the eighteenth century. The few exceptions to this rule include Blind Harry (c. 1440–92), William Dunbar (b. 1459 or 1460), and Robert Louis Stevenson (1850–94). Joyce draws upon the poetry of Robert Burns to convey the demotic, musical atmosphere of HCE's bar; to elaborate on the theme of duality in the *Wake*; and as a symbol with which to point out the partial and enduring "Scottishness" of the north of Ireland. The poetry of James Macpherson is, in general, employed by Joyce as an emblem of the constructed repetitions of art and life as well as to highlight the shared cultural heritage of Ireland and Scotland. James Hogg's masterpiece *The Private Memoirs and Confessions of a Justified Sinner* is a key pretext for Joyce's treatment of split personality in the *Wake*. Joyce also alludes to the work of the poet Thomas Campbell (1777–1844), with the poem "The Exile of Erin" used in a passage describing Shem in I.vi (*FW*, 148.33). In addition, there are a number of allusions to the texts of Tobias Smollett in the *Wake*—"lice nittle clinkers" (*FW*, 29.08) (i.e., *The Expedition of Humphry Clinker* [1771]), "Roderick Random" (*FW*, 381.11–12) (i.e., *The Adventures of Roderick Random* [1748])—and the works of the Unionist poet and novelist Walter Scott are also referred to on a number of occasions.

According to Scott Klein, the novels of Scott were an important influence on *A Portrait of the Artist as a Young Man*. While there is a possible connection in this case (as in two of the short stories of *Dubliners*), it would be hard to argue that Scott's fiction provided any real inspiration for Joyce's work as a whole, especially since Scott's works are found discarded in a pile of "old useless papers" in "Araby" (*D*, 21). However, there are a number of allusions to Scott in *Finnegans Wake*.

References are made to the novels *Rob Roy* (*FW*, 546.18) and *Ivanhoe* (*FW*, 178.01), and to the poem "The Lady of the Lake" (*FW*, 465.36). The allusion to *Ivanhoe*, or "hivanhoesed" (*FW*, 178.01), comes in I.vii, a section based on the writing career of Shem and his "boasting of his literary ability while drunk" (Benstock, xviii). This passage includes references to Scott as well as to Charles Dickens and William Makepeace Thackeray in the less than complimentary-sounding phrase "greet scoot, duckings and thuggery" (*FW*, 177.35). When Stanislaus Joyce discusses his own juvenile and "questionable" literary taste in *My Brother's Keeper*, he mentions his interest in Scott and Dickens, writers whom his brother "could not stand" (94). We can probably add Thackeray to this blacklist, since, as we have seen, the unfortunate three are thrown together in the *Wake*.

The Heart of Midlothian is transplanted into Ireland with "the heart of Midleinster" (*FW*, 381.16) at the end of II.iii, the Roderick O'Conor section where Roderick/HCE finishes off the dregs of his departed customers' drinks and collapses onto the floor. The earliest version of this episode was the first installment of *Finnegans Wake* Joyce composed, commencing work on it in March 1923. The phrase, not present in the first draft, is a reference to HCE as well as a new epithet for the Hibernian Metropolis itself. This relocation from "Midlothian" (the Scottish county which includes Edinburgh) to "Midleinster" (Leinster being the Irish province that contains Dublin) provides a small link between the capitals of Scotland and Ireland. HCE is being described as "the heart of Midleinster" here as a way of demonstrating his own deluded sense of centrality and importance to his community, in contrast to the relatively lowly status he actually enjoys (or suffers). Alternatively, the phrase can be read as an ironic Walter Scott–style romanticized, nostalgic view of the fallen king/barman. Often in Joyce's work allusions to Scott are utilized to give a romantic veneer to a more sordid or mundane situation, as is the case in the stories "An Encounter" and "Araby."

The phrase "roberoyed" (*FW*, 546.18) is placed next to a mention of the "faineans" (*FW*, 546.18), binding Irish republicanism with the famous Scottish outlaw and the novel that bears his name. This strange juxtaposition suggests the essentially "romantic" nature of the Irish Republican Brotherhood and the Fenian Brotherhood. As Thomas Hofheinz notes, references to modern Ireland in conjunction with allusions to mythology or legend "foreground the dense romantic mythography of Irish nationalist resurgence doctrines" (35). Scott's retrospective work is connected to the dreams and voids of *Finnegans Wake* itself here, as the phrases "surrounded by obscurity" (*FW*, 546.19) and "inher light" (*FW*, 546.21) suggest. The word "roberoyed" echoes "hivanhoesed" in that Joyce has reconfigured the original proper nouns into terms resembling verbs in the past tense with the suffix -*ed*. These conversions, conveying completed actions of the past and suggesting that history is actually capable of conclusions or resolutions, are apt microdescriptions of the content and concerns of Walter Scott's historical novels and of "the Scottish Enlightenment paradigm in which what is sacrificed to progress is retrieved imaginatively as nostalgia" (Whelan, 60). The romantic, poetic, nostalgic side of the Scottish Enlightenment is involved in *Finnegans Wake* alongside its more rational and scientific areas. This dual presentation of the contrasting aspects of the Scottish Enlightenment provides a further indication of the various quality of Scotland's written culture, both romantic and scientific, both backward looking and progressive.

The works of Scott and *Finnegans Wake* share a preoccupation with reviving and adapting the stories of history, legend, and folklore. However, Scott and Joyce have their roots in very different political traditions (Scott's Unionism contrasts with Joyce's family connections to Fenianism and Parnellism). Furthermore, Scott's relatively "goahead"[1] and teleological novels, in which individuals are caught in the midst of vast and "necessary" social change and which display a faith in progress and the possibility of concrete, permanent (Unionist) resolution, are in contrast to the presentation of history as a cyclical and basically unchanging process in the *Wake*. Moreover, Scott's almost painterly priority is with the external realm of events and landscapes, rather than any focus on psychological exploration: "Scott is not, on the whole, a novelist who explores the psychological depths of motivation and introspection" (R. Watson, 259).

Indeed, texts such as *Waverley* (1814) present us with purposefully one-dimensional and "simple" main characters whose role is simply to exist at the flashpoint of historical change as antagonistic sections of a society clash (Scott was interested, as was Adam Smith, in the stages of history).[2] In other words, Scott details the advance of a dialectical process which engulfs middling, average figures such as Edward Waverley (hence his appeal for Marxist critics such as Georg Lukács and Fredric Jameson). With *Finnegans Wake*, on the other hand, history "occurs" within the mind of the dreamer, and there is no real sense of a superficial "change" or "progress," only a nightmarish carousel of repetition and re-semblance. Scott's works are at variance to the spirit of Joyce's enterprise and not nearly as useful to Joyce as the novels of Stevenson or Hogg. Hogg's *Private Memoirs and Confessions of a Justified Sinner* (1824) and Stevenson's *Strange Case of Dr. Jekyll and Mr. Hyde* (1886) are important blueprints for Joyce's treatment of internal division and split personality in the *Wake*. Unlike the references to Scott, allusions to Hogg, Stevenson, and Hume in *Finnegans Wake* all relate to the internal situation of the dreamer and help construct the Celtic unconscious of the *Wake*. As Ian Duncan has noted, "Walter Scott was the major novelist of the nine-teenth century [but his] achievement was comprehensively sidelined by the aesthetic revolutions of modernism" ("Scott and the Historical Novel," 103).

The philosophical branch of the Scottish Enlightenment is as useful to Joyce as its literary counterpart—if not more so. In particular, the skepticism and idealism of David Hume's philosophy form a basis for the general sense of uncertainty in *Finnegans Wake* (often reproduced in the reading experience through its distorting use of language and inten-tional obscurity) and its focus on the inner, mental world. Moreover, Hume's skepticism is an important precursor to the sense of disbelief or rejection of tradition in much of modernist literature. Although work has begun relating Hume to postmodern thought,[3] there is a gap to be filled here in terms of Hume's connections with modernism, especially with its "inward turn." The influence of philosophers such as Friedrich Nietzsche and Karl Marx on modernism is well documented by now. Perhaps it is time to move beyond the study of these two in relation to the movement, especially considering the general skepticism and idealism (in the mental sense) of many kinds inherent in the modernist era. I would suggest that the idea that there is a "collapse in idealism" in the modernist era needs to be revised (see Bell, Michael, 18).

Hume's work in general forms a stark contrast to the work of fellow Scottish Enlightenment writer Walter Scott in that it offered to Joyce a way of describing the uncertain and limited situation of the dreamer in *Finnegans Wake* (and, by extension, in all of us). Later, we will consider the theory of the "Caledonian antisyzygy," the hypothesis that Scottish literature is marked by the coming together of various contraries. There is a certain duality in Joyce's inclusion of references to both Scott and Hume, stressing the disparity between two branches of Scottish Enlightenment literature—romantic fiction or poetry and rational, scientific philosophical enquiry. Furthermore, Joyce's use of James Hogg and Robert Louis Stevenson indicates a skeptical attitude towards the idea of a coherent and stable "self."

Joyce's skepticism towards a conception of the self as a consistent, stable, identifiable entity is shared by the "Bundle theory" of Hume, who "endeavors to demonstrate how there is no Self . . . only . . . particular ideas, impressions" (Žižek, 720). This conception—or lack of conception—of the self will be familiar to anyone who has attempted to pin down the central identity of the hypothetical "dreamer" of the *Wake* and has been confronted only with varying "perceptions." For Hume, notions of the self are

> nothing but a bundle or collection of different perceptions, which succeed each other with an inconceivable rapidity, and are in a perpetual flux and movement. Our eyes cannot turn in their sockets without varying our perceptions. Our thought is still more variable than our sight; and all our other senses and faculties contribute to this change; nor is there any single power of the soul, which remains unalterably the same, perhaps for one moment. The mind is a kind of theatre, where several perceptions successively make their appearance; pass, re-pass, glide away, and mingle in an infinite variety of postures and situations. There is properly no *simplicity* in it at one time, nor *identity* in different; whatever natural propension we may have to imagine that simplicity and identity. The comparison of the theatre must not mislead us. They are the successive perceptions only, that constitute the mind; nor have we the most distant notion of the place, where these scenes are represented, or of the materials, of which it is compos'd. (Hume, *Treatise*, 300–301)[4]

It is striking just how close this is in spirit to the conception and style of *Finnegans Wake*. The *Wake*—with its sense of shifting, kaleidoscopic flux; its lack of a single, discrete central character or identity; its constant confusion or mingling of "bundles" of figures, ideas, words, or languages; its similar portrayal of the mind "as a kind of theatre" and of the total disconnection between this "theatre" and the "reality" of its "scenes" or "materials"—resembles Hume's understanding of our mental faculties. With his various engagements with Hume, we can see a radical and sustained form of skepticism in Joyce, one that questions the connections between the representations of our minds and the "reality" or otherwise of the external material world.[5]

As he walks along the sands of Sandymount Strand in the "Proteus" episode of *Ulysses*, Stephen Dedalus's meandering philosophical musings turn to the final line of the Gloria Patri hymn: "Open your eyes now. I will. One moment. Has all vanished since? If I open and am for ever in the black adiaphane. *Basta!* I will see if I can see. See now. There all the time without you: and ever shall be, world without end" (*U*, 3.25–28).[6] As was mentioned earlier, Stephen associates this line with his brief speculation that the external world does not depend upon his perception of it. Stephen's thoughts contrast with the idealist notion that nothing exists outside of our minds, or that only mental representations exist, that our inner life is the only genuine or accessible reality. As I stated previously, one alternative sense of the phrase "end of the world" in *Ulysses* is the idealist position that, in a sense, the world "ends" when we are not perceiving it. According to Hume, our faith in the continuing existence of external objects when we stop perceiving them is based on nothing but habit or custom rather than reason: "For Hume, the common belief in an external world is not based on any sort of reasoning to begin with, and cannot be supported by sound reasoning after the fact. . . . Hume holds that reasoning, by itself, is generally incapable of fixing belief and, in this particular case, incapable of establishing a belief in the existence of an external world" (Fogelin, 211). Hume describes this position in a pamphlet introducing his 1738 work *Treatise of Human Nature*: "Almost all reasoning is there reduced to experience, and the belief, which attends experience, is explained to be nothing but a peculiar sentiment, or lively conception produced by habit. Nor is this all. When we believe any thing of *external* existence, or suppose any object to exist a moment after it is no longer perceived, this belief is nothing but a sentiment of the same kind" (*Abstract*, 27). Similar comments are made by Hume in the *Treatise* itself (italics are mine):

Now since nothing is ever present to the mind but perceptions, and since all ideas are deriv'd from something antecedently present to the mind; it follows, that 'tis impossible for us to conceive or form an idea of any thing specifically different from ideas and impressions. Let us fix our attention out of ourselves as much as possible : Let us chase our imagination to the heavens, or to the utmost limits of the universe; we never really advance a step beyond those perceptions, which have appear'd in that narrow compass. *This is the universe of the imagination, nor have we any idea but what is there produc'd.* (116)

It is noteworthy that an interest in Humean views on consciousness or "the universe of the imagination" comes directly following the colonial and historical concerns of "Telemachus" and "Nestor" as Stephen walks along the beach. So, the coast functions as a place of threat and invasion but also as a space of potential alternatives. As Jon Hegglund comments: "In the first two chapters, Stephen is cast into narrow versions of stereo-typed Irishness, first by the Englishman Haines, then by his employer, the Ulster Unionist schoolmaster Deasy. Significantly, it takes a walk on the beach—the border between land and sea—for Stephen to imagine a way out of this confinement" (73). Stephen seeks some form of inner lib-eration from the historical realities of colonialism. At this point in the text, his musings strongly resemble the idealist world of David Hume's philosophy. For Andrew Gibson, Stephen does eventually find some release from a state of "confinement." By the time we reach "Circe," "Stephen has . . . made progress. He has resisted his own depressed con-viction of imprisonment within ineluctable conditions, and reasserted the project of an open art, one dedicated to the exploration of pos-sibilities" (*Revenge*, 196).

Joyce associated Hume strongly with skepticism and considered Hume to be a part of a specifically skeptical Scottish school of philo-sophical thought, along with the Conservative politician Arthur Balfour. However, he also associated Hume strongly with the type of idealism displayed by the passage above. That Joyce's main conception of David Hume was as an idealist/skeptic combination is shown by remarks made by Joyce in conversation and in print. Elsewhere he comments on a "Scottish school" of philosophy. In the article "La Cometa dell''Home Rule,'" which first appeared in Trieste's *Il Piccolo della Sera* in December

1910, Joyce discusses the "political situation in England [*sic*]" (*OCPW*, 155) before describing the various party leaders. Arthur Balfour, the Scottish leader of the Conservative Party, is described as being "more of a sceptic than a politician" (*OCPW*, 157). Joyce goes on to state that "he is a worthy disciple of the Scottish school" (*OCPW*, 157).[7] Joyce interprets skepticism as a Scottish phenomenon, or at least believes that Scottish (or Celtic) philosophy has a decidedly skeptical "essence."

Joyce's remark creates a problem for a comment Willy Maley makes about Joyce, Scots, and Arthur Balfour: "My own impression, tinged with sadness, is that Joyce appears to have shared the prejudice of those Irish of the time who assumed that all Scots were incorrigibly Protestant, Conservative, and Unionist. Certainly, in Arthur Balfour they had a prime example of that type" ("Kilt by Kelt," 216). Strangely, despite his position as the Conservative party leader, this does not lead Joyce to view Balfour himself as a philosophical conservative. Joyce's article is partly about the confusion or "contradictions" (*OCPW*, 157) of the London political scene of this period. As he writes, "the English [*sic*] parties no longer answer to their names" (*OCPW*, 155). Later on the same page he comments that "this paradoxical situation is accurately reflected in the persons who are party leaders." So, Joyce's position in 1910 was that Balfour was not really a Conservative at all. Neither is Balfour the ideal candidate for an embodiment of Protestantism. As Joyce remarks of Balfour: "His biographer . . . will be able to say of him that in his philosophical essays he skilfully dissected and stripped bare the secret fibres of the religious and psychological principles whose champion he became by a turn of the parliamentary wheel of fortune" (*OCPW*, 157). In any case, Balfour is unlikely to be remembered in Ireland for his supposedly skillful philosophical dissections, since he was chief secretary for Ireland at the time of the Mitchelstown Massacre of 1887, when three Land League supporters were shot dead in County Cork (hence the sobriquet "Bloody" Balfour), and since as British prime minister from 1902 to 1905 he ruthlessly implemented severe and draconian legislation in the application of his Unionist agenda.[8]

To return to the subject of Hume and skepticism, in a lecture given at Trieste in March 1912, Joyce links Hume to the type of philosophy that he elsewhere designates "the Scottish school" (*OCPW*, 157). During a section on Blake in the paper "Realism and Idealism in English Litera-ture," Joyce offers the following comments:

> If we were to lay a charge of madness against every great genius who does not share the science undergraduate's fatuous belief in headlong materialism now held in such high regard, little would remain of world art and history. Such a slaughter of the innocents would in-clude most of the peripatetic system, all medieval metaphysics, an entire wing in the immense, symmetrical edifice built by the angelic doctor, St Thomas Aquinas, the idealism of Berkeley and (note the coincidence) the very scepticism that leads us to Hume. (*OCPW*, 179–80)

It is slightly strange that on the one hand Joyce names skepticism "the Scottish school," presumably including Hume as a member of this school, and on the other he discusses skepticism as a process that *leads* to Hume. However, Joyce's comments reveal that he both regarded Hume as a part of skepticism and considered the tradition a "Scottish school." Furthermore, Hume's skepticism "coincides" with the Irishman George Berkeley's idealism. Given his comments in the *Exiles* notes (see below), this coincidence must relate to his conception of the connections of skep-ticism and idealism in Celtic thought. Crucially for our understand-ing of Hume's role in *Finnegans Wake*, Joyce regards Hume as the *end* of a process of philosophical development. Is there not a similarity be-tween Hume and Joyce in relation to their positions as "conclusions" of their respective "schools"? It is commonplace, as Richard Ellmann points out, to conceive of Western philosophy as beginning with Aristotle and ending with Hume (*Liffey*, 94). Likewise, there is also the sense that with *Ulysses* and *Finnegans Wake* the radical experimentation of literary modernism—along with modernism itself—reaches its limit. T. S. Eliot wondered how anyone could write again after "Penelope" (*JJII*, 528), while Joyce considered himself at the "end of English"[9] during the writ-ing of *Finnegans Wake*, a text that describes itself as the "last word" (*FW*, 424.35) and was published in the final years of what we now consider the modernist era. The texts of Joyce and Hume function as the extreme limits, the *ne plus ultra* of their respective fields.

In his Trieste library, the collection gathered during the period from 1904 to 1920, Joyce held copies of the following works by David Hume: *An Enquiry concerning Human Understanding*, *An Enquiry concerning the Principles of Morals*, and *The History of England* (Ellmann, *Consciousness*, 113).[10] As Richard Ellmann notes in his biography, Joyce probed Hume's theories and writings in conversation at the time of the composition of *Finnegans Wake*. Ellmann reports a rather awkward-sounding conversation in Paris between Joyce and Samuel Beckett on the subject of Hume: "Beckett was addicted to silences, and so was Joyce; they engaged in conversations which consisted often of silences directed towards each other, both suffused with sadness, Beckett mostly for the world, Joyce mostly for himself. . . . Joyce suddenly asked some such question as, 'How could the idealist Hume write a history?' Beckett replied, 'A history of representation.' Joyce said nothing. . . . Later, 'For me,' he said, 'there is only one alternative to scholasticism, scepticism'" (*JJII*, 648).[11] It is tempting to read this exchange as Joyce attempting to overcome the internal contradictions of *Finnegans Wake* itself, a history *as* representation, that is to say, a synchronic history of external events presented through the secondary representation of internal dream.

It is also tempting to view Joyce's interest in idealist, indeterminate philosophy in the context of his own failing eyesight and his diminishing connections with the "audible-visible-gnosible-edible world" (*FW*, 88.06). In any case, Joyce now refers to Hume as an idealist rather than a skeptic. According to Ellmann, however, Joyce probably saw Hume as a mixture of the two (see *Liffey*, 93–96). Skepticism, "the view that nothing can be known with certainty; that at best, there can only be some private probable opinion" (Mautner, 552), or "a set of arguments intended to undercut claims for knowledge or even rational belief" (Fogelin, 221), is compatible with idealism, the view that "only minds and mental representations exist; there is no independently existing external material world" (Mautner, 292). They are similar positions insofar as value or importance is placed on the individual, limited, and private functions of the mind as opposed to the external material world—and its attendant history—which is either unknowable or does not exist independently. In both, our connections with certainties about the external world are tenuous and fragile. When one adopts a framework that dispenses with an external world, it follows that realism must also be dispensed with. Fredric Jameson:

> If realism is grasped as the expression of some commonsense experience of a recognizably real world, then empirical examination of any work we care to categorize as "modernist" will reveal a starting point in that conventional real world, a realist core as it were, which the various telltale modernist deformations and "unrealistic" distortions, sublimations or gross characterizations, take as their pretext and their raw material, and without which their alleged "obscurity" and "incomprehensibility" would not be possible. (*Modernity*, 120)

However, if there is no "commonsense experience of a recognizably real world" to begin with, then the "deformations," "distortions," and so on can be read as a disconnection from a "realist core" rather than having their "starting point" in such a core.[12]

Presumably Joyce saw an inherent contradiction here in that an idealist philosopher such as Hume could write about history when Hume held the view that the existence of an exterior reality can never be properly verified. Beckett's witty solution to this problem seems to gain Joyce's silent approval while Joyce's further comment on skepticism as an alternative to scholasticism indicates that his earlier attachment to the work of Thomas Aquinas had diminished somewhat by this time (furthermore, it also suggests that English materialism was, for Joyce, not a viable alternative). These fragments of evidence also reveal that Joyce maintained an enthusiasm for Hume from his time in Trieste, through to the period of the composition of *Finnegans Wake* in Paris. Incidentally, this latter period coincides roughly with the era in which unbiased critical scholarship on Hume finally began to become available.[13]

Joyce's notes also indicate his somewhat idiosyncratic conception of Scottish philosophy existing as part of a broader Celtic school of skepticism: "Joyce's notes preliminary to *Exiles*, composed about November 1913, indicate a fellow-feeling towards Hume as a Celt: 'All Celtic philosophers seem to have inclined towards incertitude or scepticism—Hume, Berkeley, Balfour, Bergson'" (Ellmann, *Liffey*, 94).[14] Instead of associating Scotland with any particularly reductive value system or creed, Joyce sees Scottish thinkers as sharing in a Celtic tradition of "incertitude or scepticism" and views Scottish and Irish thought as being part of the same philosophical tradition.

This conception of Hume as a "Celtic" philosopher is somewhat ironic, since, for Hume in his *History of England*, the historical Celts were a race of "degenerate" and "abject" Britons.[15] Furthermore, Balfour, Berkeley, and Bergson are scarcely classic Celtic figures (Balfour was from East Lothian [in the East of Scotland, not the West], Berkeley was born into an Anglo-Irish family, and Bergson was a Parisian although he did have connections to Ireland on his mother's side), but this is a categorization based on perceived habits of mind rather than strict genealogy or geographical background. Joyce's conception of what counts as Celtic is fairly broad and inclusive. But whatever our reservations about Joyce's grouping here, it is certainly true that there are important connections in Irish and Scottish philosophy. As Terry Eagleton has noted, the Scottish-Irish Francis Hutcheson—who was born in County Down to Ulster Scot parents and became chair of moral philosophy at the University of Glasgow—was the "founder of the most fertile current of intellectual enquiry in eighteenth-century Scotland" (*Heathcliff*, 122). Eagleton also mentions that Hutcheson's "economic doctrine descended to his student Adam Smith, thus laying one of the intellectual foundations of the modern world" (122), and speaks of David Hume as Hutcheson's "disciple" (110). In addition, a good deal of Hume's work on perception is a revision and extension of ideas originally found in the work of Berkeley (see Fogelin, 230). Furthermore, Joyce himself used the Scottish philosopher Alexander Campbell Fraser's text on Berkeley when working on the "Proteus" episode of *Ulysses* (see Rabaté, xv).

David Berman has discussed "the Irish contribution to the Scottish Enlightenment, a contribution which . . . was more considerable than is usually supposed" (379):

> The very term "Scottish Enlightenment" was coined by an Irishman, W. R. Scott, who was born in Omagh in Northern Ireland and educated in Dublin. It was also an Irishman—Thomas Sheridan, father of the playwright—who first described eighteenth-century Edinburgh as the "Athens" of Britain. . . . In Scotland probably the chief external influence was Irish—Berkeley, who, acting upon

Hume, brought about the questioning and creative response which constitutes much of Scottish philosophy. That, at any rate, is how Thomas Reid seemed to see his own philosophical development: "I once believed [the] doctrine of ideas so firmly as to embrace the whole of Berkeley's system in consequence of it; till, finding other consequences to follow from it, which gave me more uneasiness than the want of a material world. . . ." That the other consequences were of a Humean nature seems clear from Reid's statement in the introduction to his *Inquiry into the Human Mind* (1764), that "by giving up the material world [Berkeley] hoped . . . to secure the world of spirits. But alas! [Hume's] *Treatise of Human Nature* wantonly sapped the foundation . . . and drowned all in one universal deluge." So Berkeleianism radicalized by Hume was the danger against which Scottish common-sense philosophy responded and flourished. (379–82)

So, perhaps Joyce's conception of a unified—albeit varied—field of Celtic philosophy is not as far-fetched as it may originally appear.[16] As Jean-Michel Rabaté has suggested, Joyce's comments on Celtic philosophy point to "a tradition or a line of descent in which Joyce clearly wants to be inscribed" (24). Of course, an integrated Celtic philosophy of skepticism ties Scotland and Ireland in a way that religion could not, while also linking to Joyce's own vehement rejection of the Catholic Church.[17]

Richard Ellmann has noted what he regarded as Hume's influence on the latter chapters of *Ulysses*:

Aristotle is a much less active presence in the episodes beginning with the *Wandering Rocks* than their predecessors. I would suggest that there is a new philosophical presence, and that this can probably be identified as David Hume. . . . Joyce must have seen Hume as a mixture of sceptic and idealist, akin to Berkeley. . . . For a sceptical philosophy, Hume was Joyce's obvious source. The unknowability of Hume's universe was an excellent contrary to the knowability of Aristotle's. Aristotle was, as Dante said, and as Stephen quotes, *il maestro di color che sanno*, and Hume was the master of those who do not know. Hume is not prepared to assert, as Stephen is, that the soul is the form of forms, and instead declares that questions about the soul's essence, such as its degree of materiality, are unintelligible. . . . The dominant mood from the *Wandering Rocks* through *Circe* is scepticism, Bloom's day but also, for the nine hours from three to midnight, Hume's day. (*Liffey*, 93–96)[18]

So, unknowability and unintelligibility begin to exert an influence on the latter stage of *Ulysses*, and Joyce based this on the work of David Hume. Dublin is gradually injected with dubium. Furthermore, sections of the "Oxen of the Sun" episode—a chapter that features the first appearance of a non-Irish Celtic character (J. Crotthers) in the book and in which the shifting styles portray reality as ultimately "ineffable" (French, 185)—are modeled on Hume's distinctive prose style.

Despite these connections between Hume and *Ulysses*, Hume's philosophy is more suited to the interior, "interred" mind-set of *Finnegans Wake*, given the pervasive atmosphere of doubt or "unknowability" in a work where "the unfacts, did we possess them, are too imprecisely few to warrant our certitude" (*FW*, 57.16–17). Indeed, the text's description of itself here is based on comments made in Arthur Balfour's *The Foundations of Belief* (see Henkes). Balfour, as we have seen, is both a member of the "Scottish school" and of Joyce's conception of a Celtic philosophical grouping. As Richard Beckman points out, "Joyce especially liked Hume" because "Hume blithely pointed out how little was knowable" (*Rare View*, 75–76). The "unknowability of Hume's universe" or his "radical doubt" (Fogelin, 213) is fitting for a book in which definite knowledge or certainty, even about the basic plot and "characters" of the work, is elusive or totally unattainable, an "Epistlemadethemology for deep dorfy doubtlings" (*FW*, 374.17–18). Herring notes that the "most startling examples of Joyce's uncertainty principle are to be found in *Finnegans Wake*, where language, plot, character, and motivation are all destabilized to produce literature's most famous enigma" (Herring, xiii–xiv). Elsewhere Herring writes that

Joyce's seemingly contradictory strategy of producing both ambiguous texts and the keys to interpreting them may have the effect of keeping professors busy, one of his stated purposes, but it also reveals a genuine skepticism about our ability to get at the truth except in fragments, to understand finally and completely the impressions that our senses bring us, to analyze and interpret experience with a high degree of certainty, and to express ourselves unambiguously in eel-slippery language. . . . Incertitude may be the dominant theme of the *Wake*. (182–83)

Furthermore, according to Beckman, Hume's undermining of the concept of causation allows for a freer type of associative configuration in Joyce's text:

> In the *Wake* Humean skepticism prevails. Hume's demolition of the knowability of casual connections made room for associative connections, and this affects the method of the *Wake*, where a profusion of extremely free associations is held together not noticeably by plot or logic but by allusions, recurrences, and, readers agree, subtle—just about invisible—structures. . . . Emphasizing free associations diminishes the role of perception. The epistemological mode here is Humean: what was perceived is in doubt, while the unknowability of things is glossed over by custom. (*Rare View*, 68)

Hume's philosophy undermines the very idea of intelligible casual connections, whereas Joyce's fiction promotes a system of associative connections.

Joyce's interest in Hume is revealed at a number of points in *Finnegans Wake* where references to the philosopher evoke his concepts of skepticism/idealism, and, furthermore, through the latent linguistic possibilities of Hume's name, Joyce evokes the situation of the text's dreamer himself, what Thomas Hofheinz has termed "the weird ontology of sleep" (162). In section I.iv of the *Wake*, during the section in which "Kate Strong recalls old times in the midden heap in Phoenix Park" (Benstock, xvii) and following the "burial in Lough Neagh" (xvii), Hume's name makes an intriguing double appearance:

> What subtler timeplace of the weald than such wolfsbelly castrament to will hide a leabhar from Thursmen's brandihands or a loveletter, lostfully hers, that would be lust on Ma, than then when ructions ended, than here where race began: and by four hands of

forethought the first babe of reconcilement is laid in its last cradle of hume sweet hume. Give over it! And no more of it! So pass the pick for child sake! O men! (*FW*, 80.12–19)

Although Kate is recalling the pile of rubbish in which the letter has been buried and recovered—called a "dumplan" (*FW*, 79.29) as well as a "Tiptip!" (*FW*, 79.27)—the subject of this section is to some extent HCE himself, as evidenced by a phrase bearing his initials: "homelick cottage of elvanstone" (*FW*, 79.29), and a play on the name Earwicker in the words "her weaker" (*FW*, 79.33).[19] As we shall see, Joyce brings together the situation of the central "character" (closely related to the dreamer) with ideas of burial and burial places. As was mentioned earlier, Joyce viewed Hume as the terminus of a particular route in philosophy, and here the grave of "last cradle" and the ominous warped prayer ending "O men" express this sense of finality.[20]

Mabel Worthington has dissected this passage of *Finnegans Wake* as part of an examination of the role of folk music in the work. "Home Sweet Home" is a well-known American song, and Worthington considers the use Joyce puts the title of this tune to:

> Joyce uses the word "home" to refer to "home," literally, for *Finnegans Wake* is, on one level, a domestic drama. "Home" also refers to the spiritual home, the church ("Rome"). It refers to our last home, the grave ("hume"). And it refers to our first home, woman, the womb. The paragraph on pages 79–80 deals with a mound of earth which is the world (full of relics of the past, guarded by woman), the tomb, and also the bed in which the All-Father and his woman were making love when the thunderclap announcing the end of a cycle was heard. . . . Here, "where race began," "the first babe of reconcilement is laid in its last cradle of hume sweet hume." The union of the two opposites . . . results in the child. In Joyce the child reconciles the man and woman, makes them one, ends (for them, for the time being) the battle of the sexes. At the same time, in creating children, the parents pronounce their own doom, for the children will succeed them. In time, the children will return to "hume sweet hume," replaced by *their* children. (200)[21]

If Worthington is correct that "home" refers in part to the church and to religion, then it is ironic that Hume is alluded to here, since "The Great Infidel" was probably an atheist (see P. Russell, "Hume on Religion"). Interestingly, Edinburgh—the center of the secular Scottish Enlightenment—is rendered in *Finnegans Wake* as "Heidenburgh" (*FW*, 18.23), a name that contains the German *heiden* or "heathen."

As was suggested earlier, and as Worthington hints at, the possibilities open to Joyce in Hume's name are also utilized here. The conversion of "home" into "hume" works as a reference to the philosophy of David Hume but also signifies the earth—*humus* being the Latin for soil—in which HCE is buried. All of the references to Hume in *Finnegans Wake* carry the echo of *humus* and so are linked to soil and death, perhaps also to human culture as a whole: "In Latin, it was the verb *humare*, to bury, which gave the primary and proper meaning to the noun *humanitas*, human civilization" (Vico, 8). Burial in the *Wake* expresses the unknowing experience of the *Wake*'s dreamer:

> Etymologically, the word "bed" derives from the proto-Indo-European root **bhedh-*, meaning "to dig or bury" or, in nominal form, "a hollow in the ground, for sleeping." . . . If the man "tropped head" "in bed" at the *Wake* is indeed "dead to the world" and can largely only "no," how can he "know" that the "bed" in which he lies is not, "as a murder effect" (345.7), a "bed of soil?" Or, to bend the same question back into the experience of "our own nighttime," how does anyone fully asleep and "dead to the world" know that he is not really dead to the world? And conversely, how does anyone actually dead to the world know that he is not simply asleep? (Bishop, 66–67)

Bishop here highlights the uncertain, ambiguous connections between the earth, beds, burial, and sleep in *Finnegans Wake*. Joyce's use of the word Hume relates to these connections, since it can simultaneously evoke the earth or burial and also—through the skepticism and doubt associated with Hume's philosophy—convey the doubt and incertitude of sleeping and dreaming.

In an article based on the passage of *Finnegans Wake* we are presently considering, Richard Beckman makes the following remarks on the figure of Kate, the cleaner: "Kate, who merges with Katherine Strong the scavenger, oversees the journey from cradle to grave in the creepiest sense possible, the return to vacuity of 'the first babe of reconcilement' to 'its last cradle of hume sweet hume' (80.17–18), where Hume's realm of unknowable causation transforms home sweet home into a rather sour metaphysical aporia" ("Jove's Word," 373–74). There is little to suggest that Joyce is specifically addressing the question of causation here. Rather, Joyce is utilizing the overall spirit of Hume's philosophy. Ellmann's position was that Hume's work was, for Joyce, a fusion of idealism and skepticism. However, idealist aspects are most pertinent when considering Hume's function in *Finnegans Wake*. Idealism, with its focus on mental representations and its rejection of the exterior world, is a perfect description of the tenuous void of *Finnegans Wake* itself. The buried subject of the *Wake*, being asleep or "*Dead to the World*" (*FW*, 105.29), and confined within the limits of his own unconscious mind, has only his internal, mental representations available to him; there is no external reality in *Finnegans Wake* (except through the limited stimuli of sound or sensation): "Joyce identified 'the hidden or subconscious world' as the 'most exciting,' and this 'unexplored and hallucinatory world' is developed in *Finnegans Wake* to the near exclusion of the world of experience" (Kimball, 141–42).

As David Sidorsky has astutely observed, "In *Finnegans Wake* . . . the agents and actions of history are admitted only as thoughts, appearances, images, or sounds. Since these images and sounds take place within a nightmare, the only form of reality that is being ascribed to them is that of illusion or dream" (316). Joyce sees unconsciousness as casting all humans into an imprisoned and limited state similar to the idealist conception of reality, where only the interior mental life can be known. Similarly, there is no "real" history as such in Joyce's final work, only a present-time reconstruction of the past: "Joyce's prime assumption routinely baffles newcomers: that there is, cognitively speaking, no 'past.' There is only what we can experience, as it streams through 'the eye of a noodle' (*FW*, 143.09). True, we can write what we call 'history,' . . . but such 'histories' are stories—fictions—and themselves exist in the present, alongside what they propose to explain" (Kenner, "Present," 853).

Here we may detect a similarity between this presentation of history as *the present* and what Terry Eagleton describes as a particularly Irish mode of "time-warping" (*Heathcliff*, 279):

> The Irish are supposed to fetishize the past; but in quite what sense that constitutes a backward-looking spirit is debatable. As with Walter Benjamin's anti-historicist spirit, it would seem less a question of grasping the past as the prehistory of the present, than of constellating an image plucked from that past with a quick sense of the contemporary. . . . What is recent is not last week, but antiquity. . . . Anti-historicist consciousness blends the archaic with the absolutely contemporary, squeezing out the dreary continuum between them; and this . . . is as true of Ireland's modernism as it is of nationalism. (*Heathcliff*, 278–79)[22]

This tension or mixing of the "archaic" and the "absolutely contemporary" in Irish nationalist consciousness and in Irish modernism arises, for Eagleton, out of specific historical conditions:

> What is afoot in nineteenth century Ireland, with the cataclysm of the Famine, the agrarian revolution, the sharp decline of the language and the sea changes in popular culture, is the transformation *within living memory* of a social order in some ways still quite traditional, and so a peculiarly shocking collision of the customary and the contemporary. The time of artistic modernism is a curiously suspended medium, a surreally foreshortened temporality in which the laws of orderly narrative are lifted so that time, much as in the dream or the unconscious mind, seems at once fantastically speeded up and fixated upon certain images dredged from the depths of some ancient collective memory. (280)

We might read the Humean, idealist consciousness of the *Wake* as constantly mixing "the archaic with the absolutely contemporary," while "several perceptions successively make their appearance; pass, re-pass, glide away, and mingle in an infinite variety of postures and situations" (Hume, *Treatise*, 301).

In the night lessons of II.ii, where the children Shem, Shaun, and Issy are studying, there is a further subterranean reference to Hume:

> When who was wist was ware. En elv, et fjaell. And the whirr of the whins humming us howe. His hume. Hencetaking tides we happly return, trumpeted by prawns and ensigned with seakale, to befinding ourself when old is said in one and maker mates with made (O my!); having conned the cones and meditated the mured and pondered the pensils and ogled the olymp and delighted in her dianaphous and cacchinated behind his culosses, before a moso-leum . . . highlyfictional, tumulous under his chthonic exterior but plain Mr Tumulty in mufti-life. (*FW*, 261.2–19)

Again, the context involves a figure that is "chthonic" (*FW*, 261.18) or dwelling underground like an underworld deity (ironic, given the Hu-mean context), under a "tumulous" (*FW*, 261.18), a pile of earth and stones over a grave, or a burial mound: "howe" (*FW*, 261.04). A focus on burial is also revealed by the play on mausoleum in "mosoleum" (*FW*, 261.13), and death is present in the phrase "when old is said in one," which is, of course, a play on the saying "when all is said and done."[23] However, as with the sections of the *Wake* indebted to Hogg and Steven-son, duality is present here:

> The *Wake* explicitly states at points that the dreamer has two domi-nant personae—"tumulous under his chthonic exterior but plain Mr Tumulty in mufti-life" (*FW* 261)—one of which assumes the in-flated proportions of a god (chthonic: pertaining to deities) or of an imaginary giant embedded in the landscape (cthonial: dwelling un-derground), the other assuming the more realistic dimensions of a "plain" man in "mufti," an ordinary mortal—most frequently a publican—stripped of his dignifying uniforms and his elevating masks ("his chthonic exterior"). The postscript to the final version of the Wakean letter hints that the inflated vision of the self is an imago appropriated from geographical folklore: "Hence we've lived in two worlds. He is another he what stays under the himp of holth." (K. Devlin, *Wandering*, 64)

Again, Joyce links sleep and death/burial to the idealism and skepticism of Hume while also involving the dualities of a fractured psyche and the experience of a life divided between day and night. In this section Hume is in the esteemed company of other philosophers (*FW*, 260.8–261.22), appearing alongside the Italian "Vico" (*FW*, 260.15) and the Irishman "Berkeley" (*FW*, 260.11) in keeping with the general theme of learning in the chapter. The skepticism of Berkeley and Hume meets the repetition of Vico in the interior history of the *Wake*.

The final mention of Hume is also made in connection with the buried body of HCE—or the "erected . . . century . . . hen" (*FW*, 606.16–17), whose body forms the "three Benns" (*FW*, 606.14) of Howth—and with a focus on the clash of idealism and history:

> Bisships, bevel to rock's rite! Sarver buoy, extinguish! Nuotabene. The rare view from the three Benns under the bald heaven is on the other end, askan your blixom on dimmen and blastun, something to right hume about. They were erected in a purvious century, as a hen fine coops and, if you know your Bristol and have trudged the trolly ways and elventurns of that old cobbold city, you will sortofficially scribble a mental Peny-Knox-Gore. Whether they were franklings by name also has not been fully probed. Their design is a whosold word and the charming details of light in dark are freshed from the feminiairity which breathes content. *O ferax culpa!* (*FW*, 606.13–23)

This section comes from book IV, the final part of *Finnegans Wake*. The reference to Biddy the hen links Hume again with the rubbish heap where the mysterious and elusive letter of the *Wake* has been inhumed. The letter itself is alluded to in the same paragraph: "What will not arky paper, anticidingly inked with penmark, push, per sample prof, kuvertly falted, when style, stink and stigmataphoron are of one sum in the same person?" (*FW*, 606.25–28). Since this appears in the chapter of reawakening, the sleeping or buried body "comes out of the soil very well" (*FW*, 606.28–29).

Once again Hume is associated with the soil, with Joyce seeing a similarity between the mind of the dead or sleeping subject and the unknowable universe of Hume's philosophy. To adopt Hume's terminology, the world of *Finnegans Wake* is a synthesized nocturnal agglomeration of "idea" versions of earlier "impressions."[24] As well as the entombing soil of the grave, finality is suggested by the phrases "Nuotabene," "the other end," "extinguish," and "bald heaven." The hallucinatory visions of the dreamer are expressed in the phrase "charming details of light in dark," reminiscent of the phrase "united states of Scotia Picta" (*FW*, 43.29–30), which also represents the imagery or pictures of dreams as seen in the obscurity of sleep and night (this phrase will be looked at in more detail in chapter 4). The contrasting expression "light in dark" is also a description of a chessboard, connecting with bishops and rooks or "Bisships" and "rock's." The use of the word "mental" also highlights the focus on cerebral processes in the passage. Furthermore, in the above passage Hume is once again linked to history and the act of writing—"right hume" and "scribble"—through a connection to the elusive letter. The cyclical scheme of civilization advanced by Vico is also present in the section, through the lightning clap that marks the beginning of a historical cycle: "blixom" is based on the Swedish and Dutch words for lightning, *blixtar* and *bliksem* respectively. The phrase "right Hume" in place of "write Hume" signals Joyce's positive estimation of the philosopher's theories.

Sections where David Hume is pitched into the black vault of *Finnegans Wake* also involve imagery of burial, through words related to earth or graves such as "tumulous" (*FW*, 261.18), "chthonic" (*FW*, 261.18), "last cradle" (*FW*, 80.17), or to HCE's interred body as landscape with "three Benns" (*FW*, 606.14). HCE is "under" the "exterior" (*FW*, 261.18). Each passage in which Hume's name is buried also relates to the enigmatic letter through references to writing—"ensigned" (*FW*, 261.06), "loveletter" (*FW*, 80.14), "right hume" (*FW*, 606.16), "petsybluse" (*FW*, 261.2)—and to the hen who discovers the letter: "as a hen fine coops" (*FW*, 606.17). Thus the historian Hume is linked to a history that cannot be properly known or understood. A central problem of *Finnegans Wake* is how we are to interpret the past, something that is by definition not accessible to us: "How could the idealist Hume write a history?" (*JJII*, 648).

All of the Humean allusions relate to HCE, as shown by the appearance of his initials in close proximity to the name Hume in each case. These instances are "homelike cottage of elvanstone" (*FW*, 79.29) in the

paragraph that runs from 79.27 to 80.19; "enthewsyass cuckling a hoy-
den" (*FW*, 260.18), "him, a chump of the evums" (*FW*, 261.13–14), and
"highly fictional, tumulous under his chthonic exterior" (*FW*, 261.17–
18) in the paragraph from 260.8 to 261.22; and "erected in a purvious
century, as a hen fine coops" (*FW*, 606.16–17) in the paragraph from
606.13 to 607.16. Hume's name forms a nexus at three points in the text
where the themes of fiction, history, skeptical philosophy, burial imagery,
and explorations of the death-like nature of sleep all converge. Joyce
creates a resemblance between the idealism of Hume and the situation
in which the dreamer of *Finnegans Wake* finds himself, inhumed within
the "fictional" limits of his mental faculties.

Joyce also associates Hume with the grave so often in *Finnegans
Wake* because—along with Bertrand Russell—he regarded Hume as
representing the end of philosophy, or at least of a certain branch of
philosophy: "David Hume . . . is one of the most important among
philosophers, because he developed to its logical conclusion the empirical philosophy of Locke and Berkeley. . . . He represents, in a certain
sense, a dead end: in his direction it is impossible to go further" (B. Russell, 600).[25] For Russell, Hume's work advances down a philosophical
cul-de-sac that "represents the bankruptcy of eighteenth-century reason-
ableness," arriving at "the disastrous conclusion that from experience and
observation nothing is to be learnt" (610–11). A central plank of Hume's
thought is his assertion that "no argument can establish the existence of
external objects resembling our perceptions" (Fogelin, 228). Of course,
all of this presented a major problem for empiricism and scientific
method.[26] Joyce writes of "the very scepticism that leads us to Hume,"
conceiving Hume's work as a terminal point (*OCPW*, 179–80). Joyce
then applies this idea in *Finnegans Wake*, where Hume also symbolizes a
"dead end," with his name constantly associated with conclusions and
burials. This idea, coupled with the linguistic possibilities opened up by
the earthy name "Hume," means that in *Finnegans Wake* Hume is associated with the grave and with burial, the endings both of human life and
of philosophy itself.

Hume's *An Enquiry concerning Human Understanding* was more
valuable to Joyce in thinking of ways to develop the inner world of
Finnegans Wake than *An Enquiry concerning the Principles of Morals* or
The History of England, since the first deals with mental faculties and

processes (Hume's *Treatise* does not appear in the published lists of Joyce's libraries, but the two *Enquiries* are largely revised versions of material found in that work). Hume's name is joined in *Finnegans Wake* by the words "sweet" and "right." Joyce's interest in Hume can be attributed to a conception of Hume as a "Celtic" philosopher, part of what he saw as a general inclination towards incertitude in Irish and Scottish philosophy. As such, Hume is used to construct the darkened Celtic burial chamber of *Finnegans Wake*.

The opposition to certainty in Hume's work is a key to *Finnegans Wake*, Joyce's own undogmatic slumber. In the conclusion to *An Enquiry concerning the Principles of Morals*, Hume writes:

> I am sensible, that nothing can be more unphilosophical than to be positive or dogmatical on any subject; and that, even if excessive scepticism could be maintained, it would not be more destructive to all just reasoning and enquiry. I am convinced, that, where men are the most sure and arrogant, they are commonly the most mistaken, and have there given reins to passion, without that proper deliberation and suspense, which can alone secure them from the grossest absurdities. (78)

Rather than adhering to or advancing any type of "dogmad" ideology (*FW*, 158.03), Hume stresses a skeptical detachment or "suspense." Hume is a writer whose work is based not upon any particular religious or political agenda and recommends the reserving of judgment and the adoption of scepticism and an enlightened liberation from emphatic, confident certainties. Likewise, doubt is a constant in Joyce's texts and in his worldview:

> The role of doubt in Joyce's own mental history had been framed in *A Portrait of the Artist as a Young Man*. Stephen's artistic convictions depend upon freeing himself from religion and nationalism. In Joyce's other books the same state of mind appears in their heroes. Shem in *Finnegans Wake* is "of twosome twiminds fornenst gods" and a "national apostate." In *Exiles* Richard discovers in his wife's possible infidelity a trial of his faith . . . and accepts doubt . . . as the air he must breathe. (Ellmann, *Liffey*, 92–93)

This description of Shem used by Ellmann in the section above draws together the theme of divided consciousness with the related issue of doubt or skepticism; both are areas with strong Scottish connections. The phrase "of twosome twiminds" here combines two of the main conceptual subjects of this study, interiority and mental division. We shall now proceed to study how Joyce bases the inhumed "twiminds" of *Finnegans Wake* on Scottish literary precedents.

THREE

Celtic Antisyzygy

Hogg, Stevenson, Joyce

During the composition of *Finnegans Wake* in the years following the partition of Ireland into the Free State and Northern Ireland, the itinerant Joyce reflected upon the outward wanderings and meanderings of his own "race," paying close attention to those who came from outside the island to settle in Ireland (and vice versa), while considering the mixed, fluid, and divided identities these oceanic movements had brought about over time. Joyce's exploration of Ireland's past—including his reading of history texts by Irish authors such as Stephen Gwynn, Benedict Fitzpatrick, and J. M. Flood—led him to an interest in Scottish history. Here Joyce read that Scottish history begins with an Irish-assisted birth. For Joyce, Scotland seemed to some extent an offshoot or separate development from the main course of Irish history. He also saw the countries as being related in some underlying way, members of an estranged family. Joyce describes Scotland as being Ireland's doomed "sister" in the poem "Gas from a Burner" (*PE*, 109), and in *Finnegans Wake* he casts Irish and Scottish tribes as fraternal rivals.

Joyce's interest in Scottish subject matters becomes more pronounced as his career develops, with his greatest attention to the country appearing in his most ambitious, demanding, and obscure text. *Finnegans Wake*, with its warring twin brothers and its preoccupation with internal division, contrasts, and clashing contraries, is where Joyce creates his own history of the contacts and interpenetrations that make up the constantly evolving relationship between Ireland and Scotland. It is here that Joyce expresses his vision of the "Celtic world" (*OCPW*, 124) through the presentation of a Humean, internal, unconscious state. In Scottish history and literature Joyce found material that could form the foundations of his work on psychological and national dualities, pressing concerns of his final text. Furthermore, the strategy of combined opposites—which is constantly linked by Joyce to Scotland—acts as a denial of history just as the *Wake*'s Humean "setting" acts as an alternative to the exterior world:

> In *Finnegans Wake*, virtually each and every reference to a specific historical event or figure is immediately modified by means of a verbal ambiguity or contrary incident that complicates its univocal reality and negates its significance or purposiveness. If, then, one were to posit or affirm as a governing myth the whole of the course of history, as exhibited in Vico's *The New Science*, the method of "the coincidence of opposites" would enable and entail the undoing or negation of that entire plot. . . . A fictional retelling of a dream in which the Vichian phenomenon of historical recurrence is transformed into a random series of nonteleological happenings undermines any conception of a historical process. Since the language of the narration of the series or sequence of episodes combines disparate events in its single words or phrases, it obscures sequentiality. The denial of temporal sequentiality leads, beyond the negation of teleology, to the affirmation of the illusory unreality of history. The strategy of "the coincidence of opposites" is used by Joyce both to reject the teleology of any historical movement and to deny the reality of any historical event. (Sidorsky, 303–4)

As we shall see when we encounter the Picts and the Scots, an evasion of "sequentiality" is linked by Joyce to Scottish historical events, just as a response to the material world is created via Scottish philosophy.

Crucially for our understanding of Joyce and Scottish literature, *Finnegans Wake* was written in the aftermath of Irish partition or "partitioned Irskaholm" (*FW*, 132.33), the division of Ireland into "a price partitional of twenty six and six" (*FW*, 264.22–23), the twenty-six counties of the Irish Free State and the remaining six counties of Northern Ireland. Partition began with the Government of Ireland Act of 1920 but became fixed with the establishment of the Free State in 1922 and the inevitable opt-out of the predominantly Protestant northern counties allowed by the Anglo-Irish Treaty of 1921. Conflict over that act led to the Irish Civil War of June 1922 to May 1923. In March 1923, Joyce began the early sketches for what would become *Finnegans Wake*. Joyce's commentary on "Irrland's split" (*FW*, 171.06) in *Finnegans Wake*—which can be read both as a commentary on the civil war and on partition—includes an awareness of the Scottish contribution to the situation in the north through the attention paid to the Scottish Presbyterian presence, "the settler nation . . . which is at the same time an anti-nation" (Pocock, 33).

In a section of II.iii of the *Wake*, where the interrogation of Yawn/Shaun (an authoritarian figure and a "son"/element of the main presence, HCE) takes a distinctly northern Irish accent, there are numerous references to Scottish matters, and the divisions of the four Irish provinces into three Free State provinces and one northern zone are highlighted: "Three to one!" (*FW*, 521.31).[1] The "split hour" of partition is evoked (*FW*, 519.35), alongside references to the rival Scottish and Irish peoples the Picts and the Scots.[2] The preoccupation in *Finnegans Wake* with division must be partly attributable to this traumatic event. As Emer Nolan has noted, "[Joyce's] writings about Ireland may not provide a coherent critique of either colonised or colonialist; but their very ambiguities and hesitations testify to the uncertain, divided consciousness of the colonial subject" (*Nationalism*, 130).

For Nicholas Allen, meanwhile, the tensions and dualities of the *Wake* must be read in the context of the Irish Civil War: "Joyce's grand scheme, with its warring opposites, its conflicting testimonies and furious linguistic blurring, both registers and readjusts the experience of civil war, partition and state formation" (34). As we shall see in the following chapter, Joyce saw in Scottish history some of the origins of partition and its attendant civil war (as well as the Irish role in ancient Scotland's own "state formation").[3] But that is not the only division in Irish life: "Across this small island, a partitionist mentality has divided North from South, Unionist from Nationalist, Anglo-Irish from Gael; in even the smallest parishes we have built separate Protestant and Catholic schools; and in the schools themselves we have parcelled up the literature of the island into two separate packages. It is not surprising that our schizophrenia has assumed notorious and war-like form" (Kiberd, "Quarantine," 21).

Similarly, Eoghan Ó Tuairisc has written that the modern Irish writer suffers from a "divided mind" and a "cultural schizophrenia" due to inheriting literary traditions in two languages: "It is not too much to say that the political partition of the island and the storm and stress of emotion it involves is but the external symbol of the inner dichotomy of the spirit experienced by every sensitive Irishman" (171). In Scottish literature, Joyce finds ways of registering this "partitionist mentality" or, as Ó Tuairisc puts it, this "psychic partition" (171).

In chapter 1 we saw how the Scottish medical student of the "Oxen of the Sun" and "Circe" episodes of *Ulysses*, J. Crotthers, is a dual or compound character, representing merged identities and societies but also embodying division and contrast. Split personalities and the figure of the double or "doppelgänger" are dominant themes of nineteenth-century Scottish literature, featuring in James Hogg's *Private Memoirs and Confessions of a Justified Sinner* (1824) and Robert Louis Stevenson's *Strange Case of Dr. Jekyll and Mr. Hyde* (1886), both of which Joyce utilizes and alludes to in *Finnegans Wake*, his book of "Doublends Jined" (*FW*, 20.16). Louis Mink first researched the use Joyce made of James Hogg's work in his *A "Finnegans Wake" Gazetteer*, published in 1978 (Mink, 41–42). Building on this important discovery, Luke Thurston has written on the influence of nineteenth-century novelists on Joyce's treatment of the "uncanny double" in a subsection of his Lacanian study *James Joyce and the Problem of Psychoanalysis* (2004). In a subsection of the chapter "Egomen and Women," entitled "Satan's Signature: Doubles and Diables," Thurston discusses the importance of the works of Oscar Wilde, Robert Louis Stevenson, and James Hogg to Joyce's handling of doubles and psychological division. It is striking and noteworthy that in Thurston's study, two of Joyce's three main influences for his representation of the related themes of demonic possession, multiple personalities, and the concept of the "double" come from the comparatively small canon of Scottish literature (the other is, of course, by an Irish writer). Thurston even claims that Wilde's *The Picture of Dorian Gray* (1890), the source for Joyce in Wilde's work, which is concerned with doubles, was itself influenced by Stevenson's text (Thurston, *Problem*, 119). This shows just how indebted *Finnegans Wake* is to Scottish literary precedents and preoccupations, especially in its concerns with and representations of "double life" (*FW*, 490.06).

There is a twofold outcrop of texts focusing on mental or spiritual duality in Europe during the late nineteenth and early twentieth century, growing out of Scottish and Irish cultures. Could we include Yeats—with his interest in internal divisions—in this group? Richard Ellmann has discussed the literary attention to mental doubling at the end of the nineteenth century with reference to Yeats, without noticing the dual-provenance of this trend: "In literature the splitting up of the mind into two parts is accomplished near the end of the century by two books, *Dr. Jekyll and Mr. Hyde* (1885) and *The Picture of Dorian Gray*, published in magazine form in 1890" (Ellmann, *Yeats*, 75). Ellmann claims that these texts had no influence on the poet: "Yeats came to maturity in this atmosphere of doubling and splitting of the self, but his mental growth was parallel to that of other writers and did not derive from them" (77). Quite how Ellmann knows that there is no connection here is not disclosed, although he does at least admit that Yeats attended "a dramatized version of *Dr. Jekyll and Mr. Hyde* in October 1888" (77).

Unlike Ellmann, Luke Thurston has noticed how the duplications of modern Irish literature are direct engagements with the Scottish writers Hogg and Stevenson:

> In *Finnegans Wake*, Joyce spells out an intricate response to Hogg's *Justified Sinner*, with "a multiplicity of personalities inflicted on the documents" (*FW* 107.24–25). The semantic duplicity of "characters"—veritable "open doubleyous" (*FW* 120.28)—is insistently exploited at every turn in the *Wake*, so that identities and letters can never be untangled or properly ascribed. In particular, Joyce relishes Hogg's invention of a character to embody the fall of a formerly stable or "realistic" world into a condition of multiplicity, of *dubium*. (Thurston, *Problem*, 115)

While noting the importance of Hogg and Stevenson to Joyce's works, Thurston overlooks the significant fact that both writers are part of the same literary tradition. One of the main attractions for Joyce in Scottish writing was its treatment of the "double" or multiple personality, and his interest here is part of a more general concern in his work with different models of Celtic interiority.

Following the nineteenth-century works of Hogg and Stevenson, the concept of the coming together of contraries retained its prominence in Scottish literature into the twentieth century and is an important feature of Scottish poetry contemporaneous to the writing of *Finnegans Wake*. According to Patrick Crotty, "Scottish poetry prides itself on paradox" (Crotty, "Caledonian Antisyzygy," 89). Paradox, or, more accurately, the meeting of contraries, is the principal concept of Hugh MacDiarmid's 1926 book-length poem, the somewhat neglected modernist masterpiece *A Drunk Man Looks at the Thistle*:

> I'll ha'e nae hauf-way hoose, but aye be whaur
> Extremes meet—it's the only way I ken
> To dodge the curst conceit o' bein' richt
> That damns the vast majority o' men. (MacDiarmid, *Drunk Man*,
>   l.141–44)[4]

MacDiarmid (a Scottish nationalist and a committed Communist, as well as a Joycean), whose later vision of "World Language" is entitled *In Memoriam James Joyce* (1955), saw Joyce's literary innovations as an important source of inspiration in his struggle to provoke a new phase of cultural and political regeneration in Scotland. MacDiarmid's *Drunk Man* (itself partly inspired by *Ulysses*), a poetic stream of consciousness bemoaning the contemporary state of affairs in a Scottish wasteland, and a text that fluctuates between various philosophical and poetic extremes, was heavily influenced by the critical work of G. Gregory Smith. Smith, professor of English literature at Queen's University Belfast from 1909 to 1930, developed the quasi-Hegelian theory of the "Caledonian Antisyzygy" in the seminal 1919 study *Scottish Literature: Its Character and Influence*. He viewed Scottish literature as being unique and distinctive due to its concentration on merged oppositions: "Does literature anywhere, of this small compass, show such a mixture of contraries as his [the Scot's] in outlook, subject, and method; real life and romance, everyday fact and the supernatural, things holy and profane, gentle and simple, convention and 'cantrip,' thistles and thistledown?" (20). Smith's book advances the idea that the varied and contrasting nature of Scottish history and life are reflected in Scottish prose and poetry through the fusion of divergent styles of expression and a general tendency towards duality, "almost a zigzag of contradictions" (4). Smith defines the "Caledonian Antisyzygy" as

> a reflection of the contrasts which the Scots shows at every turn, in his political and ecclesiastical history, in his polemical restlessness, in his adaptability, which is another way of saying that he has made allowance for new conditions, in his practical judgement, which is the admission that two sides of the matter have been considered. If therefore Scottish history and life are, as an old northern writer said of something else, "varied with a clean contrair spirit," we need not be surprised to find that in his literature the Scot presents two aspects which appear contradictory. Oxymoron was ever the bravest figure, and we must not forget that disorderly order is order after all. (4–5)

More recently Murray Pittock considered the causes and effects of the dualities of Scottish literature, which, like Smith, he finds in the conflicts and schisms of Scottish history:

> If identity, as Edward Said and others argue, is defined by opposition, the Scottish habit of opposing each other rather than the common foe can be seen as compromising the development of a consistent sense of nationality. In the Wars of Independence . . . Scottish magnates took the English side; in the later Middle Ages, the Lords of the Isles did the same thing; from the 1640s to the 1740s, Scotland was riven by religious and dynastic conflict, which cut across the issue of political independence and in the end secured its destruction . . . even the country's imaginative literature continued to provide image after image of the "divided self" as a source for the theme of the irreconcilability of personal and political dualities. (*Scottish Nationality*, 5–6)

The "Caledonian Antisyzygy" may be seen then as a literary manifestation of Scotland's divided identity or identities, as represented by its struggles for self-determination and its current union with England; its three languages, Gaelic, Scots, and English; the tensions between Presbyterianism and Catholicism (or Episcopalianism); the geographical and cultural split between the Highlands and the Lowlands; and so on. According to George Watson, "Scottish writers have felt . . . history as fractured by Calvinism or distorted by Scott's Enlightenment progressivism. . . . The regionalism of Scottish literature, its diversity and even fragmentation—if that's what it is—might well function as a strengthening example or ally to us in Ireland as we contemplate our own divided society and its differing imaginative constituencies" (39). The ways in which the "fragmentation" of Scottish literature does indeed "function as a strengthening example" for Irish fiction, particularly throughout *Finnegans Wake*, will be traced here and in the following chapter. While the Caledonian Antisyzygy might be overused in the study of Scottish literature, it may be instructive when adapted and transferred to Irish texts.

According to Smith's theory, the deep rifts of Scottish history have given a distinctly divided character to Scottish poetry and prose and created a preoccupation with contrast, polarities, and dualities in Scottish writing. Arguably, even as recently as 1980 this sense of division has featured prominently in Scottish literature, which has in turn drawn on Joycean developments. For example, Alasdair Gray's *Lanark: A Life in Four Books* (1981) is, as the title suggests, divided into four sections, two of which are a portrait of the young Glasgow art student Duncan Thaw. The remaining two books relate the dystopian existence of his counterpart or double, Lanark. As in James Hogg's *Confessions*, mental breakdown is a possible reason in *Lanark* for the projection or splitting of one subject or person into two "selves." But the dualities of Scottish culture and politics are also registered here.

While examples of the Caledonian Antisyzygy could be said to exist in poetry predating James Hogg's 1824 satire of religious fanaticism, *Private Memoirs and Confessions of a Justified Sinner* (note the paradox[es] of the title), this is probably the earliest prose work that can be said to demonstrate features of the concept. The tensions or dualities of Hogg's masterwork can perhaps be traced to the contrasts of his background:

> James Hogg was born in the Borders. He inherited an awareness
> of rigorous Presbyterianism from his shepherd father; and from his

mother he inherited his fascination for the supernatural and the folk-traditional. . . . Hogg came from a world that had created the Border ballads, a world in contact with "the other landscape" of enchantment. Scotland's legendary medieval seer, Thomas the Rhymer, came from this country; Hogg's grandfather, the celebrated Will O' Phaup, was believed to have conversed with the people of the other world. Hogg's background was thus rooted in the oral tradition, and centuries away from the culture of Enlightenment Edinburgh, where he came in 1810 to make his way as a man of letters. . . . The oral tradition underlying Hogg's work was sophisticated; his mother was a "tradition bearer," who gave many great songs to Walter Scott when he was collecting for his *Minstrelsy of the Scottish Border*. She told Scott that these songs "were made for singin' an' no for readin', but ye hae broken the charm noo, an; they'll never be sung mair" . . . Hogg's whole creative identity can be seen as held in tension between these oral and written traditions. (Gifford et al., 288–89)

Hogg's life was divided between the enchantment of the Borders and the Enlightenment of Edinburgh. His *Confessions* present the story of one Robert Wringhim, a religious fanatic who goes on a "justified" killing spree in seventeenth-century Calvinist Scotland. Robert is encouraged to commit his crimes by an enigmatic figure named Gil-Martin, who is either the Devil himself or an illusion emanating from Robert's own deranged mind. Throughout the novel we are deliberately left in doubt as to the solution of this mystery.

This duality is a key precedent for Joyce's presentation of the psyche in *Finnegans Wake*. Robert's version of events is framed by a fictional modern (i.e., scientific, rational, enlightened) editor who gives his own account of the mysterious, seemingly supernatural happenings that occurred a century before his investigations. However, this editor—who embarks on a farcical quest on an "excellent pony" (Hogg, 202) to find Wringhim's remains at the book's close—cannot be treated as an authority. At one point he adds eight and five and comes up with twelve (Hogg, 10). The editor's narrative becomes a satire on the certainties of the Enlightenment project, and the book as a whole has a kind of Humean skepticism towards the accessibility of truth. However, as a satire on the dangers of religious fanaticism, the book also holds the supernatural in suspicion. With its conflicting viewpoints, narrative games (Hogg himself appears within the text as a shepherd and is uninterested in helping the search for the sinner's bones: "Od bless ye, lad! . . . I hae mair ado than I can manage the day, foreby ganging to houk up hunder-year auld banes" [Hogg, 202]), sense of "play," self-conscious attention to texts, and unresolved obscurities, Hogg's text is a pre-echo of modernism and postmodernism. The powerful sense of ambivalence and doubt generated in the clash between contrasting supernatural and rational accounts in the text is a crucial precursor to the overwhelming atmosphere of Humean incertitude in *Finnegans Wake*:

> Uncertainty, ambivalence, and mystification prevail throughout Hogg's masterpiece, *The Private Memoirs and Confessions of a Justified Sinner* (1824). As the fictional "editor" says in the brief coda allotted to him: "With regard to the work itself, I dare not venture a judgement, for I do not understand it. . . . Neither of course, did the writer—poor deluded Robert Wringhim; it is only towards the end of his memoir that he begins to realise the true identity of his distinguished friend, the incognito prince of a far country, who is so bound to him as to be almost part of him, who urged him and helped him to murder first, a blameless "moderate" clergyman, then his own brother, his father, his mother, and who made it possible for him to debauch young girls and be "fou for weeks thegither" without being aware of his orgies. And that identity is—the Devil himself. Or is it? Is the puzzled, rationalistic editor perhaps right after all? Were the "Confessions" an "allegory" produced by "dreaming or madness," and was their deranged author Wringhim one "who wrote and wrote about a deluded creature, till he arrived at that height of madness, that he believed himself the very object whom he had been all along describing"? (T. Crawford, 100)

Like Hogg's *Confessions*, *Finnegans Wake* is suspended in a void of incertitude. There is no single truth to be accessed in Hogg's work, and even the text's fictional editor—commenting on Wringhim's confession—admits that he does not "comprehend the writer's drift" (Hogg, 208). Elsewhere he asks, "What can this work be?" (Hogg, 197). Furthermore, the original 1824 edition of the text carried a frontispiece with a letter purportedly handwritten by Robert Wringhim himself, an almost supernatural relic from a darker, more mysterious age. This hoax letter—and the device of presenting an editor who himself presents a supposedly "found" manuscript, the "Confessions" themselves—shows Hogg playing with ideas of the genuine and authentic while inviting readers to question the reality of the novel's contents (Macpherson's poetry, which we shall consider later, also lies in the tradition of the Scottish hoax). Likewise, Joyce prizes a sense of the uncertain and of the unknown. The works of Joyce and Hogg share this disposition as well as a related preoccupation with duality.

In his article on Joyce and Scotland, Willy Maley notes that both Stevenson's *Dr. Jekyll and Mr. Hyde* and Hogg's *Confessions* are "instances of what critics have called 'Caledonian Antisyzygy'" ("Kilt by Kelt," 215). Strangely enough, Smith's *Scottish Literature* refers on a number of occasions to James Hogg's poetic works but never actually mentions his *Confessions*, thereby ignoring some of the most convincing evidence for his own thesis. However, *Finnegans Wake* includes several obvious allusions to *Confessions*, undermining somewhat the received notion that the French author André Gide "rediscovered" Hogg's work in the 1940s, thereby bringing it back into the mainstream of European culture. Luke Thurston: "Joyce acknowledges his literary debt to James Hogg's *The Private Memoirs and Confessions of a Justified Sinner* (1824) by daubing *Finnegans Wake* liberally with 'hogsfat' (doubling 'Hogg's fact,' a deed or document perpetrated by Hogg: *FW* 483.25). The *Justified Sinner* is both an astonishing premonition of Freud's discovery and a turbulent proto-modernist stylistic experiment" (Thurston, *Problem*, 114).

The most clear and sustained of Joyce's allusions to Hogg comes in III.iii of the *Wake*. In this section, Yawn, a version of Shaun, is being interrogated by "the Four" and is asked a question regarding "complementary characters, voices apart" (*FW*, 487.3–4), a query that clearly relates to his "complementary" relationship with his twin Shem and to the numerous disembodied "voices" sounding within the brain of the text's "dreamer" (Hogg's text contains the "twins" of Robert and George, Robert and Gil-Martin, and Robert and the Editor). Shaun's answer (or confession) begins with a very thinly veiled reference to James Hogg himself (this phrase can also be read as an expression of gratitude from Joyce to Hogg):

> —I'm thinking to, thogged be thenked! I was just trying to think when I thought I felt a flea. I might have. I cannot say for it is of no significance at all. Once or twice when I was in odinburgh with my addlefoes, Jake Jones the handscabby, when I thinkled I wore trying on my garden substisuit, boy's apert, at my nexword nighboor's, and maybe more largely nor you quosh yet you, messmate, realise. A few times, so to shape, I chanced to be stretching, in the shadow as I thought, the liferight out of myself in my ericulous imaginating. I felt feeling a half Scotch and pottage like roung my middle ageing like Bewley in the baste so that I indicate out to myself and I swear my gots how that I'm not meself at all, no jolly fear, when I realise bimiselves how becomingly I to be going to become. (*FW*, 487.7–19)

Yawn's answer concerns Shem, who he regards as his "addlefoes." Shem is Yawn's enemy or "foe" as well as his αδελφός (*adelphos*, "brother" in Greek). They are "complementary characters." The passage as a whole here refers to the possessed or insane character Robert Wringhim's killing (*nex*, Latin for "violent death") in *Confessions* of his brother George in Edinburgh ("odinburgh"), a pivotal gothic scene of Hogg's novel (George and Robert are Shem and Shaun-like in their antagonism). As Stefanie Lehner has pointed out, "The history of Irish literature, in particular, but also that of Scottish writing, charts a long tradition of engagement with the gothic genre (for example in the works by writers such as Sheridan le Fanu, Charles Robert Maturin, Bram Stoker; and James Hogg . . . Walter Scott, Robert Louis Stevenson)" (55). Lehner links this tradition to the Irish experience of colonialism and to the stateless situation of Scotland.

The section from the *Wake* above also refers to an incident in Hogg's *Confessions* where George goes walking on Arthur's Seat, the tallest hill in the city of Edinburgh, and sees what he thinks is a spirit in the surrounding mist. Here is part of the passage from the "Editor's Narrative" section of Hogg's novel to which Joyce refers:

George conceived it to be a spirit. He could conceive it to be nothing else; and he took it for some horrid demon by which he was haunted, that had assumed the features of his brother in every lineament, but in taking on itself the human form, had miscalculated dreadfully on the size, and had presented itself thus to him in a blown-up, dilated frame of embodied air, exhaled from the caverns of death or the regions of devouring fire. (34–35)

In the novel, George turns to run and immediately encounters his fanatical Calvinist brother Robert. The projection may be George's own magnified shadow, cast as a "brocken spectre."[5] The reader is left in doubt as to whether it is George's image projected into the vapors in an enlarged and warped form or a "horrible monster" associated with Robert (34). The distorted and magnified figure cast into the clouds from this scene in *Confessions* returns to haunt Joyce's text in the phrases "largely," "so to shape," "stretching," and "in the shadow" on page 487 of the *Wake*. Elsewhere in Joyce's text, this crucial scene of mist and mystification from Hogg is referred to in a phrase discussing HCE. In the opening chapter we are told a "meandertale, aloss and again, of our old Heidenburgh in the days when Head-in-Clouds walked the earth" (*FW*, 18.22–24).

The passage ends with Yawn admitting that he does not constitute a single, consistent entity, echoing Robert Wringhim's internal schism: "I generally conceived myself to be two people" (Hogg, 125). Although obsessed with the idea of the self (note how many occurrences of the words "I" and "my" appear in the passage), Yawn admits he is "not meself at all." He is "*bi*miselves" (my italics), and "half Scotch," composed of two substances like whisky and a drop of water. As I shall discuss later, elsewhere Joyce considers the extent to which Ireland (or at least its northern part), through the Ulster Plantation, has been rendered "half Scotch." Shaun, like Ireland itself, has split into two selves. As a result, he has "become of twosome twiminds" (*FW*, 188.14). The phrase "once or twice" suggests duality, and "I'm thinking to" can be read as "I'm thinking two." Furthermore, "felt feeling" is a strange chronological and linguistic clash of past and present tenses. Joyce's vision of Shaun's duality has been created, in part, by way of reference to Hogg's work and to Hogg himself. The personality of Shaun is split in two, with one half of his identity taking the form of an uncanny doppelgänger, his "addlefoes"

Shem. His brother/enemy is a mental projection, "stretching . . . the liferight out" of him in the manner of a brocken spectre. In much the same way, the enigmatic figure Gil-Martin of Hogg's *Confessions* can be read as deriving from Wringhim's mental disorder, part of Wringhim's personality transmitted outwards and taking the shape of a satanic outsider, "a deil" (Hogg, 160).

The name of the figure "Gaping Gill" in *Finnegans Wake* derives from the Gil-Martin of Hogg's *Confessions* (see Glasheen, 57). Gill is the name of the cad who approaches Earwicker (one of the many names of HCE) in the Phoenix Park to ask the time. Joyce appropriates the name of Hogg's satanic figure / mental projection for the *Wake*, as well as Hogg's technique for presenting separate fragments of a singular psychology as independent characters. Luke Thurston has discussed Gil-Martin and Gaping Gill in relation to psychoanalysis:

> The narrative ego grapples with its own inability to reduce itself, split away from proper self-recognition, to a theoretical truth: "This was an anomaly not to be accounted for by any philosophy of mine. . . . To be in a state of consciousness and unconsciousness, at the same time, in the same spirit, was impossible." . . . This untheorisable self-division, identified as an anomaly (the Greek *anomalos*, "not identical with itself," etymologically encodes a lack of "law," *nomos*, and of "name," *onoma*), cannot belong to a reality governed by the spatio-temporal unity of "mememormee" (*FW*, 628.14), where the French for "same" doubles into a surplus "I." . . . But Hogg's inspired move is to incarnate this lack-of-reality, to make it into a character . . . Gil-Martin, McGill, Gil . . . "Gaping Gill" (*FW*, 36.35), as he or she is named in the *Wake*, is precisely a hole, a point of visible lack. (Thurston, *Problem*, 114)

The attention to "hogsheads" (*FW*, 581.12) and a "hogsheaded firkin family" (*FW*, 381.35–36) in the *Wake* can also be explained with reference to Hogg. On the subject of hogsheads, John Bishop has discussed the relevance of barrels in *Finnegans Wake*:

> The notoriously strange "barrel" in which Shaun appears ("I am as plain as portable enveloped" "care of one of Mooseyeare Goonness's

registered andouterthus barrels" [414.10–12]) is . . . simply a cipher for the imperceived and "unknown body" of HCE (96.29), within which the "fumiform[ed]" Shaun and all kinds of letters are in fact "enveloped": etymologically, the English word "body" derives from the Old English *bodig* ("a cask" or barrel) and is cognate with the Middle Low German *boddig* ("a tub for brewing") because then as now the body was perceived as a container of better things ("spirits"). (Bishop, 140)

In other words, HCE is/has a "hogshead" in the sense that he contains the contrasting "spirits" of Shem and Shaun. However, the "hogshead" is also a signal that this presentation of "heads" or identities and their internal natures is derived from the work of "The Ettrick Shepherd." Elsewhere, the phrase "caledosian capacity" (*FW*, 187.07) brilliantly combines the sense that the sleeping ("doze") head of the dreamer (*caput*—Latin—head) is "Caledonian." The brain of the dreamer displays a typically Scottish division as well as being utterly closed off to the exterior world in the manner of Humean idealist philosophy.

For Thurston, the doublings of *Confessions* and *The Wake* function as a Derridean deconstruction of truth itself. Commenting on the work of Sarah Kofman, Thurston discusses how "the double figure as an allegory or *mise en abîme* of an originary difference" is inherent in "*all* representation": "The multiplication of selves would thus be only a radical exposure of how all language 'doubles' the world, triggering the philosophical anxiety—as old as Plato—that its simulcra constitute a 'structure of duplicity' and thus obscure or dismantle the truth. Joycean writing . . . is an exemplary site of truth-dismantling—also known as deconstruction—and has been ascribed a privileged status as such by Derrida" (Thurston, *Problem*, 111). Of course, deconstruction bears close similarities to Scottish Enlightenment philosophy: "David Hume . . . called scepticism 'a malady which can never be radically cured, but must return upon us every moment, however we may chase it away. . . . Carelessness and inattention alone can afford us any remedy.' . . . Deconstruction works at the same giddy limit, suspending all that we take for granted about language, experience and the "normal" possibilities of human communication" (C. Norris, xi).

Appropriately enough for this study of doubles and duality, Joyce has another Scottish author from which to draw for the *dubium* of *Finnegans Wake*. Robert Louis Stevenson's 1886 gothic novella *Strange Case of Dr. Jekyll and Mr. Hyde* provided a further Scottish prototype for Joyce's treatment of fractured character and dual identity in the *Wake*.[6] *Jekyll and Hyde* is not the first or last of Stevenson's texts to address duality. He also tackled this theme in his 1880 play *Deacon Brodie, or the Double Life*, which, interestingly for students of the *Wake*, features an Irish character named Humphrey (Humphrey Chimpden Earwicker being one of the names given to the central figure of the *Wake*: HCE). Furthermore, Stevenson's 1886 historical adventure novel *Kidnapped* sets the heroic and charismatic Highlander Alan Breck Stewart in diametric opposition to the prosaic and colorless Lowlander David Balfour.[7] Bizarrely, G. Gregory Smith's *Scottish Literature* manages to omit any reference to *Dr. Jekyll and Mr. Hyde*, as well as to Hogg's *Confessions*. It is a strange set of circumstances where these two works, which are thought of today as the most obvious examples of the idea of Caledonian Antisyzygy in prose, do not actually feature in the original text that advances the theory. Furthermore, Smith never makes the point that duality—especially duality in narration—can lead to all kinds of uncertainties. This is certainly the case in Hogg's *Confessions*.

As with James Hogg, Stevenson's personal background provides important context for a consideration of his interest in duality:

> Throughout his life Stevenson was fascinated by man's double being, by "those provinces of good and ill which divide and compound man's dual nature." He had been intrigued by the career of William Brodie (1741–88), a respected Edinburgh businessman who was simultaneously an unscrupulous thief. Moreover his own character and imagination were irrevocably marked by the strict Calvinism of his early environment and by his rebellion against the narrow morality of Victorian Scotland. . . . The story is much more than a simple allegory of good versus evil; it is a profound study of hypocrisy. Part of Jekyll's ambivalence lies in his attitude to evil, in the fact that he regards the throwing off of moral control as a liberation. It is not so much that he wishes to embark on an orgy of lust and

violence as that he cannot tolerate the notion that certain forms of behaviour are not permissible. In this ambivalence Jekyll embodies that hypocrisy which Stevenson sought to expose and criticise. . . . The story is then a parable both on the dual nature of man and on the double standards man applies to his own behaviour. (Hammond, 123–24)

Stevenson's severely religious childhood clashed with the blithe bohemian freedom of his teenage and student years at Edinburgh. Furthermore, Edinburgh's clean, bright, orderly and respectable eighteenth century New Town provided a stark contrast to the shadowy, dirty, dangerous, and labyrinth-like underworld of its medieval Old Town. Although set in London, the city in *Dr. Jekyll and Mr. Hyde* is—as has been pointed out by numerous critics—noticeably reminiscent of Edinburgh. According to Alan Sandison, Stevenson's interest in the inherent contrasts of the city relates to a broader interest in duality:

[Stevenson's] subject . . . dictated that his location should be the city but his *treatment* of that subject dictated it too. As has already been suggested, its "doubleness"—the contrast between façade and interior, its capacity to sustain a complex secret life, the contrast between its day- and night-time existence, the multifariousness of its aspects which can change from being one moment concretely physical to disconcertingly surreal the next—all these dualities and ambivalences contribute to the working-out of his dominant pluralist vision. (Sandison, 224–25)

For Sandison, Stevenson is a "harbinger of Modernism" whose work displays "artistic self-consciousness" and "metafictional structures" (4, 224). Elsewhere, Ronald R. Thomas notes that "*Jekyll and Hyde* . . . launch[es] an elaborate assault on the ideals of the individual personality and the cult of character that dominated the nineteenth century, striking at the heart of that ideology: the life story" (158). Furthermore, *Dr. Jekyll and Mr. Hyde* is the "beginning of a tradition subversive to conventional self-narration that can be traced through the central modernist . . . writers of fictional autobiography [including] Joyce" (158).

The theme of psychological duality of Stevenson's work was itself influenced by Hogg's *Confessions*. Hogg's text is subtly alluded to within Stevenson's work as part of a more general scheme of indeterminacy: "The various 'objective' and 'subjective' accounts, in a structure which echoes Hogg's *Justified Sinner*, offer shifting perspectives on the central events, provoking thoughts about what constitutes 'truth.'. . . The echoes of Hogg are telling, for just as *The Justified Sinner* undermines any single or fixed notion of truth, so too does Stevenson's novella, which, foreshadowing post-modern fiction, is hauntingly 'indeterminate'" (Gifford et al., 411–19). Again, Joyce involves Scottish writers whose texts either "undermine" a single or fixed notion of truth or insist that no such truth is actually attainable. Hume, Hogg, and Stevenson, in different ways, all add to the cultural response against the certainties of rationality and materialism in *Finnegans Wake*. Linked to this, as with the use of Hogg's work, Stevenson is also incorporated into the *Wake* in order to develop the text's sense of uncanny duality. According to Thurston, "the starting point of Freud's discussion of the uncanny [is] Schelling's definition of the latter as 'the name for everything that ought to have remained secret and hidden but has now come to light.' It is therefore no surprise that the texts by Hogg, Wilde and Stevenson dealing with double existences (or 'doublin existents,' *FW*, 578.14) are profoundly embroiled in the apparitional problematic of truth, of *alethia* or revelation" (Thurston, *Problem*, 114). In the final section of Stevenson's text, entitled "Henry Jekyll's Full Statement of the Case," Jekyll offers his own insight into the dissociations of human psychology, one that has considerable bearing on *Finnegans Wake*:

> Others will follow, others will outstrip me on the same lines; and I hazard the guess that man will be ultimately known for a mere polity of multifarious, incongruous and independent denizens. . . . I learned to recognize the thorough and primitive duality of man; I saw that, of the two natures that contended in the field of my consciousness, even if I could rightly be said to be either, it was only because I was radically both. (Stevenson, 70)

The idea that a person may be composed of "multifarious, incongruous and independent denizens" is certainly present in the *Wake*, where HCE is described as being "more mob than man" (*FW*, 261.21–22) and consists of (at least) "two natures," the rebellious, unorthodox writer Shem and the conservative, establishment figure Shaun. Furthermore, the lawyer Henry Jekyll resembles Shaun to a certain extent, in that they represent repressive order and strict authority. As we shall see in the following chapter, HCE "contains" the twins in the same way that Ireland encompasses divergent identities or cultures.

Stevenson's *Dr. Jekyll and Mr. Hyde* is not given as prominent a treatment in *Finnegans Wake* as Hogg's *Confessions*, though there are a number of important allusions to the work: "though I shall promptly prove his whole account of the Sennacherib as distinct from the Shalmanesir Sanitational reforms and of the Mr. Skekels and Dr. Hydes problem in the same connection differs *toto coelo* from the fruit of my own investigations . . . as being again hopelessly vitiated by what I have now resolved to call the dime and cash diamond fallacy" (*FW*, 150.15–24). The allusion to *Dr. Jekyll and Mr. Hyde* here, in I.vi, continues in the sketching out of the polarities and underlying links of Shaun and Shem ("distinct," "differs"/"same," "connection") also developed in other sections of the *Wake* such as "The Mookse and the Gripes" and the story of Burrus and Caseous. Another "binary figure," Douglas Hyde, must also be present here. Despite Shaun's protestations to the contrary, the similarity of the brothers is stressed at the end of the chapter during an extended question-and-answer session:

> The twelfth and last question and answer . . . hint at the eventual reunion of the twins. Phrased as an imperative but punctuated as a question, Shaun's "*Sacer esto?*" expresses perfectly the complex moral vision of the *Wake*: Shaun's command is both a curse and a blessing, and his question is not only whether his brother will be accursed but also whether he will be blessed (both meanings are implicit in Latin *sacer*). Shem's answer, "*Semus sumus!*," is, as Tindall observes, "both singular and plural" and "means I am Shem and we are the same." (McCarthy, "Three Approaches," 411)

The allusion to *Dr. Jekyll and Mr. Hyde* shows that even though the twins take radically opposed forms and display starkly different characteristics—"differs *toto coelo*"—they have always been, like Stevenson's character(s), essentially the same entity—"same connection." The twin brothers "resolve" themselves within the father figure HCE. Or to put it another way, Shem and Shaun are divergent tendencies *of* HCE. In the following chapter we shall see how the twin brother figures relate to Ireland and Scotland and how the countries themselves are represented as twins.

Elsewhere in *Finnegans Wake* there is a fascinating allusion to Stevenson's tale in ALP's list of poisoned gifts for a group of children. Along with "snakes in clover, picked and scotched, and a vaticanned viper catcher's visa for Patsy Presbys" (*FW*, 210.26–27), ALP's "colonial ... bagful" (*FW*, 212.20) also includes "a jackal with hide for Browne but Nolan" (*FW*, 211.31–32). Here, as in the following allusion to Stevenson, there is an emphasis on hiding or concealment, as well as to animals or to untamed aspects of human psychology. The reference to Bruno the Nolan connects Stevenson's portrayal of divided consciousness to the sixteenth-century Italian Dominican friar Giordano Bruno's philosophical concept of the "coincidence of contraries" (Koch, 237). The works of Hogg and Stevenson may then be read as literary equivalents for the theories Joyce finds in Bruno. Ronald J. Koch has summarized the critical responses to Joyce's use of Bruno's "doctrine":

> *Wake* criticism has tended to accept this doctrine as an explanation of the numerous pairs of opposites in *Finnegans Wake*—usually read as attributes of the opposite and feuding sons Shem and Shaun. . . . W. Y. Tindall suggests, "Maybe [Joyce] got his quarreling twins from Bruno, without whose intrusion one son to replace the father might have seemed sufficient. Maybe Shem is Bruno's thesis, Shaun his antithesis, and godlike H. C. E., in whom these contraries coincide, their synthesis. Anyway, before and after taking father's place, the equal and opposite twins agree." This seems sound enough, for it is clear that the sons have to get together to replace the father, and the pattern of the twins' exchanging of roles is clearly related to Bruno. (237–38)

Tindall's suggestion that Joyce found the idea of the quarrelling twins in Bruno is intriguing. However, there are also important literary pretexts—namely Hogg and Stevenson—for the presentation of incongruent identities existing within the same person. Interestingly, Joyce writes "Browne but Nolan" rather than "Browne and Nolan" (Here Joyce is also referring to a Dublin bookshop named Browne and Nolan). The use of "but" here implies exclusions, contradictions, or contrasts rather than the simple connection or continuation that would be implied with the use of the simpler conjunction "and." In the passage from page 211 of the *Wake*, the literary opposites or dualism of Stevenson meet the coincidence of contraries of Bruno. By mingling these important and disparate influences here, Joyce highlights their essential similarity. The philosophical precedent for *Finnegans Wake* may have been Bruno, but here Joyce links this source to the Scottish literary tradition.

Just before the eventual morning of book IV of *Finnegans Wake*, a final reference to Stevenson's *Dr. Jekyll and Mr. Hyde* appears: "How did he bank it up, swank it up, the whaler in the punt, a guinea by a groat, his index on the balance and such wealth into the bargain, with the boguey which he snatched in the baggage coach ahead? Going forth on the prowl, master jackill, under night and creeping back, dog to hide, over morning. Humbly to fall and cheaply to rise, exposition of failures" (*FW*, 589.12–17). This section (linked to HCE through the appearance of his initials in "Humbly," "cheaply," and "exposition") displays some of the duality of Stevenson's work with the contrasts of "under"/"over," "night"/"morning," and "going forth"/"creeping back." Joyce now applies Stevenson's representation of a divided consciousness to the situation of the sleeping brain "under night" and the lucidity, inhibition, and clarity returning "over morning." The passage also suggests the emergence of some animal-like, feral, or prehuman aspect of the personality that is free to go "on the prowl" during dreams only to be forced to "hide" once dreams end in the morning and consciousness (as well as civilization itself) returns. The movement from "jackill" to "dog" hints at an untamed or wild aspect of human psychology at night being neutered into a safer, domesticated version during the day. This emphasis on repression is a suitable context for an allusion to Stevenson's text. Are the "failures" alluded to here an inability to reconcile the contrasting elements of HCE's identity, or is the animal side of his psychology something he has failed to "master"? Despite the seemingly psychoanalytic nature of this passage I would suggest that the exploration of an interior world in *Finnegans Wake* is as much Humean as it is Freudian.

So, HCE is composed of warring, contradictory elements in technique derived in part from Scottish literature. As we shall see, this representation is linked by Joyce to his portrayal of the connections of Irish and Scottish histories. Although the presentation of HCE as a divided psyche is partly achieved through allusion to Stevenson, Joyce also alludes to the Edinburgh writer in a more atavistic discussion of racial identity during a lecture on Charles Dickens:

> To arrive at a just appreciation of Dickens, to estimate more accurately his place in what we may call the national gallery of English literature it would be well to read not only the eulogies of the London-born but also the opinion of representative writers of Scotland, or the colonies or Ireland. It would be interesting to hear an appreciation of Dickens written, so to speak, at a proper focus from the original by writers of his own class and of a like (if somewhat lesser) stature, near enough to him in aim and in form and in speech to understand, far enough from him in spirit and in blood to criticize. One is curious to know how the great cockney would fare at the hands of R. L. S. (*OCPW*, 184–85)

These seemingly nonironic remarks tell us a number of important things about Joyce's views on Stevenson and on Scotland. Firstly, that Joyce regarded Stevenson as a "representative writer" of Scotland. They also show that Joyce (more so than T. S. Eliot; see his plainly odd essay "Was There a Scottish Literature?") conceived of Scottish writing as a separate tradition from English literature, able to offer divergent insights into English texts (free from what Joyce sees as a "London-born" bias towards English writers). These insights are possible despite the similarities existing between Stevenson and Dickens in "class," "stature," "aim," "form," and "speech."

What then is it that distinguishes Stevenson from Dickens? Joyce makes the bold assertion that Scotland—as well as Ireland (represented by Moore)—is removed from England not only in literary tradition but also in the charged terms of racial discourse—"spirit" and "blood." Compare the very different assertion of Thomas MacDonagh in *Literature in Ireland* (1916) that "Scots literature was born brother to English, the literature of men of the lowland race; and the blood relationship has proved a strong bond" (20). Anglo-Irish writing, on the other hand, was, for MacDonagh, "a new literature . . . with the difference of nationality" (22). MacDonagh was a lecturer in Irish literature at Joyce's alma mater, University College Dublin, and was executed after taking part in the 1916 Easter Rising. Unlike Joyce, MacDonagh stresses the racial links between the lowland Scots and the English. MacDonagh ignores Scottish Gaelic literature and is rather selective in his demonstration of a supposed "kinship" (22) felt by Scottish poets to their English counterparts.

Clearly Joyce believed at the time of his paper "The Centenary of Charles Dickens" (1912) that there were fundamental—even *essential*—differences between Scotland and England in terms of their ethnicity but also in some vague spiritual sense. According to critics such as Len Platt and Vincent Cheng, Joyce later undermines essentialized ideas of nationality and race in the *Wake*.[8] At this earlier stage in his career, however, Joyce employs such notions, with an emphasis on "blood" and "spirit."[9] If Joyce *totally* abandons his belief in such notions, it represents a major volte-face.[10] In any case, as Emer Nolan points out, Joyce's rejection of conceptions of racial purity or national homogeneity never stops him from investigating racial or national identity (see *Nationalism*, 148). Likewise, Platt notes that various ethnic identities are simultaneously present and not present in the *Wake* (see *Joyce, Race*, 50). I argue that Joyce's belief in a Celtic "spirit" survives well into *Finnegans Wake*, through the deployment of a neo-Revivalist conception of Irish (and Scottish) identity based on interiority, skepticism, and duality. Ironically, Stevenson is a "representative" of Scotland here—suggesting there must be some quintessentially Scottish essence to represent in the first place—while later in Joyce's career, Stevenson's work becomes a touchstone for Joyce's representation of fragmentation in individual and national identities.

With the works of Robert Louis Stevenson and James Hogg, Scottish literature provided Joyce with a means of splitting identities in his fiction and offered a multifaceted view of human psychology, allowing the exploration of various possibilities or aspects rather than one static essence. The representation of the dreamer's mind (or the figure of HCE) as being composed of opposing tendencies or aspects owes much to Scottish literature. Joyce's treatment of the dream state in *Finnegans*

Wake required a strategy wherein his dreamer could contain the various divergent tendencies, emotions, and ideas that exist in the sleeping brain. The bisected mental space, wherein the opposed son-figures Shem and Shaun are also somehow resolved or contained within the father-figure HCE, is a development of ideas with its roots in nineteenth-century Scottish literature. In the following chapter we will see how Joyce expands on the techniques offered by Hogg and Stevenson and, in the spirit of the Caledonian Antisyzygy, creates a mutating and evolving network of phrases in *Finnegans Wake* based on the connections and contrasts of Irish and Scottish ancient and modern history. This motif, based on the originally rival but eventually partner tribes the Picts and the Scots, helps to define the binary relationship of the rival twins of the *Wake*, Joyce's version of Robert and Gil-Martin or Jekyll and Hyde. Here Joyce develops the Hogg/Stevenson polarities of the *Wake* to examine the uncanny connections of Scotland and Ireland but also their internal racial, religious, and cultural dualities.

FOUR

The United States of Scotia Picta

The Celtic Unconscious of *Finnegans Wake*

THE STRUCTURE OF A WAKEAN TEXTUAL NETWORK

Surveying the realms of world mythology and history in his Parisian exile, Joyce encounters some notable earlier Irish expatriates. In J. M. Flood's *Ireland: Its Saints and Scholars* (1917), Benedict Fitzpatrick's *Ireland and the Making of Great Britain* (1922), and Stephen Gwynn's *History of Ireland* (1923) he discovered the story of the ancient Scoti tribe.[1] He would also have stumbled upon the Scoti's counterparts, the Picts, in these works as well as in James Frazer's groundbreaking work of anthropology, *The Golden Bough* (1890).[2] These two ethnic groups eventually merged to form the forerunner to medieval Scotland in the period 850–1000. Joyce not only repeatedly alludes to the historical origins of ancient Scotland in *Finnegans Wake* with a textual system of references to the Picts and the Scots; he also deliberately links this network to his own versions of innovations from nineteenth-century Scottish literature. These features form a Celtic trail through the Scotch mist of *Finnegans Wake*, contributing to a sense of the contrasting mental tendencies of the "dreamer" of the *Wake* and to the constantly evolving relations between Ireland and Scotland. This chapter traces how Joyce exploits the malleable potential of the words Pict and Scot to help project some of the pervasive, thematically interrelated concerns of the *Wake*—the experience of dreaming, familial rivalry, sexuality, and national histories, to name a few—through the prism of the divided Antisyzygy-like psychology of the text's "dreamer." In *Finnegans Wake* Joyce presents a vision of intra-Celtic events that is submerged into his presentation of an interior, Humean mind. As we have seen, this modernist and idealist aesthetic is created as a response to what Joyce saw as a "fatuous" modern materialist civilization (*OCPW*, 179). Alongside the duality of Anglo-Saxon and Celt, we will now consider the inter-Celtic binary opposition of Pict and Scot. Again, this relationship is attached to Joyce's presentation of an "inhumed" mind.

The Pict/Scot "nodal system" in *Finnegans Wake* adheres to the broader structure of the work.[3] There are six occurrences of phrases involving a pair of words based on "Pict" and "Scot" in book I, two in book III, and one in book IV. The motif does not appear at all in book II. The references always deal with the Picts and the Scots in pairs; they perform as a double act, much like Hogg's Robert and Gil-Martin or Stevenson's Jekyll and Hyde. There is one exception to this rule: late in the text the Picts are appointed a very different partner, the Saxons. The phrases containing semantic distortion of the words Pict and Scot signal the relationship of the brothers Shaun and Shem—in keeping with a general focus in *Finnegans Wake* on the division of a central personality into separate elements—but resist the assignment of either brother to a particular tribe or word. In a similarly ambiguous fashion, the motif of the Picts and the Scots represents both a convergence of competing energies and an identity constantly under pressure from centrifugal forces, moving away from the center in different directions.

The system also functions to some extent as a model of the structure of the *Wake* in miniature form. As was mentioned earlier, the Picts-and-Scots motif does not appear in book II. I would suggest that this absence is related to Joyce's treatment of the progression (or otherwise) of the two brother figures Shem and Shaun and how this connects to the larger structure of the *Wake*. Book II acts as the focal point at which the divergent personalities of the brother figures Shem and Shaun meet and fuse together. As Clive Hart notes, "Around a central section, Book II, Joyce builds two opposing cycles consisting of Books I and III" (*Structure*, 66–67). Prior to book II Shem's personality is most prominent, especially in the last two answers of the quiz show of I.vi. Towards the end of II.ii, the brothers become united and merged, before Shaun takes center stage: "As the previous vignettes have defined Shem far more clearly than Shaun, exploring the possibilities the artist-critic-outsider presents, from this point on [book II], Shaun will be the dominant presence" (Kitcher, 172). Because of the *Wake*'s broad structure, consisting of opposing sections joined by a central axis, the Picts and the Scots are absent in II. The series of motifs concerning the two ethnic groups tends to stress various types of opposition and contrast. They are absent in the middle section of the book, where a merging occurs and "where extremes meet" (*FW*, 440.34–35). It is only on either side of this area of convergence that the motif appears.

In the following sections, I will follow this network through the text to show the different inflections created as it develops and offer close readings of these sections. This approach will give a sense of both the "local" environment in which the phrases are found and how these locations affect the motif examples themselves. This methodology will also reveal the connective thematic bonds between the various iterations of the design and give a sense of how the ideas Joyce is working with here mutate and modulate through their multiple occurrences in the text in accordance with its overall structure. Such a technique will provide a reconstructed survey of a meandering and revealing pattern—a "plot" even—which brings together Scottish and Irish histories with the double focus on consciousness and duality we have encountered in the previous chapters.

"THE BLEW OF THE GAELS"

After his encounter with the James Hogg–derived figure, Gaping Gill, in a park, rumors about HCE's unseemly conduct coalesce into a humiliating comic song entitled the "Ballad of Persse O'Reilly" (the song itself appears on page 44), which goes on tour across a considerable geographic expanse:

The wararrow went round, so it did, (a nation wants a gaze) and the ballad, in the felibrine trancoped metre affectioned by Taiocebo in his *Casudas de Poulichinello Artahut*, stumpstampaded on to a slip of blancovide and headed by an excessively rough and red woodcut, privately printed at the rimepress of Delville, soon fluttered its secret on white highway and brown byway to the rose of the winds and the blew of the gaels, from archway to lattice and from black hand to pink ear, village crying to village, through the five pussyfours green of the united states of Scotia Picta. (*FW*, 43.21–30)

Joyce's words based on the terms "Pict" and "Scot'" always appear in pairs, and pairings extend to the context of the phrases, as in the passage above. For example, in the above section we have the paired phrases "from archway to lattice" and "from black hand to pink ear." As well as evoking a temporal theme through allusion to music—"the ballad"—a spatial aspect is also included by the singing of this tune "from village to village."

In its primary function the phrase "the united states of Scotia Picta" is obviously concerned with states in the sense of territories, with its allusions to the United States of America; it is also concerned with Scotia, an old name for Scotland (but, confusingly, also a Roman name for Ireland—the name crossed the Irish Sea with the Scoti), and with the five ancient and four current provinces of Ireland. There is already a trace of the sense of division that will accompany all the phrases we will encounter in the doubling of terms but also in the contradiction of "the united states of Scotia Picta." If the unification was complete, one name would suffice, as in "the United States of America" (*FW*, 130.28) or "the United Stars of Ourania" (185.31). Furthermore, a contrast is drawn between the "United Kingdom" of England and Scotland and these "united states," with Joyce drawing attention to earlier political unions of Scottish history.

The foundation of what was to become Scotland begins with the uniting of "states," one of which had its origins in Ireland. Stephen Gwynn's 1923 work *The History of Ireland*, one of Joyce's source texts for *Finnegans Wake*, describes the partly "Irish" origins of "Scotland" (these terms must be used in the knowledge that "we are talking of a time before the emergence of the modern idea of a nation or a country" [Stewart, 34]):

In the fifth century nearly all of Alba, which we now call Scotland, was held by the Picts. . . . There was no organised Gaelic state in Alba till in A.D. 470 Fergus Mac Erc, King of Dalriada, crossed over and established his kingship on the eastern shore [i.e., Scotland]. For three hundred years his successors ruled on both sides of the Irish channel as Kings of Dalriada; then, in the break-up caused by the Scandinavian invasions, they lost their territory in Ireland. But long before this the new conquest had become the main part of their possessions, and they ruled from Alba—of which country they finally became complete masters, defeating Picts and Britons, Angles and Norsemen. (Gwynn, 19)

The Gaelic kingdom of Alba is thought to have come into being with the coming together of the previously rival kingdoms of Dál Riata (or Dalriada), which consisted of the south-western lands of the originally Irish "Scoti" and the northern and eastern territory of Pictland in the years around 900 CE (see Lynch, *Scotland*, 43–47). As Gwynn notes, "The race which by the close of the fifth century had spread out of Ireland into Scotland . . . were known to themselves as the Gaels, but to the Latin world as the Scoti" (20). According to Fitzpatrick, "The Gaelic form of Argyle is Airer-Gaedhil, that is territory of the Gael, or Irish" (114). And as A. T. Q. Stewart writes, "We usually think of eastern Ulster as an extension of Scotland, but it is just as true that western Scotland was once an extension of the Ulster kingdom of Dalriada" (34). Given Joyce's knowledge of this chapter of Irish history—his reading of these pages is shown by notes in *"Finnegans Wake" Notebooks* VI.B.6 (V. Deane et al.)—the phrase "united states of Scotia Picta" must in part be an allusion to, and inspired by, the history of the formation of Scotland with its roots in Irish colonialism, the "green" of "Scotia Picta." Gaelic was introduced to Scotland by the Scoti (see Ball, 145) and "spread beyond its initial 6th century limits until, by 1100, it was spoken throughout virtually the whole of Scotland" (Lynch, *Companion*, 378). The references to this aspect of Irish history and Gaelic maritime movements, "the blew of the Gael," act as a small counterbalance to the usual presentation of Ireland suffering repeatedly from invasions in the *Wake*, leaving Joyce open to accusations of creating an ambivalent and neutral uniformity in his presentation of different forms and eras of colonialism.

Joyce is also linking some of the earliest Irish migrations to Scotland with one of the preferred destinations of his own diasporic generation: the United States of America.

Given its formation through amalgamation of different peoples, Scotland would fail to adhere to Leopold Bloom's definition of a nation given in the "Cyclops" chapter of *Ulysses*: "A nation is the same people living in the same place" (*U*, 12.1422–23). It is this idea of Scotland being composed of separate entities, as well as the Irish catalyst, which made this aspect of ancient history of such interest to Joyce. As Joyce notes in his 1907 lecture "Ireland: Island of Saints and Sages," "[The Irish] civilization is an immense woven fabric in which very different elements are mixed" (*OCPW*, 118). Joyce's attention to, and interest in, differing ethnic or national elements here and in his later fiction must be partly attributable to the cosmopolitan atmosphere of the city in which he delivered this lecture and in which he lived for ten years. As John McCourt has shown, Trieste, then a thriving port of the Habsburg Empire but with a strong Irredentist movement working towards joining Italy, had a powerful effect on Joyce's work.[4] So much of Joyce's life was spent in occupied or contested spaces—Ireland, Trieste—that the attention he pays to other "anomalous" European areas, such as Scotland, should not be surprising.[5] Joyce was particularly well positioned to view the national and regional variations existing within imperial or state structures and to appreciate the nonfixed nature of such institutions.

Paul Robichaud has written that "Ireland's history of invasions and settlement, its mixture of various peoples and languages, makes it specially resistant to essentializing definitions" ("Narrative," 186–87). Joyce's reading of Scottish history would have shown him that Scotland is similar to Ireland in this respect, that it is also a mixture of ethnicities and cultures and therefore resistant to such definitions: "What Joyce grew increasingly to understand is that, whereas racism and ethnocentrism depend on static essences and absolute difference, peoples and populations contain multiplicitous and heterogenous characteristics of both individual and cultural difference that cannot be so conveniently . . . named and labelled" (Cheng, *Joyce, Race, and Empire*, 53). Scotland, as seen in Joyce's "book of breedings" (*FW*, 410.1–2), is a population containing "multiplicitous and heterogeneous characteristics," including a crucially important Irish element. Irish historians working in the same era as Joyce, such as Stephen Gwynn, are keen to point out that Scotland has a secondary, replicated position as a product of Irish invasion and colonization. Joyce, however, values replications, copies, and processes of transition or metamorphosis. The allusion to "Puss in the Corner," a game in which children move between fixed points, strengthens the impression that Joyce is playing with ideas of immigration as evoked by the allusion to the founding of Alba. The crossing (and returning) of peoples across the Northern Channel and the Irish Sea is, of course, a hugely significant part of Ireland and Scotland's historical relationship.[6]

So, the phrase "united states of Scotia Picta," while evoking entwined Irish and Scottish histories, also has a strong spatial or geographical dimension and is placed in a context suggesting the passage of time. However, of critical importance to the phrase is the word "states." A meaning other than its geographical or political sense is intended here, that of states of consciousness. The Greek for darkness or obscurity is σκότος (*skotos*), while the word "Pict" derives from the Latin for painter: *pictor*. With this sharply contrasting semantic material Joyce paints a de-*pict*ion of the dream "state" itself, of the darkness of sleep and night, "Scotia," with the dream imagery or pictures suggested by "Picta"—a picture which exists in a Humean darkness.[7]

John Bishop, in *Joyce's Book of the Dark*, has argued convincingly that Joyce's repeated use of terms related to darkness is a method of constructing the dream state of "one stable somebody" (*FW*, 107.30). The above passage is one exception to this rule, filled as it is with colors and shades. We have "red," "white," "brown," "rose," "blew," "pink," and "green." The vividness of this part of the dream is rendered through a palette of colors befitting a painter, or *pictor*. There is also the contradiction of dream vision in a "blank" sleep with "blancovide" (*videre*, Latin, "to see"). Since *vide* is also the French for "empty," the unreal, phantasmal nature of dream imagery is also hinted at here, the essential immateriality of our nighttime visions. The reduction from five to four is also suggestive of our senses as we sleep: with our eyes closed we lose our sight (though it is replaced in a sense by dream imagery), but our hearing and senses of touch, taste, and smell all, to varying degrees, remain. The "united states of Scotia Picta" is an area where the opposites of consciousness and unconsciousness and darkness and light meet, as well as a reference to the creation of Alba, or the historical "united states" of Dál Riata and Pictland. By linking a representation of the dream state to opposing Celtic tribes the phrase functions as a representation of a particularly Celtic divided and totally internal "reality." If, as Joyce suggests, "nations, like individuals, have their egos" (*OCPW*, 108), then the individual ego must, like the nations he examines, be divided or mixed.

HCE himself is synthesised from "opposites"—a condition lifted straight from the pages of Stevenson and Hogg. Likewise—as Joyce highlights—Scottish history begins with the combination of different components. These contrasting inner tendencies begin to develop into Shem- and Shaun-like figures during the trial of a figure named Festy King, which appears at *FW*, 85.20–93.21. Towards the end of this section the following disguised reference to the Picts and the Scots appears while Festy King, a Shem-type figure (see Swartzlander, 465), is acquitted: "Untius, Muncius, Punchus and Pylax but could do no worse than promulgate their standing verdict of Nolans Brumans whereoneafter King, having murdered all the English he knew, picked out his pockets and left the tribunal scotfree, trailing his Tommeylommey's tunic in his hurry, thereinunder proudly showing off the blink patch to his britgits to prove himself (an't plase yous!) a rael genteel" (*FW*, 92.35–93.5). England and Scotland, cause and effect, and the Browne and Nolan bookshop in Dublin are all connected with Giordano Bruno of Nolan here, "who discussed the coincidence of opposed contraries and whose name is made to illustrate the principle" (McHugh, *Annotations*, xv).[8] Marian Eide has discussed Joyce's interest in Giordano Bruno as an influence on the relationship between "oppositional entities" (Eide, 473) in the *Wake*: "According to Joyce's 1903 essay, 'The Bruno Philosophy,' Bruno professes that 'every power in nature or in spirit must evolve an opposite as the sole condition and means of its manifestation; and every opposition is, therefore, a tendency, a tendency to reunification' (*CW* 134). . . . Joyce sets Bruno's theory at the center of his text and illustrates it in multiple contexts that emerge from the central metaphor of the warring and yet mutually dependent brothers" (474). The motif of the Picts and Scots, and therefore the representation of Scotland itself, is an example of a more general obsession with duality in the *Wake* and of one of the "multiple contexts" in which Joyce illustrates Bruno's theory. The "Caledonian Antisyzygy" literature of Hogg and Stevenson is another of these contexts. The Picts and Scots also take on the roles of the feuding brothers who are central to the *Wake*'s treatment of Bruno's philosophy. Taken together, these features create an atmosphere of multiplicity or *"dubium"* (Thurston, *Problem*, 115), deepening the sense of uncertainty created by the text's Humean "reality."

Doubles—such as Shem and Shaun—are a vital aspect of the structure of *Finnegans Wake*: "Duality of being is perhaps the most important of all the basic structural concepts in *Finnegans Wake*. There are two of everything—so that any crux can always be related to some analogous passage for enlightenment" (C. Hart, *Structure*, 153). Here Hart provides a crucial method of interpreting the *Wake*, the comparison and connection of one passage with an "analogous" one. Finn Fordham has noted the importance for Joyce of doubling as a method of composition: "Doubling is a major process of the way Joyce generated text, not along some linear structure but by returning to what he'd done and repeating what was already there, in a slightly different way each time. Words, phrases, or narratives always grow into some related form. They have morphed versions of themselves making connections, either nearby or with distant echoes further away" (46). Helpfully, Joyce highlights the analogous nature of the passages discussed here with interrelated terms based on two basic, opposed lexical units—"Pict" and "Scot."

The Picts and the Scots function as opposing principles, forces existing in relation to other forces, reflecting Joyce's world of endless conflict. The Celt exists in opposition to the Anglo-Saxon, but within the Celtic world the Pict exists in opposition to the Scot. Like the linguistic landscape in *Finnegans Wake*, everything can be broken down into constituent parts (for example, a Wakean portmanteau can express the singular and individual meanings of its components well as the meaning of the full or complete unit). However, this lack of essential unity or harmony in terms of identities, ideas, or words does not mean that there is not also some kind of underlying connection between discrete units. Furthermore, that an identity such as "Irish" or "Celtic" is revealed as essentially "constructed" in the *Wake* does not mean that it has no validity as an identity.

The evocation of contrasting darkness and color or light—which featured in the first appearance of the Pict/Scot motif—also appears in conjunction with a third, slightly risqué phrase. This case appears in the "Burrus and Caseous" section of the eleventh quiz show answer in I.vi:

> Positing, as above, two males pooles, the one the pictor of the other
> and the omber the *Skotia* of the one, and looking wantingly around
> our undistributed middle between males we feel we must waistfully
> woent a female to focus and on this stage there pleasantly appears
> the cowrymaid M. whom we shall often meet below who introduces
> herself upon us at some precise hour which we shall again agree to
> call absolute zero or the babbling pumpt of platinism. (164.4–11)

Paired oppositional terms appear again, with the contrasting temperatures of "absolute zero" and "babbling pumpt." Division and difference
is also provided by the reference to the fallacy of the undistributed
middle, an expression in philosophy which states, wrongly, that if all *a*
are *b* then its converse is also true, that all *b* must be *a*. Here, Shem and
Shaun are the opposing terms of a categorical proposition. The sister
figure Issy is cast as the middle term that links the two but is not "dis-
tributed." Contrast is also produced by the juxtaposition of two related
but different foodstuffs, with HCE being "made" in a "churn" out of
butter and cheese, the two differing sections of his personality, which are
also the twin brothers. The two males are "polarised" through the introduction of Nuvoletta, a version of Issy, in the form of margarine (Tindall, 123–24).

The setting for the third passage of the Pict/Scots network (*FW*,
164.4–11) is a picture house or theater, which allows the darkness and
light of the first phrase to recur. The darkness of the auditorium, as
well as the blackened mind of the dreamer—Hume's "theatre" (*Treatise*,
301)—is cast by "*Skotia*" (σκότος/*skotos*, Greek for "darkness") and
"omber" (*ombre*, French for "shadow"; *umber*, Latin for "shade"); the film
reel loops into "males pooles," there is a reference to Poole's Myriorama,
which was a traveling proto-cinema (McHugh, *Annotations*, 164), and
the words "focus" and "stage" develop the sense that this is a cinematic
and theatrical scene.[9] Projected through the gloom onto the screen is the
"pictor," just as "highlyfictional" (*FW*, 261.17–18) images may be "seen"
or experienced in the mind during sleep, despite the darkness of night
and shut eyes. This particular "film"—though not exactly X-rated—may
contain some adult content and scenes of a sexual nature, as it stars "two
males" looking "wantingly" for a "female to focus."[10]

Although the reference to the Picts and Scots in the Festy King trial section hinted at a possible connection to the figures Festy King and the Wet Pinter, this sexual and cinematic picture-show is the first of the motifs in which the ancient Scottish tribes are embodied in masculine characters or figures, "two males." Any two paired male figures in the *Wake* with a resemblance to each other, "the one the pictor of the other," must inevitably be identified with the rival brothers Shem and Shaun, especially when the figures appear in contexts dealing with opposed pairings: contrasting heat and cold, darkness and light, space and time, butter and cheese. The twins Shem and Shaun themselves are polar opposites; Shaun represents allegiance to tradition, whereas Shem is the rebellious, artist figure and is often linked in the text to Joyce himself. The sense of a paradoxical division and union in this second passage is added to by the words "mutuearly polarised" at *FW*, 164.2. John Gordon writes that in I.vi HCE is looking at a mirror and in this act Shem and Shaun stare at each other (*Plot Summary*, 151).

This underlying concept of having HCE split into two opposed, reflected twin figures—based largely on the presentation of divided characters in the works of Hogg and Stevenson—carries on through the following two chapters, where the next two occurrences of the motif occur. As Attridge and Howes have suggested, this is typical of Joyce:

> Philosophically he could be said to have been both a separatist and a unionist, thinking constantly in terms of oppositions and that which dissolves (or reverses) oppositions. He even extended this preference for undecidability or hybridity to the very opposition between separation and union as distinct principles of thought . . . so that even these terms cannot finally operate in isolation from each other. To identify points of difference, for Joyce, is to articulate a kind of connection. (2)

Since these opposing twins are connected to rival Scottish and Irish tribes, this motif also—by extension—presents Ireland and Scotland as nonidentical "twins." This idea tallies with a general trend in Joyce's writing where he casts the Celtic countries as family members, such as the line "Poor sister Scotland" in "Gas from a Burner" and his discussion of the "Celtic family" in "Ireland: Island of Saints and Sages" (*OCPW*, 119). However, the "simultaneously complicating oppositions" also amount to a denial of historical progression (see Sidorsky, 303–4). In casting the twins Shem and Shaun into Pictish and Scottish roles, Joyce traces the connections of Irish and Scottish history while setting up HCE's divided mental state as a specifically Celtic zone. However, since the twins exist in an uncanny affiliation—"at once utterly familiar and irreducibly strange" (McDonald, 50)—this points to a conception of Scotland and Ireland themselves as existing in an essentially *uncanny* relationship. For Joyce, Scotland is at once alien and familiar.

"ALLSTAR BOUT WAS HARRILY THE RAGE"

Although Joyce alludes to a combined ancient Irish and Scottish history to create the mental "state" of HCE, this is not a presentation of some sort of inner Celtic harmony. As a sequel to the slightly seedy cinematic exploits of I.vi, the following section introduces two elements to our present chronicle which will echo throughout the *Wake*, modifying the words Pict and Scot to create images relating to animals and to warfare. This passage is probably the most oblique reference to the Picts and the Scots in *Finnegans Wake*, and it is the only section where these paired terms are placed more than a line apart:

> Now it is notoriously known how on that surprisingly bludgeony Unity Sunday when the grand germogall allstar bout was harrily the rage between our weltingtoms extraordinary and our pettythicks the marshalaisy and Irish eyes of welcome were smiling daggers down their backs, when the roth, vice and blause met the noyr blank and rogues and the grim white and cold bet the black fighting tans, categorically unimperatived by the maxims, a rank funk getting the better of him, the scut in a bad fit of pyjamas fled like a leveret for his bare lives, Talviland ahone ahaza, pursued by the scented curses of all the village belles and, without having struck one blow, (pig stole on him was lust he lagging it was becaused dust he shook) kuskykorked himself up tight in his inkbattle house. (176.19–30)

That Joyce is referring to the tribes with the words "scut" and "pig stole" is apparent when these terms are compared to the phrases "pigs and scuts" at *FW*, 619.11 and "scotty pictail" at *FW*, 521.11. On the subject of tails, a scut is the short tail of a rabbit, hare, or deer, and a leveret is a young hare. So, a Shem-and-Shaun contrast is set up here between hares and pigs. Of course, "scut" can also mean an objectionable person, as it is used in the "Cyclops" episode of *Ulysses*: "Courthouse my eye and your pockets hanging down with gold and silver. Mean bloody scut" (12.1759–60). A further gloss to "scut" is to flee, as it is used in *A Portrait*: "I know why they scut" (40). This last meaning tallies well with the historical Scoti, since they originally "fled" from Ireland, and also suggests the cowardly behavior of Shem. The close proximity of the passage from page 176 to the "pictor" (*FW*, 164.4) and "*Skotia*" (164.5) of I.vi is note-worthy because most of the passages with Pict/Scot motifs are often placed near to a "twin" passage. Furthermore, there are two appearances of the Pict/Scot motif in the Shaun-dominated book III. The pairing of the passages from I.vi and I.vii means that the Shem-influenced latter stages of book I also contain two occurrences of the motif, providing a neat symmetry, mirroring perfectly the themes of duality and reflection that the motif is so concerned with.[11]

Shaun provided the first substantial descriptions of his altered, in-verted image Shem in the previous chapter and carries on portraying his brother in I.vii as "HCE continues to stare into the mantelpiece mirror, communing with himself" (Gordon, *Plot Summary*, 159). This passage displays fewer examples of contrasting imagery than the other sections to be examined, but this can be explained with reference to Shaun's nar-ration. In the previous chapter he attempts to deny his connection to his brother, an attempt that results in imagery evocative of both division and unity. Here Shaun's denunciation of Shem's cowardice sets up a different kind of contrast to the examples previously discussed. Shaun describes warfare in glowing terms; it is "grand," an "allstar bout" and "extraordi-nary." Shaun's militarism clashes with Shem's pacifism here. The narrator and his subject are on opposing sides, like "when the roth, vice, and blause met the noyr blank and rogues and the grim white and cold bet the black fighting tans" (*FW*, 176.20–25). Shem's unwillingness to fight is regarded by Shaun as part of his "lowness" (170.25) and the retreat of Shem to his "inkbattle" suggests that, like Joyce himself, his strategy will depend upon a retreat into creativity and interiority: "Joyce . . . could be accused, like Shem, of cowardice, of being a 'zürichschicken' . . . or a 'chicken' of Zürich, for not taking part either in the Easter Rebellion of 1916 or in the World War. Instead, 'without having struck one blow,' he kuskykorked himself up tight in his ink battle house, with his booze and his writing materials" (Manganiello, 159).

This passage in I.vii carries on from the work begun in the last two questions and answers of the quiz show section in constructing the figure of Shem. In contrast with the more belligerent Shaun we meet in III, here Shem's avoidance of conflict is stressed. The references on page 176 to the first Bloody Sunday (176.19–20) and the Black and Tans (176.24–25) and other allusions relating to warfare appear in an atmosphere of conflict—"the grand germogall allstar bout was harrily the rage" (176.20–21)—from which the frightened Shem flees for the safety of his "inkbattle house" (176.31).[12] This passage, mired in hostilities, is a fitting place to find the contending clans. Here Joyce brings together the violence of the early twentieth century with an earlier conflict, the clash of the Picts and the Scots (before their eventual merger). The collision and comparison of modern British imperial violence with ancient Irish colonialism is arresting in its jarring boldness and demonstrates Joyce's conception of cyclical conflict. Again Joyce leaves himself wide open to accusations of fencesitting, or "mug's wumping" (*FW*, 268.11). It could be argued that his critique of colonial expansion or violence simply extends to Irish military excursions in order to avoid the politics of victimhood or grievance. However, despite these hostilities, Shem and Shaun are not the binary opposites they would first appear to be.

The Picts and Scots are set up in *Finnegans Wake* as oppositional forces not only through Joyce's semantic and etymological play but also by contexts stressing contrast. For example, the backgrounds to the references contain images of opposing temperatures, light conditions, and foods. It may, however, be better to regard these terms as differing degrees of the same substance rather than true opposites. Darkness is not the opposite of light, merely a lack of it. The same is true for temperature, since the "opposites" of boiling point and absolute zero to which Joyce refers are both points on the same scale. In a similar way, butter and cheese are, of course, both dairy products. Pigs and hares are different species of animals but are animals nonetheless. So, the presentation of the brothers as isolated and contrasting opposites is only half true; they are, of course, fundamentally connected. Shaun's bungling efforts to present himself and his brother as "mutuearly polarised" (164.2) have backfired badly. Every comparison he offers during I.vi in an attempt to highlight their opposition only serves to stress their underlying similarity. How does this relate to Joyce's view of Scotland and Ireland?

In a rather deconstruction-like move, Joyce creates a binary opposition only to overturn or undermine it. As well as his failed butter-and-cheese analogy, Shaun rather stupidly compares the relationship with his brother to the two identical points B and C on an isosceles triangle and to the historical allies Brutus and Cassius (C. Hart, *Structure*, 158). Kimberly Devlin has considered this relationship with reference to Freudian psychology: "In the Wakean dream, self and other are superficially represented as disparate figures, but the differences between them are continually collapsing. The various versions all establish clear correlative dichotomies—license/inhibition, native/invader, insurgence/authority— that are undermined by clues suggesting that self and other are similar, interconnected" ("Self and Other," 38–39). The Picts and the Scots fit with the "correlative dichotomy" of the native and the invader, with the Picts as the natives of Scotland and the Scots as the intruders. The motif, if we adopt Devlin's theory, may be seen as part of a theme in *Finnegans Wake* in which the dreamer attempts—without much success—to keep separate the Shem and Shaun aspects of his psyche or identity. This attempt is constantly disrupted by the underlying similarities of the figures in which the dreamer casts these divergent impulses.

That Joyce used the Picts and the Scots as part of this scheme shows that he realized these groups were antagonistic but ultimately connected, through a shared "Celtic" lineage and by the fact that they eventually merged to form Scotland. We can extrapolate from Joyce's use of these "Scottish" and "Irish" tribes that he saw Scotland and Ireland as also fundamentally linked and intermixed despite their obvious cultural, religious, and political differences; they are contrasting yet connected. The warpings of the words Picts and Scots are, in a related way, associated with each other despite an obvious oppositional tendency. They are always—with one important exception—placed together, another representation of the rival twin brothers Shaun and Shem. As Philip Kitcher discusses in *Joyce's Kaleidoscope*, the brothers merge or amalgamate into the personality of HCE and convey differing and conflicting aspects of his psyche. Similarly, historically speaking, the Picts and Scots united to form what later became the Scottish nation after an era of hostility. If we place the Picts-and-Scots motif in the general context of the duality and unity of Shem and Shaun, then they are both opposed tribes and related peoples. Indeed, the Picts were a Celtic tribe and so part of the same people as the Scoti. For a discussion of the Celtic idea in relation to Joyce's work, see the chapter "Celt, Teuton and Aryan" in Len Platt's *Joyce, Race and "Finnegans Wake."*[13]

"TWO LADS IN SCOUTSCH BREECHES"

Book I.viii of *Finnegans Wake*, which deals primarily with the maternal figure ALP, consists of the gossip of two washerwomen working away on the opposite banks of a river. These women continue the polar relationship of Shem and Shaun set up in the previous chapter (Gordon, *Plot Summary*, 165). Two instances of the Pict/Scot motif occur here at the opposed riverbanks, and in such close proximity that it is tempting to regard them—like the gossips busy with their laundry—as a pair. There is also a spatial resemblance between the figures on the opposite sides of the river and the Picts and the Scots, since these rival peoples began as groups separated by a body of water. Indeed, the word "rival" itself originates in the Latin for "one using the same stream," *rivalis*. As with Crotthers, Joyce associates these tribes with fluidity, with the constant flux of the flowing river. Single male roles, present in the previous section, are maintained in the first of the passages: "And wasn't she the naughty Livvy? Nautic Naama's now her navn. Two lads in scoutsch breeches went through her before that, Barefoot Burn and Wallowme Wade, Lugnaquillia's noblesse pickts, before she had a hint of a hair at her fanny to hide or a bossom to tempt a birch canoedler not to mention a bulgic porterhouse barge" (204.4–9). Here two boys, or scouts, are identified with the Picts and the Scots and are included in a discussion regarding the adventurous love life—expressed through phallic canoes and "bulgic" barges—of the young ALP. However, as the section is dealing with adolescent or childhood sexuality—the phrase "not a hair at her fanny" indicates a prepubescent state—the young girl represents Issy as well as the young ALP. The two young "scoutsch," because of their sexual interest in the girl, must be versions of the brothers Shaun and Shem. Thus the scene is reminiscent of the passage from page 164 with its representation of "two males pooles" who "waistfully woent a female to focus" (164.4–7).

In fact, the entire Earwicker crew is present in the above passage. HCE is present in the word "porterhouse," "Porter" being another of HCE's names as well as linking to his profession as the manager of a pub or "porter house." Furthermore, HCE is often associated with mountains, and here we have a reference to Lugnaquilla, a peak in County Wicklow. There is also an indirect reference to Ben Bulben through the allusion to the "Noble Six," a group of IRA soldiers killed at the famous mountain in Sligo during the Irish Civil War. The allusion to the civil war also suggests fraternal rivalry and therefore also points to the adversarial twins Shem and Shaun. Again, Scotland is linked here to the rifts of early twentieth-century Ireland, while Ireland itself is connected to earlier "civil wars" and the beginnings of a different political entity—the contemporary and the archaic become merged, and a sense of progress disappears. The oppositional tendencies of the rival brothers are conveyed in the above section by contrasting primary elements: namely the fire of "Burn" and water of "Wade." Paradoxically, however, *burn* is also the Scots word for "stream," and *bùrn* is a Lewis-dialect Gaelic term for "water." The two figures are somehow both contrasting and not contrasting, distinct and yet the same. Joyce again links the exchanges and connections of Irish and Scottish events to water, not only to stress the maritime conduit by which these links were created, but also to highlight the essential ethnic "fluidity" of the two nations and their essentially "tidal" or repetitive nature. "Wade" also carries the association of General George Wade, the Anglo-Irish soldier who organized the building of an extensive network of military roads in the Scottish Highlands between 1726 and 1727 as a means of better controlling Jacobite sympathizers (Lynch, *Companion*, 601). Actually this measure had the opposite effect, since the Jacobites made good use of these roads in the 1745 uprising. One notable Jacobite sympathizer, Robert Burns, appears as a means of balancing out the politics of the passage.

Any mention of the military rivals the Picts and the Scots will suggest conflict, and this impression becomes more prominent with the reference to the "Noble Six" of Yeats Country and with the forceful, aggressive language of "went through her," "barge," and "breeches." An unsettling brew of violence and sex emerges—as well as a merging of opposites—through the allusion to Yeats's "Leda and the Swan": "leada, laida, all unraidy" (*FW*, 204.10). The slightly queasy sexual content of the passage offers further insight into a troubled mental state, as the various lovers of ALP's life before her relationship with HCE begin to cause some anxiety. In merging the identities of ALP's "lads" with HCE's sons, we can detect HCE's fear that he may at some point fall, with his authority and prowess being usurped in a Freudian (and Frazerian) process. Indeed, this event comes to pass in book II of the *Wake*.

The sexual content present here can be exposed to varying degrees in most of the motifs of the first half of the *Wake*, contained in the "pussyfours" of the first instance, and more obviously in "we must waistfully woent a female to focus" in the third. Any reader of *Finnegans Wake* will have been struck by the sheer amount of amusing sexual humor present, and how this adds greatly to the fun of the work. In *Joyce, Race and "Finnegans Wake"* Len Platt discusses the unusual sexuality of the Earwicker family with reference to the European race policies and propaganda in the 1920s and 1930s:

> Far from imaging the hygienic state, the family unit is a hotbed of jealousy and desire, with territorial insecurities and incestuous instincts becoming normalised as part of the psychological landscape of everyday family life. . . . Against this background, stereotypes of gender roles within families become hugely distorted—to the point where Finnegan the patriarch is a literal country; HCE, "folkenfather of familyans" (328.18), a literal state, and ALP, again, literally turned to nature as a river. (Platt, *Joyce, Race*, 154–55)

We have already witnessed the distortion of HCE into a territory, the linking of the political and the psychological, in "the united states of Scotia Picta" (*FW*, 43.29–30), and because of the echoes of this original phrase throughout the *Wake*, this distortion is present in all of the sections discussed in this chapter.

The above passage, featuring the young ALP and her lovers, is an example of Platt's observation that ALP is at various moments in the *Wake* "turned to nature as a river." The male figures "went through her,"

and their names are both associated with water and there are also references to canoes and barges. However, any idea that she could represent
some kind of natural, feminine principle or be the embodiment of "normal" maternal instinct is deliberately undermined. She is, in one sense,
engaged in a ménage-a-trois "canoodle" session with her two sons. Another way of viewing the scene is as a sexual encounter between Shem,
Shaun, and Issy. Either scenario serves as a method of offering some
rather "alternative" or "nontraditional" family activities and relationships,
"entirely transgressive of idealised gender roles" (Platt, *Joyce, Race*, 155).

Platt goes on to discuss how Joyce's parodic and undermining tactics
in relation to familial or sexual matters are also linked to an attempt to
debunk ideas of racial purity. Seen in the light of Platt's work on race
in the *Wake*, the relationship of the Picts and Scots cannot be considered
as some kind of harmonious Celtic reconciliation between peoples of
Scotland and Ireland, a happy family gathering. Rather, Joyce is, to some
extent, parodying the conception of a supposed Celtic racial identity that
had become popular in the Irish Revival of the late nineteenth and early
twentieth centuries: "Woefully integrated, assimilated, contaminated
and vandalised, the Celt, like the Frank, the Gaul, the Anglo-Saxon and
all the other race identities in the *Wake*, is both there and not there. It
exists, but only as a cultural construction" (Platt, *Joyce, Race*, 50). Under
any real pressure or scrutiny, much like the identity of HCE, "Celtic" or
"Aryan" racial identity will fall apart to some extent. Platt points out that
ideas of shared racial purity are mocked in the lines Willy Maley chose
for the title of his essay, "Kilt by kelt shell kithagain with kinagain" (*FW*,
594.3–4). This line does seem to poke fun at the idea of some kind of
Celtic reunion between family members or "kith" and "kin," but the conversion of "shall" into "shell" points again to beaches and the sea, to the
position the sea serves as a convenient interface connecting Ireland and
Scotland. Furthermore, something like this occurs with Crotthers and
the medical students in "Oxen of the Sun." The use of the word is ambiguous, however, suggesting also the emptiness of ideas of racial purity.
Violent death is of course present in the word "kilt," which combines
"killed" with "kilt," a traditional item of Scottish clothing. The aural
similarity between "kinagain" and "Finnegan" is also worth stressing,
representing a link between the Celts themselves and HCE. Despite the
Wake's suggestion that all races are "contaminated" or "vandalised," a fas-

cination with the idea or concept of the Celtic race persists in Joyce's work. Furthermore, while no fixed or stable racial constructions can be discerned in the *Wake*, this is a specific expression of a more general atmosphere of doubt and uncertainty—a setting that can be read as Joyce's expression of the character of Celtic thought.

So, Joyce makes use of the Picts and Scots not as signifiers of some elusive, ancient Celtic racial purity and cohesion but—in tandem with his Celtic inhumed consciousness—mainly to construct a literary mental state consisting of polarized tendencies. He also links this divided psyche to the essentially mixed nature of nations. Indeed, Joyce would have known well that Scotland's history shows the extent to which nations are composed of a mixture of different races rather than a singular homogenous people. *Finnegans Wake* plays with the idea that both the mind and the nation consist of varied and sometimes conflicting substrata, and Scotland was an ideal location and subject for Joyce to work with in order to create this theme. Platt makes a convincing case for the idea that Joyce parodies early twentieth-century race politics in the *Wake*. However, in the case of the Picts and the Scots motif, Joyce's interest is also in keeping with the construction (or perhaps the deconstruction) of HCE. As has been suggested throughout this study, rather than searching for a lost Celtic identity based on racial purity, blood ties, or the resuscitation of ancient codes of heroism or active life, Joyce constructs a hazy, uncertain, nonmaterial Celtic sleep text based on idealism, skepticism, contrasts, inversions, and underlying connections.

The second appearance of the Pict/Scot pair found in I.viii appears six pages after the image of the three frolicking youths at the riverbank. This is the last phrase dealing with the Picts and the Scots for 307 pages, a prolonged absence that helps in a small way to define the structural center of *Finnegans Wake*. It is here in I.viii, at this crucial point, that the most important historical difference between Ireland and Scotland is finally evoked, in the list of ALP's nasty gifts: "snakes in clover, picked and scotched, and a vaticanned viper catcher's visa for Patsy Presbys" (210.26–27). Tellingly, this dubious present originates from a "colonial . . . bagful" (212.20), thus clearly situating the picking of Presbyterians to scotch Ireland within colonial terms. Placed in close proximity are the related but opposed doctrines of Catholicism in "vaticanned" and Presbyterianism in "Presbys," similar to the darkness/light, pigs/hares contrasts of earlier passages. The mention of Presbyterianism inevitably evokes the religious history of Scotland, where that doctrine mainly developed. But does the word "snakes" portray the Scottish settlers as insidious and creeping threats lurking in the Irish clover? Or, since it is "Patsy Presbys" who is given a "catcher's visa" to trap a "vaticanned viper," is Joyce pointing to a Protestant sectarian fear of the Catholic Irish here? As R. F. Foster notes, the Irish were "a disadvantaged minority [in Scotland] until the 1920s" (*Modern Ireland*, 368). In further complications, "Patsy" hints at St. Patrick, thereby linking him with the Protestant settlers and drawing a comparison between different types of "conversion" in Ireland but also to a person or persons who have, perhaps, been wrongfully blamed for a crime. Finally, the phrase also relates to the union of the Protestant HCE and the Catholic ALP through the ongoing "marriage" problems of Protestant Scots and Catholic Irish. A settled, confident and reductive conclusion is impossible here and deliberately so. As with the majority of *Finnegans Wake*, incertitude prevails.

Why is it that out of all of the Pict/Scot phrases, one that stresses difference so strongly is placed before book II, where the identities of Shaun and Shem merge? Would it not make more sense for the phrases to become more related to peace and accord towards the center of the book, in keeping with the progress of the brothers? In fact, the opposite process occurs. While the Picts and Scots phrases at the beginning and the end of the *Wake* tend to be more harmonious, the phrases nearer the middle of the book tend to be more troubled. In keeping with the paradoxical nature of the phrases, their overall progress actually runs counter to the trends of the twins with whom they are so closely identified. Every new phrase offers a variation on the Picts-and-Scots network. The overall effect of studying this network in isolation is that we are presented with an intricate and developing network of issues vital to the *Wake*, held together by the underlying key words Pict and Scot. The phrases began by setting up the Celtic territory of "Scotia Picta" (43.30) as a metaphor for the experience of dreams. Moving from the darkness of the early passages, which focus on rendering the contrasts of the dream state and the presence of HCE, we arrive at a point where HCE has dissolved into the background, the contrasting presences of Shem and Shaun have been foregrounded, and the other members of the Earwicker family come into clearer focus and clarity. With this sharper view of the Earwickers, the themes of racial purity (or otherwise) and religious difference have emerged.

"NORTHERN IRE" AND "INVERTEDNESS": *MACBETH*, THE *WAKE*, AND THE NORTH OF IRELAND

On either side of book II of *Finnegans Wake* a phrase using the words Pict and Scot as a foundation appears, framing the point at which Shem's dominance and prominence in *Finnegans Wake* recedes and Shaun's unstable identity surfaces. On one side we have the sections that feature Shem and Shaun, expressed through an emphasis on duality, with ALP and Issy also making cameo appearances. The pair of phrases placed after book II appear at III.iii and have an alcoholic context in common. Now HCE's drunken persona is beginning to seep through the phrases. HCE has been at something of a distance since the first Pict/Scot passage, though never completely absent. His job as an innkeeper, together with his fondness for the drink, suggests his presence lurking in the following passage, where Joyce's strategy of remodeling the words Pict and Scot as a representation of the confrontational and oppositional brothers is most apparent: "—They did not know the war was over and were only berebelling or bereppelling one another by chance or necessity with sham bottles, mere and woiney, as betwinst Picturshirts and Scutticules, like their caractacurs in an Irish Ruman to sorowbrate the expeltsion of the Danos? What sayest thou, scusascmerul?" (518.19–23). That Shem and Shaun are present here is shown by the "twin" of "betwinst," as well the context of "mere and woiney" (a reversal of война и миръ, Russian for "war and peace"). Shem is also frequently described as a "sham" in the text, for example: "Shem was a sham and a low sham" (170.25). Beer and wine can also be sampled here, which, along with the "bottles," raise the specter of the publican figure HCE. "Picturshirts" sounds vaguely fascistic, not unlike the Irish "Blueshirts" or the Italian "Blackshirts." However, instead of the sartorial predilection for a single color of the "Irish" Army Comrades Association / National Guard and the "Ruman" Milizia Volontaria per la Sicurezza Nazionale, these shirts—tellingly—display the various hues of a "picture." Any reference to radical nationalist organizations of the 1930s at this point would be part of Joyce's general attack on fascism and racism, here through a system that draws attention to the "miscegenations" (18.20) on which nations such as Ireland and Scotland themselves are founded.

The motif of the Picts and Scots, a paradoxical symbol of division and unity, had its absence extended through II but also through the first two chapters of III until it emerges here. It is not until the four old men chance upon the postman—now named Yaun—on the midden heap, where he has become an excavation site and a scattered "complex of discordant voices" (Kitcher, 215), that the ancient remains of the Picts and Scots are unearthed and forensically examined. The word "Scutticules" brings in a possible etymology of the word Scot, which Joyce would have read about in Stephen Gwynn's *The History of Ireland*. Gwynn notes that "Scoti . . . is the latinised form of a Gaelic word meaning The Cutters . . . and this was used as if it were the name of a people" (16). "Scutticules"— a play on the Latin for skin, *cuticula*—is at variance with the clothing of the word Picturshirts and the morpheme "pelt" of "expeltsion."[14]

At this point in the *Wake* the interrogation of Shaun turns to the subject of the wake ceremony itself, so HCE cannot be far from the mind of the dreamer. HCE is slowly beginning to reappear, and his presence will be most keenly felt in the "final" phrase, where Picts and Scots are found as a pair (if we accept that *Finnegans Wake* has a conclusion at all). The usual imagery of doubling or duality is here in "berebelling or bereppelling," "chance or necessity," and "mere and woiney," and the differing emotions of conflict or "sham bottles" are present in "sorowbrate," obviously combining "celebrate" and "sorrow." The reference to "an Irish Ruman" alludes to Stephen's writing of his name "Doubly, by appending his signature in Irish and Roman characters" in "Ithaca" (*U*, 17.775). Historically, of course, the Roman Empire never occupied the island of Ireland (and they gave up on their attempt to control what is now Scotland, building walls to demarcate the empire). The focus on alcohol continues into the second of the pair of phrases of III.iii, placed three pages later in the interrogation of Shaun/Yawn: "Come now, Johnny! We weren't born yesterday. *Pro tanto quid retribuamus?* I ask you to say on your scotty pictail you were promised fines times with some staggerjuice or deadhorse, on strip or in larges, at the Raven and Sugarloaf, either Jones's lame or Jamesy's gait, anyhow?" (521.10–14). The Picts and Scots are now united in the identity of Shaun/Yawn. Philip Kitcher argues that during the course of the chapter we find that HCE appears as "the deepest stratum in Shaun's many layers" (Kitcher, 216). Even as "scotty pictail" serves here as a reminder of Shaun's duality, the alcoholic context—with references to the Guinness brewery, the Power's distillery, and the Bushmills distillery—reveals the subterranean, ghostly spirit of HCE. Yet again, pairings are evident with "staggerjuice or deadhorse" and "in strip or in larges."

This method of doubling or coupling is of great importance here considering the context, which is an extended passage dealing with Ulster but which, perhaps unsurprisingly, includes some arrestingly Scottish material. For example, we have an allusion to Robert Burns's "Is There for Honest Poverty" in "Should brothers be for awe then?" (520.23)—and a play on the song "Loch Lomond" which features a further evocation of Scotland's national poet: "So let use off be octo while oil bike the bil and wheel whang till wabblin befoul you but mere and my trullopes will knaver mate a game on the bibby bobby burns of" (520.24–26). Aptly, "Loch Lomond'" concerns the separation of two individuals, one taking the "high road" and one the "low road," and so also stresses partings, division, and duality. There are also mentions of a "highlandman's trousertree" (521.7), a "dram" (521.8), the phrase dealing with Picts and Scots itself, and an intriguing play on Inverness in "invertedness" (522.31).

Is it possible that Joyce saw Scottish history to some extent, to paraphrase Declan Kiberd, as a process of *inverting* Ireland? That is to say, Alba essentially began with a short-haul Irish migration, and so the new country must have originally resembled it in terms of location, weather, landscape, culture, religion, law, and linguistics (of course, some of these similarities remain intact). However, over time the Scots became radically altered from their original "family," through a fairly radical brand of Protestantism (though not before a conversion to Catholic Christianity through Irish missionaries), through its part as an imperial subordinate and junior partner in the British Empire, and through its role in the Ulster Plantation, into something recognizable yet distorted, an uncanny and reversed mirror-image. The confrontational nature of the passage here, with its emphasis on the Scottish impact on the north of Ireland and the oppositional relationship of the brothers, makes this reading a distinct possibility. It is worth remembering here that Shem and Shaun themselves—who are closely connected to the Picts and the Scots by Joyce—appear in *Finnegans Wake* as mirror images. But does the *vert* of "invertedness" in III.iii seek to remind us of the lasting Irish green hue of the Scottish cultural landscape, much like the phrase the "green of the united states of Scotia Picta" (43.29–30)? Alternatively, perhaps it is the north of Ireland that has also been "inverted" through its associations with Scotland, in particular the Ulster Plantation.

References to the Highlands city of Inverness in *Finnegans Wake* such as "in vanessy" (3.11–12), "inverness" (35.10), "at Idleness" (289.28), and "Inverleffy" (332.28) also function as allusions to Shakespeare's *Macbeth* (Cheng, *Shakespeare and Joyce*, 209). *Macbeth*—along with the plays *Hamlet, Julius Caesar*, and *A Midsummer Night's Dream*—frequently takes the stage in *Finnegans Wake*. Through allusions to the play, Scotland—indirectly—supplies an important reserve of material relating to the theme of the overthrown father figure of the *Wake*, as well as being part of "a notable anxiety about unstable borders" (Plock, 216):

> If HCE's family name is indeed "Porter," then it . . . suggests the role of a *Macbethian* gate-keeper for the *Wake*'s protagonist—a protagonist threatened to be overthrown by violent assaults from the next generation. The *Macbeth* intertext thus assisted Joyce in conceptualizing the archetypal family feud central to the *Wake*'s structural process. . . . Porters, it seems, are very common obstacles for Celtic heroes, [indicating] how much Celtic territories had started to feature as netherworlds in the popular imagination of Shakespeare's time. Scotland, Wales, and Ireland, these unruly tribal regions beyond England's national borders, inspired both fear and curiosity in Elizabethan and Jacobean times. (216)

Alongside its function as a signal of this anxiety, the role of *Macbeth* is well suited to this adversarial section of the *Wake*. The power struggle of Macbeth and Macduff, ghosts of a rancorous past haunting the present—along with the violent and bloody nature of the play itself—makes it a grimly apposite work to reference in a section dedicated to the north of Ireland, perhaps even more so in relation to the troubled years since the publication of *Finnegans Wake*. Although *Macbeth* is of course an English play, the play's Celtic location and subject matter were what interested Joyce, alongside its being a work about a power struggle with an overthrown father figure (King Duncan) and a preoccupation with the night and sleep.[15] In lieu of a Shakespeare play actually based in Ireland from which to draw upon (such a work would have detained Joyce no end), "The Scottish Play" is the closest available alternative. After all, Joyce speaks of Macbeth not as a Scottish claimant but rather as a "Celtic usurper" (*OCPW*, 164), thus placing him in a wider, Irish-related context.[16]

The "Scotch philosophaster with a turn for witchroasting" (*U*, 9.751–52), James VI of Scotland / James I of England—in his role as architect of the Ulster Plantation—is also suggested obliquely here, since *Macbeth*, with its weird sisters, was written partly in tribute to the new king (of England). The seventeenth-century plantation of Scottish settlers in Ireland by James VI of Scotland / James I of England was the critical factor in creating the religious and political divide between the north and south of Ireland (and within the north itself). Previously Ulster had been the least Anglicized area in Ireland, and during the period 1300–1500 areas north of the River Boyne had more in common culturally and linguistically with the Gaelic-speaking Highlands of Scotland than with England, and "in 1600 Ulster was synonymous with wildness and untamed Gaelicism" (Foster, *Modern Ireland*, 7). Through a shared language (or at least mutually intelligible languages: Gàidhlig and Gaeilge / Scottish Gaelic and Irish) and maritime links a cultural connection remained between the peoples of Ulster and the Highlands and Isles of Scotland, a heritage dating back to the formation of Alba and before. According to R. F. Foster, "Scots had been spilling back and forth across the narrow straits since time immemorial, and Antrim and Down were densely Scottish in population. In many ways the Antrim coast was closer to the mainland than to its own hinterland" (*Modern Ireland*, 60). However, the majority of settlers drafted into Ireland during the seventeenth century did not share a common religion, language, or culture with their new neighbors. Presbyterian Lowlanders who subscribed to a form of Puritanism that regarded the papacy as the antichrist made up the vast majority of the settlers planted into counties Antrim and Down (S. Connolly, 501). Centuries of discord and conflict have been the result of this disastrous policy, as has the "different" nature of Ulster within Ireland: "What must be grasped from the early seventeenth century is the importance of the plantation idea, with its emphasis on segregation and on native unreliability. These attitudes helped Ulster solidify into a different mould" (Foster, *Modern Ireland*, 78).

Fittingly, the reference to *Macbeth* on page 522 is embedded into roughly two pages of the *Wake* where the interrogation of Shaun takes on a distinctly northern Irish character and tone. Coming immediately after the short section evoking Robert Burns and the song "Loch Lomond," Scots vocabulary and an allusion to the Annals of Ulster are delivered in Joyce's finest Ulster accent:

> —What hill ar yu fluking about ye lamelookond fyats! I'll discipline ye! Will you swear or affirm the day to yur second sight noo and recant that all yu affirmed to profetised at first sight for his southerly accent was all paddyflaherty? Will ye, ay or nay?
> —Ay say aye. I affirmly swear to it that it rooly and cooly boolyhooly was with my holyhagionous lips continuously poised upon the rubricated annuals of saint ulstar.
> —That's very guid of ye, R.C.! (520.24–35)

The aggressive or suspicious mentions of a "southerly accent" and "paddyflaherty" set up the passage as having a distinctly northern perspective. On the following page the remaining provinces of Ireland—Leinster, Connacht, and Munster—are combined into a separate, cohesive territory as "the Four" begin to argue amongst themselves: "Will you repeat that to me outside, leinconnmuns?" (521.28). Clearly the issues of partition, separation and exclusion are at stake here in this tense, volatile exchange. As with previous references to the Black and Tans, contemporary twentieth-century concerns are linked back to inverted historical counterparts. Ulster Scots appear on the same page as the original Irish Scoti, and colonists of different eras—who traveled in different directions across the North Channel—begin to clash and merge.

Joyce approximates a heavy northern Irish accent here with "yu," "ye," and "yur," while "ay or nay" and "noo" are examples of Scots or Ulster Scots vocabulary. "Guid" is Scots for "good." This is the section of Joyce's writing most replete with Scots language since the "Oxen of the Sun" episode of *Ulysses*. Loch Lomond again appears rearranged in "lamelookond" (520.27). The split personalities of HCE and Shaun reflect not only the literature of the Caledonian Antisyzygy but also the Scottish-assisted—if that is the word—division of Ireland itself. The presentation of HCE as a divided entity originates partly in Scottish literature, in particular the works of Hogg and Stevenson. Therefore, an Irish split with a historical Scottish influence is actually *rendered* through techniques found in Scottish writing, especially the works of Stevenson and Hogg. The animosity and tension of the interrogation scene of the *Wake* brings the most divisive aspects of Irish history to the fore because the more Yawn attempts to give the impression of a cohesive whole, the more the cracks begin to appear. With these divisions comes the raised specter of HCE, the "lowest stratum" (Kitcher, 216) of Shaun's identity.

As in the Pict/Scot phrase from I.viii, the religious divisions of Ireland are evoked in close proximity to allusions to Scottish culture. The religions of Ireland and Scotland are collapsed in the name "Robman Calvinic" (519.26), suggestive of theft and a "conversion" from Catholic to Calvinist. Towards the end of this northern-influenced section Shaun is asked the question, "Did any orangepeelers or greengoaters appear periodically up your sylvan family tree?" (522.16–17), probing Shaun's religious and ethnic background. Scottish poetry, songs, and geography appear during a border dispute characterized by "Northern Ire" (522.4). The context of the "scotty pictail" points to a type of internal psychological division that involves national identity or identities, a schism that continues to "ail." The Belfast civic motto *"Pro tanto quid retribuamus?"* is included in an accusation that Shaun has been bribed to give certain answers in his interrogation: "That's very guid of ye, R.C.! Maybe yu wouldn't mind talling us, my labrose lad, how very much bright cabbage or paperming comfirts d'yu draw for all yur swearin? The spanglers, kiddy?" (520.35–521.2). As the questioning becomes more fraught, some threatening and abusive language is issued in the Ulster accent: "Ef I chuse to put a bullet like yu through the grill for heckling what business is that of yours, yu bullock?" (522.1–2).

Clearly, the Ulster Scots here are associated with bullying authority, threats, and violence. However, by drawing a parallel between the Irish colonization of Scotland (the Picts and Scots) and the Ulster Plantation, the text loses any real condemnation of the seventeenth-century process of colonization. This is despite an obvious historical difference in that the Scoti eventually became absorbed into, and formed, the original

Scottish nation of Alba, whereas the Ulster Scots went on to create what J. G. A. Pocock has termed an "anti-nation" within Ireland (33), commenting further that "Scottish Ulster . . . may be thought of as Scotland without the Moderate Enlightenment" (Pocock, 33, 112). The phrases "split hour" (*FW*, 519.35), "partition footsteps" (475.25), "dogumen number one" (482.20), and "Doggymens' nimmer win" (528.32–33) appear in this section of the *Wake*, linking the fragmented personalities of HCE and Shaun in *Finnegans Wake* to the Ulster Scot "anti-nation" within Ireland as well as to the 1921 Anglo-Irish Treaty. The partition of the island of Ireland into Northern Ireland and the Free State in the period of 1921–22 was, for Joyce, a division with an obvious Scottish dimension because of the presence of the Ulster Scots in the North.

Joyce presents Irish/Scottish events as a cyclical and mirrored process of colonization attended by internal divisions, beginning with the Scoti and continuing with the Plantation. This presentation creates uniformity in the face of categorical difference, and there is a definite sense that, in highlighting the recurrent and somewhat balanced nature of these contacts, Joyce assumes his default God-of-the-creation position— removed, neutral, and uncommitted, "paring his fingernails" (*P*, 233). Allusions to *Macbeth* appear in a section stressing internal strife in Ireland. This section is given a Scots / Ulster Scots context through links to Scottish culture and through the offstage figure of James VI. This "Northern Ire" (*FW*, 522.04) obviously has a Scottish connection, and this is part of a larger theme of confessional division or "bisectualism" (524.12), linked contraries and entities within entities explored in the chapter. Particular attention is paid to the presence of foreign influences, and this is linked to HCE's status as an outsider: "HCE, as others see him, [is] an outsider, impious [and] destructive" (Kitcher, 219).

As John Gordon has pointed out, III.iii is a "ghost-raising" (*Plot Summary*, 237). At this séance, the voices of HCE, Shem, and ALP are within Yawn and speaking through him: "ouija ouija" (*FW*, 532.18), "I have something inside of me talking to myself" (522.26). Similarly, attention is paid to the Scottish presence within Ireland (through allusions to *Macbeth* and Burns and through the use of Scots vocabulary) and the Irish presence within Scotland (through allusions to the Scoti people). "There are sordidly tales within tales" (522.05). So, Shem, HCE, and ALP existing within Shaun is like the vestiges of Scottish culture within

Ireland or the vestiges of Irish culture within Scotland. Furthermore, the mirrored relationship of Scotland and Ireland complements that of the twins Shaun and Shem, and is part of Joyce's representation of the divided consciousness of the dreamer and the partitioned terrain of Ireland.

"HERE GIVES YOUR ANSWER"

Book IV is the final section of *Finnegans Wake* but is—as is well known—also its circuitous "ricorso," with the "final" word of IV and the *Wake*, "the" (628.16), flowing in a cyclical movement back to the beginning of "riverrun" (3.1) in I.i. If we take the Picts and Saxons' convergence of III. iv as being an end to the textual relationship between the Picts and the Scots, then a new start is heralded in IV as ALP defends her husband's conduct in a letter for the morning mail:

> Well, we simply like their demb cheeks, the Rathgarries, wagging here about around the rhythms in me amphybed and he being as bothered that he pausably could by the fallth of hampty damp. Certified reformed peoples, we may add to this stage, are proptably saying to quite agreeable deef. Here gives your answer, pigs and scuts! Hence we've lived in two worlds. He is another he what stays under the himp of holth. The herewaker of our hamefame is his real namesame who will get himself up and erect, confident and heroic when but, young as of old, for my daily comfreshenall, a wee one woos. (619.6–15)

In this first (or final) ripple of the Pict/Scot stream we have the same Scottish division of consciousness that we will find again in the next phrase, in book I. Scots vocabulary emerges again with "wee" and "hame," meaning "small" and "home," respectively. The "wagging" of the "Rathgarries" recalls the gossiping washerwomen at the river, and "amphybed" suggests a "damp" riverbed as well as the bed of the dreamer. Once again, the Picts and the Scots are linked to the circular waters of history and to the dividing lines created by bodies of water.

The use of the somewhat pejorative terms "pigs" and "scuts" here can be explained by considering ALP's anger at those who have criticized the sexual relationship of herself and HCE. This prying attitude towards the sex life of HCE and ALP mirrors the first appearance of the Pict/Scot motif on page 43, in which, as Clive Hart points out, the "rough and red woodcut" (43.25) mentioned in connection with the making of the ballad hints at "'excessively rough and red' love-making" (C. Hart, *Structure*, 127), linking the section with earlier suggestions of fertilization.[17] Animal imagery appears throughout IV in a series of allusions to the "turgid outpourings of H. P. Blavatsky" (C. Hart, *Structure*, 49). The nineteenth-century Russian occultist Helena Blavatsky's theory of mystical cycles or ages ends with an "intermediate space . . . filled with strange beings" (52), and this is parodied in the final threshold of the *Wake*. However, animal imagery has been present in many of the Pict/Scot passages. On page 176 we have the words "scut" (176.26), "leveret" (176.27), and "pig" (176.29). The passages also feature "snakes" (210.26) and a "pictail" (521.11).

On first reading, "Here gives your answer, pigs and scuts!" would seem to be some kind of reply or rebuke with some ambiguity as to whether the phrase is a request or a statement ("gives" can be read as a blurring of "give us" and "is"). However, it can also be read that ALP's answer *is* "pigs and scuts." That is to say, ALP's defense and explanation of her husband and his behavior are based on his internal Shaun/Shem division, his personal Caledonian (or Hibernian) Antisyzygy. HCE's dual identity is expressed through the phrases "two worlds" and "[he] is another." As with the characters of James Hogg's and Robert Louis Stevenson's fiction, there appear to be two versions of HCE, one that sleeps under the Hill of Howth and one who will "get himself up," one who is dead or asleep and one who is alive or awake. John Gordon has demonstrated that the material from 615.12 to 619.16 concerns ALP "abusing her nemesis who . . . is consubstantial with her husband's buried Shem-past" (*Plot Summary*, 272). The resurfacing of the Pict/Scot motif at this point must mean that she must also be engaging with her husband's "Shaun-past" as well. Finally, the dreamer is able to find self-understanding through the voice of ALP, through a tenuous Good Friday agreement of internal contrasts, variations, and disharmony.

ALP's letter for the morning post, which brings about this sense of "unionist" harmony in IV, has some distinctly Scottish aspects. In a number of its appearances throughout the *Wake*, the letter involves Scotland. For example, in I.iii there is an inquiry relating to the missing missive:

> Will it ever be next morning the postal unionist's (officially called carrier's, Letters Scotch, Limited) strange fate (Fierceendgiddyex he's hight, d.e., the losel that hucks around missivemaids' gummibacks) to hand in a huge chain envelope, written in divers stages of ink, from blanchessance to lavandaiette, every pothook and pancrook bespaking the wisherwife, superscribed and subpencilled by yours A Laughable Party, with afterwite, S.A.G., to Hyde and Cheek, Edenberry, Dubblenn, WC? Will whatever written in lappish language with inbursts of Maggyer always seem semposed, black looking white and white guarding black, in that siamixed twoatalk used twist stern swift and jolly roger? (66.10–21)

The elusive document is being carried by "Letters Scotch" to "Hyde and Cheek, Edenberry." The allusions to Edinburgh and to *Strange Case of Dr. Jekyll and Mr. Hyde* give the letter a divided nature existing *between* two subjects—the writer and the reader—suggesting that the way communication and art themselves function depends on duality. There is also a link here to Joyce's reading of James Hogg and Robert Louis Stevenson. As Luke Thurston notes, "We recall that in Hogg's *Justified Sinner*, one effect of Gil's diabolic presence was the subversion of the legal validity of a signature; and likewise, when the autograph of Jekyll is compared with that of Hyde, a decisive difference is visible: 'the two hands are in many points identical; only differently sloped'" (*Problem*, 121). Thurston goes on to point out that "duplicity of character in Hogg and Stevenson" is "made manifest in the narrative incidents of the letter, of name-changing and sinister handwriting" (126). The letter is "Scotch" since—for Joyce—this assignation signals duplication.

This sense of duplication is also signaled by the involvement of both of the twin brothers with the letter: Shem has composed or "semposed" the "siamixed twoatalk," and Shaun, in his role as the postman, delivers it. The language of contrasting shades present in the first passages crops up here again in "black looking white and white guarding black" as well as in the black-and-white pirate flag, the Jolly Roger (is the suggestion here, in relation to the Picts and Scots, that all maritime colonialism is essentially banditry?). Doubled words occur with "Hyde and Cheek" and "Edenberry, Dubblenn," where the capitals of Scotland and Ireland are set against each other.[18] "Edenberry" refers primarily to Edenderry in County Offaly (or its namesake in County Down), but the switching from a "d" to a "b" means that Edinburgh is also present here. Allusions to Scottish history and literature in connection with the letter continue throughout the *Wake*. In I.v, which deals primarily with an examination of the letter, there is a warning against impatience that refers to Robert and Edward Bruce: "both brothers Bruce with whom are incorporated their Scotch spider" (108.14–15). Furthermore, the discussion of the envelope on page 109 is written in the style of the nineteenth-century Scots writer Thomas Carlyle's *Sartor Resartus*.[19]

Mentioning the Picts-and-Scots motif in ALP's letter ensures that Irish and Scottish histories are permanently embedded into the system of the *Wake*. The letter is destined to be lost in a pile of refuse, meaning that Scottish-Irish history will be both present and concealed in *Finnegans Wake*. The theme has been discarded into the Humean obscurity of what John Bishop calls the dreamer's "mnemonic dump" (134). When Scottish-Irish history—in keeping with the paradoxical nature of allusions to it in the *Wake*—does come to light, it is associated with a will to repress inner tendencies and a consequential duality. There are both psychological and familial aspects and cultural and political aspects of this repression and duality. Joyce also hints at a possible future opportunity to overcome these problems, in the form of ALP's letter. However, as we shall see, this history is also a "nightmail" (*FW*, 565.32).

"THE PICKTS ARE HACKING THE SAXUMS"

At bedtime the twins "jerry" (*FW*, 565.10) and "keve" (565.15), versions of Shem and Shaun, respectively, are slightly traumatized by the nocturnal sight of their father's less than callipygian bare arse. This view becomes Phoenix Park, "Finn his park" (564.8), the site of HCE's mysterious crime (see Gordon, *Plot Summary*, 256–67). The mother attempts to calm the boys by reassuring them that they were only "dreamend" (*FW*, 565.18) or having a "nightmail":

Sonly all in your imagination, dim. Poor little brittle magic nation, dim of mind! Shoe to me now, dear! Shoom of me! While elvery stream winds seling on for to keep this barrel of bounty rolling and the nightmail afarfrom morning nears.

When you're coaching through Lucalised, on the sulphur spa to visit, it's safer to hit than miss it, stop at his inn! The hammers are telling the cobbles, the pickts are hacking the saxums, it's snugger to burrow abed than ballet on broadway. Tuck in your blank. (565.29–566.1)[20]

As with the "united states of Scotia Picta" (43.29–30), a link is made here between dreams, or the imagination, and countries in the phrase "magic nation." Much like Benedict Anderson's conception of the "imagined community," the suggestion is that nations are illusory mental constructions. In the same chapter HCE is described as "The old humburgh" (560.7), recalling Hogg's "odinburgh" (487.9–10) and the earlier passage alluding to *Private Memoirs and Confessions of a Justified Sinner*. Further adding to the sense of opposition or doubling, the prose is again set into twinned phrases with "The hammers are telling the cobbles" complementing "the pickts are hacking the saxums."

The boys are settled in their beds—"burrow abed . . . Tuck in your blank"—and the song "The Heavens Are Telling the Glories" is sung as a lullaby (McHugh, *Annotations*, 565). Superficially, the song becomes an image of construction or building. The word "pickt" contains "pick," and *saxum* is Latin for "stone." So, "the Picts are carving the stones"—an activity the historical Picts were constantly engaged in—which tallies with "the hammers are telling the cobbles."[21] However, the lullaby is not as reassuring as the mother intended. Lurking not very far beneath the surface, in keeping with past tweaked occurrences of the word Pict, are disturbing images of ethnic conflict and violence. The "pickts" are "hacking" the "saxums." Simultaneously suggestive of both construction and destruction, this possesses signature Wakean double—or multiple—connotations. The famous letter, which will bring some relief, has not yet arrived, but "the nightmail afarfrom morning nears."

Why then do the Saxons replace the Scots as the opposition of the Picts at this critical juncture? Chapter III.iv, as John Gordon points out, is a "home-coming" of sorts (*Plot Summary*, 254). There is a feeling in the chapter that events are drawing to a close as the family prepares to bunk down in bed. The parents check on the young girl on page 561 and on the boys on page 562. In this context the appearance of the Saxons arrives at a time when past exertions are supposedly over and everything is settled. Considering the location of the phrase in the broader structure of the *Wake*, we may regard it as putting the long development of the merging of "Irish" (the Scots) and "Scottish" (the Picts) peoples to an end. This appearance of the Saxons at the last moment reads like a consideration of later Scottish history, marking the decline of Scotland's Gaelic past and its connections with Ireland and an increase in English or Anglo-Saxon influence.

This phrase also indicates Joyce's awareness of Scotland's fraught relationship with England, or at least the antagonism between northern tribes and southern tribes. This awareness is also demonstrated by references in the Willingdone Museyroom section of the text to the battles of Bannockburn or "panickburns" (9.25) and Flodden or "floodens" (9.24). Always concerned with contrasts, Joyce's work features allusions to Scotland's role in the Empire but also to its conflicts with England. The Battle of Bannockburn (1314) was a decisive victory for Scotland during the Wars of Independence and led to centuries of independence for the country. Flodden (1513), fought as part of Scotland's obligations to France during the time of the "Auld Alliance'" between the two nations, resulted in a heavy loss for the invading Scottish army who were routed in Northumberland. The *Wake* casts Scotland as a dominating power (or at least part of one) but also explores its history of resistance to English power.

The positioning of this violent meeting of Picts and Saxons in the context of a chapter dealing with things coming to a close suggests that Joyce saw Scottish history, and history in general, as a constantly evolving pattern of new configurations of different peoples, never reaching a final state, with all arrangements equally unstable and liable to shift. There is no comforting unity for the two frightened boys, no suggestion that this new amalgamation will bring any stability or harmony. The old divisions between Shaun and Shem linger in this chapter: "feud fionghalian. Talkingtree and sinningstone stay on either hand" (564.30–31).[22] This representation of violence and instability, the "feud" of Anglo-

Scottish relations, is a stark contrast to the nineteenth-century conception of this history as exemplified in the works of Walter Scott: "Within that fiction, there is inscribed an end to history—that is, an end to the bitter relationships between England and Scotland and a final reconciliation of which marriage is the stock analogue" (S. Deane, *Strange Country*, 40). Joyce offers no such reconciliation or resolution. Joyce's conception of history is at one with his conception of the constantly chaotic activities of the mind. As Hume noted, "The mind is a kind of theatre, where several perceptions successively make their appearance; pass, re-pass, glide away, and mingle in an infinite variety of postures and situations" (*Treatise*, 301).

We may also view this Pict/Saxon convergence as being an unhappy prologue to the swelling acts of the Pict/Scot theme rather than its epilogue. In fact, there was an important battle between the Picts and a people usually regarded as being Anglo-Saxon: the Northumbrians. The Pictish victory at the Battle of Dun Nechtain in 685 "enabled the emergence of a distinct polity to the north of Saxon England" (Pittock, *Scottish Nationality*, 20). In the centuries following Dun Nechtain, the Pictish and Scottish kingdoms began to unite to form Alba. If the Pict/Scot motif follows a general historical trend, we can read the phrase "the pickts are hacking the saxums" of III.iv as a necessary prelude to the unification of the "pigs and scuts" in IV. Thus, the above passage is both an introduction and a conclusion. Joyce created an ambiguous circularity for Scotland's historical progress in *Finnegans Wake*, moving both towards southern domination as we progress through the work and away into a Gaelic interlude as we pass through the ricorso.

Presumably Joyce could have selected any two rival-then-merged tribes at random from world history for his motif on rivalry, the fluidity of nations, and diverging psychologies. Would two ethnic groups from Irish history not be sufficient for his purposes? Why did he choose two peoples who merged in ancient Scotland? The Scottish literary precedent—outlined in the previous chapter—in dealing with personalities consisting of conflicting tendencies meant that Scotland was the perfect location on which to map out the divided mental territory of HCE. Just as a personality or identity has no single tendency or voice but comprises conflicting and sometimes contradictory drives, so the nation is founded by the merging of diverse and sometimes competing peoples.

Finnegans Wake's "merging of characters . . . becomes a hugely comic version of races merging, a "confusioning of human races" (35.5), which has the effect of utterly destroying any notion of race purity and singularity of race origin" (Platt, *Joyce, Race*, 11). Joyce simultaneously debunks ideas of national or racial purity and explores the schisms of individual human psychology through his attention to ancient and literary Scotland. However, the creation of the internally divided HCE through references to Scottish literature and history exists in the uncertain domain of a Celtic and idealist mind-set. The very idea of a motif that never resolves itself or settles into one fixed meaning is illustrative of a similar atmosphere of incertitude at work in the "Oxen of the Sun" episode of *Ulysses*: "The terrible fact that truth is not Truth, or that many bits of truth add up not to a final great knowledge but to a final great confusion and incertitude, need not be underlined" (French, 176, 179).

The words Pict and Scot provided the raw linguistic material needed to create a mutating motif spanning the vast expanse of *Finnegans Wake*, helping to construct a multiple personality for the dreamer based on Scottish literary precedents. Joyce highlights these textual associations while forming a commentary on Irish and Scottish history, a vision of cyclical colonialism, ethnic mixing, and national "doubles." Scotland has played a crucial, often divisive, role in Ireland's past and could not be ignored in the *Wake*, since this text addresses the history of the world through a focus on Ireland. Joyce's polysemy—incorporating a knowledge of ancient Scottish history and working in tandem with advances made by Scots literature—allowed Scottish culture to be channeled into the turbulent maelstrom of the *Wake* in a way that powerfully articulates the fluid, evolving nature of Scotland and Ireland as twinned spaces pictured in the obscurity of an uncertain, unconscious "state."

FIVE

The Dream of Ossian

Macpherson and Joyce

"PHALL IF YOU BUT WILL, RISE YOU MUST"

In a letter to Paul Léon dated September 11, 1937 (Fahy, 27), Joyce re-
quests a copy of Macpherson's *Ossian*, so he must have wished to consult
the work even in the advanced stages of work on *Finnegans Wake* (which
was published in May 1939). Joyce held copies of Macpherson's work as
part of his Trieste library, a collection that predates the composition of
Finnegans Wake (Ellmann, *Consciousness*, 122). In one of the many notebooks from the *Finnegans Wake* period, Joyce writes that "dream thoughts
are wake thoughts of centuries ago: unconscious memory: great recurrence: race memory" (T. Connolly, *Scribbledehobble*, 104). According to
George Cinclair Gibson this means that "the *Wake* may have an ancient
and mythic key" (4). For Joyce there is a connection between race, repetition, and mythology. In James Macpherson's "forged" versions of stories
from the mythological cycles of Ireland and Scotland, "the amorphous
Celtic *Odyssey*" (*OCPW*, 148), Joyce finds a symbol of the replications
and repetitions he sees as central to art, existence, and "race memory,"
while adding another layer of *dubium* through an incertitude regarding
authenticity, priority, and origins. Like the multiplicity of Hogg's and

Stevenson's texts, the "hoax" reputation of Macpherson's *Ossian* adds to the sense that definitive, genuine reality cannot be found in the *Wake*, only the sham or the counterfeit. So, the Celtic interior world Joyce creates in *Finnegans Wake* is idealist, skeptical, marked by internal contrast, and, crucially, a forgery.

We have seen that in using the work of David Hume to create a world of Celtic interiority in *Finnegans Wake*, Joyce is continuing in a Celticist tradition that casts the idealist Celt in opposition to the materialist Anglo-Saxon. Arguably, Celticism has its origins in *Ossian*: "The construction of Celticism and the discourses associated with it effectively begin with [Macpherson's *Ossian*]" (G. Watson, "Aspects," 130–31). As Malcolm Chapman has argued, the Celtic/Anglo-Saxon system of opposition originates to a large extent in Macpherson's work: "The Ossianic controversy promoted a picture of the Celt as natural, emotional, naïve, and a failure in the rough and tumble of the modern world. This Celt soon began to occupy a place in European history" (82).[1] Drawing on Macpherson's primitivist and romantic texts, theorists such as Ernest Renan ("himself a Breton Celt" [*OCPW*, 113]) and Matthew Arnold began to cast the Celtic and Saxon races as being fundamentally and essentially contrasting. This work also laid the foundations for the Celtic Revival: "It was Ossian by way of Matthew Arnold who structured the Celtic Twilight in Ireland and Scotland" (G. Watson, "Aspects," 131).[2] The Celtic/Saxon contrast presents the Celt as having artistic, spiritual, and emotional characteristics while the Anglo-Saxon is a materialist:

> We can see that Renan's Celt . . . takes much of his shape in opposition to rationality, intellectuality, and a materialist world of scientific and political manipulation. Instead of these the Celt has an artistic capacity beyond the ordinary, a religious instinct of unusual depth, a strength and profundity of thought and feeling but a weakness in the external world of action, a ready emotionality and an easy communion with nature, a strength in domesticity but a weakness in a wider political sphere. . . . Passion, irrationality, obscure consciousness, sensitiveness, affection and nature are opposed to and thus defined by contrast to intellectuality, reasonings, hard scholasticism, merciless dissection and science. The opposition of the Celt to the

qualities ascribed to science is made more explicitly by Arnold. (Chapman, 86–87)

Developing Renan's work, Matthew Arnold wished to find a perfect synthesis of "the idealist Celt and the materialist Anglo-Saxon" (Chapman, 94).[3] Of course, this is undertaken for ideological and political reasons:

> The major nineteenth-century theorist of Celticism in the Anglophone world, Matthew Arnold, published *On the Study of Celtic Literature* in 1866. In this famous work, Celticism is very much deployed for assimilative purposes: its subtext is how to bring Ireland more firmly into the Union. Arnold, who knew very little about the philology of the Celtic languages, and not very much even about their literary history (which he knew only at second hand), nevertheless presents a sympathetic, even attractive picture of the Celt, as spiritual, melancholy, natural and poetic. The contrast is with the materialist, philistine, utilitarian, excessively rational, artificial, industrialized and urbanized Saxon. (G. Watson, "Aspects," 136)

But, being childlike dreamers, the Celts, in Arnold's view, always need the Saxons to hold their hands and to take care of all of the practical work: "Not only is the Celt impractical, he has a fatal 'readiness to revolt against the despotism of fact.' . . . So, Arnold's repressive tolerance suggests that the Celt is lucky to have the dull and muddy-mettled Saxon to run his affairs for him; in return the Celt will serve to leaven the Saxon lump, bringing with him to the heavy imperial dining table his wit and his visionary and spiritual qualities" (G. Watson, "Aspects," 136). Arnold's other racial binary—that of the Jew and the Greek in his *Culture and Anarchy*—is an important background text of *Ulysses* (see Tymoczko, 41). Indeed, the Hellenic/Hebraic axis and the Celtic/Anglo-Saxon structure are variations of the same theme: "The governing idea of Hellenism is spontaneity of consciousness; that of Hebraism, strictness of consciousness" (Arnold, *Culture and Anarchy*, 132). For Arnold, "it is clear that the world of tangible, material affairs, of instrumental activity, is opposed to creativity and the world of ideas, the former being the talent of the Anglo-Saxon and the latter the talent of the Celt" (Chapman, 91). Arnold's conception proved enormously popular and enduring, as Chapman has noted: "[Arnold's] picture of the Celt was adopted with enthusiasm by people in all fields of study, and became an established fact, a security with which an argument could be begun rather than a conclusion to be reached. The spirituality of the Celt and the materialism of the Anglo-Saxon, and all their other associated qualities, are continually referred to in journals of Scottish and Gaelic studies from the 1880s onwards" (99).[4] It is this conception, albeit in a divergent form, which finds its way into the work of Joyce. In short, the idealist/materialist binary system which, as we have seen, Joyce comments on and adapts in his own work, stems indirectly from the work of James Macpherson (via Arnold).[5] It is therefore fitting that Joyce's own world of Celtic idealism should feature Macpherson's work so prominently. As Watson rightly points out, Celticism in general "may be anodyne in itself, but is pernicious in its promiscuous co-operation with colonial attitudes" (G. Watson, "Aspects," 129). With Joyce a form of neo-Celticism is created entirely at odds with colonial values. However, it could be argued that Joyce's work shares with Celticism an attempt to "re-create or assert a cultural identity for the people of Ireland . . . which will distinguish them from the majority inhabitants of the British Isles, the English" (129).

Text lifted from the work of Macpherson, adapted and placed into *Finnegans Wake*, is a prime example of Joyce's magpie-like literary "borrowing," with the added value that this work had already been reused once before. *Finnegans Wake* continues the recycling of *Ossian* by making a "new" artistic product out of old poetry, which itself was composed of ancient, constantly remade remnants. Indeed, Watson's description of the Ossianic text as being "synthetic and ambiguous" (G. Watson, "Aspects," 132) could easily be applied to the *Wake*. This particular process is also an ongoing exchange between Irish and Scottish cultures, which bears out one of the central ideas of *Finnegans Wake*, that nothing in art can be ever truly new, only a transformed replication of older prototypes or precedents, or a "tissue of citations, resulting from the thousand sources of culture" (Barthes, 146). Again, this ties in with the Humean conception of the operations of the mind itself as consisting of clashing copied representations of numerous external materials (see Hume, *Treatise*, 300–301).

Macpherson's texts have a decidedly hotchpotch quality—a medley of disconnected units of folklore—gathered in what was, for Joyce, something of a hybrid nation (as we have seen in the previous chapters). *Finnegans Wake* constantly insists upon the mixed and rehashed nature of both texts and nations. After all, Scottish Gaelic culture is to some extent a legacy from the Irish Scoti people we encountered earlier, another uncanny—familiar yet strange—occurrence. Now, while Macpherson and a great deal of Celtic matters are associated with interiority in *Finnegans Wake*, there is no sense that this equates to some "pure" Celtic racial identity. Although there are strong associations between idealism, skepticism, and Celticism in the *Wake*, it is also suggested that Celtic culture, or any culture for that matter, is an evolving and recycled compound of disparate elements. Indeed, this skepticism regarding national or racial cohesion also relates to personal integrity or unity.

In the previous chapters we have looked at how Joyce adapts the theme of the double from texts of Scottish literature. As Nick Groom has noted, the figure of the forger in eighteenth-century culture is closely related to that of the doppelgänger: "The impersonator is potentially as transgressive a figure as the forger—disturbing or mad or supernatural or criminal, yet also a celebrity and a walking example of the contradictions of Romantic subjectivity and its sinister possibilities. It is no surprise that this period saw the composition of uncanny works of doppelgänger fiction such as . . . James Hogg's *Private Memoirs and Confessions of a Justified Sinner*" (Groom, 1645). Forgery and the doppelgänger are both threatening challenges to the very idea of uniqueness and cohesion, whether personal or textual. Whereas Hogg and Stevenson relate to national and psychological duality in Joyce's work, Macpherson is implicated in questions of literary authenticity and exclusivity. All three authors are involved in creating the atmosphere of uncertainty and feeling of instability in the *Wake*.

James Macpherson (Seumas MacMhuirich), a native Gaelic speaker, was born at Ruthven in the Scottish Highlands in 1736 and educated at universities in Aberdeen and Edinburgh. He came to international attention and acclaim with the publication of *Fragments of Ancient Poetry Collected in the Scottish Highlands* (1760) and *Fingal, an Ancient Epic Poem in Six Books, together with Several Other Poems composed by Ossian, the Son of Fingal, translated from the Gaelic Language* (1761). In 1763 *Temora* was published, followed by a collected volume entitled *The Works of Ossian* (1765). Collectively, these translations are now known as Macpherson's *Ossian*. James Porter has summed up the enormous influence *Ossian* had on European culture:

> Literary lions felt the impact of *Ossian*, including Blake, Burns, Byron, Coleridge, Scott, Wordsworth, and Yeats. . . . Goethe modeled his best-selling *Die Leiden des jungen Werthers* . . . on the elegiac mood established by Macpherson's poems. His contemporaries in Germany—Hölderlin, Klopstock, and Lenz—were also deeply affected by *Ossian* . . . as were Chateaubriand, Diderot, and Mme. de Staël-Holstein in France, Lermontov in Russia, and a host of other creative artists, including painters like Gérard, Girodet, and Ingres, all of whom contributed to the Ossianic canvasses commissioned by Napoleon at Malmaison. . . . *Ossian* captivated Beethoven, Schubert, Brahms, and especially Felix Mendelssohn, who visited Scotland and whose evocative tone-poem, the "Hebrides Overture," was originally titled "Fingal's Cave." . . . In America, James Fenimore Cooper and Edgar Allan Poe came under *Ossian*'s spell. . . . Folklorists and cultural historians alike in the 19th century felt the power of the poems: notably Herder and the Grimms in Germany and Elias Lönnrot in Finland. In Scotland, John Francis Campbell, who designed an innovative and accurate fieldwork method for recording Gaelic folktales, devoted much time and energy to Ossianic matters. Indeed, it is no exaggeration to say that the poems of *Ossian* are not just the key to European Romanticism—with its emphasis on individual sensibility and the sense of loss associated with a glorious past—but the key also to the beginnings of interest in a collective cultural history and oral tradition. (Porter, 396–97)

According to Paul Robichaud, antiquarian or "anthropological" writers such as Macpherson, Burns, and Scott acted as precursors to "professional anthropologists" such as the Scot James Frazer:

> Writers as diverse as James Macpherson, Robert Burns, and . . . Walter Scott approach Scottish society as a proto-anthropological site

rich in endangered cultural practices, to be textually preserved and passed down as part of a continuous Scottish identity. Macpherson's *Ossian* fragments and the ballads collected by Burns and Scott are early examples of what would later be called fieldwork in a residually oral culture. Their efforts anticipate the work of professional anthropologists like . . . James Frazer, who "knew also that his own land was invested with sacred sites, and that topography, lore, and landscape were bound together" . . . A common theme uniting Macpherson's *Ossian*, Scott's *Waverley*, and Frazer's *Golden Bough* is the persistence of the "primitive" in spite of the relentless progress of modernity, and this is intimately linked to Scottish Enlightenment ideas concerning the development of societies "out of barbarism into refinement." (Robichaud, "MacDiarmid and Muir," 136)[6]

Strangely, despite its roots in an investigation of "the persistence of the 'primitive,'" Macpherson's work becomes part of the background to literary modernism since it is a forerunner of Frazer's inquiries, which, in turn, proved to be so influential for writers such as Joyce and T. S. Eliot.[7]

The Irish Literary Revival also displayed a marked interest in legend and folklore. In Yeats's early work "Wanderings of Oisin" (1889) the task of the poet figure Oisin (Ossian is Macpherson's name for Oisín/Oisin, son of the heroic Fionn mac Cumhaill in the Fenian cycle of Celtic mythology) is to memorialize the epic character of his community and to mourn its loss as it vanishes in a clash of pre-Christian and Christian civilizations: "Sad to remember, sick with years / The swift innumerable spears" (1). Oisin belongs to a "godless and passionate age" (31). Patrick, the harbinger of a new order, informs Oisin that he is "still wrecked among heathen dreams" (2). Similarly, Macpherson's poetry is concerned with memory. Ossian is a blind figure, lacking vision of the external world but experiencing inner visions (similar to the temporarily "blinded" dreamer of the *Wake* and perhaps to the older Joyce himself, with his constant eye difficulties and near blindness). His role is that of one who remembers, the figure who mentally stores the dreams of a community, and it is this feature that Joyce utilizes in the *Wake*. Furthermore, as we shall see, Macpherson's work was itself an attempt to preserve and record his own receding culture. Tellingly, Joyce does not use Yeats's poem in the *Wake*. Macpherson's texts, recyclings of found objects, more powerfully convey the theme of consciousness and texts as a recycled forms. While Yeats reverses the Arnoldian binary to make Celtic spirituality a heroic attribute, Joyce is far more ambivalent. However, Joyce certainly explores the idea of a Celtic "'interiority."

Macpherson's texts, with their vague materiality and largely fluid characters, create a poetic world similar to that of Joyce's final work: "Many of the peculiarities of *The Poems of Ossian* can, indeed, be seen to function as creative catalysts for the reader. . . . The repetitious nature of the language, imagery, metre and even the plots, has an almost mesmeric quality, while at the same time evoking a landscape and cast of characters sufficiently imprecise to allow the reader's full participation in the creative experience" (Stafford, introduction, xvi). On a similar note, Nick Groom has commented that Macpherson's poetry is "a self-consciously remote translation, a derelict monument to a lost age, a vast memento mori of the Celtic twilight. The characters Ossian describes are already dead and appear as transient ghosts, the topography is elusive, the landscape is fading" (Groom, 1626). Macpherson claimed that his works were recovered epics of ancient Scotland. Significantly, Macpherson's texts appear in the wake of the doomed Jacobite rising of 1745/1746 (a movement named after another exiled James—James VII of Scotland / James II of England) and the subsequent assault and near destruction of Scottish Gaelic culture by the British state. Macpherson's work was, in part, an attempt to preserve something of this vanishing way of life in the face of what Joyce would later call "the vast Anglo-Saxon civilization" (*OCPW*, 125), as well as encroaching aspects of modernity.[8] If Macpherson's work was an effort to construct a memorial for a endangered civilization in the face of modernity and imperialism, *Finnegans Wake* replicates the attempt to create a spectral "memory," an inner Celtic state as an alternative to materialism.

The Joyce critics Fritz Senn and Ward Swinson carried out invaluable early work on Macpherson and *Finnegans Wake* by compiling lists collating Joyce's many allusions to Macpherson's work, adding to material in James Atherton's *The Books at the Wake* and Adaline Glasheen's *Second Census of Finnegans Wake*. Senn's list was published in 1966, in the new series of the now sadly defunct *A Wake Newslitter*, with the following remarks: "*Ossian* tends to be somewhat repetitive in its evocations and descriptions of nature and of battle-scenes. This often makes it difficult to indicate, with any degree of assurance, to which passage in *Ossian* an allusion in *Finnegans Wake* refers. Sometimes Joyce seems to have been content merely to create an atmosphere reminiscent of the Ossianic poems" (Senn, "Echoes," 25). While it is true that Joyce wishes frequently in the *Wake* to create an *Ossian*-like atmosphere, there is more to Joyce's use of Macpherson than as a simple tonal device. Fritz Senn's paper was updated by Ward Swinson's list in 1972, also published in *A Wake Newslitter*, and the work of Senn and Swinson was eventually included in Roland McHugh's *Annotations to Finnegans Wake*. However, study in this area came to an abrupt halt at this point. Unfortunately, neither Senn nor Swinson provided much in the way of explanation as to why Joyce used Macpherson's poetry so extensively, other than Senn's comments above.

As Senn points out, it is often difficult to ascertain which of Macpherson's poems Joyce is referring to with his Macpherson allusions in the *Wake*. However, this is usually almost irrelevant. The meaning of the specific Ossianic vocabulary used can sometimes be of significance, but generally Joyce's allusions relate to the *idea* of *Ossian*, rather than to the internal concerns of Macpherson's poetry itself. This idea involves the poetry's status as a fake or hoax and its nature as something created (or re-created) out of previously existing material. Fiona Stafford has discussed the reputation of *Ossian* as hoax in her introduction to Macpherson's works: "Although the relationship between *The Poems of Ossian* and traditional Gaelic verse has been the subject of major scholarly investigations since the 1760s, and it has long been established that Macpherson drew on traditional sources to produce imaginative texts not modelled closely on any single identifiable original, the idea that he was the author of an elaborate hoax persists" (Stafford, introduction, vii). The belief that *The Poems of Ossian* were "an elaborate hoax"—which took root in Macpherson's day with Samuel Johnson among his detractors—was certainly still prevalent at the time of publication of *Finnegans Wake*. Joyce's erstwhile towermate Oliver Gogarty declared in an *Observer* review of the *Wake* that Joyce's final work was "the most colossal leg pull in literature since Macpherson's *Ossian*" (*JJII*, 722). *Ossian*'s questionable, suspicious status—and the initial mystery surrounding its publication—makes it fitting for inclusion in a text like the *Wake*, where so much is uncertain. Despite the unenviable reputation *Ossian* has acquired, Macpherson did in fact conduct genuine field research and work with real sources: "Macpherson had . . . in his travels gathered together an important collection of manuscripts which, but for his intervention, might have been entirely lost. Important among them were the early sixteenth-century work now known as *The Book of the Dean of Lismore*, *An Leabhar Dearg* or *The Red Book* which Macpherson acquired from Neil Mac-Mhuirich, a member of the famous bardic dynasty, and *An Duanaire Ruadh* or *The Red Rhymer*, from the archives of Clanranald" (Chapman, 39).[9] Though Macpherson did search the Highlands and Islands of Scotland for oral and textual examples of ancient Gaelic poetry on tours in 1760 and 1761, he reworked and embellished his source material, making it accessible and palatable for a late eighteenth-century Anglophone audience. Unfortunately for Macpherson's status in the long run, he was, unlike Joyce, never open about his artistic methods, and his name has become synonymous with hoax, forgery, and cultural corruption.[10]

Indeed, Macpherson's work appeared in an era preoccupied with questions of authenticity and origins, as Nick Groom has noted: "Literary forgery was a perpetual concern in the second-half of the eighteenth century. . . . Broadly speaking, this fascination with the legitimacy of the past emerged from the heightened need for a sense of national identity engendered by the Act of Union in 1707" (1625). Of course, the "nation" in question here is the newly established United Kingdom—not Scotland. This political construct was in need of an ennobling lost epic that could provide some sense of a cohesive identity for its divergent constituent nations and peoples (however, *Ossian* has also been read as a salvage operation mounted in the ruins of late eighteenth-century Gaelic culture). It is into this environment that Macpherson's works appeared. His slightly underhanded activities received mixed responses in Scotland and England but met with almost universal opprobrium in Ireland: "*Fingal* and *Temora* were greeted by a barrage of objections from Dublin, as scholars such as Charles O'Connor and Sylvester O'Halloran criticised Macpherson's free-handling of Gaelic poetry, and particularly the way in which stories from the Fionn and Ulster cycles had been confused. Even more aggravating was his appropriation of Irish heroes, and the refusal to accept that the Scots were originally inhabitants of Ireland" (Stafford, introduction, vii).

The touchy Irish critics who wished to maintain Ireland's position as the primary, original Celtic nation also pointed to Scotland's more advanced modernity as a signal that it was now somehow less Celtic (although this relatively advanced state had actually helped to bring Celtic literature to European attention): "As Hardiman and Theophilus O'Flanagan and a host of others had combatively asserted, Ireland could claim priority over Scotland as the 'original' Gaelic culture precisely because the Scots had not kept their Gaelic tradition intact in any comparable way. Scotland had yielded itself to print much earlier than Ireland; it had, therefore, a less enduring manuscript tradition; it was therefore less 'pure,' less authentic" (S. Deane, *Strange Country*, 108). It is precisely these spurious notions of "purity," "priority," and "authenticity" that Joyce wishes to attack with his inclusion of Macpherson in *Finnegans Wake*. His treatment intimates that almost everything is in some sense "forged'" or a "rehash" and that purity and authenticity are, ultimately, chimeras. Like Mangan and Wilde, Joyce understood "the value of the false, the insincere and the artificial, over whatever purported to be 'real,' genuine or authentic art" (Sturgeon, 115).

Using Macpherson to make this point is somewhat ironic, since Macpherson's own defense of the supposed authenticity of his decidedly "mixed" works rested to some extent on their origins in a purportedly "unmixed" society: "The dialect of the Celtic tongue, spoken in the north of Scotland, is much more pure, more agreeable to its mother language, and more abounding with primitives, than that now spoken, or even that which has been writ for some centuries back, amongst the most unmixed part of the Irish nation. . . . *Scotch Galic* is the most original, and, consequently, the language of a more antient and unmixed people" (Macpherson, 216–17). Furthermore, the use of myths in literary modernism gestures towards the essentially *constructed* nature of "the human world": "This recognition of the self-grounding character of the human world is the truest meaning of the Modernist use of myth. Myth could be many things, including nostalgia for a lost unity, a fascistic regression, or a literary structure, but its most important meaning was as an emblem of the human world as self-created" (Bell, 14). Joyce's synthesized use of Macpherson attests to the manufactured nature of writing, consciousness, and identity just as his work on the Picts and Scots had explored the "impure" constitution of nations. Macpherson's work is also used to illustrate Joyce's conception of consciousness itself as a type of "hoax" or deception.

It now seems bizarre that Hardiman and O'Flanagan could grumble about the supposed nonconformity of Macpherson's poetry, considering Celtic mythology had already been in a constant state of flux for hundreds of years. Joyce may well have been aware of these early objections or reservations, but his own readings of traditional Irish/Gaelic poetry would perhaps have allowed him to detect the nature of Macpherson's "free-handling" for himself. For example, his knowledge of the Irish mythological cycles would probably have been good enough for him to realize that Macpherson's work had "confused the chronology of the legends by making Fingal and Cuchullin contemporaries" (Stafford, *Sublime Savage*, 165). In fact, this confusion had actually existed in Gaelic culture before Macpherson began his work, and *Ossian* merely continued it (see Stafford, *Sublime Savage*, 165). Furthermore, given the purposefully mixed "thisorder" (*FW*, 540.19) of *Finnegans Wake*, it is reasonable to assume that Joyce might not have been particularly offended or perturbed by Macpherson's liberty-taking and rearranging. Indeed, Joyce does not place much faith in supposedly "authentic" or "pure" Celtic mythology; during the "Cyclops" episode of *Ulysses* the "twelve tribes of Iar" feature "the tribe of Ossian" (*U*, 12.1125–29).

Alongside revering the supposed sanctity and purity of stories from Gaelic mythology, Irish critics of the period also jealously guarded Ireland's status as the "original" Celtic nation (or at least "more original" than Scotland): "All through the late eighteenth and well into the nineteenth century, Irish commentators had fought the *Ossian* battle over and over, denying the Scots the primacy they claimed in the Celtic hierarchy, insisting instead that it was the Irish who had been the original founders of the culture of which Scotland was a derivative" (S. Deane, *Strange Country*, 43). Joyce's work demonstrates little interest in such controversies (apart from his work on the Picts and the Scots), promoting and promoting the rehashed, the transformed, the "derivative," and the processes of "metamorphoseous" (*FW*, 190.31) while linking these processes to the internal functions of the mind itself. However, much of Joyce's later interest in Scotland can be traced to its partial status as an Irish "derivative." *Finnegans Wake* is based around the concept of recurrence, and we have seen how his system of allusions to the Picts and Scots functioned as a reminder of the cyclical nature of Irish and Scottish interpenetrations. Macpherson's *Ossian* is not simply a literary forgery to Joyce. It is a heavily distorted echo of Irish culture, a reminder of the historical and linguistic heritage shared between Scotland and Ireland.

Joyce's treatment of Macpherson's work in the *Wake* shows an understanding that *Ossian* was not a total "fibfib fabrication" (*FW*, 36.34), an appreciation that there were elements of genuine Gaelic poetry in the work that had been copied, modified, and pieced together in a bricolage fashion.[11] While *Ossian* is used in *Finnegans Wake* to evoke ideas of fabrication and hoax, it also becomes a symbol of resurrection or recurrence since—at least according to Macpherson—the traditional epic poetry he had gathered had been lost until his miraculous "discovery." We must remember that Macpherson's poetry was presented to the public as a series of genuine historical artefacts rescued from obscurity. Joyce takes advantage of the latent symbolic quality of *Ossian* as a fake but also as something retrieved from a buried and distant past, from the "fossilized evidence of the history of . . . a society" (Lévi-Strauss, 22). Like Frazer's dying and reviving god, Macpherson's work was—supposedly—something that had miraculously been resurrected from oblivion.

RECYCLED TEXTS

There is an arresting resemblance between Macpherson's research and composition methods and Joyce's process of gathering and altering preexisting material for insertion into *Finnegans Wake*. As ought to be well known by now, the *Wake* cannot be regarded as a "pure" and spontaneous product of Joyce's imagination and creativity. The book is an immense recycling center, a textual collection consisting of countless elements of culture amassed in Joyce's notebooks, modified, and gradually assembled as the final compilation. Hillary A. Clark has discussed this approach in an article entitled "Encyclopedic Discourse": "Joyce's task in composing *Finnegans Wake* (and to some extent in *Ulysses*) involves rearranging ready-made narratives and . . . knowledge. Joyce works like the encyclopedist, his method of 'interpolation' and 'recycling' involves continually working elaborations, revisions and supplements into the text, while retaining the earlier drafts alongside the new material" (H. Clark, 105). This method is close to Macpherson's technique of reusing "ready-made narratives" for the patchwork of *The Poems of Ossian*. Vincent Cheng has also highlighted this aspect of Joyce's work: "Joyce himself was accused (and self-accused) of simply cannibalizing the past and its great works of literature, of sometimes lifting entire passages from other works and placing them in his own books; furthermore, the author admitted his own lack of originality. . . . Forgery, theft, and plagiarism appear to be givens in Joyce's concept of the literary world" (*Shakespeare and Joyce*, 96–97). Joyce himself seemed perfectly at ease with the idea of himself working in this way: "I am quite content to go down to posterity as a scissors and paste man for that seems to me a harsh but not unjust description" (*LI*, 297). As Philip Herring has suggested, "Joyce . . . accepts as given that the artist is a forger of meaning and of identity" (117).

In III.i of *Finnegans Wake*, a section dominated by the authority figure Shaun, the "insufficiently malestimated notesnatcher" (125. 21–22), Shem is compared to Macpherson:

> Let me see, do. Beerman's bluff was what began it, Old Knoll and his borrowing! And then the liliens of the veldt, Nancy Nickies and Folletta Lajambe! Then mem and hem and the jaquejack. All about Wucherer and righting his name for him. I regret to announce, after laying out his litterery bed, for two days she kept squealing down for noisy priors and bawling out to her jameymock farceson in Shemish like a mouther of the incas. (422.31–423.1)

Here the birth of Shem, the "farceson," is being discussed, and, again, birth or human origins are related to "litterery" or textual concerns. Here "litterery" stresses Joyce's concern with texts that have been constructed from "litter," abandoned, leftover remains or fragments, such as the fragments of Gaelic poetry and myth Macpherson salvaged to create *Ossian*. William York Tindall has made the following comments on this allusion to Macpherson: "Shem, that forger of farces, is as bad as 'jameymock farceson,' the forger of *Ossian*" (233). Certainly this partly explains the allusion, but another "jamey" is comparing himself to Macpherson here, since the rebellious artist figure Shem is partly modeled on Joyce himself. Of course, the name Shem derives in part from the Irish *Seamus*, the English version of which Macpherson and Joyce share as first name.[12] This connection amounts to Joyce celebrating the status of his art as part of an endlessly mutating development rather than as an isolated and autonomous project. In a modernist self-reflexive gesture, Joyce also highlights the "artificial" or "simulated" nature of his text through the use of the term "mock." Indeed, Joyce preferred to consider his own artistic processes as reproductive or imitative rather than purely creative: "Joyce was always an arranger rather than a creator, for, like a mediaeval artist, he seems superstitiously to have feared the presumption of human attempts at creation" (C. Hart, *Structure*, 44).

In the section above, Shaun is being interviewed about the *Wake*'s enigmatic letter, and he takes the opportunity to castigate his brother Shem. As with the passage from page 294, Macpherson's name is connected with origins—as well as oral tradition—through mother or "mouther." The initial material of the passage is a "concise account of the incident in the park" (Kitcher, 196). So here Macpherson is again linked with human reproduction and also with HCE's shadowy and originary indiscretion. Interestingly, Shaun reports the arrival of Shem as though it were a death, with the words "I regret to announce." The beginning and the end of life are conjoined here by Shaun, which connects with the idea of literary recycling. The phrase "litterary bed" describes *Finnegans Wake* itself—a textual dreamstate, constructed from the "litter" of leftover literature. Of course, the phrase also refers to the "setting" of the *Wake* itself. Shaun's denunciation ends with familiar accusations of forgery: "Every dimmed letter in it is a copy and not a few of the silbils and wholly words I can show you in my Kingdom of Heaven. The lowquacity of him! With his threestar monothong! Thaw! The last word in stolentelling!" (424.32–35). Allusions to James Macpherson in *Finnegans Wake* relate to reproduction and renewal, suggesting forgery or copying is an essential or unavoidable process in the act of creation or textual production. Macpherson becomes a convenient symbol for Joyce's treatment of birth as he is the "creator," or re-creator, of something unoriginal, fashioned from preexisting materials. Allusions to Macpherson appear in order to create the recycled nature of the famous letter, an object that in turn stands for *Finnegans Wake* itself, a four-part square wheel built around recurrences and constructed from found materials.[13]

Book I, chapter vii of *Finnegans Wake* also concentrates on the Joyce-like artist figure Shem. As well as a physical description of the "hybrid" Shem (169.9), his eating habits, and a portrayal of his cowardice, we are also informed of Shem's methods of artistic (re)production: "What do you think Vulgariano did but study with stolen fruit how cutely to copy all their various styles of signature so as one day to utter an epical forged cheque on the public for his own private profit" (181.14–17). The themes of copying, forging, and plagiarism are also present here: "How few or how many of the most venerated public impostures, how very many piously forged palimpsests slipped in the first place by this morbid process from his pelagiarist pen?" (182.1–3).[14] Of course, the *Wake* itself was a palimpsest for Joyce in the sense that what had already been composed— by himself and previous authors—was constantly being written on top of. Also noteworthy in the second passage is the mention of a "process." Shem's activity is an ongoing activity, part of an artistic continuum. His texts are, like Macpherson's, "impostures."[15]

Page 182 of the *Wake* is based on Joyce's life and career on the continent, for example his alcohol-assisted stint as a teacher at the Berlitz language school in Trieste ("beerlitz" [182.7]) and his writing of *A Portrait of the Artist as a Young Man* ("inartistic portraits" [182.19]). The allusions to *Ossian* at this point come as something of a surprise, bringing a suggestion of falsity or fraud to Joyce's oblique look at his own early artistic career. Joyce, through allusion to Macpherson, admits that he is also in some ways a "copyist" (121.30), while Shem's attempts to find or create his own singular identity through exile and art are compared to the creative methods of James Macpherson. Like Hume's sense of self consisting of bundles of perceptions or the divided psyches of Hogg and Stevenson, disparate elements will need to be pieced together by Shem. Indeed, Joyce stresses the similarities between artistic production and the production of human identities—true "originals" or definite "origins" are impossible to come by. Philip Kitcher has reflected on Shem's quest to forge an identity for himself:

> Shem's preference . . . is not for what we ought to imbibe from the
> past, from tradition, from the history of his community, but a rotten
> version of it. To change the metaphor, in forging his consciousness
> he must rely on conceptions and categories that have been handed
> down to him. . . . If Shem . . . supposes that he can begin completely
> afresh, fashioning his own identity from some point completely out-
> side history and tradition, then he is deeply deceived. There is no
> such point to be found. (Kitcher, 34–35)

Does Macpherson's poetry qualify as a decomposed form, a "rotten version," of the history of the larger Gaelic community? The contemporary
Irish critics of his work such as O'Connor and O'Halloran might have
thought so. Previously Macpherson's work has functioned as a reminder
of the constant repetition of history through the exhumed letter, through
the comparison to childbirth, and to the routine of sleep. Although
Finnegans Wake itself is a response to materialism and imperialism, Macpherson's work is used in the *Wake* here as a reminder that history can
never be fully escaped, that any new beginnings are always in some way
reliant on the past (or, since historical events are cyclical, there is no historical "sequence" as such). At the very point where Shem should be associated with newness and originality he is identified with Macpherson's
poetry—something conspicuously unoriginal. However, this could also
be regarded as a necessary, even healthy process. Macpherson's Ossianic
poetry is associated with Shem because it is a body of work created out
of the materials of the past. Shem's own forged identity may also be
brought about in a similar way, not a new creation but a different configuration of preexisting elements, much like *Finnegans Wake* itself. A
forgery requires some previous form to replicate. The creation of Shem's
art works in the same way, with the artist writing his "cyclewheeling history" (186.2) out of ink created from his own bodily waste, "a no uncertain quantity of obscene matter not protected by copriright" (185.29–30).
For Joyce, artistic "output" depends on the inputs of tradition, language,
and history. If the categories of identity and consciousness are seen as
hopelessly "constructed" in *Finnegans Wake*, this is an unavoidable situation. That Joyce links these ideas to "inauthentic" Celtic mythology
suggests that the Celtic idea itself may ultimately be a sham, but it is one
that is likely both to endure and to be endlessly reproduced.

RECYCLED CONSCIOUSNESS

Book I, chapter v, of *Finnegans Wake* is concerned with ALP's (or Shem's) recurring and mutating letter, her "untitled mamafesta" (104.4), which represents, among other things, the text of the *Wake* itself. Like Macpherson's work, it has seemingly been recovered from obscurity, having been dug up from a rubbish tip by a scratching hen. The letter is also in a constant state of fluctuation or instability, with the wording continuously in transition through the *Wake*. We can never arrive at a definitive and fixed version of the letter's contents, in much the same way that the fluid events and figures of the *Wake* remain impossible to pin down with any degree of certainty. In a further similarity, Macpherson's poetry is an artistic or cultural product of content that has undergone countless mutations over time and through the processes of oral folk tradition, movement overseas from one territory to another, translation from Gaelic into English and through Macpherson's own alterations and embellishments. Finally, the poetry has ended up being further modified by Joyce and fed into the textual machine of *Finnegans Wake*.

A reference to Macpherson's *Ossian* appears towards the end of this chapter in a particularly dense section. As with the Scottish character Crotthers in *Ulysses*, a distinct maritime theme is involved here: "In the case of the littleknown periplic bestteller popularly associated with the names of the wretched mariner (trianforan deffwedoff our plumsucked pattern shapekeeper) a Punic admiralty report, *From MacPerson's Oshean Round by the Tides of Jason's Cruise*, had been cleverly capsized and saucily republished as a dodecanesian baedeker of the every-tale-a-treat-in-itself variety which could hope satisfactorily to tickle me gander as game as your goose" (123.22–29). The allusions to the *Ancient Mariner* and to Jason and the Argonauts; the conversion of the word "Ossian" into something approaching "ocean"; and the terms "capsized," "admiralty," and "*Cruise*" all link to the sea and seafaring here. In addition to maritime imagery, "dodecanesian baedeker" conveys travel, since "dodecanesian" refers to Greek islands and "baedeker" to the popular travel guidebooks. Furthermore, the references to geese also suggest migration. These images of movement and the sea are brought together with the names of works of literature and terms connected with writing, such as "bestteller," "reports," and the allusions to Greek myths, to Shakespeare, and to Macpherson's *Ossian* itself. The neologism "periplic" looks like a portmanteau of the words "periplus," meaning a circumnavigation or an account of a circumnavigation, and "epic." The word "periplus" chimes with the nautical imagery, and "epic" links up with Jason and the Argonauts and *Ossian*.[16] The italicized section could serve as alternative title for the *Wake* itself.

Ossian—as well as Scotland itself—is a product of overseas migration with the ancient Gaelic poetry it was based on brought across the "Moylean Main" (*FW*, 25.27) from Ireland to Scotland, part of the shared cultural heritage of the two nations. This cultural inheritance has been sustained by the maritime links that Joyce foregrounds here. Literature is being compared to ALP's letter, which has been "transhipt" (111.9) across the sea and is also a communication between a divided consciousness; hence the focus on "*Schizophrenesis*" (123.18–19) in the paragraph as a whole. All texts are attempted acts of communication similar to the voyages mentioned in the passage in the sense that meaning has to make a type of movement like the delivery of the letter. The sea and the letter are often conflated in *Finnegans Wake*, for example through allusion to the shouts of "Thalatta! Thalatta!" (Sea! Sea!) of Xenophon's ten thousand men: "The letter! The litter!" (93.24).

Ossian, the letter, and seafaring are also linked in the *Wake* through an attention to progress and transformation. As Clive Hart has discussed, Joyce was fascinated by processes rather than by finished articles:

He was remarkably uninterested in achievements—either his own personal and artistic achievements or the socio-political achievements of Europe—but the flux of the moment never failed to hold his attention. In art as in life it was process rather than result that appealed to him most—how a thing comes to be, rather than what it is. Physical and spiritual gestation of all kinds delighted him. Nora's pregnancies, which to her were simple human conditions, became for him mystical events worthy of the deepest study. He spent a thousand hours, according to his own reckoning, trying to reproduce the physical process linguistically in the "Oxen of the Sun" episode of *Ulysses*, and even contrived to make the whole of another book, *A Portrait*, reflect the stages of development of the human

> foetus. This interest in the process of creation is yet more pro-
> nounced in *Finnegans Wake*, in which everything, as has frequently
> been said, is in a constant state of becoming. (*Structure*, 51)

In the passage from page 123 the imagery implies continuity, "becoming," and also fluctuation, in keeping with the presentation of ALP as a
river. The play on Jesus Christ hints at resurrection, circularity is provided with "*Round*," and repetition is present in the word '*Tides.*' As *mac*
is Gaelic for "son," "*MacPerson*" can be read as "son of the person," again
suggestive of renewal. All of these linguistic constructions suggest
echoes, perpetuation, or ongoing processes. The images of travel also
connect to continuation since they stress movement, and the sea features
because it provides a sense of fluidity. Elsewhere in the *Wake* vocabulary
from *Ossian* is used to stress the wave-like, repetitive nature of sleeping
and waking (or a Frazerian pattern of death and revival): "Phall if you
but will, rise you must" (4.15–16). The word "report" can mean to repeat
or echo as well as to relate. Given that the context deals with repetition
and seafaring, it can also be read as "re-port." This appellation can be
explained in part by the fact that the dream the dreamer is experiencing
is a type of report. The connection between *Ossian* and dreams is a subject matter that predates *Finnegans Wake*. For example, the French neo-
classicist painter Jean-Auguste-Dominique Ingres was commissioned by
Napoleon (who is reputed to have carried a copy of Macpherson's poetry
into battle) to create a work based on *Ossian*. His painting, *Le Rêve
d'Ossian* or *The Dream of Ossian* (1813), depicts the mythical poet asleep
at his harp with a cast of heroic figures in the spectral background.

In the passage above, Joyce is shaping a concept of continuity in
change. This theme, combined with the suggestion of imitation provided
by the reference to *Ossian*, suggests that dreams (as well as racial and cultural exchange) continue through repetition and constant transformation, through processes akin to the instability and repetitive actions of
the sea. Also implied is the idea that texts are not stagnant, fixed, discrete
units but parts of a larger, shifting, unified "sea" of discourse or ideas.
Neither life nor art is considered by Joyce to be a process in which the
creation of anything genuinely new—be it a text, a singular consciousness or a nation—or totally "itself" is possible because both life and art
necessarily contain elements of previous iterations. Instead they, and

Finnegans Wake itself, progress through variations on—and transformations of—what has previously existed. According to Joyce's copy principle, everything is a work in progress and nothing is ever completed. Most importantly, the above passage is also a consideration of dream production similar to the "united states of Scotia Picta" section we considered earlier (43.29–30). As John Bishop discusses in *Joyce's Book of the Dark*, our nighttime hallucinations can be stimulated by the sound of blood pumping in the ear. Bishop points out that Joyce alludes to this idea in the *Wake* with phrases such as "pulse of our slumber" (428.16) and "the heartbeats of sleep" (403.5). Bishop also explains how Joyce exploits this idea in the "Anna Livia Plurabelle" chapter of *Finnegans Wake*, and how water imagery can be traced to Joyce's interest in the mental process of dream production.

The passage on page 123 states that a "report"—an anagram of "Porter," another name for HCE or a possible candidate for the identity of the dreamer—has been "cleverly capsized" (in the "Finnegan's Wake" drinking song the corpse has a barrel of porter at his head). Here "cleverly" relates to mental processes and in "capsized"—aside from signifying a sinking vessel—something is being fitted to or into the human head, since "cap" derives from the Latin for head: *caput*. Furthermore, "saucily" is redolent of "souse," which is "A sound as of water surging against something" (*OED*). The word "republished" implies that the events of the "report" have previously been told and are to be retold. As a whole, the passage is a commentary on how the quotidian events of waking life and history are copied or recycled and "republished" as present hallucination, converted for the brain into something imitative, constructed, and secondary like Macpherson's *Ossian* or any history text. *Finnegans Wake* promotes the validity of the internally "forged," the mentally replicated, the inner simulacrum, the fake. In the Celtic core of the *Wake*, Hume's idealist philosophy meets Macpherson's "hoax" as a rejection of the "real" or material world.

The water imagery is crucial to this reading, as it shows the dreamer being influenced by external stimuli in the creation of his virtual world (though the dreamer still remains trapped in his own mind, *unaware* of the exterior world). The allusions to literature connect to the internal stories formed by the dreamer himself during the night. So, the reference to *Ossian* functions as a reminder that a dream is an altered "forgery" or a mutated simulation of reality. For Joyce, this forged reality, whether created in the mind or in the "smithy" of the soul, is always linked to a wider community, to the situation of the Irish and Celtic races. Here this link is highlighted through allusion to Macpherson. The oceanic imagery—as with the "Proteus" episode of *Ulysses*—provides the sense that dreams or the imagination can offer some sort of escape route from the concerns of the more fixed, stable "land" of reality.

As with the other Scottish writers Joyce employs in the *Wake*—especially Hume, Stevenson, and Hogg—Macpherson is used to describe the nature of (un)consciousness itself. Two main themes Joyce associates with Scotland are merged here, the sea (pointing to the ancient maritime links of the two nations) and consciousness (linked to the idealist "setting" of the text). In the children's lessons of II.ii, Joyce again alludes to Macpherson: "Allow me anchore, I bring down noth and carry awe. Now, then, take this in! One of the most murmurable loose carollaries ever Ellis threw his cookingclass. With Olaf as centrum and Olaf's lambtail for his spokesman circumscript a cyclone. Allow ter! Hoop! As round as the calf of an egg! O, dear me! O, dear me now! Another grand discobely! After Makefearsome's Ocean" (294.5–13). Crucially, the word "Ossian" switches to "Ocean," echoing the maritime language from page 123. A further maritime image is present in "anchore," which also indicates repetition through the Italian and French words for "again"—*ancora* and *encore*, respectively. Water generally signifies repetition and return in the *Wake*, as it does in its opening lines, for example: "riverrun, past Eve and Adam's, from swerve of shore to bend of bay, brings us by a commodius vicus of recirculation back to Howth Castle and Environs" (3.1–3). As with the character Crotthers in the "Oxen of the Sun" chapter of *Ulysses* and the Picts-and-Scots references of *Finnegans Wake*, Scotland is closely associated with the sea, with the "cordial waters" (*U*, 14.742) which connect Ireland and Scotland and which helped to create the shared mythological cycles upon which Macpherson drew for his poetry. Earlier, we saw how sea crossings to Scotland were a potential means of flight from Dublin for characters such as Mrs Malins. So, water in Joyce is "a conduit for the linkages of cultures as well as a means of escape" (Hegglund, 71). The connection of Macpherson and water also highlights the essentially pliant, constantly changing nature of folk "texts."

Here "Olaf," or alpha, and "lambtail," or lambda, refer to the geometrical figure on the previous page, 293. This figure consists of two overlapping circles and two triangles. Clive Hart has suggested that the diagram forms a map with the circles centered on the ancient ceremonial site of Uisneach in County Westmeath and Lambay Island, which lies off the coast of County Dublin (see C. Hart, *Structure*, 248–49). If so, the right-hand circle of the figure stretches out towards southwestern Scotland, encompassing the sea routes through which Gaelic mythology disseminated across the Irish Sea. As John Gordon points out, the illustration also represents the mother's vagina (*Plot Summary*, 191), with the triangle being "the Wake's premier symbol of origins" (185) since it represents, among other things, a river delta. So here Macpherson's supposed "discovery" of *Ossian* is compared to Shem and Shaun's introduction to their own origins. Joyce ties Macpherson's *Ossian* to birth, (re)creation, renewal, and continuation. The word "lambtail" also refers to Charles Lamb's children's book *Tales from Shakespeare* (1807), a further image of literary recycling.

As Jennifer Schiffer Levine has noted, "The problem of origins is connected at several points [in the *Wake*] to the notion of the writer as copyist and cheat" (109). This observation is especially pertinent here, since human origins are being specifically linked to James Macpherson. The conversion of "Mac" into "Make" stresses that Joyce is exploring themes relating to creation at this point, perhaps of humans through "fear," since the homophone *fir* is the Irish word for men. This reading would be appropriate given that the two boys are uncovering the place of their birth here.[17] In the Irish and Scottish mythology from which Macpherson created his poetry, Ossian/Oisín is the son of Finn/Fionn. Given that Finn is one of the many "avatars" of HCE in *Finnegans Wake*, it is unsurprising that Joyce associates *Ossian* with sons. In this section on reproduction the text itself is also, self-reflexively, commenting on its own artificial or "made" status through allusion to Macpherson.

Macpherson's work is also included at this point because it symbolizes continuation or "recirculation" (*FW*, 3.2), and ALP is the main figure in the *Wake* representing renewal through her identification as a river. The reproduction of life itself, expressed through the geometric image of the vagina, is compared to literature that was copied from an older source—a reproduction. For John B. Vickery, this is the essence of the *Wake*: "What *Finnegans Wake* as a whole constitutes [is] a metaphor or trope for the ceaselessly metamorphic actions of life itself" ("Sexual Metamorphosis," 217). Levine has commented on *Finnegans Wake* and its treatment of origins linking the production of people to the nature of language and literature: "We are born, we breed, we die. Our children in turn repeat the process and their children after them. What looks like change is only, perhaps, recycling, and we are bound to a wheel of repetition. For the word too it is recycling, repetition, quotation. Words have always already been spoken, it is impossible to return to their points of origin, to deny all of the uses they have already been put to" (111). Joyce's use of references to James Macpherson is related to the ideas that Levine discusses here. The passage of *Finnegans Wake* from II.ii includes circular imagery, which links to the diagram itself and expresses eternal continuation or the meetings of endings with beginnings. For example, "Olaf" alters Alpha, replacing an "A" with an "O" and evoking the Bible's "Alpha and Omega." "Olaf" is also a reference to the ninth-century Viking king of Dublin or to Olaf Sihtricson. Either way, the Norse origins of Dublin are evoked here. The circular words "spokesman," "circumspect," "cyclone," "Hoop!," and "discobely" (a play on the Greek Δισκοβόλος/*diskobolos*, "discus thrower"), point towards a spinning "wheel of repetition," and the rounded letter/word "O" is used repeatedly, for example, "O, dear me now!" In addition, "Hoop!" is heavily reminiscent of the birth at the beginning of the "Oxen of the Sun" episode of *Ulysses*: "Hoopsa boyaboy hoopsa!" (*U*, 14.5).

Macpherson is linked with renewal and with mental interiority from the very onset of *Finnegans Wake*. On the first page of the text, at the end of the fourth paragraph, we are presented with the following wisdom: "Phall if you but will, rise you must: and none so soon either shall the pharce for the nunce come to a setdown secular phoenish" (4.15–17). The first part of this sentence is based on a line from Macpherson's "Fingal II": "Let me be forgot in their cave; for I will not fly from Swaran,—If I must fall, my tomb shall rise amidst the fame of future times" (Macpherson, 66). It is not difficult to understand why Joyce selected this particular phrase from *Ossian* for inclusion in this prominent position in the *Wake*, since it speaks of falling and rising, or resurrection, and can be used to express the ascent/descent of HCE and the sleep and waking of the dreamer. Rising and falling are constantly linked to circularity and renewal in the *Wake*: "The genuine mystery lying at the heart of all resurrection and solar myths, emerges in miniature, but with undiminished strangeness, in any thinking about 'solarsystemised' process of sleep (263.24), which draws everybody in the world 'seriocosmically' (263.24–25) through periodic cycles of nonbeing and being, snuffing out and resurrecting lives like 'Finnegans'" (Bishop, 76). The passage on page 4 addresses the routine of nightly unconsciousness with a head "setdown" so that someone may "Phall" asleep "for the nunce," or temporarily. The onset of *Finnegans Wake* includes a "phoenish" where the beginning meets the end. The Macpherson allusion highlights the recycled and constructed nature of our mental contents while linking this to the position of a wider Celtic community.

Looking closely at this early reference to Macpherson, the first part of Joyce's adapted Ossianic line remains very close to unaltered English by Wakean standards. Only the "f" of "fall" is replaced by a "ph," a process repeated with "pharce" and "phoenish." Joyce here is linking the biblical fall, farce, and the Phoenix Park, as well as endings and beginnings through the myth of the phoenix rising from its ashes. According to Levine, "Throughout the *Wake* we are confronted with the dilemma of origins. . . . Sexual experience, the fall from grace, the fall into knowledge: *Finnegans Wake* explores their interconnections" (109). The passage directly precedes the introduction of HCE and is linked to his fall and resurrection. Phrases originating in Macpherson's work in the *Wake* are, as with allusions to Macpherson's name, habitually attached to imagery suggesting repetitions, renewal, or continuity. Indeed, the first two pages in which the above phrase is found are full of words and phrases suggesting repetition—"recirculation" (3.2), "rearrived" (3.5), "retaled" (3.17). Throughout *Finnegans Wake* Joyce uses *Ossian* to convey the idea that "the old order changeth and lasts like the first" (486.10).[18] Joyce tells us from the very onset of *Finnegans Wake* that this work will be concerned with repetitions and uses a key work of Scottish literature to introduce the reader to this theme. However, this trope is also linked in the *Wake* to Italian philosophy in the shape of Giambattista Vico's cyclical patterns of history. This connection between the "oceanic" cycles of Macpherson and Vico's cycles of history is made most explicit in the book's opening section.[19]

In the first chapter of *Finnegans Wake* there is also a meteorologically converted mention of Fingal, Macpherson's name for the Irish/Scottish mythological hero Fionn MacCumhaill: "And Jarl van Hoother bleet-hered atter her with a loud fingale: Stop domb stop come back with my earring stop" (22.9–10). This allusion to Fingal is placed deliberately within a specific section of the tale of the Prankquean, a vignette that takes up only three pages of the *Wake* but that reverberates throughout the work, particularly through distorted echoes of the Prankquean's baf-fling riddle: "Why do I am alook alike a poss of porterpease?" (21.18–19). The tale of the Prankquean is based partially on the story of the sixteenth-century Irish pirate Gráinne Ní Mháille and her kidnapping of the son of the Earl of Howth, as well as the Celtic legend of Diarmuid and Gráinne.

In Joyce's version, the Prankquean arrives at the castle of Jarl van Hoother and poses a riddle similar to Shem's "first riddle of the universe" (170.04) and to the children's games of II.i. Jarl van Hoother refuses to solve the conundrum, and the Prankquean responds—unreasonably enough—by abducting one of van Hoother's sons.[20] This process is re-peated until peace is restored at the third attempt, as is customary in myths or folk tales. The relevance of Macpherson to this story has been explained by Michael H. Begnal with reference to the theory of human history advanced by Vico:

> Vico's idea is reflected here in the combinations of threes which occur throughout the Prankquean's adventure. She asks her riddle three times, van Hoother has three children, each significant phrase is stated three different ways ("be dermot," "be redtom," "be dom ter," etc.), and, most important, the Prankquean makes three trips to van Hoother's castle. It is these three forays which clearly point to Vico, for each occurs in one of the Viconian ages. She first appears in the divine age . . . she returns in the heroic age, as evidenced by the allusions to such heroes of the past as Finn MacCool ("finegale" recalls "Fingal," name for Finn in the "Ossian" poems). (Begnal, "Prankquean," 14)

Joyce includes an allusion to Macpherson's poetry here in accordance with a section representing the "heroic age" of Vico's cyclical model of human history. Further uses of Macpherson's poetry can also be explained by referring to Joyce's use of Vico's theory on the ages of history. In particular, the "Mime of Mick, Nick and the Maggies" shares a tripartite structure with the story of the Prankquean and also features references to Macpherson's poetry. Macpherson's work is more useful to Joyce compared to other, more "legitimate" or "authentic" sources of Celtic mythology, since the "cyclical" nature of history is already inherent in the work as it is largely a reproduction of previous myths and folklore. Whereas references to Hogg and Stevenson worked in conjunction with Joyce's engagements with the concepts of Giordano Bruno, the work of Macpherson fits into a Viconian pattern of repeated cycles.

As with Joyce's use of Hume, there is certainly something otherworldly or ghostly about the use of Macpherson in *Finnegans Wake*. Take, for example, this extended misty, and imprecise, section:

> lo you there, Cathmon-Carbery and thank Movies from the innermost depths of my still attrite heart, Wherein the days of youyouth are evermixed mimine, now ere the compline hour of being alone athands itself and a puff or so before we yield our spiritus to the wind, for . . . it is to you, firstborn and firstfruit of woe, to me branded sheep, pick of the wastepaperbaskel, by the tremours of Thundery and Ulerin's dogstar, you alone, windblasted tree of the knowledge of beautiful andevil, ay, clothed upon with the meteur and shimmering like the horescens, astroglodynamonologos, the child of Nilfit's father, blzb, to me unseen blusher in an obscene coalhole, the cubilibum of your secret sigh, dweller in the downand-outermost where voice only of the dead may come. (194.2–20, section in parenthesis omitted)

The plays on Ossianic materal here include "Cathmon-Carbery," "the days of youyouth are evermixed mimine," "hour of being alone," "athands," "we yield our spiritus to the wind," "tremours of Thundery," "Ulerin," "treeblasted," clothed upon the meteur," "secret sigh," and "voice only of the dead." Without the missing central parenthetical passage the two sections become a large cluster of allusions to the work of Macpherson.[21]

The passage has an ominous feel to it, with "meteur" (Latin *metuor*, I am feared) and "horescens" (Latin *horrescens*, shuddering) adding to the sense of foreboding provided by the allusion to Campbell's poem, while "spiritus" and "voice of the dead" give the passage a supernatural feel. Vico's theory that language began when our thunderstruck ancestors were frightened into caves by celestial disturbances is present here, with "Thundery"; "astroglodynamonologos," which alludes to τρωγλοδύται/ *tröglodytai*, Greek for "cave dwellers"; and λόγος/*logos*, Greek for "word, study, wisdom, reasoning." Furthermore, "unseen," "coalhole," and "dweller in the downandoutermost" suggest the habitation of caves. This combination of caves, spirits, and ghosts with Celtic subject material recalls the mausoleums and chthonic dwelling-places of the sections connected with David Hume.

As we have seen before, vocabulary from Macpherson's poetry is connected with the question of recurrence, to represent continuation by copying, and to develop the idea that nothing is new, only recreated: "Nilfit," from Latin *nil* [*nihil*] *fit*, "nothing is made." By a process of continual copying we still carry with us behaviors and ways of thinking that have developed over generations. Macpherson's poetry is used by Joyce to signal this inescapable debt to the past. As John Bishop has written: "If consciousness is a man-made property that changes in historical time, then each individual owes the way in which he thinks to the generation of his parents; yet his parents owe his thinking and behaviour to the generation of their parents; and so forth . . . 'in the modifications of our own human minds'—'the traditions of all dead generations weighing like an Alp on the brains of the living,' in one of Marx's psychoanalytical phrases" (Bishop, 183). Joyce's use of Macpherson's otherworldly poetry here connects the deathly and ghostly condition of sleep—"dweller in the downandoutermost"—with a suggestion of the essentially unchanging nature of human consciousness and humanity itself—"the child of Nilfit's father."[22]

The parenthetical section separating the two passages deals with "ricorso": "all that has been done has yet to be done and done again, when day's woe, and lo, you're doomed, joyday dawns and la, you dominate" (*FW*, 194.10–12). Indeed, as the page becomes an introduction to ALP, the wider subject of the end of the chapter seems to be ricorso or "racecourseful" (194.26). The lines "all that has been done has yet to be done and done again, when's day's woe, and lo, you're doomed, joyday dawns and la, you dominate" (194.10–12) match the Ossianic passage from page 131 we considered earlier. ALP's coming is heralded with words relating to water: "spring," "drops," "bridges," "weirs," "bog," "pools." All water has been through the cycle from clouds, fallen as rain, flowed through rivers to the sea and been evaporated back into the air. Joyce uses this imagery in the *Wake*, in a similar way to the fashion in which Macpherson's poetry is used, to express his conviction that nothing is new, only a fluid repetition. Again, aquatic imagery is linked to *Ossian*, with the production of dreams being linked to the forgeries of Macpherson. While Hogg and Stevenson undermine the idea that there may be a single and unchanging reality and Hume maintains that truth is never really attainable, Macpherson's recycled work is "mesmeric" and "imprecise," appropriate enough for the representation of a foggy and mesmerized consciousness.

JOYCE, MACPHERSON, AND SCOTLAND

The example of James Macpherson is valuable to Joyce for a number of reasons. Macpherson's poetry—which was supposedly a lost and rediscovered body of epic poetry—helps Joyce in maintaining the theme of disappearance and reappearance, connected to the fall and rise of HCE and the fall into sleep and ascent into consciousness. Joyce could easily have used solely "authentic" Irish or Gaelic mythology in *Finnegans Wake*, but the deliberate inclusion of material based on Macpherson's work provides connotations of discovery, forgery, and the recycling processes of textual, mythological, and mental "matter" that would not have been supplied by the "genuine article." The Irish mythology, which the contemporary critics O'Connor and O'Halloran had sought to defend, had not disappeared into obscurity and been "rediscovered" in the way Macpherson claimed his poetry had been. "Real" Irish mythology does not connote artificiality or reprocessing for Joyce, since it had not been deliberately processed or forged in the same way. Furthermore, enlisting Macpherson's *Ossian* expands Joyce's program of linking the Celtic world in his texts to visions, dreams, and memory. *Ossian* can be considered another example of the aftereffects of an ancient Irish thalassocracy, since it is a rehash of a shared culture, a "rinvention of vestiges" (*FW*, 602.26) which exists as a result of ancient Irish emigration to Scotland and the maritime proliferation of Gaelic civilization. Along with the motif of the Picts and the Scots, Macpherson in *Finnegans Wake* is a submerged causeway between the cultures and shared historical events of Ireland and Scotland.

As we shall see, the many links between *Ossian* and the word "ocean" can be explained by Joyce's view of the work as representing the maritime links between the two nations. Something similar occurs with the briny amalgam figure Crotthers in the "Oxen of the Sun" and "Circe" episodes of *Ulysses*. But as early as *Dubliners* Joyce is writing about sea crossings between the two countries. The motif of the Picts and Scots developed the idea of the Irish beginning of Scottish history and the divisions and connections between Ireland and Scotland while linking this to the fragmented mental state of the dreamer. References to the accumulated, collected, and processed works of Macpherson stress recurrences rather than resemblances, hinting at the duplication or doubling of an originally Irish culture across the water in Scotland.

Finnegans Wake was constructed by collecting and working with and on fragments of previously existing concepts, designs, and textual material. These found objects are "reclaimed," reconfigured, set out in new forms with new functions. Like everything else in the *Wake*, texts are conceived of as continual processes of copying, replication, and recycling. Works of art are seen here as not new, standing alone, or complete in themselves. In *Finnegans Wake* cultural artefacts are manifestations of a continuing process, steps on an evolutionary pathway. Through comparison of James Macpherson and Shem, Joyce uses a major work of Scottish literature to comment on the nature of his own artistic venture. Similarly, Joyce suggests, human identities are constructed from leftovers of the past in the form of cultural inheritance. Dreams also operate in an analogous fashion, arising from old memories, fears, and aspirations woven together into something new but also "fake," — history repeated as illusion. Consciousness is, for Joyce, an unreal report of an inaccessible and removed reality.

In using Macpherson's poetry for his own purposes, Joyce is also reviving writing which was in part an attempt to preserve something of the Gaelic culture of the Highlands. This culture was under threat of destruction due to the punitive measures carried out by the British state following the Jacobite defeat at Culloden in 1746 which marked the end of the failed "furtivfired" campaign (*FW*, 514.27) led by Charles Edward

Stuart.[23] Fiona Stafford has discussed Macpherson in relation to his historical background in her introduction to his poetry:

> Between the ages of ten and eighteen, James Macpherson . . . lived through scenes of appalling violence, and saw his home and family under the constant threat of further oppression. During this period, a series of measures were implemented to crush the distinctive Highland way of life, and render the region safe for ever. After 1746, the tartan plaid was banned, and no Highlander allowed to carry arms or play the bagpipes. . . . Such measures were a more Draconian development from the earlier, relatively peaceful, attempts to open communications and transport networks in the Highlands, and to encourage the use of English rather than Gaelic. But it is in the context of systematic cultural destruction that Macpherson's efforts to collect the old heroic poetry can be seen; they were, at least in part, an attempt to repair some of the damage to the Highlands sustained in the wake of the Jacobite Risings. (introduction, ix–x)

The rising of 1745–46 was an attempt to return the Catholic Stuart dynasty to the British throne.[24] However, the "Young Pretender" Charles Stuart had promised in his manifesto at Glenfinnan to dissolve the union between Scotland and England following victory, and "No Union" was a common flag motto of the movement (Devine, *Nation*, 37). Joyce is writing into *Finnegans Wake* strands of Gaelic and anti-Union Scottish history through allusions both to the events of that history and to the culture those historical circumstances produced.

Joyce wished to give a large-scale depiction of the totality of Irish history in the *Wake*, so an inclusion of the impact of Ireland on the outside world was necessary. As the Gaelic dimension of Scotland can be traced back to Ireland and Irish emigration, the background to *Ossian* has a direct link to Ireland. Furthermore, Joyce counters the inclusion of material relating to the occupations and invasions of Ireland by working with cultures connected to an Irish overseas conquest. The movement of the "Scoti" across the "moylean Main" (*FW*, 25.27) is a rare instance of Irish overseas territorial expansion, and Joyce's attention to Scottish Gaelic culture is linked to these events, a reversal of the familiar pattern. Furthermore, a large number of Irish troops were involved in the '45 campaign on the side of Charles Stuart. Finally, as Colin MacCabe points out, "*Finnegans Wake*, with its sustained dismemberment of the English linguistic and literary heritage, is perhaps best understood in relation to the struggle against imperialism" ("Finnegans," 4). Joyce can thus be read as an instance of literature connected to Scottish resistance to the British state (although Macpherson himself later became secretary to the governor in colonial Florida and then a member of the British Parliament) as part of a broader look at the history of London-based domination and the various cultural reactions against it. Joyce's Ossianic allusions function as a way of bringing together a consideration of the recycled nature of our mental activity with a portrayal of the importance of dream and memory in Celtic culture. But perhaps the allusions also bring a certain gravitas to *Finnegans Wake*. When singing a favorite song from Massenet's *Werther* to his friend Ottacaro Weiss, Joyce would point out the origins of this section of the libretto: "As though to add dignity to it, he said more than once to Weiss, 'You know, the words are taken from Ossian'" (*JJII*, 393–94).

SIX

Joyce's Burns Night

PROTEAN POET

Themes of mental duality, imperialism, and racial mixing all converge when one studies Joyce's use of Robert Burns in *Finnegans Wake*. As the Joyce scholar Adaline Glasheen once noted, "There's an awful lot of Burns in *FW*" (Burns and Gaylord, 31). While this is certainly true, some of the Scottish songs in *Finnegans Wake* could be designated as Burns songs or simply as traditional Scottish songs. Such is the nature of the folk music tradition in Scotland—as in Ireland—where lyrics and tunes can vary over time and from singer to singer, a process similar to the transmission of Celtic folklore or mythology.[1] Indeed, the initial popularity of Burns needs to be put into the context of romantic-era Celticism: "Burns' adoption of the mantle of 'bard' played to the faux-Celticism that came into vogue in the eighteenth century, attested to in the literary taste of the Scottish Enlightenment for 'Ossian'" (Carruthers, *Robert Burns*, 14). Despite his own Lowland origins, Burns's numerous appearances in the *Wake* also need to be read in a Celtic context.

Joyce held two collections of Burns's poetry in his Trieste library. These were *The Poetical Works*, published by the Oxford University Press in 1919, and *The Poetical Works of Robert Burns*, published by Milner and Sowerby in 1855 (Ellmann, *Consciousness*, 103). Since there is a relatively small amount of Burns in *Ulysses*—the composition of which corre-sponds to the existence of the Trieste library—we can conclude with relative safety that Joyce kept the works for enjoyment's sake at this time, rather than utilizing them in his own creative endeavors. Certainly Stanislaus Joyce was an admirer: "Scotland, too, has its Gaelic poets; but it has a host of poets even before Burns, in comparison with whose songs Anglo-Irish love poetry until Yeats is a very thin vintage" (S. Joyce, 164). As *Finnegans Wake* contains a great deal of material relating to Burns, the poetry must have become of more use or importance to Joyce during work on this project.[2]

Why is it that *Finnegans Wake* has so many more allusions to Burns's work than *Ulysses*? One reason is that Burns's work suits the ambience of HCE's bar and of the wake ceremony itself. Singing, particularly the performance of popular folk or traditional songs such as the work of Burns, though a subject and thematic device of *Ulysses*, is arguably much more important to the structure of *Finnegans Wake*, since the latter text's "plot," such as it is, deals in part with the lively, alcoholic, and musical atmosphere of an Irish wake. The increase in attention to Burns fits in with Joyce's amplified interest in Scotland generally, as he worked more Scottish history and culture into the *Wake* than his previous works. This is an important element of Joyce's attempts to include representative work of all of European culture in the *Wake* as part of its encyclopedic nature but also as a feature of his look at the nature of the "relations" of Ireland in the text, those nations who are "racially" linked to Ireland. The Picts-and-Scots nodal system is a further example of this project (and this is, as we shall see, linked to Burns in the *Wake*). Finally, Burns is involved more in the *Wake* since using his poetry allows Joyce to attend to the various divisions of Irish society, including those brought about through Scottish plantation.

The songs of Burns would have been well known in late nineteenth-/early twentieth-century Dublin, so it is fairly plausible that a Chapelizod pub would resound to the melodies of Burns tunes along with other popular music. As has been noted, the folk music endlessly playing in *Finnegans Wake* is not exclusively Irish: "It would be wrong to overstress the Irishness of the songs in *Finnegans Wake*. The demotic culture on which the book is based may be primarily Dublin-Irish, but . . . there are several quotations from Scottish songs, particularly Burns's" (Hodgart and Worthington, 16). Burns's material adds to this musical representation of "demotic culture" and reflects the tastes of "average" men and women in Dublin. Only Thomas Moore would have surpassed "the bard" in terms of fame and popularity as a songwriter at this place and time. The use of allusions to Burns's songs in the *Wake* is comparable to the use of Moore, though less extensive. In fact, the example of Burns and the musical adaptations of his work was a direct precedent for the production of Moore's *Melodies*, while the latter works had their roots in a spate of antiquarianism associated with the United Irishmen:

> Moore's *Melodies* have recently attracted serious attention from readers of Irish literature and students of Irish music. They are a strange synthetic mix: working with the music collected by the United Irish antiquarian Edward Bunting, in 1807 Moore undertook to produce a series of songs based on Irish tunes for his publisher William Power. These songs would match English lyrics composed by Moore, to melodies originally performed on the Irish harp. . . . It was hoped that the series would repeat the great success of the settings made by many composers of the Scottish songs of Robert Burns. (M. Campbell, 189)[3]

The example of the "synthetic" matching of Burns to music was a key inspiration behind the production of Moore's *Melodies*. Matthew Hodgart and Mabel Worthington discuss the vast number of allusions in the *Wake* to the songs of Moore, and some of their main conclusions can be applied to Joyce's incorporation of Burns's songs:

> It may be asked with Joyce why Joyce went to such fantastic lengths to work in most or all of the *Melodies*: the answer is that these songs were entirely suitable to his purpose. First, their use is naturalistic, since every household that could afford it possessed a copy of the *Melodies* with the music, and the songs were on everybody's lips. Secondly, they provide a complete cycle, covering almost every topic of interest to the Irish and as such prefiguring *Finnegans Wake*. Though faintly absurd on the printed page, they come to life when sung, expressing simple feelings in subtle rhythmical patterns. Apart from Burns, Moore is almost the only writer of true songs since the

end of the seventeenth century. Thirdly Joyce must have enjoyed them as art. (11)

The use of Burns's songs would certainly be naturalistic, as many would have been well known in Dublin in the late nineteenth and early twentieth centuries, so the inclusion of Burns's songs adds to the "realism" — such as it is—of *Finnegans Wake*. The musical traditions of Scotland would be pretty much unavoidable in the writing of such an enterprise, especially given Scotland's proximity to Ireland, the historical connections between the two countries, and Joyce's own personal acquaintance with the country and its cultures.

The year 2009 marked Robert Burns's 250th birthday (it was also the 70th anniversary of the publication of *Finnegans Wake*). This occasion was used as an opportunity to hold a yearlong promotion throughout Scotland of Scottish culture as part of an attempt to lure back members of the worldwide Scottish diaspora, with the largest clan gathering in history taking place in Edinburgh during that summer. The series of events, named The Homecoming (an inspiration behind Ireland's similar and much criticized 2013 event The Gathering), appropriated the image of Robert Burns throughout its campaign. Burns's likeness even appeared on specially commissioned Coca-Cola bottles in Scotland. Of course, this commodification of Burns is nothing new. For example, Burns appears on the Bank of Scotland £5 note, sharing a distinction with Joyce in being featured on the currency of the land of their birth. In the twenty-first century Robert Burns remains symbolic of Scotland. Joyce's works have also seized upon Burns in his capacity as Caledonian emblem. However, this is a deeply complex and ambiguous symbol. While Burns has been championed as a patriotic Scottish radical mourning the loss of Scottish independence, his likeness can also be seen adorning the walls of Orange Lodges in the west of Scotland. Joyce adopts this duality (another "Celtic" contradiction), linking Burns to a broader anti-imperialist program but also to the nascent project of empire itself through an association with the Ulster-Scots. Adding to the complications, Owen Dudley Edwards suggests that Joyce may not even have thought of Burns as being Scottish: "Everyone in Ireland knew Burns's songs and nearly everyone tried to sing them. They were the new vernacular as Gaelic was dying. Burns was so Irish they used *Sweet*

Afton as the name of the best-known Irish cigarette, manufactured by Carroll's of Dundalk: Rabbie's face on the front, Rabbie's opening lines of Afton Water underneath a suitably idyllically tragic landscape" (Edwards, "Scotching Joyce," 15). Alongside this supposed Irishness, Burns is strongly associated with Scotland in *Finnegans Wake*; he is not simply a detached, nonaligned source of quotable poetry. At crucial junctures in the *Wake* where Joyce alludes to Burns and/or his poetry, Joyce is also clearly exploring Scottish history and identity. However, Burns in *Finnegans Wake* also represents the Scots presence in Ulster and a meeting of contrary cultures. The Scottish poet functions as part of Joyce's commentary on the divisions and tensions of Ireland, particularly the north of the island. Rather than existing as solely Irish or Scottish, Burns becomes—like the Picts and Scots, Crotthers and *Ossian*—emblematic of the cross-cultural currents flowing between Ireland and Scotland and the resultant plural and hybrid identities. Fittingly, the word Burns is used to signify both fire and water in *Finnegans Wake*. *Burn*, apart from meaning "to combust" or "to incinerate," is also the Scots term for "stream" (as in "Bannockburn," where the fourteenth-century battlefield was situated at the Bannock Burn near Falkirk). Furthermore, although *uisge* is the more commonly used term in Gaelic, *bùrn* is a Lewis dialect Gaelic word for water. Both fire and water are symbolic of renewal or ongoing developments in *Finnegans Wake*, since they are associated with the mythical Phoenix and natural cycles, respectively. Both burning and flowing are *processes*, however, and Burns—like Macpherson—is linked by Joyce to the continuously variable or shifting nature of both art and human communities.

In a volume of essays sketching the links between Burns and Ulster, Frank Ferguson and Andrew R. Holmes have made the following comments:

> Robert Burns is a protean poet. . . . Championed and censored in equal measure since his entry into public life, no Scottish poet before or since has been woven so prominently into the weft of Scotland's national fabric. However, his reputation was such that he did not remain the property of Scotland. A poet of global renown, many nations, regions and individuals have declared their devotion to him. Indeed, one does not need to travel far from his Ayrshire birthplace

to the northern counties of Ireland to find communities in the eighteenth and nineteenth centuries who made special claims as his audience, brother poets and critics. . . . Burns, as an inhabitant of Ayr in the south west of Scotland, would have been fully aware of the proximity of Ireland and the traffic across the North Channel. Irish melodies and songs found their way into his poetry, Irish poets sought him out on their literary pilgrimages and, later, members of his family settled in Dundalk and Belfast. . . . Burns symbolizes major connections between Scotland and the north of Ireland in terms of literature, religion, politics and culture. (9)

Unsurprisingly—given Burns's long-standing popularity in Ulster and the general Scottish religious and cultural influence there—whenever Burns is connected to Irish matters in *Finnegans Wake*, it is to the north of Ireland. As with Crotthers and the Picts and Scots, Burns is part of the blurring of identities of Scottish and Irish relations in *Ulysses* and *Finnegans Wake*. The function of Burns in Joyce's work is as an inversion of Macpherson's role in a sense, since passages cited from Macpherson highlighted the Irish influence on Scotland. Sections alluding to Burns provide a commentary on the opposite process, the Scottish impact on Ireland.

The "temporal conflation" (Mackay, 106) of Joyce's works has the strange effect of giving chronologically distant historical occurrences equal prominence. Seemingly unrelated conflicts are also merged together in the *Wake*. In *Finnegans Wake* all history is given equivalent value or importance, suggesting that all human activity is of significance, or that everything is equally insignificant when viewed from a "cosmic" perspective (or that it is essentially "unreal"). As Seamus Deane has pointed out, it could be argued that this has the effect of producing an indifferent uniformity in Joyce's texts: "The pluralism of [Joyce's] styles and languages, the absorbent nature of his controlling myths and systems, finally gives a certain harmony to varied experience. But, it could be argued, it is the harmony of indifference, one in which everything is a version of something else, where sameness rules over diversity, where contradiction is finally and disquietingly written out" (*Heroic Styles*, 15). Certainly Joyce's look at Irish/Scottish history tends to seek the common and the corresponding in the midst of the diverse and the different. Although—

as Joyce was well aware—Scotland was complicit at later stages of English-dominated imperialism in the form of the now largely obsolete and moribund British Empire, Joyce's writing displays a "memory" or historical awareness that stretches from 1939 back, past the union of 1707, to the era of Scottish resistance to English power. Of course, Ireland and Scotland share experiences of being at the end of English domination and control. Both aspects of Scotland's relationship to imperialism are alluded to in Joyce's works, its opposition and its eventual compliance through the capitulation of its elites (although its current independence movement also has a significant Joycean connection).[4] One way out of this bind is to view Joyce's form of a static or unreal history as part of his form of Celtic idealism and skepticism, a riposte to Anglo-Saxon materialism.

Unfortunately there has been very little critical analysis of Joyce's use of Burns songs and poetry, a negligence that is part of a larger dearth of critical attention paid to Scottish subjects in Joyce's works. Kimberly J. Devlin has written an essay entitled "'See Ourselves as Others See Us': The Role of the Other in Indeterminate Selfhood," using a line of Burns's poetry as part of its title.[5] However, the essay is more concerned with Lacanian psychoanalysis than Scottish poetry. Zack Bowen's *Bloom's Old Sweet Song: Essays on Joyce and Music* mentions Burns only once, where Bowen points out that "Love's old sweet song" has become the "Auld Lang Syne" of the Joycean community (137). As with almost any set of song lyrics, Burns songs make "sense" only when sung, and Burns's lyrics add, in no small fashion, to the musical quality of *Finnegans Wake*. But they also help to create the "weird ontology" (Hofheinz, 162) of the book.

Of all the Burns songs and poems alluded to in *Finnegans Wake*, probably "Auld Lang Syne" has received the most critical attention. Of course, it should not be particularly surprising that "Auld Lang Syne" appears in the *Wake*, considering the primary subject matter of the song is the passing of time, and that it is a drinking song, well suited to the ambience of a public house. It barely needs pointing out that *Finnegans Wake* is saturated in the songs and atmosphere of the bar and that alcohol is central to the elusive "plot" of the *Wake*. In *Joyce's Kaleidoscope*, Philip Kitcher discusses the appearances of "Auld Lang Syne" with reference to the "Four Masters," who seem to have adopted Burns's song as their group anthem: "Auld Lang Syne, the song that traditionally cele-brates the passing of the year, with its evocations of the old days, is an appropriate song for the four old men, and it recurs through their con-versation: here, the cup of kindness—'kindest yet'—is a palliative, a mo-mentary relief for the condition to which they find themselves reduced" (184). For Kitcher, the use of the song in association with the four old men is primarily as a means of blocking out reality. The song is fre-quently associated with these decrepit drunks. In II.iv where "the Four" are spying on the journey of the Celtic lovers Tristan and Iseult there are a number of references to the song: "auld lang syne" (384.17; 393.16); "for a cup of kindness yet" (386.8–9; 397.19); "for auld acquaintance" (389.11; 398.14); "never brought to mind" (390.21); "be forgot" (390.23); and "auld luke syne" (398.26).

Aside from the facts that "the Four" are generally nostalgic or ob-sessed with the past and that they enjoy a drink or two, a further reason they are so fond of "Auld Lang Syne" is that one of their group, as with the posse of merry medical students in "Oxen of the Sun," has a semi-Scottish derivation. Usually the four old men are associated with the four provinces of Ireland. However, Johnny MacDougal is described as "Poor Johnny of the clan of the Dougals, the poor Scuitsman (Hohannes!), nothing if not amorous, dinna forget" (*FW*, 391.4–5), a description that contains the Scots "dinna" meaning "do not." Is Johnny singing "Auld Lang Syne" in a drunken fit of homesickness? The appearance of a Scot-tish or partly Scottish character here is attended with Scottish song in the same way that the Crotthers is surrounded by Scottish language and cultural references in "Oxen of the Sun."

While Philip Kitcher identifies "Auld Lang Syne" primarily with "the Four" and sees it as indicative of the desire of "the Four" to forget or to erase reality, John Bishop stresses how Joyce adapts Burns's lyrics as a way of creating the obscurity, amnesia, and confused chronology of sleep: "Evidence given about exact dates and times ('he would be there to remember the filth of November . . . the dates of ould lanxiety') designates as well the absence of perceived historical time altogether— discrete 'fifth' slipping into blacked-out 'filth' and 'the days of our anxiety' blurring away into 'Auld Lang Syne' (where 'auld acquaintance' 'be forgot' and is 'never brought to mind'" (Bishop, 46). The allusions to "Auld Lang Syne" work both as descriptive of the old men and also of the experience of sleep; once again the situation of the *Wake* is linked to Scottish culture. As with the material on David Hume, Joyce uses Burns's anthem to describe the idealist entrapment of sleep in the *Wake*, an imprisoned space where historical time and the external, material world are absent, where everything is "forgot" and cannot properly be "brought to mind" (this is linked to an assault on Protestant authority with the reference to the Gunpowder Plot, "filth of November"). As is well known, "Auld Lang Syne" is traditionally sung at New Year's Eve / Hogmanay, and this liminal phase between two years is where we find these old men attempting to escape history and time itself.

JOYCE, SCOTLAND, AND ULSTER

During a particularly volatile, hot-tempered section of the interrogation of Shaun by "the Four," an unmistakable Ulster accent begins to reverberate (and berate) as the exchange descends into something of a stramash. A northern brogue can be heard amid a cacophony of allusions to various Scottish songs, poems, writers, locations and items, including a striking and prominent reference to Robert Burns:

> —Angly as arrows, but you have right, my celtslinger! Nils, Mugn and Cannut. Should brothers be for awe then?
> —So let use off be octo while oil bike the bil and wheel whang till wabblin befoul you but mere and mire trullopes will knaver mate a game on the bibby bobby burns of.
> —Quatsch! What hill ar yu fluking about ye lamelookond fyats! I'll discipline ye! Will you swear or affirm the day to yur second sight noo and recant that all yu affirmed to profetised at first sight for his southerly accent was all paddyflaherty? Will ye, ay or nay? (520.22–31)

Further signals of the text taking on a Scottish slant here include references to a "highlandman's trousertree" (521.7); a "dram" (521.8), which is a Scottish measure of whisky; a "scotty pictail" (521.11), which alludes to the ancient tribes the Picts and the Scots; and a use of "Guid," the Scots word for "good" (521.31). Furthermore, the word "invertedness"

(522.31) appears, in which the Highland city Inverness is alluded to (see chapter 4 for a discussion on "invertedness").[6]

Alongside these Scottish elements, the primary subject of the exchange is obviously Ulster anger or "Northern Ire" (522.4), as signified in part by references to Bushmills distillery or "Bushmillah!" (521.15), the Belfast civic motto "*Pro tanto quid retribuamus?*" (521.10–11), and Queen's University Belfast: "Queen's" (521.35). [7] The text also begins to mimic the Ulster accent: "Ef I chuse to put a bullet like yu through the grill for heckling what business is that of yours, yu bullock?" (522.1–2). A raw religious and political divide becomes apparent in the section: "Did any orangepeelers or greengoaters appear periodically up your sylvan family tree?" (522.16–17). The dispute here between Shaun and his interrogators begins to display the tensions and divisions of the north of Ireland.

The paragraph that reads "So let use off be octo while oil bike the bil and wheel whang till wabblin befoul you but mere and mire trullopes will knaver mate a game on the bibby bobby burns of" not only namedrops Robert Burns as "bobby burns" and alludes to his poem "A Man's a Man for A' That,"[8] but is set to the tune of the well-known Scottish traditional song "Loch Lomond." Since "Loch Lomond" is concerned with death—me an' my true love will ne'er meet again"—it is not difficult to see why it became a useful tool for Joyce in the writing of the *Wake*. In fact, the song was a favorite of Joyce's own social circle in Paris. Jacques Mercanton and Lloyd Parks have described how Joyce and his clique would entertain themselves in the autumn of 1938 as "the threat of war loomed over the forthcoming publication of [Joyce's] book" (105):

> Music alone could cheer those anxious hearts. Mrs. Jolas sang a few Negro spirituals, Joyce, old Irish songs in that warm voice of his, capable of such gentle modulations. Seated around the table, we took up the refrain in a chorus, or else accompanied his light singing with our humming, "Loch Lomond" or "Drink to me only with thine eyes," which he sang in a restrained, an almost interior, voice, his face illuminated by the grace of the moment. (Mercanton, 106)

As with the melodies of Thomas Moore, one of the reasons "Loch Lomond" (not an old Irish song as Mercanton and Parks perhaps think) appears in *Finnegans Wake* is simply that Joyce enjoyed it, as the above anecdote shows. Joyce developed a soft spot in the '30s for the more touristy aspects of Scottish culture, with his singing of "Loch Lomond" and his eye-catching tartan attire.[9] However, the singing of "Loch Lomond"—a song of war, loss, and separation—must have held a special poignancy in the fraught Paris of 1938.

The passage from page 520 is not the only occasion in *Finnegans Wake* where the lyrics of "Loch Lomond" are sung. In II.iii, during the Butt and Taff section, where two television personalities, who are also versions of the brothers Shem and Shaun, perform, there are three separate units of allusion:

> Scutterer of guld, he is retourious on every roudery! The lyewdsky so so sewn of a fitchid! With his walshbrushup? And his boney bogey braggs?
>   BUTT (*after his tongues in his cheeks, with pinkpoker pointing out in rutene to impassible abjects beyond the mistomist towards Lissnaluhy such as the Djublian Alps and the Hoofd Ribeiro as where he and his trulock may ever make a game*). The field of karhags and that bloasted tree. Forget not the felled! For the lomondations of Oghrem! (340.1–9)

The three allusions are, of course, "boney bogey braggs," "*where he and his trulock may ever make a game*," and "lomondations." On previous pages the descriptions of Butt and Taff's own utterances include a reference to the Scottish traditional song "The Flowers of the Forest" or "the florahs of the follest" (339.25), a lament over Scotland's catastrophic defeat at the Battle of Flodden in 1513, and an allusion to Burns's poem "Sweet Afton" in "Till even so aften" (338.14). In the above passage, the phrase "boney bogey braggs" represents Shem and his emaciated condition ("boney"), his quasi-demonic status ("bogey"), and his tendency to boast ("braggs"). Butt, the Shemish figure, is named a "Scutterer," which echoes "Scuts" (245.28) or "Scots." As a play on the word "stutterer," it also links Butt to the guilty speech impediment of HCE. Through an allusion to Thomas Moore's "Forget Not the Field," also known as "The Lamentations of Aughrim"—a song that commemorates James II's defeat at Aughrim in 1691, in which Scottish troops fought on the

Williamite side—Joyce once again unites the figures of Burns and Moore. As Vincent Cheng has made clear, "It was the Irish defeat at Aughrim a year after the Boyne that finally sealed English domination of Ireland," and as such it is "a poignant symbol of domination and colonization" (*Joyce, Race, and Empire*, 144). Joyce thus links Shem to decisive losses of Scottish and Irish histories: Flodden and Aughrim. Here Scotland and Ireland's subaltern situations are compared, or, alternatively, Scotland's involvement in British domination of Ireland is highlighted.[10]

Turning again to the section from page 520 of *Finnegans Wake* in which Burns appears in an Ulster context, the funeral amusements or rituals covered in previous pages of the *Wake* are again being discussed: "With the funeral comes 'funeral games,'" and the meeting of Shem and Shaun "becomes the subject of a trial" where the testimony regards "the antagonists rolling around 'togutter' in the 'Black Pig's Dyke' (517.13–15)" (Gordon, *Plot Summary*, 245). There has been an altercation involving Shem and Shaun in the dirt, or "some clever play in the mud" (517.3), indicated in the passage "they rolled togutter into the ditch together?" (517.14). This discussion of the confrontations between the brothers continues on page 518 with an allusion to the Picts and the Scots.[11]

The various streams of Scottish material and allusion form a confluence in this section, against the backdrop of a northern Irish dispute. This section is another of *Finnegans Wake*'s Scottish/Irish "nodal points." The fighting in the "ditch"—or bed, since they are virtually indistinguishable in *Finnegans Wake*—continues in the section that alludes to Burns. The word "octo" relates to the eight hours of the day spent in sleep. *Whang* is a Scots word meaning "a stroke, blow; a cut with a whip," according to the *Concise Scots Dictionary*.[12] *Wabble* is another Scots word, meaning to "walk unsteadily, totter, waddle" (*CSD*), while "wheel" provides a sense of cyclical repetition. So, the "wheel whang till wabblin befoul you" on page 520 translates into English as something like "we'll constantly beat each other up until your unsteadiness upsets you and you are covered with filth." Of course, such a "translation" lacks both Joyce's economical use of language and the lilting melody of "Loch Lomond." The filth they are liable to descend into is the earth of the grave, which in *Finnegans Wake* also functions as a cipher for the obscurity and "burial'" of sleep. If a fall into death or sleep occurs to the brothers here, they may also end up "lamelookond" (520.27) or "limelooking" (95.14). In other words, sleep/death has rendered the brothers literally or figuratively "blind." The word "limelooking" is also suggestive of the burying of bodies covered in lime. Furthermore, if the brothers are deceased, then "lomondations" (340.9) or lamentations may need to be sung. In a sense, the song "Loch Lomond" is a song of mourning since its subject matter is a couple who "will never meet again," as one has died in battle and is taking the "high road," an "ascent" to Scotland. Thus, "Loch Lomond" represents a Shem/Shaun–type separation: "You tak the high road and I'll tak the low and I'll be in Scotland afore ye." As was previously noted, the song was also a staple of Joyce's soirées in the tense evenings of prewar Paris. The song has a similarly gloomy purpose in *Finnegans Wake*, where it functions as part of sections on burial, death, and separation.

Furthermore, "but mere and mire trullopes will knaver mate a game on the bibby bobby burns of" indicates the unending nature of the fraternal struggle of Shem and Shaun. The phrase "mate a game" hints at victory in competition, since *mate* can be used as a verb meaning to "overcome, defeat, subdue" (*OED*), as in chess for example. Such a victory may "knaver," or never, occur in the confrontation between Shaun and Shem, however. This endless struggle has landed both participants in the "mire." Since "befoul" can mean to become foul in a moral sense,[13] this fight has had an unpleasant, degrading effect on the fraternal adversaries.

In *The Narrow Ground: The Roots of the Conflict in Ulster*[14] A. T. Q. Stewart argues that "The distinctive Ulster-Scottish culture, isolated from the mainstream of Catholic and Gaelic culture, would appear to have been created not by the specific and artificial plantation of the early seventeenth century, but by the continuous natural influx of Scottish settlers both before and after that episode: in particular the heavy immigration which took place in the later seventeenth century seems to have laid the foundations of the Ulster colony" (39). Stewart covers the long story of "Scottish" and "Irish" convergences/divergences, a subject Joyce displays a keen interest in:

> At the core of the Ulster problem is the problem of the Scots. . . . It is . . . often assumed that it began only in the reign of James I. In fact, it was then already centuries old. At the narrowest part of the

North Channel, Scotland is a mere twelve miles from the Antrim coast. From the time of the earliest human occupation of the region this proximity has been the cause of migrations in both directions. It is now generally accepted that the Early Mesolithic people who were Ireland's first inhabitants arrived by this route. Of the many later migrations one of the most important was that which occurred in the second half of the fifth century, a migration of the gaelicized Ulaid into Argyll. We usually think of eastern Ulster as an extension of Scotland, but it is just as true that western Scotland was once an extension of the Ulster kingdom of Dalriada. The medieval Latin word for Irishman was *Scotus* and these emigrations actually "gave Scotland her name, her first kings, her Gaelic language and her faith." Some at least of the planters who arrived in Ulster in the early seventeenth century were direct descendants of earlier Ulster invaders of Scotland. (34; Stewart quotes Heslinga, 118)

Stewart's overview treats the recent "Troubles" of the north of Ireland as the regrettable but inevitable consequence of some kind of natural, organic process rather than as one of the many disastrous results of British imperialism. Stewart almost displays a Haines-like disavowal of British responsibility here. As R. F. Foster has noted in his discussion of the seventeenth-century "symbiotic relationship" (*Modern Ireland*, 79) of Ireland and Scotland, this view of Ulster history, "the argument that the 'real' Ulster plantation was that carried out 'invisibly' by the Scots, both before the initiatives of 1609–10 and later in the century . . . would later provide an argument used by Unionists that Ulster's different nature is immemorial and uncontrollable, and stems from something more basic than English governmental policy" (78). Nevertheless, Stewart's capsule history of the cyclical patterns of Irish and Scottish migrations can help to explain why Joyce links the postplantation divisions of Ireland to the ancient merger of the Picts and Scots. Joyce's representations of the almost organic constant interpenetrations of Irish and Scottish histories are very close in spirit to Stewart's overview, leaving Joyce vulnerable to charges of "indifference" (see S. Deane, *Heroic Styles*, 15).

For Joyce, these historical events are all components of one large, unified phenomenon in *Finnegans Wake*: "[Joyce] conceived of his book as the dream of old Finn, lying in death beside the river Liffey and watching the history of Ireland and the world—past and future—flow through his mind like flotsam on the river of life" (*JJII*, 544). The *Wake* takes a cosmic, as well as a comic, view of history. In this vision, distant events such as the maritime migration of the Scoti to Argyll are considered alongside modern history and culture such as the work of Robert Burns. The intervening time is collapsed, and all events gain an equal level of importance. Joyce's technique in *Finnegans Wake* attempts to provide an expansive, panoramic overview of the convergences, divergences, and recurrences of all of human history. In the case of the recurrent, cyclical, shared histories of Ireland and Scotland, Joyce achieves the formidable task of presenting a network of allusions to poets and poetry, migrations and mergers, conflicts and incursions, which provides a representation of an epic span of Scottish and Irish interconnections, spanning from the foundation of Scotland to the twentieth century. But there is a definite sense that, in highlighting the recurrent and balanced nature of these contacts, Joyce assumes his default God-of-the-creation position, removed, neutral, and uncommitted, "paring his fingernails" (*P*, 233). Despite this almost blasé *sub specie aeternitatis* authorial remoteness, the discord of modern Ireland is still clearly registered in the text through images of collision such as the Pict/Scot material. As Nicholas Allen has commented of *Finnegans Wake*, "If the book's pages contain no declaration of a political position, there is the representation of a troubled terrain" (22).

The fraternal altercations of page 520 may at first sight seem to be a negative, cyclical commentary on Irish and Scottish confrontations and the "doubled" population of Ulster. However, the line "mere and mire trullopes will knaver mate a game" is highly ambiguous. The word "mate" points to sexual reproduction, and *mère* is French for "mother," as well as being suggestive of *mer*, French for "sea." Previously in the *Wake*, in another Scottish and Irish encounter, the early sexual life of the mother figure ALP is detailed in the following terms: "O, wasn't he the bold priest? And wasn't she the naughty Livvy? Nautic Naama's now her navn. Two lads in scoutsch breeches went through her before that, Barefoot Burn and Wallowme Wade, Lugnaquillia's noblesse pickts, before she had a hint of hair at her fanny to hide or a bossom to tempt a birch canoedler not to mention a bulgic porterhouse barge" (204.4–9). Two young boys are wading through the water here, but since ALP is conceived as a river in the *Wake*, this is also an act with an erotic dimension. The two washerwomen, whose riverside gossip forms this conversation, also discuss how ALP was "first licked by a hound" (204.11–12). Bestiality aside, this representation really makes sense only if we remember ALP's representation as a river. Here again Burns or "Barefoot Burn" is associated with violence, with "breeches"—through "breaches"—also suggestive of sexual activity. The word "noblesse" hints at the French *blessé*, meaning "having been hurt," in an emotional or physical sense. This adds to the fogginess of a passage that mixes sexual activity with violence or pain. The burning here, since it is in connection with the river-goddess figure ALP, points towards fertility, to the type of fecundity restored to fields after fires. The convergence of conflict and sex is also displayed in the other allusion to "Loch Lomond" mentioned earlier: "*trulock may ever make a game*" (340.7). The word "trulock" is obviously based on the words "true love" of the lyrics of "Loch Lomond"; however, Trulock was also a Dublin gun manufacturer (McHugh, *Annotations*, 340).

In the above passage Joyce takes advantage of the ambiguity of the word "Burn," which could of course relate either to the physical sensation of a youthful sexual encounter or to the destruction of warfare. The connections between sex and war are famously explored by Yeats's great poem "Leda and the Swan," and this work is alluded to in the lines following the section: "And ere that again, leada, laida, all unraidy, to faint to buoy the fairiest rider, too frail to flirt with a cygnet's plume" (204.9–11). Here "Burn" signifies a stream-like fertility of foreign influx (as well as paradoxically hinting at the damage cause by this influx), in much the same way that the HCE-related Scandinavian invasion of Ireland is conceived of as both destructive and creative in *Finnegans Wake*. So—bizarrely, we might think—there is little in the way of explicit condemnation of the Plantation from Joyce.

Burns functions as another part of the splits and divergences of *Finnegans Wake* in connection with the mergings and schisms of Irish and Scottish histories. In the ALP section above, the two boys are versions of the brothers Shem and Shaun, who form the main binary opposition of the *Wake*. Coupled with this is the inherent fire-and-water duality of Burns's name that Joyce sought to take advantage of. Burns, in the sense of heat or injuries—"scalds and burns and blisters" (189.32)—

is present along with the violent associations the word carries, while the context carries a number of military allusions. For example, there is a reference to "Sligo's Noble Six" or "noblesse pickts" (McHugh, *Annotations*, 204). However, Burns here is also used to signify water, since, as noted earlier, *burn* is a Scots term for "stream." That Joyce is using "Burn" in this way seems likely, considering the aquatic nature of the section. Furthermore, it is demonstrable that Joyce was aware of the Scots word *burn*, since he also uses a variation of it in relation to bodies of water: "No, he skid like a skate and berthed on her byrnie and never a fear they'll land him yet, slitheryscales on liffeybank, times and times and halve a time a pillow of sand to polster him" (*FW*, 525.35–526.2).[15]

As discussed in chapter 4, on the Picts and the Scots, pages 518 to 522 of *Finnegans Wake* concentrate the binary and contrasting relationship of Shaun and Shem into a presentation of the different occurrences of Scottish and Irish meetings or confrontations. What is most interesting here for a study of Burns is that his name, barely altered, appears in Joyce's presentation of Scottish influence on Ulster. As Liam McIlvanney has noted, Burns's initial popularity outside of Scotland was at its greatest in Ulster: "In the wake of the Kilmarnock volume, Burns appears to have been almost as popular in the North of Ireland as in Scotland. The first edition of Burns's poems outside Scotland appeared in Belfast in 1787, and there were sixteen editions of his poems locally printed from 1787 to 1826. If in England Burns was received as something of a literary curiosity, in Ulster he achieved what one historian calls an 'immense and immediate popularity'" (*Radical*, 224). The popularity and influence of Burns in the north of Ireland is reflected in this section of *Finnegans Wake*. Furthermore, Burns's poetry became an inspiration for the poets associated with the ill-fated United Irish uprising of 1798:

> Perhaps the most intense and instructive contemporary engagement with Burns' politics took place in Ireland—and particularly in Ulster. . . . In Scotland and England, the reform movement was effectively hamstrung by government intimidation: in Ireland it struggled on to the great conflagration of 1798 and the abortive United Irish Rebellion. The role played by Burns' poetry in the cultural and political life of Ireland during this turbulent period is both significant and unwarrantably neglected. In Ulster, Burns was the inspiration and

figurehead for a whole school of radical poets (often writing in vernacular Scots) who attached themselves to the United Irish movement and to its party newspaper, the Belfast *Northern Star*. (McIlvanney, *Radical*, 220–21)

It does not seem that this intriguing aspect of Burns's connection with
Ireland is utilized by Joyce in *Finnegans Wake*; he was perhaps unaware
of the extent of Burns's influence on the radical poets of the north. In
general, references to the name Burns are used simply as a signifier of the
partial Scottishness of Ireland, in particular the north of Ireland. This is
the reverse side of the motif of the Picts and Scots and the allusions to
James Macpherson, which showed the partially Irish roots of Scotland
and the survival of an originally Irish culture in Scotland. Joyce—rather
indifferently—demonstrates the inverted symmetries of Irish and Scottish histories by not only working on the Irish roots of the Scottish
nation but, through the figure of Burns, stressing the impact of later
Scottish influences in Ireland. Burns is used by Joyce as a convenient
cipher for the Scottish impact on Ireland, sometimes in direct contrast
with phrases that highlight the Irish effect on Scotland. Allusions to
Burns function as part of a larger look at the recurring patterns of mutual
interference or effects created by each country on the other.

Whereas Macpherson in *Finnegans Wake* represents the idea of repetition and the recycling of ancient Gaelic material, and therefore Ireland's influence on Scotland and the connections between the cultures of
the two countries, allusions to Burns represent something quite different.
These references function as part of a representation of the more modern
presence of Scottish culture and Scots language in Ireland. Joyce alludes
to Burns's poetry for various, varying purposes befitting the "protean"
(Ferguson and Holmes, 9) nature of the poet—in order to conjure up the
rowdy, musical atmosphere of HCE's bar; as part of the demotic culture
of *Finnegans Wake*; as an ironic call to arms. The song "Auld Lang Syne"
is a favorite of the four historians of the *Wake* and is used to express the
forgetful, amnesia-like situation of the dreamer and an attempt to deny
reality and history. Crucially, Joyce also uses Burns as a symbol of Scotland when he wishes to address the Scottish influence on the north of
Ireland.[16] Taken together, the themes of divided identity and inhumed
perspective again point to the creation of a specifically Celtic uncon-

scious, a portrait of an "idealist leading a double life" (*FW*, 490.06). Allusions to Burns's poetry are also part of a number of instances where Joyce evokes the history of Scotland's wars with England and poetic responses to those wars, highlighting a radical side of Scottish culture and politics as an alternative to the "Protestant, Conservative, and Unionist" creeds with which it has been supposed Joyce associated Scotland (Maley, "Kilt by Kelt," 216).

NOTES ON A POSTCARD: BURNS AND THE BRUCES

In an amusing correspondence sent to Ezra Pound postmarked December 22, 1920, Joyce bases some semihumorous and rather self-pitying lines on Burns's well-known 1793 song "Robert Bruce's Address to His Troops at Bannockburn—*or* Scots Wha Hae":

> Bis Dat Qui Cito Dat
>   [flourish]
> Yanks who hae wi' Wallace read,
> Yanks whom Joyce has often bled,
> Welcome to the hard plank bed,
> And bolshevistic flea
> Who for Bloom and Inisfail
> Longs to pine in Singsing jail,
> Picking oakum, without bail,
> Let him publish me.

On the reverse of the card the following correspondence is written:

> Best Xmas greetings to Mrs Pound and yourself from us all (see other side). <u>Circe</u> finished this morning at last. Will revise, type and forward soon. No news <u>re</u> above. (*LIII*)[17]

The Latin phrase preceding the poem translates as "He gives twice who gives promptly," a joke regarding the length of time Joyce took to complete the "Circe" episode of *Ulysses*. The adaptation of "Scots Wha Hae" begins on the third line. This postcard is one instance of Joyce's writing

that, through allusion to Burns, evokes the long history of Scottish resistance to London rule prior to 1707. Allusions to this aspect of Scottish history continue through Joyce's texts and appear again repeatedly
throughout *Finnegans Wake*. Here Joyce adapts a Burns song that is concerned with Scotland's pre-Union history and its various struggles for
self-determination, a work that also has connections with both French
Jacobin and Scottish Jacobite politics:

> This was the Burns who "knelt at the tomb of Sir John the Graham,
> the gallant friend of the immortal Wallace" and "said a fervent prayer
> for old Caledonia over the hole in a blue whinstone, where Robert
> de Bruce fixed his royal standard on the banks of Bannockburn. . . ."
> But this historical nostalgia was associated with his sympathy for the
> American and French Revolutions. "For Burns in 1793"—the year
> in which he composed *Scots Wha hae*—"Bannockburn is directly as-
> sociated with the French Revolution," . . . in the sense that "Scot-
> land's fight for independence could be the channel of expression, the
> 'objective correlative,' for feelings of independence that were not con-
> fined to Scotland." (Nairn, 144–45; quotations are from J. Smith)

The Wallace of Joyce's postcard may have a double (or triple) significance.
First, Joyce may be referring to Hugh Campbell Wallace, the US ambas-
sador to France from 1919 to 1921, since this diplomat is referred to in
a letter to Pound dated December 12, 1920. Hugh Campbell Wallace is
mentioned in connection to the legal difficulties surrounding the publication of *Ulysses*. Also mentioned in this letter is one Richard Wallace,
an American book illustrator.

The Wallace of Burns's poem is, of course, William Wallace, a
prominent leader of a revolt against the rule in Scotland of the English
king Edward I. After a promising start for the Scottish revolutionaries,
including victory at the Battle of Stirling Bridge in 1297, this particular
rising ended with the torture and execution of Wallace in London in
1305. In 1296, the year before Wallace's rebellion, the "Stone of Destiny"
was taken to England by Edward I.[18] The Stone of Destiny (or The
Stone of Scone) is mentioned very early in *Finnegans Wake* as a support
that has been placed under the fallen Finnegan: "Sharpen his pillowscone, tap up his bier!" (6.23–24). Traditionally, the Stone of Destiny

is the biblical pillow on which Jacob rests and dreams of steps leading to the heavens, hence "pillowscone." However, another phrase from the same section, also with a Scottish connection, indicates that this state of hibernation may not be permanent: "Phall if you but will, rise you must" (4.15–16).[19] In fact, since the stone may have originated in Ireland, here is another display of the contact points of Irish and Scottish histories in the *Wake*. The MacAlpin reign, a period that consolidated the beginnings of the Scottish nation or the "united states of Scotia Picta" (43.29–30), possibly involved the bringing of the ceremonial Lia Fáil from Tara in County Meath—the seat of the ancient High Kings of Ireland—to the seat of the new nation in Scotland, something intimated in the portmanteau "tarrascone" (227.35), a term cementing together relics of Irish and Scottish royal histories.[20] Once again Joyce highlights the Irish roots of Scotland as he follows the journeys of Irish history beyond the shores of Ireland while linking these roots and journeys to the unconscious dreamer. The opening funeral is juxtaposed with Irish and Scottish royalty, suggesting that the void of sleep is the only place in which total Celtic ascendancy can ever be possible. In this reading the situation of the *Wake* is an indictment, not a celebration.

To return to the subject of Wallace and his rebellion against Edward I and English rule, Paul H. Scott has written that "Edward I of England seized the opportunity of [a] disputed succession to attempt to take over Scotland, first by diplomatic manipulation and then, when that failed, by force. It was a pattern that was to be repeated frequently for the next 300 years, with the slaughter and destruction renewed in each attack" (1). According to Scott, this amounts to "the longest war in European history" (2). When Joyce alludes to Burns's song, he is also referring to this crucial period of Scottish history, namely Scotland's self-defense, its medieval struggle for self-determination, and an extended period of "slaughter and destruction." The Christmas postcard sent to Pound may only be a throwaway and not meant to be taken too seriously, but it does at least reveal the breadth of Joyce's awareness regarding Burns's works. It also shows an awareness of the Burns poetry that deals with a period of Scottish history previous to the union with England, characterized by opposition to England. This is linked by Joyce to *Ulysses*, which has been described as a form of "Celtic revenge" (Gibson, *Joyce's Revenge*, 1).

In his 1920 postcard Joyce replaces the word "Scots" with "Yanks" and substitutes his own name in place of "Bruce," Scotland's fourteenth-century guerrilla-fighter Robert de Brus / Robert the Bruce. Burns's song takes the form of an address to the Scottish army before the decisive Battle of Bannockburn in 1314. The Scottish victory at Bannockburn over the troops of Edward II of England, son of Edward I, is one of the most famous and celebrated events in Scottish history, since it guaranteed total Scottish independence until the 1603 Union of the Crowns. Independence was declared six years later after Bannockburn in the 1320 "Declaration of Arbroath," a letter sent to Pope John XXII. The Battle of Bannockburn itself appears in the first chapter of *Finnegans Wake* thinly disguised as "panickburns" (9.25).[21] In typically Wakean fashion the battle is balanced alongside the disastrous defeat of Scotland by the English in 1513 at Flodden Field or "floodens" (9.24), and the clashes appear as part of a compendium of allusions to confrontations from across the globe and from various points in human history. What is specifically Wakean here is the coincidence of opposites; triumph and disaster meet in the same passage, and history collapses in on itself.

In the postcard version of Burns's song, however, Joyce is less focused on matters of national independence and more concerned with complaining about his own perilous situation as a writer struggling to find a publisher for *Ulysses*: "He hoped to finish *Circe*, 'the last adventure,' by Christmas, and finally, on December 20, after having rewritten from start to finish six or seven or eight or nine times (the count varied), he pronounced it done. . . . It would have been agreeable to know who would publish *Ulysses*, but for the moment no plan was firm" (*JJII*, 497). Why then did Joyce choose a Burns song on medieval Scottish warfare (though with links to the politics of Burns's own lifetime) to describe his plight as a struggling artist? And why did he not adapt an Irish poem, something by James Clarence Mangan perhaps? The simplicity of Burns's call to arms is one to which Joyce could relate:

SCOTS, wha hae wi' WALLACE bled,
Scots, wham BRUCE has aften led,
Welcome to your gory bed,—
Or to victorie.—

Now's the day, and now's the hour;
See the front o' battle lour;
See approach proud EDWARD's power,
Chains and Slaverie.—

Wha will be a traitor-knave?
Wha can fill a coward's grave?
Wha sae base as be a Slave?
Let him turn and flie:—

Wha for SCOTLAND's king and law,
Freedom's sword will strongly draw,
FREE-MAN stand, or FREE-MAN fa'
Let him follow me.—

By oppression's woes & pains!
By your sons in servile chains!
We will drain our dearest veins,
But they *shall* be free!

Lay the proud usurper low!
Tyrants fall in every foe!
LIBERTY'S in every blow!
Let US DO—or DIE!!! (Burns, 466–67)

As we can see, the song is rallying cry set at a critical, decisive moment: "The starkness of the choice facing the Scottish army determines the starkness of the language used by Burns. At this moment of action—'now's the hour'—words have grown almost irrelevant. Bruce offers no elaborate harangue, but a terse statement of the case. He has little to do but point to the scenes in front of him" (McIlvanney, *Radical*, 213). The economical austerity of the rhetoric, the setting out in plain, sparse language of the situation in Burns's song, suits Joyce's purposes as he sets out his own predicament.

While it is a joke to some extent, Joyce also regarded the search for a publisher for *Ulysses* as a serious, fateful juncture and a time for heroic, defiant action. Accordingly, he adapts the poem to implore "Yanks" not quite to "drain their dearest veins" but at least to risk doing some hard time—"who for Bloom and Inisfail / Longs to pine in Singsing Jail"— for publishing his work. As is well known, the American publishers of *Ulysses* did indeed run into significant legal difficulties, and the book was the subject of a famous indecency trial in 1933.[22] Joyce's version of the song is slightly melodramatic, since he is comparing the situation of a writer seeking help to publish a book with the grim prospects of an out-numbered army fighting for the freedom of an entire nation. While it is somewhat characteristic of Joyce to indulge in self-pity, the production and publication of his work did cause him considerable distress during his life. Also, it must be remembered that this was a private correspon-dence and was written in at least a semijovial Yuletide spirit and that Joyce has a notable habit of recasting moments of his own life into epic struggles.

In fact, Joyce's Christmas card to Pound is not the first instance where Joyce's problems with publishing his work lead him to compose poetry mentioning Bannockburn. In the 1912 work "Gas from a Burner" Joyce writes of "My Irish foreman from Bannockburn" (*PE*, 110). The man Joyce refers to is George Roberts, the Ulster-Scots publisher (see *JJII*, 336–37), who may have had sectarian reasons for rejecting Joyce's *Dubliners* (See R. Russell, "Irish Unionism"). Roberts's partial Scottish ancestry aside, the name itself must have reminded Joyce of the Scottish military commander at Bannockburn, Robert the Bruce. Joyce also writes in the same poem:

> I pity the poor—that's why I took
> A red-headed Scotchman to keep my book.
> Poor sister Scotland! Her doom is fell;
> She cannot find any more Stuarts to sell. (*PE*, 109)

Noteworthy here is the female personification of Scotland, a process that is often applied in Irish literature to Ireland through the use of the mythical figure Kathleen Ni Houlihan (the Sean-Bhean Bhocht). This similarity is increased by Joyce's use of the word "poor," which matches the Irish equivalent *bocht*. However, despite the sororal identification, the idea that Scotland is some kind of sellout is delivered in a clearly mocking, derisive tone. Compare these lines to Joyce's comments in "Ireland: Island of Saints and Sages": "Although the present race in Ireland is second-rate and backward, it merits some consideration as it is the only one in the entire Celtic family that refused to sell its birthright for a plate of lentils" (*OCPW*, 119).

But what exactly is Joyce referring to with the line "She cannot find any more Stuarts to sell"? Here Joyce confuses or conflates the events of 1603 and 1707 in a—presumably—accidentally Wakean fashion. In 1603 Scotland's James VI took up the English throne and thereby enacted the "Union of the Crowns." However, there was almost nothing in the way of financial benefit for the Scots from this union, save for the court of King James, which relocated to the wealth and privileges of London. The cash prizes of the 1707 acquisition were mainly limited to the Scottish elite, who profited from voting the act through in opposition to the wishes of the majority of the population: "In England, the debate was conducted against a background of popular celebrations; in Scotland, there were riots, protest meetings and petitions from a quarter of the shires and a third of the burghs—all of which were ignored. Later, one of the commissioners, Sir John Clerk, admitted that the Articles had been carried 'contrary to the inclinations of at least three-fourths of the Kingdom'" (Lynch, *Scotland*, 313).

Where then does Joyce derive his assertion that Scotland "sold" James Stuart? Well, the Parliamentary Union of 1707 did involve the following bribes: "places, peerages, financial compensation (including about £20,000 in cash for 'expenses' and arrears of payment to office-holders), and concessions on economic and trade matters where important economic interests, and especially those of the nobility, were involved" (Lynch, *Companion*, 606). This is more obviously a "sellout," but there is no major royal aspect to the merger. Burns himself also regretfully comments on this takeover: "We're bought and sold for English gold, / Such a parcel of rogues in a nation!" (Burns, 294). Disappointingly, Joyce simply confuses the two different events. But, according to Stephen Dedalus, "A man of genius makes no mistakes. His errors are volitional and are the portals of discovery" (*U*, 9.228–29). On the subject of a Scottish Doomsday—"Poor sister Scotland! Her doom is fell; /

She cannot find any more Stuarts to sell" (*PE*, 109)—compare Joyce's similar comments in "Ireland: Island of Saints and Sages": "Is the Celtic world . . . doomed, after centuries of struggle, finally to fall headlong into the ocean?" (*OCPW*, 124–25). As Len Platt points out in *Joyce, Race and "Finnegans Wake,"* Joyce comes to satirize the idea of a Celtic racial family. However, the idea of some kind of unity or cultural affinity between the peoples of Scotland and Ireland is present in his writing at an earlier stage and survives into *Finnegans Wake*, albeit in a new and complex form.[23]

Joyce is not the only historical personage to whom the thought of the Celtic world appealed. Edward Bruce, brother of Robert, who led a "liberation" invasion of Ireland following Bannockburn, is mentioned in the "Proteus" episode of *Ulysses* in Stephen's meditation on the "pretenders" of Irish history:

> The dog's bark ran towards him, stopped, ran back. Dog of my enemy. I just simply stood pale, silent, bayed about. *Terribilia meditans.* A primrose doublet, fortune's knave, smiled on my fear. For that are you pining, the bark of their applause? Pretenders: live their lives. The Bruce's brother, Thomas Fitzgerald, silken knight, Perkin Warbeck, York's false scion, in breeches of silk of whiterose ivory, wonder of a day, and Lambert Simnel, with a tail of nans and sutlers, a scullion crowned. All kings' sons. Paradise of pretenders then and now. (*U*, 3.310–17)

Once again in Joyce's writing there is an association between the sea and Scottish history since Stephen is, at this point in the narrative, walking along Sandymount Strand in Dublin Bay.[24] As Vincent Cheng has noted, "The beach makes [Stephen] conscious of Irish 'history' as a continuing series of foreign invasions and master-slave relationships" (*Joyce, Race, and Empire*, 161). Similarly, Jon Hegglund points out that "water has more than just a symbolic importance in the context of *Ulysses*: It also possessed a very real geopolitical and historical significance in the history of the British Empire, including relations between Britain and Ireland" (68).[25] Here the sea and the opportunities it provides for the movement of peoples is an obvious threat, and medieval Scotland is seen as an "enemy." Furthermore, the "shape-shifting" theme of "Proteus" manifests itself here in the fluid transformations brought about by the numerous arrivals of invaders from the sea.

Edward Bruce's invasion of Ireland, which is now interpreted as being "driven primarily by the dynastic ambitions of Edward Bruce, but also . . . the war aims of Robert I" (McNamee, 167), was actually pitched at the time by Bruce as another front in a campaign to rid the Gaelic-speaking lands (namely Scotland and Ireland) of the English presence, an attempt to create some kind of Celtic solidarity:

> Robert I showed a consistent interest in Ireland and visited the country on at least four occasions. Edward his brother led a Scottish invasion of Ireland in 1315, used the title "King of Ireland" and died in battle against the Anglo-Irish at Fochart in 1318. The Bruces represented their interest in terms of a pan-Celtic solidarity against the common enemy. An illustration of how they wanted to be seen in Ireland is the letter of Robert I to "all the kings of Ireland, to the prelates and clergy, and to the inhabitants of all Ireland, his friends." Enigmatic and undated, it is a letter of credence for envoys, claiming for the Irish and Scots a common national ancestry, a common language and common customs. It is justly famous for its use of the phrase "our nation," clearly intended to embrace both peoples: an expression of that pan-Celtic sentiment which occasionally surfaces in medieval literature, but only rarely in history or politics. In their appeals to the common culture and the common mythology of the Scots and Irish, and their similar overtures to the Welsh, the Bruces laid claim to leadership of a Celtic Alliance against the English; and in their interventions in Ireland from 1315 to 1318, this claim appears to have been sustained with blood and steel. (McNamee, 166–67)

In more recent times, the Scottish nationalist and communist poet Hugh MacDiarmid, one of Joyce's Scots protégés in terms of modernist artistic endeavors, concocted the rather ambitious project of a Union of Socialist Celtic nations. His activities in this case did not get very far, although we now know that the British security services considered his political activities dangerous enough to have him investigated from 1931 to 1943.[26] Murray Pittock has discussed the subject of MacDiarmid's views on a potential Celtic political or cultural union and also the influence of Irish politics on Scottish literature:

> MacDiarmid welcomed Irish immigration into Scotland, as sustaining "the ancient Gaelic commonwealth," while by 1930 the creation of Clann Albann, "a paramilitary nationalist organization," suggested that the Scottish Celticists were bent on following the Irish example to a disturbing conclusion. . . . Hugh MacDiarmid presented a strongly re-masculinized Scotland in the shape of *A Drunk Man Looks at the Thistle* (1926), while praise for the Irish example remained commonplace, MacDiarmid himself commenting that "Scottish anti-Irishness is a profound mistake" while Somhairle MacGill-Eain's (1911–96) poem on the "National Museum of Ireland" conjures up "the hero / who is dearest to me of them all . . . Connolly / in the General Post Office of Ireland / while he was preparing the sacrifice." (*Celtic Identity*, 84–85)

Pittock also points out that James Connolly's background was socialist Scotland (84).[27] Edward Bruce was not only a pretender in the sense of having declared himself king of Ireland, but also in his efforts to justify his "intervention" as part of a joint Gaelic resistance. This propagandistic stab at portraying the invasion of Ireland as a liberation attempt did not have the desired effect in Ireland. Stephen Dedalus's thoughts as he walks along the beach in "Proteus" reflect the negative status Edward Bruce gained in Ireland, one that endures and contrasts with the image of his brother.[28]

Joyce's references to either or both of the Bruces, present in *Ulysses* as well as in his personal correspondence, also appear in *Finnegans Wake*: "Now, patience; and remember patience is the great thing, and above all things else we must avoid anything like being or becoming out of patience. A good plan used by worried business folk who may not have had many momentums to mastes Kung's doctrine of the meang or the propriety codestruces of Carprimustimus is just to think of all the sinking fund of patience possessed in their conjoint names by both brothers Bruce with whom are incorporated their Scotch spider and Elberfeld's Calculating Horses" (108.8–16). This section of the *Wake*, calling for the patience of the reader and those wishing to understand ALP's "mamafesta" (104.4) and, by implication, *Finnegans Wake* itself, adapts a traditional story told of Robert the Bruce. In this folktale, Robert takes inspiration from watching a "Scotch spider" rebuild its web on seven occasions after it has been repeatedly destroyed by the elements. The persistence or "patience" of the spider was meant to have been a source of motivation for the leader in his war against England.[29] In the section above, "both brothers," as well as being a reference to the two Bruces, is an obvious reference to Shem and Shaun, who are "conjoint" and "incorporated" in HCE or "Elberfeld's Calculating Horses."[30]

But let us return to the subject of Joyce's postcard to conclude this section. The starkness of the language of Burns's original and the "moment of action" nature of its subject matter would have appealed to Joyce given the latter's difficult, precarious situation. The song deals not only with the Wars of Independence but has a wider relevance:

> The call appears to be that of Bruce, but the language of contemporary reference suggests the perpetual relevance of struggle against tyrants of all places and times. Burns has taken the idea of Scottish history as a struggle for liberty, linked both with the Wars of Independence and the Jacobites, and once again has used it as a source for a call to resistance and revolution in the age of the Terror. The "proud Usurpers" are the Hanoverians as much as the Plantagenets; the "Tyrants" are (as the poem implies if read carefully) generically English or Anglicized, the oppressing nation; while doing or dying for liberty has sharp political relevance in 1793, a relevance only mildly disguised by the historical setting. (Pittock, *Poetry and Jacobite Politics*, 219)

The song is prorevolution and proresistance, an example of politically radical poetry from Scotland that Joyce engages with. Joyce's own struggle to carry out his own act of literary revolution—in which "resistance to England" is "a central theme" (Gibson, *Joyce's Revenge*, 13)—is expressed here through a Scottish song based on the Wars of Independence.

CONCLUSION

In *Finnegans Wake* the literary and philosophical traditions of Scotland help to form a Celtic unconscious, an inhumed, internally divided, and obscured alternative reality. The divided psychology and alter-ego representation of Shem and Shaun as composing HCE is based to a significant extent on Scottish literature. In other words, the presentation of Shem and Shaun as separate, dual, contrasting tendencies derives, to a large degree, from Scottish writing. The schizoid representation of the rival brothers, contrasting tendencies of the dreamer's identity, is influenced by the studies in duality—the "Caledonian Antisyzygy"—of the writers Robert Louis Stevenson and James Hogg. Scottish writing had a major influence on the fiction of James Joyce, particularly his later work and especially *Finnegans Wake*. Joyce's construction of the Shem/Shaun binary in *Finnegans Wake* is based not only on Scottish literature but also on the Irish beginnings of the Scottish nation. This is a component of Joyce's all-encompassing treatment of Ireland's history and part of his insistence on the constant interplay and intermingling of nations as a riposte to essentialized visions of nationality. Joyce is interested in addressing, with a Humean "suspense" or reserved judgment, the complexity of Scottish history and society rather than producing a reductive, simplistic reading and representation. However, and somewhat paradoxically, Joyce is also interested in linking skepticism and idealism with a larger, unifying "Celtic spirit" (*OCPW*, 124).

The phrases Joyce uses from Macpherson's *Ossian* in *Finnegans Wake* point to the shared traditions of Irish and Scottish cultures—as with the Picts and the Scots, the Irish roots of Scottish history are also involved here—and are recycled fragments of a Highland culture which was itself part of a fading Celtic world. Macpherson and the rehashing of ancient

Gaelic poems as an eighteenth-century national epic in the *Wake* represents cycles and recyclings—the repetition of an originally Irish culture in Scotland through the movement of the Scoti, the republishing of daily events as "forged" or "faked" experiences during dreams, the revivals of parents through children. Joyce also saw in Macpherson's methodology a technique similar to his own in the composition of *Finnegans Wake*. Furthermore, Joyce's use of Macpherson is an engagement with a Celtic culture that he believed was engaged in ongoing tension with Anglo-Saxon civilization. Another Scots poet, Robert Burns, is utilized as a code for the Scottish influence on the north of Ireland through the Ulster Plantation, Joyce's somewhat neutralizing modern counterpoint to the ancient Irish impact on Scotland through the Scoti. Once again Scottish culture is linked to division or duality, in this case to the religious and political schisms of the north of Ireland.

Although he viewed Scotland as being marked by internal contrast, one tradition Joyce clearly associated with the country is skeptical philosophy, a branch of thought he regarded as fundamentally opposed to modern materialism and the only viable alternative to the scholasticism he adhered to as a youth (*OCPW*, 179, and *JJII*, 648). Joyce viewed the Scottish Enlightenment philosopher David Hume as a cross between an idealist and a skeptic and admired the doubting, questioning nature of his philosophy, drawing upon his work to create the internal, limited setting and indeterminate contents of *Finnegans Wake*. As we have seen in this study, philosophy, as with mythology, is an area for Joyce in which Ireland and Scotland are fundamentally linked. He saw "Celtic" thinkers such as George Berkeley, David Hume, and Arthur Balfour as sharing an inclination towards skepticism and incertitude. This is an odd grouping and a strange act of classification, but Joyce had an eccentric and unique habit of making peculiar connections between subjects or ideas that might usually be considered unassociated (See G. Gibson, 20). His insistence—while working on *Ulysses*—on the resemblance between the Irish and the Jews is another example of this tendency.

In many respects Joyce saw Scotland in the same way he saw Ireland, as being internally composed of different and sometimes sharply contrasting traditions, both displaying inner splits and contrasts. However, he also presents the two nations as being inverted copies of each other. As he demonstrates in *Finnegans Wake*, these inversions, this sense of mirrored and uncanny "invertedness" (*FW*, 522.31), had come about to a great extent in both countries through their proximity and through the maritime connections existing between them (this partly explains why Scotland is constantly connected with the sea in Joyce's writings). Indeed, Joyce knew from his research into Irish history that Scotland's historical origins and heritage are partly Irish, an idea that clearly appealed to him since he went to such lengths to weave an extensive motif based on the rival/partner tribes the Picts and Scots into the fabric of *Finnegans Wake*. As Joyce wished *Finnegans Wake* to cover the full extent of Irish history, it would be impossible for him to ignore Scotland, since Scotland's very inception begins with an Irish immigration in the form of the arrival of the Scoti and their eventual merging with the indigenous Picts. Furthermore, Scotland plays a crucial role in the Ulster Plantation and the subsequent development of the north of Ireland as an area "apart" from the remainder of the island.

Finnegans Wake covers both internal and external Irish history; its treatment plots the impact of the Irish on the outside world alongside the world's impact on Ireland. This idea of the family links of the two countries fascinated Joyce, and he imagined himself as being personally related to Scotland in some vague way, flaunting his association with the Murray clan through his personal stash of tartan neckties. Family "ties" are also behind the character of Crotthers of the "Oxen of the Sun" episode of *Ulysses*, a character who, rather than embodying negative stereotypes of Scotsmen, represents the maritime traffic and exchanges that have tethered Ireland and Scotland together since time immemorial. Like the motif of the Picts and the Scots, Crotthers reveals Joyce's interest in the "crossed" populations of Scotland and Ireland, how they have become intermixed over the cyclical course of history through such disparate events as the migration of the Scoti and the Ulster Plantation. Crotthers, the briny Caledonian envoy from the Mull of Galloway, is also a further example of a constant connection in Joyce's works between Scotland and the sea. Mrs Malins speaks of her supposedly beautiful sea-crossing in "The Dead"; Stephen Dedalus reflects on the pretender Edward Bruce while walking among the seaspawn and seawrack of Sandymount Strand in "Proteus," and even Scottish poetry is doused in seawater: "Makefearsome's Ocean" (*FW*, 294.13). These oceanic connections show Joyce's awareness of the extent to which the histories, societies, and cultures of the two countries have been slowly shaped by the crosscurrents of the "Moylean Main" (25.27), as well as his belief that these links had somehow sustained a "Celtic spirit" (*OCPW*, 124).

The nighttime "setting" of *Finnegans Wake* is an application of Joyce's attraction to the Humean idea that humans are always limited to the internal functions of the mind, so that they are caught in a space of detachment from the material world where incertitude prevails. At night this situation becomes more extreme and concentrated, so, for Joyce, a depiction of the sleeping and dreaming brain—of an unconscious subject—can illustrate a more general situation. Joyce's text is an internal receptacle of external events and impressions, where information becomes clouded and distorted. This is a development from the concentration on the theme of inaccessible reality in *Ulysses* and of the pervasive sense of doubt in *Exiles*. And although Joyce never directly rails against the "materialism" of the "Anglo-Saxon civilization," his work is an imaginative alternative to it since it stresses the immaterial and the internal—even the spiritual—at the expense of the worldly and the external. This formal "Celtic Revenge," an expression of Joyce's conception of the "Celtic spirit" (*OCPW*, 124), is "directed *against* the Englishness of the novel in English" (Robichaud, "Narrative," 185–86) and places his work into what he saw as a tradition of Celtic literature and philosophy but is also a method of expressing his view of life as continually suspended in doubt. The puzzling nature of *Finnegans Wake* can partly be attributed to these factors, as well as to Joyce's "rejection of dogma, of rational certitude, of reductive or simplistic visions of reality" (McCarthy, *Riddles*, 46).

What future avenues of exploration does the present study uncover? Well, while a vast amount has been written on Joyce, there are, thankfully for professors and postgraduate students, still important areas with little in the way of critical work relating to them. One area that could yield some helpful research and some useful texts would be an overview of the influence of philosophy, especially of skeptical philosophy, on Joyce's work. Studies have been undertaken on Joyce and individual philosophers such as Aristotle, Aquinas, Bruno, and Vico. However, one unified consideration of Joyce's changing tastes and interests in philosophy would be beneficial. Admittedly, this project would be a rather onerous task. Minimal work has been carried out on Joyce's various engagements with individual nations. Kristian Smidt's "'I'm Not Half Norawain for Nothing': Joyce and Norway" is an example of the kind of excellent work that can be produced when a critic seeks to evaluate Joyce's treatment of the links between Ireland and another European country and also investigates Joyce's interest in the literature and language of that country. Joyce did seem to harbor some rather questionable and essentialized views of nationality at the early stage of his career. He also had a rather peculiar interest in national traits, supposedly associating European countries with the seven deadly sins: "Gluttony, he said, was English, Pride French, Wrath Spanish, Lust German, Sloth Slavic. 'What is the Italian sin? Avarice,' he concluded, recalling how often he had been cheated by shopkeepers and how wickedly he had been robbed in Rome. As for his own people, the Irish, their deadly sin was Envy, and he quoted the song of Brangäne in *Tristan und Isolde* as a perfect expression of Celtic envy" (*JJII*, 382). One wonders if Joyce had a deadly sin in mind for Scotland. Were the Scots, part of "the Celtic family" (*OCPW*, 119), also guilty of Envy? Perhaps for Joyce the Scottish national trait is a tendency to complain: "Joyce had a story of a Scotchman and a Jew travelling on a ship which foundered and sank. They spent three days together in a lifeboat. At the end of that time, the Jew said, 'I'm a Jew.' The Scotchman said, 'I'm a hunchback'" (*JJII*, 395). This was an era before political correctness.

———

To conclude this study, let us turn to the links between Joyce, Scottish history and culture, and Irish politics. During his phase as an occasional Triestine journalist and lecturer in the 1910s, Joyce discussed the contemporary Irish home rule crisis in pieces such as "Home Rule Comes of Age" (1907) and "The Home Rule Comet" (1910). In contrast to Ireland, Scotland was lacking a viable, high-profile home-rule or independence movement at this time. The Irish novelist Colm Tóibín has detected a similarity between early twentieth-century Edinburgh and the Irish capital as presented in Joyce's *Dubliners*:

> It is easy to imagine the final story, "The Dead," happening in a number of other cities besides Dublin, capital cities which, like Dublin, did not have a parliament and in which there was no govern-

ment; cities where two languages, or two cultures, seemed to clash; cities which dreamed of sacred places in the countryside in which the soul of the citizens could be purified; cities caught between a dull, deadly provinciality and the even duller possibility of cosmopolitanism. The Dublin of "The Dead" has echoes of Barcelona or Calcutta or Edinburgh in the early years of the 20th century. . . . In all four societies—Ireland, Catalonia, Bengal, Scotland—two languages were in conflict, or at least there was an older shadow language against the one of substance. It is easy to imagine a Calcutta intellectual being attacked for not writing in his native language, Bengali, and being married to a woman from the countryside whom he, so urbanised and deracinated, will come to misunderstand and almost foolishly desire. And it is easy to imagine a Catalan intellectual attacked for not writing his book reviews in Catalan, or a Scottish intellectual berated for not wearing a kilt. (Tóibín, "Joyce's Dublin," n.p.)

It would be interesting to read Tóibín's angle on the similarity between early twentieth-century Dublin and early twenty-first-century Edinburgh.

In the 1920s the Scottish Joycean poet Hugh MacDiarmid (Christopher Murray Grieve) helped to found the National Party of Scotland, the forerunner of today's Scottish National Party (SNP), in an attempt to create what Tóibín would term "what was missing in the public world." MacDiarmid's literary debts to Joyce are well known and documented. His journal *The Scottish Chapbook* documents his excitement at the publication of Joyce's *Ulysses*: "We have been enormously struck by the resemblance—the moral resemblance—between Jamieson's Etymological Dictionary of the Scottish language and James Joyce's *Ulysses*. A *vis comica* that has not yet been liberated lies bound by desuetude and misappreciation in the recesses of the Doric; and its potential uprising would be no less prodigious, uncontrollable, and utterly at variance with conventional morality than was Joyce's tremendous outpouring" (MacDiarmid, qtd. in McCulloch, *Modernism and Nationalism*, 27). Here MacDiarmid links Joyce's artistic methods in *Ulysses* to MacDiarmid's plans for a revival of the use of the Scots language in modern literature, something that would produce a liberating, counter-conventional effect. MacDiarmid's "potential uprising" of the Scots language—which he links to Joyce's literary modernism—is part of his program for a transformed, renewed Scotland.[1] MacDiarmid's innovations developed at the same time as the emergence of the work of the great Gaelic poet Somhairle MacGill-Eain (Sorley MacLean) and the Scottish modernist novelists Neil Gunn and Lewis Grassic Gibbon. As Margery McCulloch has noted, the Scottish artistic resurgence was designed to revivify the entire national fabric: "What made this post–First World War literary revival movement unique among Scottish cultural movements was the belief of those involved that any regeneration in the nation's aesthetic culture could not be separated from revival in the nation's wider social, economic, and political life" (McCulloch, "Scottish Modernism," 766).

Joyce's influence on twentieth-century Scottish literature as a whole is significant, especially with regards to representations of consciousness. Alasdair Gray, James Kelman, and Hugh MacDiarmid are the most obvious beneficiaries in Scottish literature of Joyce's legacy (although, on the subject of Irish and Scottish connections in modern literature, Gray's debts to Flann O'Brien and Kelman's to Samuel Beckett are perhaps more substantial). Gray's *Lanark* has been described as a "portrait of the artist as a young Glaswegian" (Stevenson, "A Postmodern Scotland?," 211), while the nocturnal reveries, sexual fantasies, and formal innovations of Gray's *1982, Janine* invite comparisons with *Finnegans Wake*. However, Gray originally set out to omit anything from his text that might "move" the reader: "When I began writing [*1982, Janine*] . . . the monologue swelled up by taking in matters I had never intended to use in a book, for I agree with James Joyce when he says that great art should not move, that only improper arts (propaganda and pornography) move us, but true art arrests us in the face of eternal beauty, or truth, or something like that" (Gray, n.p.). Joyce's influence on Kelman is in terms of voice and narration:

> There was a crucial factor that I liked about the shift from first to third party: you were left with a thought process; the central character had an inner life that seemed authentic. I just kept developing that third-party narrative, finding ways to embed the thought process. This culminated in moves I made in *The Busconductor Hines*. There was something Joyce was doing, trying to be doing, Molly Bloom's soliloquy, *Finnegan's Wake* [*sic*], it was just there how some-

thing, and it was just like eh, it was just fucking obvious man just how I could not quite say. (Kelman, 183)

Joyce's influence on MacDiarmid has frequently been noted. Like Joyce, MacDiarmid was interested in an international approach to language:

> Few aspects of social life seem more irreducibly national than language. Several major languages are multinational, but none is genuinely international. There have been various attempts to construct an international tongue—whether by actual invention, as with Esperanto, or, as with Basic English, by the simplification of an existing language—but no such project has enjoyed conspicuous success; and such interest as these efforts have aroused has been overwhelmingly of a utilitarian sort. . . . Perhaps the problem can be approached in a different way. Such is the assumption which motivates two of the significant works of the twentieth century, James Joyce's *Finnegans Wake* (1939) and Hugh MacDiarmid's *In Memoriam James Joyce* (1955). These prose poems are profoundly rooted in their national traditions—the marginalized cultures of Ireland and Scotland, respectively, toward which the authors maintained intense and complicated relations—yet both also constitute extraordinarily ambitious attempts to transcend nationality and encompass a vision of world language; and MacDiarmid's project, as his title suggests, was undertaken with full awareness and appreciation of the Joycean precedent. (Freedman, 253–54)

For Alan Bold, MacDiarmid's later linguistic experimentalism in *In Memoriam* is inspired by the *Wake*, just as his earlier *Drunk Man* was by *Ulysses*:

> In addressing Joyce, who died in 1941, on the subject of world language MacDiarmid is speaking to a dead man who was once gloriously alive to all the creative possibilities of language and who attempted to create his own linguistic universe in *Finnegans Wake*. Just as *A Drunk Man Looks at the Thistle* was inspired by *Ulysses*, so *In Memoriam James Joyce* is inspired by Joyce's later and more extreme

experimental work. MacDiarmid never met Joyce, a fact he regretted, but regarded his fellow Celt as a creative colleague and the supreme linguistic innovator of the century. (223) [2]

But there may be little real Joycean influence—beyond the title—on MacDiarmid's "problematic" later work of data poetry, the "extreme" *In Memoriam James Joyce*. According to Christopher Whyte, "It is likely that the dedication to James Joyce was an afterthought" (95). However, as Roderick Watson has mentioned, "The use of exhaustive catalogues . . . has been a powerful and common device in Gaelic and Irish literature through the ages. The same penchant appears in Scots works such as *The Complaynt of Scotland*, or even Urquhart's *Rabelais*, as well as in the modern world-language poems of MacDiarmid, or in the prose of Irish writers such as James Joyce and Samuel Beckett, who delight in presenting the reader with lengthy and all-inclusive lists" (110). MacDiarmid and Joyce share an interest in composition by compilation and in "encyclopedic" texts. The two writers are also both engaged in plurilinguistic practices, partially for anti-imperial reasons: "MacDiarmid thrived on lexical vertigo. So many of his most impressive effects depend on access to areas of unusual vocabulary, whether using the Scots language or scientific terminology—'yow-trummle' or 'lithogenesis.' . . . His adoption of Scots in 1922 was a turning from the language of the Empire" (R. Crawford, *Modern Poet*, 206).

According to Fredric Jameson, "aesthetic modernism was less developed in England than in Scotland, let alone Britain's 'other island' whose extraordinary modernisms mark a sharp contrast with the commonsense empirical intellectual life of London or Cambridge" (Jameson, *Modernity*, 103). Jameson's division between Celtic and English modernisms—a dichotomy of the empirical or commonsense and their contraries—is in the same vein as Joyce's vision of a materialist-versus-idealist/skeptical opposition. For Jameson, modernism is "essentially a by-product of incomplete modernization" (103–4). This model works well for Scottish as well as Irish modernism, since both nations were incompletely modern in the political sense during this period. So, were Scottish and Irish modernisms of writers like MacDiarmid and Joyce more formally developed because of the "marginality" of these areas (resulting in aesthetic challenges to the conventions of the "center") and because of their political "incompleteness"? Certainly aesthetically innovative modernist literature acted as a vanguard for cultural (and political) change in both countries. Terry Eagleton has also discussed the blooming of "marginal" modernisms in comparison to the English modernist need to "import . . . modernist artists": "There are . . . reasons why modernism, then as now, can thrive more vigorously on the colonial or neo-colonial margins than at the metropolitan centre. In an increasingly unified world, where all times and places seem indifferently interchangeable, the 'no-time' and 'no-place' of the disregarded colony, with its fractured history and marginalized space, can become suddenly symbolic of a condition of disinheritance which now seems universal" (Eagleton, *Heathcliff*, 298). Here is an additional reason for Joyce's interest in Scottish culture, the example of another place with "fractured history and marginalized space," features that are, for Eagleton, a collective issue in the modernist era. Robert Crawford: a "cursory account of Modernism stresses its cosmopolitanism and internationalism, presenting it as a facet of 'high' metropolitan culture. But there is another, equally important, side of Modernism that is demotic and crucially 'provincial'" (*Devolving*, 218–19).

Let us return to the matter of Scottish nationalism. After the 1950s and the "high tide of Unionism" (Harvie and Jones, 65), the decline of Protestantism and empire, "the long period of Britain's post-war relative decline against international competitors" (Devine, *Scotland*, 15), and the discovery of North Sea oil, pressure for Scottish home rule increased, up until a 1979 referendum under the Conservative and Unionist administration of Margaret Thatcher (which did not command a majority in Scotland—this government also had very serious and well-documented difficulties governing the north of Ireland). The historian Tom Nairn, in his seminal 1980s text *The Break-Up of Britain*, has used some arrestingly Joycean imagery to describe Scottish nationalism during the mid-twentieth century:

> "Nationalism" in the fuller historical sense remained very weak—so weak that until the 1960s it was almost wholly resistant to even the modest organization of the SNP. In the present situation typically nationalist myths about the continuous and inevitable "rise" of the latter are bound to be invented. For nationalism time is unimportant: in its nature—mythology the soul is always there anyway, slumbering in the people, and it is of no especial importance that McFinnegan opened his eyes one hundred and fifty years after

everyone else. He had to get up *some* time, and what matters is the grandeur of the Wake. (174)

Although a majority in Scotland—a partially conscious "McFinnegan"—voted for home rule in the 1979 referendum, Thatcher's government decided that the size of the majority was insufficient and took no further action on the issue.

As a result of episodes such as the introduction of the loathed poll tax one year earlier in Scotland than in the rest of the United Kingdom, the Conservative party's support in Scotland eroded to almost nothing during the long recession-haunted days of the 1980s.[3] Famously, in the 1997 general election the Conservative party returned not one MP north of the border. In a second home-rule referendum held by a Labour administration in 1997 an overwhelming majority voted "Yes/Yes" for a parliament with tax-raising powers, and a new parliament was opened at Holyrood in Edinburgh in 1999. The Northern Irish peace process—with the final provisional IRA cease-fire of 1997 and the Good Friday Agreement of 1998 leading to power sharing in the north—attended this progress. A Labour–Liberal Democrat status quo prevailed at Holyrood until the 2007 Scottish Parliamentary election, when a minority SNP government under Alex Salmond took control of the parliament at Holyrood.[4] The rise of the left-of-center civic nationalist SNP has coincided with the gradual decline of the once-dominant Labour Party in Scotland. [5]

The SNP won a majority in 2011 following the 2010 UK general election in which a Conservative / Liberal Democrat coalition gained power in Westminster. The SNP staged an independence referendum in 2014 (perhaps chosen due its status as the seven hundredth anniversary of "panickburns" [*FW*, 9.25]), and, in the latter days of the campaign, another "crisis" gripped British politics, especially when opinion polls put the pro-Independence "Yes" campaign in the lead days before the ballot: "As the campaign reached a climax and the gap between 'Yes' and 'No' started to narrow, something close to panic gripped the very highest levels of the British state. The leaders of the unionist parties desperately searched for options to stem what seemed a rising tide drifting inexorably towards a vote for independence" (Devine, *Independence*, 233). However, in the face of considerable opposition from big business and foreign governments, and an almost uniformly hostile "Old Media," supporters of independence were unable to secure a majority in the September 2014 vote.[6] However, the "Yes" campaign was victorious in major urban areas such as Glasgow and Dundee. Furthermore, a level of support of 45 percent for Scottish Independence would have been unthinkable even recently. Perhaps the fairly evenly split Scottish electorate could be read as yet another manifestation of the ancient "Caledonian Antisyzygy." Following the referendum "Scotland remained a very restless nation" (255).

In May 2015, under Nicola Sturgeon, the SNP won a staggering fifty-six of the fifty-nine Scottish seats in the UK general election, wiping out the Labour Party in its former heartlands with the largest swings ever seen in a UK election (the Labour Party paid a heavy price for lining up in the "No" campaign alongside the right-wing Conservatives during the independence referendum). Meanwhile the Conservatives were triumphant in England. The SNP then won the 2016 Scottish Parliament election, held on May 2016, and a third term in government. Part of the SNP's 2016 manifesto stated: "We believe that the Scottish Parliament should have the right to hold another referendum if there is clear and sustained evidence that independence has become the preferred option of a majority of the Scottish people—or if there is a significant and material change in the circumstances that prevailed in 2014, such as Scotland being taken out of the EU against our will" (Scottish National Party, 24). In June 2016, England and Wales voted to leave the European Union while Scotland overwhelming voted to remain (by 62 percent to 38 percent—and with every single one of the thirty-two council areas supporting "Remain"). Northern Ireland also voted to remain, albeit by a smaller margin than in Scotland and with some areas voting to leave.[7] As Colin Kidd writes, "The result of the vote undermines Scottish unionists, one of whose central arguments in 2014 was that independence threatened Scotland's place in the EU" (Kidd, 12). With the SNP still in control of the Scottish parliament and the UK heading out of the EU, a second independence referendum—partly in response to this seismic event and the approaching "material change"—is a distinct possibility. The UK is now a little brittle, with Scotland moving in a different political direction than England and Wales. Certain voters in Scotland may relate to Robert Hand's prophecy in *Exiles*: "Some day we shall have to choose between England and Europe" (*PE*, 158).

In a strange sequence of events, Joyce, who borrowed and learned much from Scottish literature, had an important influence on the Scottish Literary Renaissance (as well as Scottish writing beyond that movement). The Scottish Literary Renaissance, also partly inspired by the achievements of modern Irish literature, was a cultural forerunner to renewed Scottish nationalist political activity that has in turn slowly developed into the present political and cultural scene in Scotland (the advent of Irish independence was also an inspiration to Scottish nationalists). As Margery Palmer McCulloch has described, "Scottish modernism of the post-1918 years . . . laid lasting foundations for the building of the confident, outward-looking culture Scotland takes for granted today" ("Scottish Modernism," 781). The political situation in Scotland now resembles—on some basic levels at least—the Irish events and sense of crisis that Joyce described in his Triestine journalism and public lectures in 1907, one hundred years before the election of the first nationalist government at Holyrood (without, of course, a corresponding "Ulster" problem or physical-force dimension).[8] And as *Finnegans Wake* powerfully attests, history is never finished; it is always work in progress.

NOTES

INTRODUCTION

1. For some prominent historians, the use of the term Britain is not even appropriate:

A. J. P. Taylor's volume of *The Oxford History of England* opens . . . with a flat and express denial that the term "Britain" has any meaning. It is, he says, the name of a Roman province, which never included the whole of modern Scotland, and was foisted upon the English by the inhabitants of the northern kingdom as part of the parliamentary union of 1707. Moreover, he continues, the term "Great Britain"—which properly denotes no more than the Anglo-Scottish union—is non-identical with the term "United Kingdom," since the latter's scope included the whole of Ireland from 1801 and the dark and bloody rump of that island from 1922. (Pocock, 24)

2. Arguably, this failure to think of the connections between Irish and Scottish writing goes back at least as far as the Irish Literary Revival. Lady Gregory once haughtily commented on the reluctance of the Irish intelligentsia to buy Scottish books: "I myself never quite understood the meaning of the 'Celtic movement,' which we were said to belong to. When I was asked about it, I used to say it was a movement meant to persuade the Scotch to begin buying our books while we continued not to buy theirs" (Gregory, 21). Well, the "old hake" (*U*, 9.1158–59) may not have been interested in Scottish literature, but Joyce certainly was. As was Lady Gregory's fellow Revivalist Yeats (although perhaps unwittingly): "One of the more interesting developments in recent Irish criticism had been the acknowledgement of Thomas Carlyle as a more potent influence on the Irish Literary Revival than Matthew Arnold. . . . Carlyle's ideas . . . permeated much that Yeats read and heard because they were mediated in the work of Carlyle's enthusiastic Irish disciple, Standish James O'Grady, whom Yeats and others saw as 'the father of the Revival'" (G. Watson, "Aspects," 140). And when Yeats was a child, his father had read

him Scott's *Redgauntlet*, a significant text because of its "celebration of the persistence of folk culture" (R. Crawford, *Devolving*, 218).

3. For a discussion Joyce's Anglophobia see the introduction to Gibson's *Joyce's Revenge*.

4. The north of Ireland is, of course, something of a special case or anomaly in a discussion of "countries" or "nations." However, as I will discuss, Joyce is also attuned to the national, religious, cultural, and linguistic variations of that contested province. The issue of Wales is well beyond the scope of this study, but the portmanteau "Englandwales" (*FW*, 242.33) may point to Joyce's awareness of England's medieval annexation of that country and of its incorporation into the English legal system.

5. Serious objections to the exclusions of *The Empire Writes Back*, in relation to Joyce's work, have been raised by critics such as Michael Mays: "[While] the historical conditions and political ramifications of Irish colonization were (and are) quite different in significant respects from those of other colonial sites, such [an omission] effectively erases the violent breach and the enmity that characterizes the history of Anglo-Irish relations. And just as it absurdly establishes an inane hierarchy of sufferers, so it glosses over that which Joyce's work takes greatest pains to map: the uncharted spaces of the conflicted identity-formations wrought by colonization in the colonizer every bit as much as in the colonized" (21). For further analysis of Scottish literature in relation to postcolonialism see Connell.

6. See also: "There was a colonial dimension to the Irish State under the union (as exemplified by its unaccountable executive and paramilitary police force), but Ireland differed from other imperial colonies in forming an integral part of the United Kingdom with all the rights, freedoms, and privileges which that entailed" (McGarry, 17).

7. I shall discuss Joyce's views on Arthur Balfour in chapter 2, on David Hume.

8. See also: "In [the stream of consciousness or interior monologue] the kaleidoscope of past and present can be constantly shaken to form transient patterns which are not essentially historical but psychological" (S. Deane, *Celtic*, 101).

9. (V. Deane et al., *"Finnegans Wake" Notebooks*, will hereafter be referred to in the customary way, by roman numeral, capital letter, and arabic numeral, e.g., VI.B.6.) The photograph in question can be seen on plate 47 of the 1982 revised edition of Ellmann's biography and also appears in Cato and Vitello, *Joyce Images*, 76–77. See pages 100–101 of the same text for a picture of Joyce wearing a tartan tie in Lucerne in the late 1930s. Joyce seems to have assigned an almost totemic significance to ties. When painting Joyce's portrait in 1924,

Patrick Tuohy stressed the importance of capturing his subject's soul. Joyce answered: "Never mind my soul. Just be sure you have my tie right" (*JJII*, 566).

10. "(O)Murry, MacMurry, Murray, MacMorrow (Gilmore). A considerable proportion of the Murrays now living in Ireland are of Scottish extraction, particularly in Ulster, where they are more numerous than in the other provinces. The old Irish surname Ó Muireadhaigh, formerly anglicized O'Murry, is now almost always Murray" (MacLysaght, 133). According to MacLysaght, Murray is the third-most-common English, Scottish, or Welsh surname in Ireland—after Smith and Brown(e) (MacLysaght, 210).

11. "Mary Jane ('May') Murray, born May 15, 1859, was ten years younger than her husband. She came on her mother's side from a family with keen musical interest; her grandfather Flynn, who had the starch mill in Back Lane mentioned in 'The Dead,' arranged for all his daughters to be trained in music. From the age of five to nineteen May Murray had lessons in piano and voice, as well as in dancing and politeness, at the 'Misses Flynn school' at 15 Usher's Island, a street which runs beside the Liffey. The school was operated by two of her mother's sisters, Mrs. Callanan and Mrs. Lyons, with the aid later on of Mrs. Callanan's daughter, Mary Ellen. It may have been from them that she learned the slightly old-fashioned courtliness of manner which she was to teach her oldest son. . . . John Joyce complained a little about the Flynns, but he drew the line at the Murrays. His finest epithets were reserved for the members of this family who had disapproved of him, and the vitriol of Thersites in the 'Cyclops' episode of *Ulysses* is modeled in part on his eloquent abuse. 'O weeping God, the things I married into'" (*JJII*, 18–19).

12. For a discussion of the Malins characters in "The Dead" see chapter 1.

13. See also: "Joyce has Bloom defeat his rival, Blazes Boylan, in Molly Bloom's mind by being the first and the last in her thoughts as she falls off to sleep" (*JJII*, 361).

14. To clarify this book's position on the identity of the "'dreamer'" of *Finnegans Wake*, this hypothetical figure is not treated as being synonymous with the father figure of the text, HCE. Instead, HCE is regarded here as a dream figure, with which the dreamer/sleeper regularly and most closely identifies. Of course, that there even is a sleeping person whose hallucinations are represented in *Finnegans Wake* is disputed. Critics such as John Bishop in *Joyce's Book of the Dark* (1986) and Philip Kitcher in *Joyce's Kaleidoscope* (2008) have worked from the starting point that the book is "set" at night and that there is a mind that "contains" the text of *Finnegans Wake*. However, Derek Attridge among others has questioned such a reading. For Attridge "the notion of the dream as an interpretive context for *Finnegans Wake* is one among a number of

such contexts which, though incompatible with one another, all have some potential value" (199). Both sides of this argument have been eloquently stated elsewhere. Suffice it to say that I find Bishop's arguments in *Joyce's Book of the Dark* convincing and that approaching the *Wake* as a text of the night and of the experience of sleep and dream offers a way to read the text productively. As Ellmann reports (though without providing a source—see Attridge, 193), "[Joyce] conceived of his book as the dream of old Finn, lying in death beside the river Liffey and watching the history of Ireland and the world—past and future—flow through his mind like flotsam on the river of life" (*JJII*, 544). Also: "In writing of the night, I really could not, I felt I could not, use words in their ordinary connections. Used in that way they do not express how things are in the night, in the different stages—conscious, then semi-conscious, then unconscious" (*JJII*, 546). Finally: "There are in a way no characters. It's like a dream. The style is also changing, and unrealistic, like the dream world. If one had to name a character, it would be just an old man. But his own connection with reality is doubtful" (*JJII*, 696). Philip Herring has discussed the connection between uncertainty and dream in the *Wake*: "One might well argue . . . that the uncertainty principle of *Finnegans Wake* is traceable directly to the dream process, which of necessity distorts meaning" (189).

15. Based on the use of Celtic languages surviving into modern times, there are generally considered to be six Celtic nations or territories: Brittany, Cornwall, Ireland, the Isle of Man, Scotland, and Wales. Which has Joyce omitted?

16. "As has been convincingly shown by, among others, Ellmann (1982), Ferrer (1985), Van Mierlo (1997) and Kimball (2003), Joyce did read widely in psychoanalysis at various points in his writing. One should emphasize, however, that this is *not* a decisive argument for using psychoanalytic ideas to read his work; what it does show is that those ideas were of great interest to him in crucial periods of his development as a writer. But had no such evidence come to light, the case for using psychoanalytic ideas to understand his work would be essentially the same, since the argument is based not on contingent historical circumstances, but on general claims about the nature of the human subject" (Thurston, "Scotographia," 410).

17. As I shall discuss later, this interiority is, for Joyce, a Celtic and Humean feature.

18. For a consideration of Joyce in connection with Freud and Jung, see Brivic, *Joyce between Freud and Jung*.

19. Joyce and Lacan have in common an intentionally difficult prose style that attempts to imitate the workings of the unconscious:

Lacan evolved a style of writing whose aim was to avoid being over-systematized and reductive, and to reflect the workings of the unconscious. Lacan's prose . . . often obeys the laws of the unconscious as they were formalized by Freud—it is full of puns, jokes, metaphors, irony and contradictions, and there are many similarities in its form to that of psychotic writing. This makes reading his essays an intellectual task of some magnitude, on a par with reading *Finnegan's Wake* [*sic*]. (Benvenuto and Kennedy, 12)

See also: "In the opening address Lacan gave at the 1975 James Joyce Symposium in Paris, he explains that as a young student he had often hung about at Adrienne Monnier's Left Bank bookshop, and it was there he had twice bumped into Joyce" (Thurston, "Scotographia," 419).

20. Deleuze's first work was *Empiricism and Subjectivity*, a study of Hume. For Delueuze's comments on Joyce see *Difference and Repetition*, 72, 86, 154–55, 157, 255.

21. For a discussion of Joyce's work as literary reprisal, see Andrew Gibson's *Joyce's Revenge*.

22. Joyce does not go so far as to call the Anglo-Saxon civilization *totally* materialist, leaving him some room to consider, for example, the "mysticism" of Blake (*OCPW*, 180). However, as Andrew Gibson has pointed out, Joyce has a unique conception of Blake as an English poet: "Joyce was drawn to Blake insofar as Blake was a poet not of England but of Albion, both an England buried and seemingly lost, and a future England, an England yet to be. He recognized the analogy between his project and Blake's, but also turned Blake's project to his own and Irish ends" (*Joyce's Revenge*, 205).

23. Patrick Parrinder has discussed the reaction in Ireland against materialism with reference to Joyce:

In Ireland, for example, University College, Dublin, which James Joyce attended, was designed to counter the British government's "godless colleges" at Belfast, Galway and Cork. (Galway and Cork later came under heavy Catholic influence.) In Joyce's autobiographical fictions we see how the student intellectual life of the Catholic university is sometimes discreetly, sometimes overtly censored by the authorities. When Joyce's hero sets out to devise an aesthetic theory, he has learnt his lesson so well that his theory is "applied Aquinas," a scholarly reinterpretation of a canonical medieval text. (Parrinder, 17)

In Joyce's later work skepticism and idealism offer liberation from both Catholic dogma and materialism.

24. Furthermore, the class hatred Woolf displays in her letters on Joyce was no barrier to her adopting his innovations (for some typical Woolf snobbery see *JJII*, 528).

25. The authorship of *The History of the Life and Adventures of Mr. Duncan Campbell* is disputed.

26. See also: "I suppose uncertainty is the handmaid of all grandiose literary projects. Many motives lay behind that 1951 decision of mine to translate Joyce's *Ulysses* into Irish. If they won't read it in English, I said to myself, bedamn but we'll put them in the situation that they can boast they won't read it in Irish aither" (O'Brien, 135).

27. For a discussion of Joyce and the Easter Rising of 1916, see Barlow, "Silent Exile?"

28. This approach contrasts with earlier attempts to reconcile Joyce with a liberal English tradition or to co-opt him into that tradition: "Michael Long, reading Joyce as 'the saving humanist of English-language modernism,' in whose work we discover 'no hate, no contempt, no foulness of mouth,' states that 'Joyce published no credo, but his writing is implicitly liberal, democratic and tolerant.' It is difficult to appreciate how attractive Joyce must appear to an English critic who wishes to appropriate a body of Irish literature for the 'mainstream' tradition" (Nolan, *Nationalism*, 105).

29. For a discussion of Joyce and the Revival see Platt, *Joyce and the Anglo-Irish.*

30. On a similar note, Declan Kiberd writes that "there is good reason to see Joyce as someone who felt himself a part (however angular a part)" of the Irish Literary Revival (Kiberd, "Joyce's Homer, Homer's Joyce," 245). Of course, the other issue here is that Joyce came from a Catholic background, whereas the Revival from the 1890s onwards was mainly an Anglo-Irish, Protestant affair. For further reading on the pre- and post-Famine cultural movements in Ireland see S. Deane, *Celtic.*

31. See also: "The near-blind exile who spins out elaborate variations on his inner vision of a primal quincunx to make the *Wake* is like a holy man who has given up the material world to meditate on a cross or mandala. . . . Having abandoned worldly power, he gained awesome spiritual power" (Brivic, *Joyce between Freud and Jung*, 203).

32. Daniel Ferrer has discussed the origin of the term Scotographia in connection with psychiatry: "In the notebook VI.B.19 . . . we find a list of psychiatric or pseudo-psychiatric terms, probably devised by Joyce himself . . . misophobia/claustrophobia/aerophobia/skotophobia/scotographia/scotoscribia. *Scotographia* (the writing of/by obscurity) is particularly interesting as a definition of *Finnegans Wake* (or of the Freudian symptom): a writing that

obscures rather than makes plain and reveals through this very process of concealment" ("Freudful," 180–81).

ONE. Crotthers

1. *The Abbot* is a significant text for the young boy of "Araby" to find:

The musty books and the boy's response to them are doubly and trebly meaningful. Joyce chose works that would objectify the themes of "Araby," works that would exemplify in the most blatant (yet unexpressed) manner the very confusions, veilings, and failures he was depicting in the priest and the boy. The books and their lurking incongruities help us arraign the priest and understand the boy. That the priest should leave a romance by Scott with a religious title that obscures the fact that it is the secular celebration of a worldly queen, Mary Queen of Scots, a queen enshrined in history as saint and harlot . . . all this is a commentary on the priest and the religion he is supposed to represent. At the same time this literary debris objectifies the boy's confusions. . . . That Scott's unblemished romantic heroine, an idolized Catholic queen by the name of Mary, should also be (though not to Scott) a "harlot queen," a passionate thrice-married woman who was regarded by many of her contemporaries as the "Whore of Babylon," as a murderess who murdered to satisfy her lust—this strange dissonance, muted and obscured by Scott's presentation, is a version of the boy's strikingly similar and equally muted dissonances. (Stone, 380)

2. In "The Sisters," "*Drapery*" is considered a "vague name" for a shop (*D*, 3).

3. Strangely, Miss Ivors's name is more suggestive of imperialism than of the Celtic Revival. Recall Stephen's Latin exercise in *Portrait*: "*India mittit ebur*" (*P*, 193).

4. The references to crosses and to fish fit in with a larger scheme of Christian allusion in "The Dead," as Adrienne Auslander Munich has discussed: "There are repeated references to crosses—twice in the dance, when the partners 'cross' just before Molly's 'cross-examination' of Gabriel, and repeatedly in Mrs. Malins's tedious recounting of her boat 'crossing' (pp. 188–90). The association between this part of the conversation and the next—a discussion of fishing and fish—prepares for the more insistently Christian references to the crucifixion at the end of the story" (180).

5. At least Scottish artists were more welcoming than their religious counterparts. For example, Hugh MacDiarmid wrote that "the growth of

Catholicism, and the influx of the Irish, are alike welcome, as undoing those accompaniments of the Reformation which have lain like a blight on Scottish arts and affairs" (MacDiarmid, *Albyn*, 3–4).

6. There are, however, a very small number of exceptions to this rule, for example the Lake of Menteith near Stirling.

7. A significant historical example of much earlier Irish immigration to Scotland also features in *Finnegans Wake*, a theme I shall discuss later in this study.

8. A variation of the name Crotthers also appears fairly prominently in Scottish literature. An early attempt at fiction by Thomas Carlyle was entitled "Cruthers and Jonson; Or, the Outskirts of Life." This story was completed in 1822 and appeared in *Fraser's Magazine* in 1831.

9. The inclusion of a Scottish medical student in "Oxen" is intriguing, given the long-standing tradition of Scots, especially students from the University of Edinburgh, studying at medical schools in Paris (Joyce also studied medicine in Paris). This tradition dates back to the early modern period. For further information see Dingwall.

10. An alternative reading of this famous line could be "History is itself the process of blaming."

11. See also "fumes of intoxication" (*U*, 13.299). Culleton suggests that this section describes another character, Bannon, rather than Crotthers (59). However, the terms "fume" and "tow" (as well as "Scotch"), used in this section, all link to Crotthers, as I shall demonstrate. Culleton also highlights the "dualism" of Crotthers, so perhaps the above section relates to both Crotthers and Bannon.

12. The work of Robert Burns also features heavily in *Finnegans Wake*; see chapter 6.

13. There is also a suggestion here of the textile industries, which attracted thousands of Irish workers to Scotland in the eighteenth and nineteenth centuries. This background is also alluded to in "Grace," where one of Mrs Kernan's sons supposedly works "in a draper's shop in Glasgow" (*D*, 156).

14. Appropriately for "Oxen of the Sun," the precursor of Bacchus—Dionysus—was often represented in the form of a bull. See Frazer, 399.

15. Leith had been one of the main centers in Scotland to receive Irish immigrants during the nineteenth century, as labor-seekers could find employment on the docks there. The area is still closely associated with Hibernian F.C., the Edinburgh football club set up by Irish newcomers in 1875. Leith was incorporated into the city of Edinburgh in 1920 (MacDonald, 104). The most famous Scottish club with Irish roots is, of course, Glasgow's Celtic F.C. This club was founded in 1888 by a Marist priest from County Sligo by the name of Brother Walfrid. Michael Davitt laid a ceremonial sod of Donegal

turf at the opening of Parkhead, the club's stadium, in 1892. The club was the first British team to win the European Cup (in 1967) and has a large following in Ireland.

16. The same confusion arises in Nabokov's *Lolita*: "I said the doctors did not quite know yet what the trouble was. Anyway something abdominal. Abominable? No, abdominal" (112).

17. Since the drunkenness of "Oxen of the Sun" is the closest *Ulysses* gets to the verbal distortions of *Finnegans Wake*, perhaps drink can also explain partly the linguistic confusions of the latter text.

18. Research into Joyce's notebooks is a vital part of the "genetic" field within Joyce studies. Genetic criticism studies the processes whereby a text came into being rather than concentrating solely on the finished article. This is not to be confused (although sometimes is) with intertextuality.

19. However, as the citizen correctly points out in "Cyclops," the harp as Irish flag was an invention of "Henry Tudor's" (*U*, 12.1308). On the subject of surnames and Celtic music, the Crotthers-like name Crowther derives from the Welsh stringed instrument the crwth. According to *The Oxford Dictionary of English Surnames*, "Crowther, Crowder, Crother, Crewther" are "a derivative of ME *crouth*, *croude*, 'fiddle, a fiddler'" (Reaney and Wilson, 119).

20. It's likely that Joyce used Frazer's work for the *Wake*: "Joyce probably used Frazer's *The Golden Bough*, and seems, like his friend T. S. Eliot, 'to have used especially the two volumes Atthis, Adonis, Osiris'" (Atherton, 193). Joyce apparently met Frazer at a drinks reception in Paris (See Jolas, 9). Alba Longa is also mentioned a number of times in Vico's *New Science*, where it is spoken of—fittingly—as Rome's mother city (See Vico, 261).

21. So this Latin tribe shares succession rules similar to those of the Picts:

> Thus it would seem that among some Aryan peoples, at a certain stage of their social evolution, it has been customary to regard women and not men as the channels in which royal blood flows, and to bestow the kingdom in each successive generation on a man of another family, and often of another country, who marries one of the princesses and reigns over his wife's people. . . . The old Danish historian Saxo Grammaticus puts this view of the kingship very clearly in the mouth of Hermutrude, a legendary queen of Scotland. "Indeed she was a queen," says Hermutrude, "and but that her sex gainsaid it, might be deemed a king; nay (and this is yet truer), whomsoever she thought worthy of her bed was at once a king, and she yielded her kingdom with herself. Thus her sceptre and her hand went together." (Frazer, 127)

For a further discussion on the Picts see chapter 3.

22. Albumin is a type of protein. The name comes from the Latin for egg white.

23. On the subject of Carlyle, *Sartor Resartus* is one of the sui generis texts—along with the work of another Scot, Tobias Smollett—that early reviewers of *Ulysses* drew comparisons with:

> Discussion of origins and lineages would be very strange to the original readers of *Ulysses*, who of course did not know what modernism was, let alone postmodernism. For many of them, *Ulysses* was a strange beast, one perhaps devoid of genealogy, and of no discernable genre. Reviewers, critics, and other novelists repeatedly expressed their consternation over what kind of book it could be. As indicated in the standard collection of contemporary reviews, notices, and comments, the only names that were regularly evoked were Sterne (repeatedly), Rabelais (frequently), and Cervantes (occasionally); other analogues suggested by Joyce's contemporaries that literary historians no longer bother to record include Carlyle, Smollett, Duchamp, Balzac, Zola. (Richardson, 1046)

Giorgio Melchiori has commented on the similarities between the texts of Smollett and Joyce, noting Smollett's "verbal ingenuity" (36) and his interest in "composite language [with a] higher concentration of meaning" (46), and pointing out that "Joyce's trick of availing himself of foreign words to complicate the polysignificance of his new vocabulary is found in Smollett" (48). Finally, "it should be noted . . . that actually it was Smollett himself who first used [the] method of presenting the same fact through different eyes leaving the reader in doubt" (48). See chapter 2 for further discussion on Joyce and doubt.

24. See also: "*A Scottish poet maun assume / The burden o' his people's doom / And dee to brak' their livin' tomb*" (MacDiarmid, *Drunk Man*, l.2638–40).

25. See D'Arcy. For a discussion on Scottish religion and the Caledonian Games Society in connection with the "U. p: up" postcard mystery in *Ulysses*, see Gibbons, *Joyce's Ghosts*, 199–206.

26. According to Terry Eagleton, Yeats's gyres and Joyce's Viconian cycles "compensate for different forms of powerlessness" (*Heathcliff*, 270).

27. Compare James Frazer's similar comments in *The Golden Bough*: "The Celtic peoples . . . inhabited the Land's End of Europe, the islands and promontories that stretch out into the Atlantic Ocean on the North-West" (730).

28. See the "Explanatory Notes" section of the "1922 Text" of *Ulysses*, 915.

29. That is not to say that *Ulysses* ceases to be "representational" at this point. For a discussion on this topic, see Gordon, "Obeying the Boss."

TWO.   Exhuming the Enlightenment

1. I take this term for Scott's presentation of history from Joyce's description of his own techniques for composing *Finnegans Wake*: "One great part of every human existence is passed in a state which cannot be rendered sensible by the use of wideawake language, cutanddry grammar and goahead plot" (*JJII*, 584–85).

2. Terence Brown on Smith, Joyce, and the decline of realism:

> It is by now a critical commonplace to associate the emergence of fictional realism as the dominant mode of the English novel in the early nineteenth century with the era of liberal capitalism in Britain. A self-regulating free market (classically defined in Adam Smith's *The Wealth of Nations*) seemed to the rational mind to be the product of a reality which, obeying principles of order, could be adequately represented in a mimetic art form. It was by contrast the determining assumption of the high Modernism of the early twentieth century . . . that such realism was no longer capable of such representation and indeed that representation itself was a misguided, because impossible, artistic ambition. It may be possible then, to read Modernism's radical eschewal of mimesis as in part a response to the changed economic conditions of late nineteenth century Britain and Europe, a century of progress being brought to a premature end by the first Great Depression of the last quarter of the century. . . . For Modernism, as it abandoned the epistemological certainties of realism and the empirical and even economic certitudes (many of the Modernist writers were obsessed with economic theory) which secured them, the matter of meaning was a central problematic. (17)

3. See, for example, Yenor, "Between Rationalism and Postmodernism."

4. Discussing Hume's position on identity, Gilles Deleuze has suggested that there is an encompassing "place"—the imagination—where identity can be performed: "The imagination is not a factor, an agent, or a determinate determination; it is a place which it is necessary to localize, that is, to fix in a determinable way. Nothing is done by the imagination, everything is done in the imagination" (Deleuze, *Empiricism and Subjectivity*, quoted in Gallagher, 26–27). Shaun Gallagher has summed up Hume's thinking on identity in this way: "In the end, human nature is constituted as the constant or fixed imagination which, in turn, dependably constitutes the fiction of identity" (27).

5. Furthermore, we may also detect Joyce's skepticism towards a notion of literary "purity" in his use of Macpherson (see chapter 5).

6. This line reappears, transformed, in *Finnegans Wake*: "whirled without end to end" (*FW*, 582.20–21).

7. Usually the term Scottish School is used to describe the "common-sense" philosophy of Scots thinkers such as Thomas Reid.

8. As Willy Maley has pointed out, Balfour appears in *Ulysses* as "Mr Allfours (Tamoshant. Con.)" (*U*, 12.865). Maley glosses this section as follows: "'con'... suggests a double-cross or sleight of hand ... 'Allfours' is both 'all force' and a quadruped, which is an apt characterization of the four-nation British state" ("Kilt by Kelt," 213). However, Joyce may also have had the following passage from Frazer's *The Golden Bough* in mind (considering the suitably bloody nature of the section and Joyce's frequent use of pig metaphors for Ireland): "At the festival of the Alfoors of Minahassa, in Northern Celebes, after a pig has been killed, the priest rushes furiously at it, thrusts his head into the carcase, and drinks the blood" (63). The Mitchelstown Massacre of 1887 is alluded to by Joyce in the same section of "Cyclops" (*U*, 12.874). See also: "Don't hesitate to shoot" (*U*, 12.877).

9. "Je suis au bout de l'anglais" (*JJII*, 546).

10. These texts were purchased in Trieste. It is surprising that Joyce neglected to work the title *Enquiry concerning Human Understanding* into *Finnegans Wake*, as it would have been an easy opportunity to include another appearance of the initials HCE, albeit in a backwards form. Joyce also missed a trick with Smollett's *The Expedition of Humphry Clinker*.

11. On the subject of Beckett and modernist indeterminacy:

Beckett once remarked that his favourite word was "perhaps." . . . Indeterminacy is a source of hope as well as scepticism, since if the world has no definitive shape to it then there is no reason why Godot may not show up after all. Instability may be a cause for comfort as well as distress. . . . Modernist culture of the mid-20th century is by and large a culture of negativity—of absence, lack, void, death, otherness, non-being. (Eagleton, "Determinacy Kills," 9)

We can also read the indeterminacy and skepticism of the *Wake* as a response to the "crazed" politics of the time of its composition. According to Philippe Sollers, "*Finnegans Wake* is the most formidably anti-fascist book produced between the two world wars" (3–4). The text is also a response to the certainties of Christian dogma.

12. On realism and Irish literature, Terry Eagleton writes,

It was not that the Irish did not know about English realism but, rather, that they could not understand what all the fuss was about. What was so marvelous about a scrupulous description of a steam engine when you could write about talking horses, ageing portraits or sinking your teeth into young women's necks? Faced with a dreary surfeit of reality in everyday life, along with a Celtic heritage of extravagant fantasy and exuberant wordplay, the Irish could see no particular virtue in photographic accuracy. Joyce could learn nothing from Thackeray or George Eliot. The point of literature was to transfigure reality, not to reflect it—which is why, from the heretical medieval philosopher John Scottus Eriugena to Bishop Berkeley and W. B. Yeats, there is such a robust Irish faith in the imagination's power to summon new worlds into existence. Philosophically, this suspicion of realism went hand in hand with a rejection of rationalism and materialism. If there is such an entity as the Irish mind, it is of a strongly idealist bent. . . . No sooner had the novel made its appearance in 18th-century England than Sterne responded with *Tristram Shandy*, a great anti-novel which showed how a text which tried to represent everything with painstaking meticulousness would simply buckle and implode. Modern Ireland was equally a source of anti-novels, such as *Ulysses*, *Finnegans Wake* and Flann O'Brien's *At Swim-Two-Birds*, as well as a purveyor of anti-drama in the work of Samuel Beckett. ("Running out of Soil," 28–30)

13. For a brief introduction to Hume's reception in Europe see Mossner.

14. Doubt is central to Joyce's treatment of the relationship issues of inheritance, paternity, and sexual fidelity. According to Joseph Voelker, the central character of *Exiles*, Richard, "has laid out his life on a Pyrrhonist principle, a distrust of the fatuous assurances that public language provides. Bertha is not really his wife. . . . Illegitimate Archie is only probably his son. Hamilton Rowan is not his heroic ancestor. . . . Richard's only source of certitude is Robert, the disciple he trusts to betray him" (503). Voelker also links *Exiles* and *Ulysses* through an attention to incertitude: "As Joyce moved away from that anxious place in the imagination, he began to delineate the homelessness of Leopold Bloom, for whom the doubtfulness of the world is sufficiently in evidence on every Dublin street" (516).

15. Cited in Platt, *Modernism and Race*, 28. It is unknown whether Joyce—an Irishman who died in Zurich—ever read David Hume's essay "Of National Characters," in which Hume states, among other observations, that the "common people in SWITZERLAND have probably more honesty than those of the same rank in IRELAND" (*Essays*, 113). With regard to the Scots, Hume's *History of England* "devoted itself to proving the superiority . . . of

Scotchmen to Englishmen; he did not consider history worthy of philosophical detachment" (B. Russell, 601).

16. For an account of the relationship between Berkeley and Joyce see Anghinetti. See also Yeats's "Blood and the Moon": "And God-appointed Berkeley proved all things a dream" (288).

17. Here then is a link back to Crotthers and the nonsectarian maternity ward of "Oxen of the Sun." For a discussion of Joyce and religious matters, see Lernout.

18. See also: "In the *Proteus* episode Stephen is firmly Aristotelean, and decides in favour of both an external world and a self. Six episodes later, in *Scylla and Charybdis*, the same questions arise and the same conclusions are reached, but less firmly. The mind is poised upon doubt as the world upon the void, Stephen concedes. After this Hume begins to have his innings" (Ellmann, *Consciousness*, 63). Karen Lawrence's *The Odyssey of Style in Ulysses* covers Joyce's skepticism "about any one mode of writing" and "about the ordering of experience in language" (108, 119).

19. The phrases "So pass the pick for child sake" and "four hands" link the historian Hume to the chroniclers of *Finnegans Wake* known as "the Four," while the presence of the four old men here can be detected by the phrase "so pass the pick for child sake," since it echoes similar phrases based on "Pass the fish for Christ sake" used in sections describing the group. "Give over it" suggests the German *übergeben*—deliver—which, along with the "pick" used to dig up the letter and the talk of "scavenging" (*FW*, 79.34), connects Hume to an attempt to uncover a past which is, like the precise details of the events in "Phornix Park" (*FW*, 80.6), essentially unknowable or "lostfully" (*FW*, 80.15). This history/writing linkage informs the context of this section: a discussion of the rubbish dump where the letter has been buried and lost.

20. Like all endings in the *Wake* and Stephen Dedalus's "allwombing tomb" (*U*, 3.402), this end is also a beginning. Birth and death are joined here, in a way reminiscent of Hume's reaction to the muted reception to his *Treatise of Human Nature*: "It fell dead-born from the press" (quoted in B. Russell, 600).

21. David Hume was in fact originally named "David Home" and changed his surname because he thought English people would not be able to pronounce it correctly. See Mossner, 8.

22. This has also been considered a Celtic, rather than a strictly Irish, phenomenon. Commenting on the great Gaelic poet Sorley MacLean, Brendan Devlin writes, "That the poet should turn so naturally and unaffectedly to an event of almost three centuries earlier is an aspect of the Gaelic mind which often seems puzzling to the Anglo-Saxon" (84).

23. One of Shem's marginal notes for this section reads, "*Dig him in the rubsh*" (*FW*, 261.17–18), which links to the rubbish pile and to the letter which represents both history itself and the processes of historiography. Furthermore, the buried letter is also alluded to with the play on "petit bleu," a type of telegram: "petsybluse" (*FW*, 261.2). For more detail on the function of the burial mounds in Irish ritual, see G. Gibson, 94–95.

24. Incidentally, this connection between impressions and ideas in Hume presents a possible problem for his refutation of causality. See B. Russell, 638.

25. Compare the comments of H. G. Wells in a 1928 letter to Joyce: "Your work is an extraordinary experiment and I will go out of my way to save it from destruction or restrictive interruption. It has its believers and its following. Let them rejoice in it. To me it is a dead end" (*LI*, 275).

26. On the subject of Hume's skepticism regarding the external world, two "possible strategies" have been formed as a way to escape Hume's "dead end." These methods are associated mainly with Thomas Reid and J. L. Austin. However, "no consensus has emerged that either of these approaches is successful in meeting Hume's challenge" (Fogelin, 230).

THREE.   Celtic Antisyzygy

1. This is a simplification, since three of the Ulster counties (Monaghan, Cavan, and Donegal) formed part of the new Free State.

2. For a discussion of how Joyce links the ancient history of the Picts and Scots to the divisions of modern Ireland, see the next chapter.

3. On the subject of partitions, it is worth pointing out that the German for Scots, *schotten*, is the same as the plural for a bulkhead. The word *schotten* appears at a number of points during *Finnegans Wake*, at 116.6–7; 138.13; 538.32–33.

4. Compare the phrase "where extremes meet" (*FW*, 440.34–35).

5. Further work on this subject is forthcoming from Katherine O'Callaghan.

6. In a piece on Joyce and Scotland, Owen Dudley Edwards states that there is "not a mention" of Stevenson in Joyce's work (Edwards, "Scotching Joyce," 15). Clearly this is not the case, as the material I examine in this section demonstrates. Aside from *Finnegans Wake*, Joyce also mentions Stevenson in the lecture "The Centenary of Charles Dickens" (*OCPW*, 185). Edwards also writes that the poem "Gas from a Burner" is the "chief reference to Scotland and the Scots in Joyce's writing" (Edwards, "Scotching Joyce," 13), despite the wealth of material relating to Scotland in *Ulysses* and *Finnegans Wake*.

7. According to Roderick Watson,

> David Balfour and Alan Breck . . . or the two sides of Dr Jekyll, represent opposed tendencies in a shifting balance between stability and adventure, or social responsibility and individual freedom. If Walter Scott proposed a similar popularity, he always ended with the *status quo*, but for Louis the condition is psychological and less easily resolved—a struggle within the hearts and minds of his heroes, who are still haunted by the booming surf, or by nights on the bare hillside, even after they have accepted a settled future. In this way Stevenson transcends the adventure novel by using its uncomplicated lines to say some rather complicated things about the tensions between imagination and convention, and the changes which take place, for better and for worse, between youth and maturity. (*Literature of Scotland*, 302)

Joyce owned a copy of Stevenson's *Catriona* (1893), the much-maligned sequel to *Kidnapped* (see Ellmann, *Consciousness*, 129).

8. See Cheng, *Joyce, Race, and Empire*, and Platt, *Joyce, Race and "Finnegans Wake."*

9. See also "the intellect of the Latin, the forbearance of the Jew, the zeal of the German . . . the sensitivity of the Slav" (*OCPW*, 174).

10. Joyce, in his later years, comes to embrace the net of nationality to some extent. Richard Ellmann reports a conversation from 1921 between Joyce and Arthur Power:

> A young Irishman named Arthur Power was brought to his table, and Joyce asked if he were "a man of letters." Power, embarrassed at the label, said he was interested. "What do you want to write?" Joyce asked. "Something on the model of the French satirists." "You will never do it," Joyce said decisively, "you are an Irishman and you must write in your own tradition. Borrowed styles are no good. You must write what is in your blood and not what is in your brain." (*JJII*, 504–5)

FOUR.   The United States of Scotia Picta

1. Stephen Gwynn's voluminous oeuvre also includes the works *Sir Walter Scott* (1930) and *Robert Louis Stevenson* (1939). Gwynn's *History of Ireland* forms part of a trend of Protestant accounts of Irish history written in this period. Gwynn was a member of John Redmond's Irish Parliamentary Party and served as an MP for Galway city.

2. Frazer's work is, of course, one of the main sources for the dying/risen god image utilized in *Finnegans Wake* and elsewhere in modernist literature.

3. For analysis of the "nodal system" of *Finnegans Wake*, see Hayman, "Nodality and the Infra-Structure." For an introduction to structuralist Joyce criticism see Roughley, *James Joyce and Critical Theory.*

4. See McCourt, *Years of Bloom.*

5. See also: "[Joyce] grew up in a city of three languages—English English, Irish English, and Gaelic—then moved to Trieste, another city where three languages interacted and reflected a history of conflict and subjugation" (Fairhall, *History*, 57).

6. This game is also mentioned in *Ulysses*: "(*He plays pussy fourcorners with ragged boys and girls.*)" (15.1601–2).

7. Adopting similar language is *Scotia Depicta; or, The Antiquities, Castles, Public Buildings, Noblemen and Gentlemen's Seats, Cities, Towns, and Picturesque Scenery of Scotland*, an 1804 collection of etchings by James Fittler. This section of the *Wake* brings to mind the Scottish-themed section of Andrew Marvell's 1681 poem "An Horatian Ode Upon Cromwell's Return from Ireland": "The Pict no shelter now shall find / Within his parti-coloured mind, / But from this valour sad / Shrinks underneath the plaid" (p. 57).

8. This passage is noteworthy as the only example of the motif where England or English is also featured. Although there is a reference to the Saxons in a later occurrence, the reference here probably relates to the treatment Joyce himself is administering to the language in *Finnegans Wake*. Usually the Picts and the Scots are paired together without any third party involvement.

9. See also: "I saw him and he not long married flirting with a young girl at Pooles Myriorama" (*U*, 18.40). As is well known, Joyce opened the first picture house in Dublin (and Ireland), the Volta. For an exploration of Joyce and cinema see McCourt, *Roll Away the Reel World*. On the subject of "Pooles," Poole is the name of Jekyll's butler in *Dr. Jekyll and Mr. Hyde.*

10. The idea of cinema as a cipher for dreams is evident elsewhere in the *Wake*, for example, "This nonday diary, this allnights newseryreel" (489.35). Motion-picture imagery combines ideas of image and duration, and so space-time polarity is again being represented, as with the first phrase mentioning the Picts and Scots on page 43 of the *Wake*.

11. Of the remaining four passages two come in ALP's section, I.viii; one is placed in I.ii; and one is found in book IV.

12. Note the convergence of opposed German and French forces in "germogall," something similar to the "united states of Scotia Picta" on page 43.

13. Given the constant mixing and blurring of identities in the *Wake*, it is not necessary (or perhaps even possible) to assign the identities of the brothers

to a specific clan of the Pict/Scot relationship, so long as we can recognize a representation of duality and contrast. However, it is tempting to relate references to the Picts etymologically through the word "painter"—the Romans named the Scottish tribe after the Pictish habit of painting their bodies—to art in general and therefore to the artist figure Shem. Shem's own artistic practices have a rather Pictish dimension, since he tattoos "every square inch of the only foolscap available, his own body" (*FW*, 185.35–36). He is also described, with another a stark reference to the notorious Black and Tans, as being a "tarandtan plaidboy" (27.9), inking himself with tartan-like patterns (see Bishop, 249). According to Finn Fordham, this is done as "defence against a hostile world" (53). Again, the modern and ancient violence of Irish history and that of Scottish history are conflated here. If "pictor" is connected to the ideas of artistic and spiritual freedom embodied in the designer Shem, then the lack of creative imagination of Shaun is implied by the darkness of "*Skotia.*"

In a parallel between Irish and Scottish history, both territories were under constant threat from Scandinavian attack and incursion at the time in which the Scottish and Pictish nations began to merge. Joyce's *Finnegans Wake* notebooks contain pages of notes on Orkney, Shetland, and the Hebrides. All of these areas of Scotland were subject to Scandinavian rule or invasion at various times up until the fifteenth century (Orkney shifted from Norwegian to Scottish control in 1472). Since the Earwicker family exists as an amalgam of the Scandinavian and the Celtic, it is unsurprising that this history would be of interest to Joyce. In general, however, Joyce's Scottish notes for *Finnegans Wake* are primarily concerned with Scotland's Irish-connected Gaelic culture. There are notes on the clan system, tartan, the Hebrides, and Jacobite songs. Joyce covers three pages of the *Finnegans Wake* notebook VI.B.6 with scrawlings relating to the Hebrides. For example, there is a note "Cuchulan Hill" (VI.B.6.155 [p]) that relates to the Cuillins on the Isle of Skye, a mountain range supposedly named after the Irish mythological figure Cúchulainn. The lines "these dyed to tartan him, rueroot, dulse, bracken, teasel, fuller's ash, sundew and cress" (*FW*, 130.24–25) are based on notes Joyce took while reading the 1918 book *The Scottish Clans and Their Tartans.* Joyce also writes notes on the various war-cries of the clans. The notes pertaining to the clans can be found in notebook VI.B.32, on pages 182 to 190. Joyce's research here centers on the original Irish colonization of Scotland and its cultural aftereffects.

14. There is a long history of guesswork regarding the etymology behind the word Scot: "Who does not feel what pleasure Zeuss brings us when he suggests that *Gael*, the name for the Irish Celt, and *Scot*, are at bottom the same word, both having their origin in a word meaning *wind*, and both signifying *the violent stormy people*?" (Arnold, 69). See also "the blew of the gaels" (*FW*, 43.27).

15. See, for example: "wicked dreams abuse / The curtailed sleep" (*Macbeth*, 2.1.50–51)"; ". . . the innocent sleep, / Sleep that knits up the ravelled sleave of care, / The death of each day's life, sore labour's bath, / Balm of hurt minds, great nature's second course, / Chief nourisher in life's feast" (2.2.33–38); "The night has been unruly" (2.3.53); "Shake off this downy sleep, death's counterfeit" (2.3.76); "Ere we will eat our meal in fear, and sleep / In the affliction of these terrible dreams / That shake us nightly" (3.2.19–21); "A great perturbation in nature, to receive at once / the benefit of sleep and do the effects of watching" (5.1.9–10).

16. The historical Macbeth is considered to be the last Celtic king of Scotland.

17. In an example of the way in which phrases are placed as twins, these two sets of images on page 43 and page 619 merge and complement each other: certain onlookers have been complaining of the "rhythms" in ALP's "amphybed" in IV. Just as other paired phrases have been positioned closely together within the space of a few pages, only the "overture" of I.i separates these two passages if the reader passes through the *Wake*'s ricorso to begin again.

18. Another merging of Edinburgh and Dublin appears in the phrase "the heart of midleinster" (*FW*, 381.16).

19. See also "Tawfulsdreck" (*FW*, 68.21), "sartor's risorted" (314.17), and "shutter reshottus" (352.25). In addition, Joyce's *Finnegans Wake* notebook VI.B.14.195 contains the notes "Letters Scotch Ltd" and "Johnny MacDougall" on the same page. That these two notes appear in such close proximity is worthy of attention. In II.iv MacDougall, one of the four old men of the *Wake*, is described as "Poor Johnny of the clan of the Dougals, the poor Scuitsman" (391.4). The Joycean playwright Thornton Wilder mentions MacDougall's partly Scottish derivation in his voluminous correspondence with the critic Adaline Glasheen: "Luke Tarpey seems to have some Welsh in him, and John McDougal some Scotch ('the poor senitsman') p. 390 [.20]—which may lead to an identification with the Three Fusileers, accosted in the Park, who likewise recur as Irish, Welsh and Scotch" (Burns and Gaylord, 591). Johnny MacDougall's name itself marks him as a shadowy outsider: "MacDubhghaill (*dubh*, black; *gall*, foreigner) is the Irish form of the name of the Scottish family of MacDugall which came from the Hebrides as gallowglasses and settled in Co. Roscommon" (MacLysaght, 79). This chapter is also augmented with allusions to Robert Burns's song "Auld Lang Syne." So, Joyce's notes suggest a link between the letter and MacDougall through a common Scottish origin. These connections mean that Scotland is central to the letter that is unearthed from the "orangeflavoured mudmound" (*FW*, 111.34). Since the letter also represents *Finnegans Wake* itself, Joyce also signals the similarity between the

Wake and Scottish literature. I would argue that this is primarily due to Joyce's association between Scottish culture and incertitude, skepticism and duality. Furthermore, "orangeflavoured" is strongly suggestive of Scotland's involvement in the north of Ireland, indicating Scottish Presbyterian links with the Orange Order.

20. The "pigs and scuts" of IV may be regarded as the last of the phrases playing on the words Pict and Scot, with the end of the network coinciding with the final chapter of *Finnegans Wake*. However—due to its position in IV—it may also be thought of as part of the "ricorso" as the new day dawns and therefore the beginning of the action. If we accept the latter interpretation, then an earlier variation on the theme in which the Picts are attached to the Saxons rather than the Scots in III.iv may be regarded as an alternative "final word" on the matter, or as a possible introduction.

21. There is also an oblique link to Tim Finnegan of the song "Finnegan's Wake" here, since his occupation is a hod-carrier.

22. Throughout *Finnegans Wake* Shem and Shaun are represented as a tree and a stone, respectively, a contrast that is continued here.

FIVE.   The Dream of Ossian

1. According to George Watson, Macpherson also created "the tone at the root of Romanticism" ("Aspects," 130–31). See also: "The romantic awakening dates from the production of Ossian" (Pound, 228).

2. Paul Kintzele has discussed Joyce's interest in Ernest Renan:

> He read Renan and maintained a long-term interest in his work; he even went to visit Renan's birthplace. . . . In [his] letters, Renan's name emerges alongside others as a decisive influence; in 1906, he wrote to Stanislaus, "If I put down a bucket into my own soul's well, sexual department, I draw up Griffith's and Ibsen's and Skeffington's and Bernard Vaughan's and St. Aloysius' and Shelley's and Renan's water along with my own." . . . A week later, Joyce cited Renan again: "Renan was right when he said we were marching toward universal Americanism." . . . Read as a whole, the critical tone in this letter shows that this kind of universality clearly held no allure for Joyce. Renan is also present in Joyce's fiction; he appears in the "Scylla and Charybdis" chapter in *Ulysses*. (Kintzele, 58)

For a discussion on Macpherson and Arnold in relation to the two Irish Revivals (pre- and post-Famine) see the chapter "Arnold, Burke and the Celts" in S. Deane, *Celtic*, 17–27.

3. Seamus Deane has provided an excellent summary of the relationship between Joyce and Matthew Arnold:

> Matthew Arnold, representative of English liberalism, created a new national vision of England by combining the idea of culture with that of mass literacy and a belief in action. This Hellenisation of England was accompanied by the recognition of the Celtic element in Ireland. Catholic Ireland was to be won over to Protestant England, Saxon morality wed to Celtic poetry. Joyce sought a release from this cultural determinism through the hero as Nietzschean renouncer, the isolate, the heretic. Joyce found the world of artistic consciousness between the actual (Hebraic) and the possible (Hellenic). In this consciousness Joyce found the possibility of the growth of the individual and the escape from history. ("Masked," 11)

4. Malcolm Chapman provides a useful list of oppositions taken from nineteenth-century discourses relating to the Celtic world: "intellectual/ emotional, rational/intuitive, science/religion, science/arts, externality/ internality, instrumentality/creativity, practicality/sentimentality, culture/ nature, materialism/idealism, objectivity/subjectivity, artificial/spontaneous, society/family, modern/ancient, male/female, Anglo-Saxon/Celt" (106).

5. Macpherson's work itself has been read—alongside Romanticism itself—as a reaction against the hitherto dominant cultures of eighteenth-century Europe: "A sensation of the intellectual inadequacy and incompleteness of rationalism and materialism, coupled with an unease at the effects of industrial success, have been argued to have engendered Romantic art, and the Ossianic Celt" (Chapman, 96).

6. For a quasi-scholarly and somewhat dated introduction to specifically Scottish folklore, see McNeill, *Silver Bough*.

7. For a discussion of the influence of Frazer's work on Joyce and other Modernists, see Vickery, *Literary Impact*. An important precursor for Frazer's work was the skeptical philosophy of David Hume. In his introduction to Frazer's *Golden Bough*, Robert Fraser has discussed Frazer's Humean education at the University of Glasgow: "These studies set the foundations of his life's work. The course-work in philosophy introduced him sequentially to the great figures of the Scottish epistemological tradition, with its marked grain of scepticism, most notably to David Hume, whose *Treatise of Human Nature*, with its investigation of the sources of human credulity, was to form the ground-plan of the treatment of human belief in *The Golden Bough*" (Fraser, introduction, xxiii). Furthermore, as Fraser points out, it would be a mistake to read *The Golden Bough* as simply an anthology of "primitive" magical or religious

practices. Instead, it is an entirely Humean undertaking: "Frazer's work might seem to be a compendium of ritual and custom. In fact it is something very different: a book on the human mind and the connections habitually made by it" (xx).

8. Macpherson had a similar aim to the two main folklore gatherers of the twentieth century in Scotland, John Francis Campbell and Alexander Carmichael: "We can see . . . in the works of the two most prominent Highland folklorists, the dominant features that were to define the field of folklore—it was disappearing before science, rationality, and modernity; it was indeed . . . already all but gone" (Chapman, 118).

9. Furthermore, Macpherson's example set a precedent for more modern gatherers of Scottish Gaelic culture such as Alexander Carmichael (1832–1912). For more information on Carmichael see the University of Edinburgh's UNESCO-registered venture "The Carmichael Watson Project."

10. Here we may detect a rather Caledonian-Antisyzygy aspect to Macpherson's works, a coincidence of the contraries of traditional, mainly oral Gaelic mythology and a printed English language poetry.

11. It seems apt to consider Claude Lévi-Strauss's term here, since he refers to "mythical thought" as "an intellectual form of 'bricolage'" built "by using the remains and debris of events" (21–22).

12. Macpherson's name in Gaelic is Seumas MacMhuirich.

13. "I am making an engine with only one wheel. No spokes of course. The wheel is a perfect square" (*JJII*, 597).

14. Stephen's words at the close of *A Portrait* are pertinent here: "I go to encounter for the millionth time the reality of experience and to forge in the smithy of my soul the uncreated conscience of my race" (276).

15. There are a number of references to *Ossian* that also help to create the image of Shem as a forger. The very inclusion of Ossianic textual matter, aside from the actual meanings of the phrases themselves, evokes Macpherson's "forgeries." For example, note the use of the phrases "the red eye of his fear in saddishness" (*FW*, 182.6–7), adopted from *Temora* I; "Uldfadar" (182.18), taken from *Fingal* V; and "in which the soulcontracted son of the secret cell" (182.34–35), which is based on phrases from *Temora* I and *The Battle of Lora*. Shem's house itself also relates to *Ossian*: "The house O'Shea or O'Shame" (182.30). In themselves these phrases and words do not relate directly to forgery, but their inclusion here links the activities of Shem to the work of Macpherson.

16. A further hidden connection between writing and seafaring exists in the passage. Pages 119 to 124 of the *Wake* relate to the illustrated manuscript known as the Book of Kells (Benstock, xvii). Joyce was aware that the Book of

Kells was written at the abbey on the Scottish island of Iona. He would have known from his reading of Edward Sullivan's *The Book of Kells* that it was produced by monks from the order which Columkille, or Columba, originally founded on this small island off the coast of Mull. The book was, for Joyce, "the most purely Irish thing we have. . . . Indeed you can compare much of my work to the intricate illuminations" (*JJII*, 545). According to Farley and Hunter, the intricate interlacings, curvilinear designs, and spirals of Celtic art were "designed to draw in and enchant the viewer" (Farley and Hunter, 51). See also Garrow and Gosden, *Technologies of Enchantment?* The Book of Kells and *Finnegans Wake* both superimpose extraordinarily complex elaborations on fairly simple outlines.

17. There is also an echo of Stephen Dedalus's list of phobias in *A Portrait*: "I fear many things: dogs, horses, firearms, the sea, thunderstorms, machinery, the country roads at night" (264). Later, in the "Proteus" episode of *Ulysses*, Stephen's fears of dogs and the sea are associated with a Scottish invasion of Ireland. I will discuss this further in the chapter on Robert Burns.

18. This is an allusion to an *Irish Independent* report on Patrick Pearse's famous oration at the funeral of Jeremiah O'Donovan Rossa in 1915. See Tóibín, "After I Am Hanged."

19. This section also has pronounced Frazerian associations:

As if to drive home the point that life's ever-changing pattern is not something dependent on human will or assertions, Joyce begins the *Wake*, as Frazer does *The Golden Bough*, with the significance of trees for man's thrust toward revival of a ceaseless order. . . . Frazer stresses the vegetative basis of primitive religion and finds one of its earliest expressions to reside in the tree worship he traces throughout Europe. He also stresses that as a result the oak was particularly singled out for worship as a sacred creature by many races including the Celts. As time went on, however, these forests gradually dwindled and with them the worship of the oak. For Joyce, this is ample grounds for imaginative extrapolation so that though the ancient oaks have been reduced to peat and ashes, their vegetative natures persist as growing elms replace dwindling ash trees. (Vickery, "Sexual Metamorphosis," 217)

20. Patrick McCarthy: "Joyce's failure to resolve all the puzzles that he sets up is an indication of his rejection of dogma, of rational certitude, of reductive or simplistic visions of reality" (*Riddles*, 46).

21. More Scottish poetry is alluded to with the phrase "Ulerin's dogstar," a pun on the title of a poem by the Scottish poet Thomas Campbell called "Lord Ullin's Daughter." The poem deals with the death of an eloping Highland couple at sea.

22. Matthew Schultz:

> Joyce uses spectral tropes—resurrection, contamination, apparition of the inapparent, and omnipresence—throughout the *Wake* to evoke and conflate multiple spaces, temporalities, and languages so that individual words and sentences, as well as the text as a whole, always mean at least "two thinks at a time" (*FW* 583.07). The result is a protean text that exhibits the characteristics of a specter defined by Derrida: "The specter is . . . what one imagines, what one thinks one sees and which one projects—on an imaginary screen where there is nothing to see" (125). It seems, then, that Joyce's working title for *Finnegans Wake* during its serialization (1923–1938), *Work in Progress*, does not refer merely to Joyce's labor as its author but also to our labor as its readers. Joyce produced a text whose spectral design invites "performative interpretation," an interpretive mode that is similarly employed by Derrida for the examination of ghosts: "that is, an interpretation that transforms the very thing it interprets" (63). (Schultz, 282–83)

The only problem here is the difficulty in distinguishing the ghostly or spectral from the remembered or imagined. In any case both are at a remove from the material world; they are essentially nonmaterial.

23. Bonnie Prince Charlie is mentioned in the *Wake* alongside Charles Darwin: "Charley, you're my darwing!" (252.28). The phrase is based on the title of a Burns / Scottish Jacobite song: "Charlie Is My Darling." Is this Darwin/Stuart (natural) history connection Joyce's observation on the nonsurvival of the Jacobite species?

24. Despite the ideological connection to Catholicism, the Jacobite risings were not totally Catholic movements: "The Catholic commitment to Jacobitism was important but, because the church had few adherents (probably around 2 per cent of the Scottish population in c. 1750), it was much less decisive than the contribution of Episcopalianism" (Devine, *Nation*, 34).

SIX.   Joyce's Burns Night

1. For example, "Auld Lang Syne" is generally considered to be a Burns composition. However, while it is largely Burns's work, there was an *ur* version of the song (see Burns, 702–3). Because the *Wake* sometimes mentions a tune only by its title, it cannot be known how Joyce found these works. In some cases it is difficult to ascertain whether Joyce knew certain songs through Burns or through an acquaintance with other, older versions of the general Scottish

folk tradition. Certainly there are songs alluded to which are completely original Burns works.

2. Here is a list, taken from Matthew Hodgart's *Song in the Works of James Joyce*, of fifteen Burns songs that appear in *Finnegans Wake*: "Rattlin, Roarin Willie," "My Heart's in the Highlands," "John Anderson My Jo," "The Rantin Dog, the Daddie o't," "Willie Brew'd a Peck o' Maut," "The Campbells Are Comin," "Afton Water," "The Deil's Awa wi' the Exciseman," "A Red, Red Rose," "Green Grow the Rashes O," "A Man's a Man for A' That," "Auld Lang Syne," "O, Whistle an' I'll Come to Ye, My Lad," "Comin Thro' the Rye," "Charlie He's My Darling."

3. As Gregory Castle has discussed (*Modernism and the Celtic Revival*), the Celtic Revival has its roots in the activities of the United Irishmen.

4. See conclusion of the present text for a discussion of this connection.

5. Bloom thinks of this line from Burns's "To a Louse" in the "Lestrygonians" episode of *Ulysses* (*U*, 8.662). Burns is not the only Scottish poet involved in *Ulysses*; Drummond of Hawthornden is mentioned during "Scylla and Charybdis" (*U*, 9.386).

6. Perhaps the line "Come now, Johnny!" (521.10) has a Scottish origin. The "Johnny" in question in the text is the figure Johnny MacDougal, one of the four historian figures of the *Wake*. However, the line is also reminiscent of the Scottish folk song "Johnny Cope": "Now, Johnnie, be as good's your word; / Come let us try with fire and sword; / And dinna rin like a frighted bird, / That's chased frae its nest i' the morning" (Crawford and Imlah, 252). The song actually has a rather Wakean taunt for a chorus, inquiring as to whether Cope—an English general—is awake: "Hey Johnnie Cope, are ye wauking yet?" (252).

7. The Old Bushmills distillery received their license to distill whisky from James VI / I in 1608.

8. This Burns poem is also alluded to in the "Oxen of the Sun" episode of *Ulysses* (see *U*, 14.650).

9. See V. Deane et al., *Finnegans Wake Notebooks*, VI.B.32.

10. Another song relating to Aughrim, "The Lass of Aughrim," features prominently in "The Dead." As has been noted by Matthew Campbell, this song was based on a Scottish tune (193).

11. Another allusion to the Picts and the Scots occurs after the reference to Burns on *FW* 520, at *FW* 521.11. See chapter 3.

12. Burns himself uses the word in his poem "The Ordination": "Nae mair the knaves shall wrang her, / For Heresy is in her pow'r, / And gloriously she'll whang her / Wi' pith this day" (185). A separate section of the *Wake* also uses the word to mean "whip," although seemingly in a more erotic/sadistic

setting: "whang her, the fine ooman, rouge to her lobster locks, the rossy, whang, God and O'Mara has it with his ruddy old Villain Rufus, wait, whang, God and you're another he hasn't for there's my spoil five of spuds's trumps, whang, whack on his pigskin's Kisser for him" (122.15–19).

13. The *OED* gives a line from Macaulay to illustrate this: "Fox had stumbled in the mire, and had not only been defeated but befouled" (*OED*).

14. Stewart takes the title for his study from Walter Scott's following lines on Ulster: "I never saw a richer country, or, to speak my mind, a finer people; the worst of them is the bitter and envenomed dislike which they have to each other. Their factions have been so long envenomed, and they have such narrow ground to do their battle in, that they are like people fighting with daggers in a hogshead" (Stewart, 1).

15. On the subject of the Scots language, although Joyce's knowledge of Scots was probably not extensive, his acquaintance with Burns and other Scottish writers who include Scots in their works—Hogg for example—would have added to his vocabulary. *Finnegans Wake* contains a considerable amount of Scots, and consequently the language can be found throughout Roland McHugh's *Annotations to "Finnegans Wake."* Incidentally, Scots is listed under the dialects-of-English section even though it is actually a separate development of a language that preceded Modern English, namely Northumbrian Anglo-Saxon. There was Scottish literature in Scots before the modern English language even existed. Scots language also absorbed a good deal of French and Scandinavian elements, due to the extensive Scottish trading links that existed before the union. Ironically, Joyce is more willing to use Scots than many Scottish writers of the early twentieth century, aside from the "Synthetic Scots" of the Joycean poet Hugh MacDiarmid and his acolytes in the Scottish Literary Renaissance. However, there has also been a general movement in recent years for writers in Scotland to abandon Standard English for different forms of Scottish language. The "foreignizing" of English (McCulloch, "Scottish Modernism," 777) in James Kelman's Booker Prize–winning novel *How Late It Was, How Late* (1994) is an example of this development. According to Francis Spufford, a mixture of dialect and sophisticated subject matter links Kelman and Irish writing:

> There is a thing—call it the bastard high style—which has preoccupied some writers ever since Villon found a fruitful union in the marriage of gutter argot and the language of the Schools. In English, in this century, it has mostly been used by Irish writers: by Joyce, with Vico and scatology, by Beckett, with velleity and bananas, and by Flann O'Brien, one paragraph of whose *At-Swim-Two-Birds* includes both an argumentum on

Rousseau and the sudden eructation of "buff-coloured puke." Now there is a new practitioner, working with a different vernacular and a different elevated diction . . . Kelman.

16. This influence did not extend to spreading the ideals of the Scottish Enlightenment to the north of Ireland. Indeed, as J. G. A. Pocock has noted (following Ian R. McBride), late eighteenth-century "Scottish Ulster . . . may be thought of as Scotland without the Moderate Enlightenment" (112).

17. A humorous verse entitled "Satire on John Eglinton: A Collaboration with Oliver St John Gogarty (in the style of Burns)," written by Joyce with Gogarty in 1903 or 1904, is based on Burns's song "John Anderson, My Jo":

John Eglinton, my Jo, John,
When last you had a   ?
I fear ye canna go, John,
Although ye are na spent.

O   begin to fel', John,
Ye canna mak' it flow,
And even if it swell, John
The lassies wadna know.

John Eglinton, my Jo, John,
I dinna like to say
Of course ye must have sinned, John
When we were young and gay

It canna be remorse, John,
That keeps ye frae a ride
Your virtue is a farce, John,
Ye cardna if ye tried (*PE*, 77; omissions not mine)

Here, instead of borrowing the radical, stirring rhetoric of "Scots Wha Hae," Joyce and Gogarty have adapted a Burns love song. However, alongside the discernible presence of the irreverent Gogarty sense of humor there is also a suggestion of the so-called vulgar works of Robert Burns. Even though the poem is based on "John Anderson, My Jo," the subject matter and the idiom are very similar to that of the erotic poetry of Robert Burns (e.g., the uncensored version of "Green Grow the Rashes O"). As the editor of *Poems and Exiles*, J. C. C. Mays, points out, the blank spaces are to be filled in by the "impure" mind of the reader. Perhaps Joyce was aware that at this stage of his life in Dublin he was considered a Burns-like figure in Dublin, a rumor which surely would have amused him: "There was some talk about my brother's wild life, in which John Eglinton, who was present, and Gogarty, the source of my information, took part. Eglinton had heard that my brother was going the way of Maginn and Burns to ruin" (S. Joyce, 247). As Nigel Leask has noted, the "troubled life" of Burns has, to some extent, diverted attention from his actual work: "The poetic achievements of Robert Burns shared the fate of Byron's poetry, and to a lesser extent the works of other Romantics, of being overshadowed by a popular fixation with the biographical narrative of a troubled, albeit inspirational, life. This was largely influenced by Dr. James Currie's 1800 biography prefaced to his edition of Burns's *Works*, the main portal through which Burns reached the nineteenth-century reader, as well as the standard edition for Romantic writers" (Leask, 83).

18. In more recent years, The Stone of Destiny was removed from Westminster Abbey in 1950 by a group of young Scottish nationalists and left in Dunfermline Abbey. The stone was recovered by the British authorities before being taken again to London. However, the stone was permanently returned to Scotland in 1996 and is currently on display in Edinburgh Castle. The restoration of the stone was mainly a public relations exercise by the Conservative government, which was deeply unpopular in Scotland. The popularity of the Tories in Scotland has improved little since. The phrase "his Tiara of scones was held unfillable till one Liam Fail felled him in Westmunster" (*FW*, 131.9–11) merges the power centers of Tara, Scone, and Westminster. Roland McHugh sees this section as a commentary on the failure of Gladstone and the defeat of the First Home Rule Bill in 1886 (McHugh, *Annotations*, 131). This conflation of Gladstone and the Stone of Scone is intriguing, since both of Gladstone's parents were Scottish (although he himself was born at Liverpool).

19. This phrase is an allusion to Macpherson's *Ossian*. See chapter 5 for a further discussion of Joyce's use of Macpherson's poetry.

20. On the subject of the Stone of Destiny:

> In the Irish Synchronisms, Kenneth is said to have been first to possess, not the kingdom of Scots, but the Kingdom of Scone, and it is in his reign that Scone, which may have been the base of Fortriu and perhaps also the place of inauguration of its kings, seems to have been deliberately cultivated anew as a holy royal centre. . . . A thirteenth-century source refers to the 'laws of mac Alpin.' What this body of laws contained is unknown. . . . Another symbolic token, which cannot be proved with any certainty, would have been, as some have suggested, the bringing to Scone

of the Stone of Destiny. The inauguration stone would have fitted well into the established rites of inauguration, which marked the marriage of king to the land and to the people he ruled. (Lynch, *Scotland*, 41–42)

21. A Scottish victory at the Battle of Bannockburn was highly unlikely, as Michael Lynch has discussed. Since we are discussing Burns in this chapter, it is worth pointing out that the Scottish army made strategic use of a *burn* in order to overcome the English army:

[Edward's] army, although almost as large as any of those of his father in terms of infantry, with some 15,000–20,000 men, had fewer archers than at Falkirk and only about 2,000 mounted men—the result of the reluctance of a number of earls to do more than send a token representation. They were confronted by a Scots force of some 8,000 men, with perhaps only about 500 of them mounted. The odds were still heavily in the English favour and by all the conventional rules of warfare an English victory was not only likely but almost inevitable. . . . The key, however, was probably the ground which the Scots had carefully chosen—a factor not easily repeated in the future. The narrowness of the front and the boggy soil prevented an effective deployment of the English cavalry. And the gorge of the Bannock Burn, which cut off a safe retreat, turned what might have been a minor but embarrassing reverse into a humiliation of English arms unparalleled since the loss of Normandy. (Lynch, *Scotland*, 124)

22. Judge John M. Woolsey of the United States District Court in New York determined that although "in many places the effect of 'Ulysses' on the reader undoubtedly is somewhat emetic, nowhere does it tend to be aphrodisiac" (*JJII*, 667).

23. See also chapter 2 of this study for a discussion of Joyce and Celtic "blood" and "spirit."

24. He has left his lodgings at the Sandycove Martello tower that, as has been noted by Greg Winston, was built by a mainly Scottish workforce (see Winston, 247). A nearby inlet is named Scotsman's Bay.

25. See also Yeats's "The Ghost of Roger Casement": "John Bull and the sea are friends" (353).

26. For details of the British state's investigation into MacDiarmid's activities, see Lyall, "The Man Is a Menace."

27. The importance of Connolly's Scottish background in forming his socialist alternative to bourgeois Irish nationalism has been noted by Owen Dudley Edwards: "Looking up from the squalid and almost lightless depths of the Cowgate, the young Connolly could learn Marxism simply by seeing the

stately folk walking far above him on the fashionable George IV Bridge which swept above the slums below. He could see he was a proletarian long before he could hear he was Irish. . . . What we know of his active life in Scotland was more that of a Scottish worker, soldier and Socialist organizer than that of an Irish emigrant's child" ("Connolly and Irish Tradition," 411–13). Meanwhile, Charles Ford has stated that "the political allegory of *Ulysses* contains no significant advocate of the national liberation who wishes to throw off not only the priest and king but landlord as well—a figure represented in real history, for example, by the trade unionist James Connolly" (754); James Fairhall has argued convincingly that Connolly is behind a "main off stage character" ("Colgan-Connolly," 303) of "Ivy Day in the Committee Room": "The solid historical reality of James Connolly underlies the vague, absent figure of the Labour candidate in 'Ivy Day'" (301). For discussions on Connolly in relation to Scottish literature, see Malcy and Lusk, *Scotland and the Easter Rising*.

28. In his study *The Wars of the Bruces: Scotland, England and Ireland, 1306–1328*, Colm McNamee has discussed the modern images of the brothers with reference to Pilkington Jackson's statue of Robert I at Bannockburn: "[The statue] was unveiled in 1964. . . . Robert I's image as a heroic defender of Scottish liberty and identity remains virtually unchallenged to this day. There is no such monument to his brother Edward Bruce, whose intervention in Ireland invited only universal opprobrium. There is some irony in this judgement of posterity as the brothers must have shared aims and values" (Mc-Namee, plate XIII). It seems that the brothers Bruce are undergoing a Shaun and Shem mode of afterlife, one glorified and the other vilified.

29. See also: "But keep on, Bruce, saith the spider" (*LI*, 396).

30. The *Wake* encompasses an impressive range of the development of Scottish poetry from the "Dark Ages" Latin of Colm Cille (185.14), through the medieval work of John Barbour, Blind Harry, and the Makar William Dunbar, whose "Lament for the Makars" is alluded to with the line "Tiemore moretis tisturb badday" (378.20), a play on the refrain "*Timor mortis conturbat me*" of Dunbar's poem (see Crawford and Imlah, 95–98). Incidentally, Scottish football also gets a mention in the same section as Dunbar through a reference to the Glaswegian team "Partick Thistle" (378.18). Probably the similarity of "Partick" and "Patrick" attracted Joyce; the team name almost brings together the patron saint of Ireland with the national symbol of Scotland. Peter J. Reichenberg has used the reference to Partick Thistle and other football teams in the *Wake* to calculate the date on which the book takes place, supposedly April 7, 1928 (See "*Finnegans Wake*"). Returning to poetry, John Barbour, the Archdeacon of Aberdeen and author of *The Brus* (1375), is—according to Roland McHugh—alluded to with the word "barbar" (108.19). Barbour's epic

poem describing the Scottish Wars of Independence includes a section where Barbour discusses how Edward Bruce halted his army at Limerick so that a washerwoman might give birth. Also mentioned in the *Wake* is Blind Harry, or "bland Harry" (484.21), the fifteenth-century poet who wrote *Wallace*, another epic poem, on the subject of "*The Actis and Deidis of the Illustere and Vailyeand Campioun Schir William Wallace, Knicht of Ellerslie*" (Crawford and Imlah, 76). The poet's nominal blindness would have attracted the attention of the glaucoma-afflicted Joyce, since representations of blindness help to render the unseeing condition of the putative "dreamer" of the *Wake*. Eighteenth-century Scottish verse is represented through the reworked Gaelic myths of Macpherson and the verse of Robert Burns. An allusion to Walter Scott's "The Lady of the Lake"—"leady on the lake" (465.36)—means that the nineteenth century is also present. In the twentieth century, Scottish poets such as Hugh MacDiarmid were influenced by Joyce's prose.

Conclusion

1. As were, briefly, his plans for a union of Socialist Celtic Republics. The lines "Scots steel tempered wi' Irish fire / Is the weapon that I desire" sum up MacDiarmid's influences and aspirations (MacDiarmid, *Selected Poetry*, 123).

2. For a poetic meeting of Joyce and MacDiarmid, see Morgan.

3. The fiction of this time shares something of Joyce's escape into the interior, or into an alteration of the interior, as a means of coping with a hostile external world, an era of high unemployment, the rise of HIV/AIDS, and a drugs epidemic: "As though in defiance of the historical reality in which it is trapped, the Scottish novel of the 1980s and 90s drew its energy from discovering a variety of routes into alternative ontologies where the imaginary can become real [as in] the mind-bending effects of drugs in Irvine Welsh's *Trainspotting* (1993)" (Craig, "Otherworlds," 268). Since Joyce's work is also concerned with creating "alternative ontologies," the consciousness of *Finnegans Wake* is not totally dissimilar from the desperate skag hits of Mark Renton and his shady Leith associates.

4. As with Joyce, Salmond's political hero appears to be Charles Stewart Parnell. Salmond is fond of quoting Parnell's declaration made at Cork in 1885 that "no man has the right to fix the boundary to the march of a nation."

5. For a discussion of the causes behind the rapid decline of the Scottish branch of the UK Labour Party (up to 2011), see G. Hassan and Shaw.

6. Scotland's most prominent historian, Tom Devine, has provided a fair-minded analysis of the various factors at work in the referendum: "'Yes' campaigners . . . anticipated a universally hostile press as the battle for votes was joined. They were not to be disappointed, though even they were perhaps surprised by the relentlessly venomous nature of many of the attacks. . . . The non-aligned agency Press Data reckoned from its analyses of stories that made the news during the campaign that the ratio in favour of the unionist cause was almost 4:1" (*Independence*, 237). In terms of business, "banks and some large companies openly talked about moving their headquarters out of Scotland in the event of a 'Yes' vote" (241). Meanwhile, "the President of the United States, the Pope, the President of the European Union and, most bizarrely of all, the Prime Minister of Australia, thought it appropriate to comment on the referendum" (233). For "No" voters, according to Devine, "all the risks associated with independence were crucial—jobs, prices, the economy, pensions and EU membership. Interestingly, these bread-and-butter issues were much more important than attachment to the UK or the promise of additional powers for the Scottish Parliament. 'Yes' voters were mainly influenced by 'disaffection with Westminster politics'" (246). Devine adds that "there was little doubt overall that 'Yes' lost mainly because it signally failed to provide convincing answers to the many economic uncertainties that had been triggered in the minds of the majority of the electorate during the campaign" (246–47). However, Devine also provocatively comments on votes cast in the referendum by those living in Scotland but born elsewhere in the UK: "The approximately 430,000 first-generation migrants to Scotland from England, Northern Ireland, Wales and elsewhere could . . . have had an impact, given the relatively small, 10 per cent difference between 'Yes' and 'No' overall. In the event, 50.2 per cent of those born in Scotland voted 'Yes,' compared to 29.8 per cent of those born in the rest of the UK" (251). In connection with the earlier discussion of Irish Catholic migration to Scotland as represented in Joyce's *Dubliners*, it is interesting to note that "significant numerically were the descendants of Irish Catholics who had migrated to Scotland in the nineteenth century. . . . Catholics were much more likely than members of the Church of Scotland to vote for independence" (248).

7. Writing in the *Guardian* on the subject of "Brexit," Fintan O'Toole states with alarm that "English nationalists have planted a bomb under the settlement that brought peace to Northern Ireland and close cordiality to relations between Britain and Ireland" (O'Toole, "The English," n.p.). Elsewhere, Daniel Finn writes that "in the short term, Brexit raises questions about the Good Friday Agreement, since the peace settlement is predicated on the Irish and British states remaining members of the EU" (Finn, 10). In the aftermath

of the EU referendum, various politicians, including the Taoiseach Enda Kenny, Fianna Fáil's Micheál Martin, and Sinn Féin's Martin McGuinness, raised the topic of a poll on Irish reunification. In the *Irish Times*, O'Toole claimed it was time to consider a union of the Republic of Ireland, Northern Ireland, and Scotland: "The new division . . . created by Brexit . . . forces the three parts of These Islands that wish to remain in the European Union to think very radically about how they relate to each other. To think, that is, about a new union—of Scotland, Ireland and Northern Ireland. . . . This is crazy talk, but sometimes history forces us all to think urgently about ideas that were previously the exclusive property of cranks" (O'Toole, "Three-State Union," n.p.).

8. According to Roy Foster, "[In Scotland] we are entering an era reminiscent of Westminster post-1885, when the votes of the Irish Home Rule party became vital to Liberal governments. . . . The groundswell of support for independence has risen to flood level, defeat in . . . [the 2014] referendum notwithstanding" ("Bribery," n.p.).

BIBLIOGRAPHY

PRIMARY WORKS

Balfour, Arthur. *The Foundations of Belief: Being Notes Introductory to the Study of Theology*. New York: Longmans, Green and Co., 1895.

Berkeley, George. *Principles of Human Knowledge, and Three Dialogues between Hylas and Philonous*. London: Penguin, 2004.

Black, Ronald, ed. *An Tuil: Anthology of 20th Century Scottish Gaelic Verse*. Edinburgh: Polygon, 1999.

Burns, Robert. *The Canongate Burns*. Edited by Andrew Noble and Patrick Scott Hogg. Edinburgh: Canongate, 2001.

Crawford, Robert, and Mick Imlah, eds. *The Penguin Book of Scottish Verse*. London: Penguin, 2006.

Crotty, Patrick, ed. *The Penguin Book of Irish Poetry*. London: Penguin, 2010.

Deane, Vincent, Daniel Ferrer, and Geert Lernout, eds. *The "Finnegans Wake" Notebooks at Buffalo*. Turnhout: Brepols, 2001–.

Gray, Alasdair. *Lanark*. Edinburgh: Canongate, 2002.

———. *1982, Janine*. Edinburgh: Canongate, 2003.

Hogg, James. *The Private Memoirs and Confessions of a Justified Sinner*. Edinburgh: Canongate, 1991.

Hume, David. *An Abstract of "A Treatise of Human Nature."* Cambridge: Cambridge University Press, 1938.

———. *Dialogues, and Natural History of Religion*. Edited by J. C. A. Gaskin. Oxford: Oxford University Press, 1993.

———. *An Enquiry concerning Human Understanding*. Edited by Peter Millican. Oxford: Oxford University Press, 2007.

———. *An Enquiry concerning the Principles of Morals*. Indianapolis: Hachett, 1983.

———. *The Philosophical Works*. Boston: Little, Brown and Company, 1854.

———. *Selected Essays*. Edited by Stephen Copley. Oxford: Oxford University Press, 2008.

———. *A Treatise of Human Nature*. London: Penguin, 1969.

Joyce, James. *Collected Poems*. New York: Viking Press, 1957.

———. *The Critical Writings of James Joyce*. Edited by Ellsworth Mason and Richard Ellmann. New York: Viking Press, 1959.

———. *Dubliners*. London: Penguin, 2000.

———. *Finnegans Wake*. New York: Viking Press, 1939.

———. *Giacomo Joyce*. New York: Viking Press, 1968.

———. *Letters of James Joyce*. Vol. 1. Edited by Stuart Gilbert. New York: Viking Press, 1957.

———. *Letters of James Joyce*. Vols. 2 and 3. Edited by Richard Ellmann. New York: Viking Press, 1966.

———. *Occasional, Critical, and Political Writings*. Edited by Kevin Barry. Oxford: Oxford University Press, 2000.

———. *Poems and Exiles*. London: Penguin, 1992.

———. *"Pomes Penyeach," and Other Verses*. London: Faber and Faber, 1966.

———. *The Restored "Finnegans Wake."* Edited by Danis Rose and John O'Hanlon. London: Penguin, 2012.

———. *Ulysses*. Edited by Jeri Johnson. 1922 text. Oxford: Oxford University Press, 1993.

———. *Ulysses*. Edited by Hans Walter Gabler. Corrected text. New York: Random House, 1986.

Joyce, Stanislaus. *My Brother's Keeper*. London: Faber and Faber, 1958.

Kelman, James. *An Old Pub Near the Angel, and Other Stories*. Edinburgh: Polygon, 2007.

MacDiarmid, Hugh. *Albyn: Shorter Books and Monographs*. Manchester: Carcanet Press, 1997.

———. *A Drunk Man Looks at the Thistle*. Edinburgh: Scottish Academic Press, 1987.

———. *In Memoriam James Joyce*. Glasgow: William MacLellan, 1955.

———. *Selected Poetry*. Edited by Alan Riach and Michael Grieve. Manchester: Carcanet Press, 2004.

Macpherson, James. *The Poems of Ossian and Related Works*. Edited by Howard Gaskill. Edinburgh: Edinburgh University Press, 1996.

Marvell, Andrew. *The Complete Poems*. Edited by Elizabeth Story Donno. London: Penguin, 2005.

Moore, George. *Hail and Farewell*. Gerrards Cross: Colin Smythe, 1976.

Morgan, Edwin. "Dialogue I: James Joyce and Hugh MacDiarmid." In *James Joyce Broadsheet*, no. 9 (1982): 5.

Nabokov, Vladimir. *Lolita*. New York: Vintage, 1997.

Shakespeare, William. *Macbeth*. In *The Oxford Shakespeare: The Complete Works*, edited by John Jowlett, William Montgomery, Harry Taylor, and Stanley Wells, 969–94. 2nd ed. Oxford: Clarendon Press, 2005.

Stevenson, Robert Louis. *Strange Case of Dr. Jekyll and Mr. Hyde*. Harmondsworth: Penguin, 1994.

Vico, Giambattista. *New Science*. Translated by David Marsh. London: Penguin, 2001.

Yeats, W. B. *The Poems*. Edited by Daniel Albright. London: Everyman, 1994.

SECONDARY WORKS

Agamben, Giorgio. *Infancy and History: The Destruction of Experience*. Translated by Liz Heron. London: Verso, 1993.

———. *Language and Death: The Place of Negativity*. Translated by Karen E. Pinkus with Michael Hardt. Minneapolis: University of Minnesota Press, 2006.

———. *Stanzas: Word and Phantasm in Western Culture*. Translated by Ronald L. Martinez. Minneapolis: University of Minnesota Press, 1993.

Alcobia-Murphy, Shane, Johanna Archbold, John Gibney, and Carol Jones, eds. *Beyond the Anchoring Grounds: More Cross-Currents in Irish and Scottish Studies*. Belfast: Cló Ollscoil na Banríona, 2005.

Allen, Nicholas. *Modernism, Ireland and Civil War*. Cambridge: Cambridge University Press, 2009.

Anderson, Benedict. *Imagined Communities*. London: Verso, 1983.

Anghinetti, Paul. "Berkeley's Influence on Joyce." *James Joyce Quarterly* 19, no. 3 (Spring 1982): 315–29.

Arnold, Matthew. *Culture and Anarchy*. Cambridge: Cambridge University Press, 1969.

———. *On the Study of Celtic Literature*. Long Acre: David Nutt, 1910.

Ashcroft, Bill, Gareth Griffiths, and Helen Tiffin, eds. *The Empire Writes Back*. London: Routledge, 1989.

Atherton, James S. *The Books at the Wake*. Carbondale: Southern Illinois University Press, 1959, 2009.

Attridge, Derek. *The Cambridge Companion to James Joyce*. 2nd ed. Cambridge: Cambridge University Press, 2004.

———. "Finnegans Awake: The Dream of Interpretation." *James Joyce Quarterly* 27, no. 1 (1989): 11–29.

Attridge, Derek, and Daniel Ferrer, eds. *Post-Structuralist Joyce*. Cambridge: Cambridge University Press, 1984.

Attridge, Derek, and Marjorie Howes, eds. *Semicolonial Joyce*. Cambridge: Cambridge University Press, 2000.

Bailey, Alan, and Dan O'Brien. *The Continuum Companion to Hume*. London: Continuum, 2012.

Ball, Martin J., ed. *The Celtic Languages*. Abingdon: Routledge, 1993.

Barlow, Richard. "Crotthers: Joyce's Scots Fellow in *Ulysses*." *Notes and Queries* 57, no. 2 (2010): 230–33.

———. "'Hume Sweet Hume': Skepticism, Idealism, and Burial in *Finnegans Wake*." *Philosophy and Literature* 38, no. 1 (2014): 266–75.

———. "James Macpherson in *Finnegans Wake*." In *Founder to Shore: Cross-Currents in Irish and Scottish Studies*, ed. S. Alcobia-Murphy et al., 33–42. Aberdeen: Research Institute of Irish and Scottish Studies, 2011.

———. "Joyce's Burns Night." *Papers on Joyce*, no. 17/18 (2011/2012): 279–311.

———. "Silent Exile? James Joyce and the Easter Rising." Easter 1916 Centenary Issue, *Moving Worlds* 16, no. 1 (2016): 17–29.

———. "The 'united states of Scotia Picta': Scottish Literature and History in *Finnegans Wake*." *James Joyce Quarterly* 48, no. 2 (2011): 305–18.

———. "What Might James Joyce Have Made of 21st-Century Scottish Independence?" *Guardian*, January 31, 2014.

Barthes, Roland. *Image – Music – Text*. Edited and translated by Stephen Heath. New York: Hill and Wang, 1977.

Baudrillard, Jean. "Simulacra and Simulations." In *Literary Theory: An Anthology*, ed. Julie Rivkin and Michael Ryan, 365–77. Oxford: Blackwell, 2004.

Beckman, Richard. "Jove's Word: *Finnegans Wake* 80.20–81.13." *Journal of Modern Literature* 22, no. 2 (1998–99): 373–84.

———. *Joyce's Rare View: The Nature of Things in Finnegans Wake*. Gainesville: University Press of Florida, 2007.

Begam, Richard. "Joyce's Trojan Horse: *Ulysses* and the Aesthetics of Decolonization." In *Modernism and Colonialism*, ed. Richard Begam and Michael Valdez Moses, 185–208. Durham, NC: Duke University Press, 2007.

Begnal, Michael H. *Dreamscheme: Narrative and Voice in Finnegans Wake*. Syracuse, NY: Syracuse University Press, 1988.

———. "The Prankquean in *Finnegans Wake*." *James Joyce Quarterly* 1, no. 3 (1964): 14–18.

Beja, Morris. *James Joyce: A Literary Life*. Basingstoke: Palgrave Macmillan, 1992.

Beja, Morris, and David Norris, eds. *Joyce in the Hibernian Metropolis: Essays.* Columbus: Ohio State University Press, 1996.

Bell, Bill. *The Edinburgh History of the Book in Scotland.* Vol. 3. Edinburgh: Edinburgh University Press, 2007.

Bell, Eleanor. *Questioning Scotland: Literature, Nationalism, Postmodernism.* Basingstoke: Palgrave, 2004.

Bell, Michael. "The Metaphysics of Modernism" in *The Cambridge Companion to Modernism.* 2nd ed. 9–32. Cambridge: Cambridge University Press, 1999, 2011.

Benjamin, Roy. "Waking the King: Faction and Fission in *Finnegans Wake.*" *James Joyce Quarterly* 46, no. 2 (2009): 305–20.

Benstock, Bernard. *Joyce-Again's Wake.* Seattle: University of Washington Press, 1965.

Benvenuto, Bice, and Roger Kennedy. *The Works of Jacques Lacan: An Introduction.* New York: St. Martin's Press, 1986.

Berman, David. "The Birth of Scottish Philosophy from the Golden Age of Irish Philosophy." *Eighteenth-Century Studies* 45, no. 3 (Spring 2012): 379–92.

Bhabha, Homi K. *The Location of Culture.* London: Routledge, 1994.

Birmingham, Kevin. *The Most Dangerous Book: The Battle for James Joyce's "Ulysses."* London: Head of Zeus, 2015.

Bishop, John. *Joyce's Book of the Dark.* Madison: University of Wisconsin Press, 1986.

Bold, Alan. *MacDiarmid: The Terrible Crystal.* London: Routledge and Kegan Paul, 1983.

Bowen, Zack. *Bloom's Old Sweet Song: Essays on Joyce and Music.* Gainesville: University Press of Florida, 1995.

Brivic, Sheldon. *Joyce between Freud and Jung.* Port Washington, NY: Kennikat, 1980.

———. *Joyce the Creator.* Madison: University of Wisconsin Press, 1985.

———. "The Mind Factory: Kabbalah in *Finnegans Wake.*" *Finnegans Wake* issue, *James Joyce Quarterly* 21, no. 1 (Fall 1983): 7–30.

Broadie, Alexander, ed. *The Cambridge Companion to the Scottish Enlightenment.* Cambridge: Cambridge University Press, 2003.

———. "What Was the Scottish Enlightenment?" in *The Scottish Enlightenment: An Anthology*, edited by Alexander Broadie, 3–31. Edinburgh: Canongate Press, 1997.

Brooker, Joseph. *Joyce's Critics: Transitions in Reading and Culture.* Madison: University of Wisconsin Press, 2004.

Brown, Bill. "Materialities of Modernism—Objects, Matter, Things." In *A Handbook of Modernism Studies*, edited by Jean-Michel Rabaté, 281–95. Chichester: John Wiley & Sons, 2013.

Brown, Richard, ed. *A Companion to James Joyce*. Oxford: Blackwell, 2008.

———. *James Joyce and Sexuality*. Cambridge: Cambridge University Press, 1989.

Brown, Terence. "Calypso: Myth, Method, Moment." In *Studies on Joyce's Ulysses*, edited by Jacqueline Genet and Wynne Hellegouarc'h, 9–20. Caen: Presses Universitaires de Caen, 1991.

Bryson, Gladys. *Man and Society: The Scottish Inquiry of the Eighteenth Century*. Princeton: Princeton University Press, 1945.

Buchan, James. *Capital of the Mind: How Edinburgh Changed the World*. Edinburgh: Birlinn, 2007.

Budgen, Frank. *James Joyce and the Making of "Ulysses," and Other Writings*. Oxford: Oxford University Press, 1972.

Burns, Edward M., and Joshua A. Gaylord, eds. *A Tour of the Darkling Plain*. Dublin: University College Dublin Press, 2001.

Cairns, David, and Shaun Richards. *Writing Ireland: Colonialism, Nationalism and Culture*. Manchester: Manchester University Press, 1988.

Campbell, Joseph, and Henry Morton Robinson. *A Skeleton Key to "Finnegans Wake."* New York: Harcourt Brace Jovanovich, 1944.

Campbell, Matthew. "Nineteenth-Century Lyric Nationalism." In *James Joyce in Context*, edited by John McCourt, 184–94. Cambridge: Cambridge University Press, 2009.

Cannadine, David, ed. *Empire, the Sea and Global History*. Basingstoke: Palgrave, 2007.

Caraher, Brian. "Irish and European Politics: Nationalism, Socialism, Empire." In *James Joyce in Context*, edited by John McCourt, 285–98. Cambridge: Cambridge University Press, 2009.

Carruthers, Gerard, ed. *The Edinburgh Companion to Robert Burns*. Edinburgh: Edinburgh University Press, 2009.

———. *Robert Burns*. Tavistock: Northcote House, 2006.

Carruthers, Gerard, and Liam McIllvanney, eds. *The Cambridge Companion to Scottish Literature*. Cambridge: Cambridge University Press, 2012.

Castle, Gregory. *Modernism and the Celtic Revival*. Cambridge: Cambridge University Press, 2001.

———. "Post-colonialism." In *James Joyce in Context*, edited by John McCourt, 99–111. Cambridge: Cambridge University Press, 2009.

Cato, Bob, and Greg Vitello. *Joyce Images*. New York: Norton, 1994.

Chapman, Malcolm. *The Gaelic Vision in Scottish Culture*. London: Croom Helm, 1978.

Cheng, Vincent J. *Inauthentic: The Anxiety over Culture and Identity*. New Brunswick, NJ: Rutgers University Press, 2004.

———. *Joyce, Race, and Empire*. Cambridge: Cambridge University Press, 1995.

———. "Of Canons, Colonies, and Critics: The Ethics and Politics of Postcolonial Joyce Studies." *Cultural Critique*, no. 35 (Winter 1996–97): 81–104.

———. *Shakespeare and Joyce*. University Park: Pennsylvania State University Press, 1984.

Cixous, Hélène. *The Exile of James Joyce*. Translated by Sally Purcell. London: John Calder, 1976.

Clark, David. "'*A Joyce Tae Prick Ilka Pluke*': Joyce and the Scottish Renaissance." *Papers on Joyce*, no. 5 (1999): 3–12.

Clark, Hillary A. "Encyclopedic Discourse." *SubStance* 21, no. 1 / issue 67 (1992): 95–110.

Cleary, Joe. *Literature, Partition and the Nation State: Culture and Conflict in Ireland, Israel and Palestine*. Cambridge: Cambridge University Press, 2002.

———. *Outrageous Fortune—Capital and Culture in Modern Ireland*. Dublin: Field Day, 2006.

Connell, Liam. "Modes of Marginality: Scottish Literature and the Uses of Postcolonial Theory." *Comparative Studies of South Asia, Africa and the Middle East* 23, no. 1/2 (2003): 41–53.

Connolly, S. J., ed. *The Oxford Companion to Irish History*. Oxford: Oxford University Press, 1998.

Connolly, Thomas E., ed. *James Joyce's Books, Portraits, Manuscripts, Notebooks, Typescripts, Page Proofs: Together with Critical Essays about Some of His Works*. Lewiston, NY: Edwin Mellen Press, 1997.

———. *The Personal Library of James Joyce*. Buffalo, NY: University of Buffalo Press, 1957.

———. *Scribbledehobble: The Ur-Workbook for "Finnegans Wake."* Evanston, IL: Northwestern University Press, 1961.

Cosgrave, Brian. *James Joyce's Negations: Irony, Indeterminacy and Nihilism in "Ulysses," and Other Writings*. Dublin: University College Dublin Press, 2007.

Craig, Cairns. *Intending Scotland: Explorations in Scottish Culture since the Enlightenment*. Edinburgh: Edinburgh University Press, 2009.

———. *The Modern Scottish Novel*. Edinburgh: Edinburgh University Press, 1999.

———. "Otherworlds: Devolution and the Scottish Novel." In *The Cambridge Companion to Scottish Literature*, edited by Gerard Carruthers and Liam McIlvanney (Cambridge: Cambridge University Press, 2012), 261–74.

———. "Postcolonial Hybridity in Scotland and Ireland." In *Ireland (Ulster) Scotland: Concepts, Contexts, Comparisons*, edited by Edna Longley, Eamonn Hughes, and Des O'Rawe, 231–43. Belfast: Cló Ollscoil na Banríona, 2003.

———. "Scotland and Hybridity." In *Beyond Scotland: New Contexts for Twentieth-Century Scottish Literature*, edited by Gerard Carruthers, David Goldie, and Alastair Renfrew, 229–53. Amsterdam: Rodopi, 2004.

Crawford, Robert. *Devolving English Literature*. 2nd ed. Edinburgh: Edinburgh University Press, 2000.

———. *The Modern Poet—Poetry, Academia, and Knowledge since the 1750s*. Oxford: Oxford University Press, 2001.

———. *Robert Burns and Cultural Authority*. Edinburgh: Polygon, 1997.

———. *Scotland's Books*. Oxford: Oxford University Press, 2009.

———, ed. *The Scottish Invention of English Literature*. Cambridge: Cambridge University Press, 1998.

Crawford, Thomas. "The Play of Region and Nation." In *The History of Scottish Literature*, edited by Douglas Gifford, 3:89–106. Aberdeen: Aberdeen University Press, 1988.

Crispi, Luca, and Sam Slote, eds. *How Joyce Wrote "Finnegans Wake."* Madison: University of Wisconsin Press, 2007.

Crotty, Patrick. "Swordsmen: W. B. Yeats and Hugh MacDiarmid." In *Modern Irish and Scottish Poetry*, edited by Peter Mackay, Edna Longley, and Fran Brearton, 20–38. Cambridge: Cambridge University Press, 2011.

———. "That Caledonian Antisyzygy" in *The Poetry Ireland Review*, no. 63 (Winter 1999): 89–93.

Cullen, L. M., and T. C. Smout, eds. *Comparative Aspects of Economic and Social History, 1600–1900*. Edinburgh: John Donald Publishers, 1977.

Culleton, Claire A. *Names and Naming in Joyce*. Madison: University of Wisconsin Press, 1994.

Cummins, Philip D. "Hume's Diffident Skepticism." *Hume Studies*, no. 25 (1999): 43–65.

Daiches, David. *The Paradox of Scottish Culture: The Eighteenth Century Experience*. Oxford: Oxford University Press, 1964.

———. "The Scottish Enlightenment." In *A Hotbed of Genius: The Scottish Enlightenment, 1730–90*, edited by David Daiches, 1–41. Edinburgh: Edinburgh University Press, 1986.

Dalton, Jack P., and Clive Hart, eds. *Twelve and a Tilly: Essays on the Occasion of the 25th Anniversary of "Finnegans Wake."* London: Faber and Faber, 1966.

Dangerfield, George. "James Joyce, James Connolly and Irish Nationalism." *Irish University Review* 16, no. 1 (1986): 5–21.

D'Arcy, Anne Marie. "Joyce and the Twoheaded Octopus of *judéo-maçonnerie.*" *Review of English Studies* 64, no. 267 (2013): 857–77.

Darwin, John. *The Empire Project: The Rise and Fall of the British World-System, 1830–1970.* Cambridge: Cambridge University Press, 2009.

Davies, Norman. *Europe: A History.* London: Pimlico, 1997.

Deane, Seamus. *Celtic Revivals: Essays in Modern Irish Literature, 1880–1980.* London: Faber and Faber, 1985.

———, ed. *The Field Day Anthology of Irish Writing.* Vol. 3. Derry: Field Day, 1991.

———. *Heroic Styles: The Tradition of an Idea.* Derry: Field Day, 1984.

———. "Joyce the Irishman." in *The Cambridge Companion to James Joyce,* edited by Derek Attridge, 31–53. Cambridge: Cambridge University Press, 1990.

———. "Masked with Matthew Arnold's Face." *Canadian Journal of Irish Studies* 12, no. 1 (June 1986): 11–22.

———. *Strange Country: Modernity and Nationhood in Irish Writing since 1790.* Oxford: Oxford University Press, 1997.

Degnan, James P. "The Encounter in Joyce's 'An Encounter.'" *Twentieth Century Literature* 35, no. 1 (1989): 89–93.

Deleuze, Giles. *Difference and Repetition.* Translated by Paul Patton. London and New York: Bloomsbury, 2014.

———. *Empiricism and Subjectivity: An Essay on Hume's Theory of Human Nature.* Translated by Constantin V. Boundas. New York: Columbia University Press, 1991.

Derrida, Jacques. *Of Grammatology.* Translated by Gayatri Chakravorty Spivak. Corrected ed. Baltimore: Johns Hopkins University Press, 1997.

Devine, T. M. *Independence or Union: Scotland's Past and Scotland's Present.* London: Allen Lane, 2016.

———. *Scotland's Empire, 1600–1815.* London: Penguin Allen Lane, 2003.

———. *The Scottish Nation, 1700–2000.* New York: Penguin, 2001.

Devlin, Brendan. "In Spite of Sea and Centuries: An Irish Gael Looks at the Poetry of Sorley MacLean." In *Sorley MacLean: Critical Essays,* edited by Raymond J. Ross and Joy Hendry, 81–89. Edinburgh: Scottish Academic Press, 1986.

Devlin, Kimberly J. "'See Ourselves as Others See Us': The Role of the Other in Indeterminate Selfhood." *PMLA* 104, no. 5 (October 1989): 882–93.

———. "Self and Other in *Finnegans Wake*: A Framework for Analyzing Versions of Shem and Shaun." *Finnegans Wake* issue, *James Joyce Quarterly* 21, no. 1 (Fall 1983): 31–50.

———. *Wandering and Return in "Finnegans Wake."* Princeton: Princeton University Press, 1991.

DiBernard, Barbara. *Alchemy and "Finnegans Wake."* Albany: State University of New York Press, 1980.

Dingwall, Helen. *A History of Scottish Medicine: Themes and Influences.* Edinburgh: Edinburgh University Press, 2003.

Duffy, Enda. "Disappearing Dublin." In *Semicolonial Joyce*, edited by Derek Attridge and Marjorie Howes, 37–57. Cambridge: Cambridge University Press, 2000.

———. *The Subaltern "Ulysses."* Minneapolis: University of Minnesota Press, 1994.

Duncan, Ian. "Scott and the Historical Novel: A Scottish Rise of the Novel." In *The Cambridge Companion to Scottish Literature*, edited by Gerard Carruthers and Liam McIlvanney, 103–16. Cambridge: Cambridge University Press, 2012.

———. *Scott's Shadow: The Novel in Romantic Edinburgh.* Princeton: Princeton University Press, 2007.

Eagleton, Terry. "Determinacy Kills." *London Review of Books* 30, no. 12 (2008): 9–10.

———. *Heathcliff and the Great Hunger.* London: Verso, 1995.

———. "Nationalism: Irony and Commitment." In *Nationalism, Colonialism, and Literature*, edited by Terry Eagleton, Fredric Jameson, and Edward Said, 23–40. Minneapolis: University of Minnesota Press, 1990.

———. "Running out of Soil." *London Review of Books* 26, no. 23 (2004): 28–30.

Edwards, Owen Dudley. "Connolly and Irish Tradition." *The Furrow* 30, no. 7 (1979): 411–24.

———. "Scotching Joyce." *Drouth*, no. 4 (2002): 13–17.

Eide, Marian. "The Language of Flows: Fluidity, Virology, and *Finnegans Wake*." *Finnegans Wake* issue, *James Joyce Quarterly* 34, no. 4 (Summer 1997): 473–88.

Eliot, T. S. "Was There a Scottish Literature?" *Athenaeum*, no. 4657 (August 1919): 680–81.

Ellmann, Richard. *The Consciousness of Joyce.* New York: Oxford University Press, 1977.

———. *James Joyce*. New York: Oxford University Press, 1959.

———. *James Joyce*. Rev. ed. New York: Oxford University Press, 1982.

———. *Ulysses on the Liffey*. New York: Oxford University Press, 1972.

———. *Yeats: The Man and the Masks*. New York: Norton, 1999.

English, Richard. *Armed Struggle: The History of the IRA*. Rev. ed. London: Pan, 2012.

Fahy, Catherine, ed. *The James Joyce–Paul Léon Papers in the National Library of Ireland: A Catalogue*. Dublin: National Library of Ireland, 1992.

Fairhall, James. "Colgan-Connolly: Another Look at the Politics of 'Ivy Day in the Committee Room.'" *James Joyce Quarterly* 25, no. 3 (1988): 289–304.

———. *James Joyce and the Question of History*. Cambridge: Cambridge University Press, 1993.

Farley, Julia, and Fraser Hunter, eds. *Celts: Art and Identity*. London: British Museum Press, 2015.

Ferguson, Frank, and Andrew R. Holmes, eds. *Revising Robert Burns and Ulster*. Dublin: Four Courts Press, 2009.

Ferrer, Daniel. "The Freudful Couchmare of ∧d: Joyce's Notes on Freud and the Composition of Chapter XVI of *Finnegans Wake*." *James Joyce Quarterly* 22, no. 4 (1985): 367–82.

Fielding, Penny. "Robert Louis Stevenson." In *The Cambridge Companion to Scottish Literature*, edited by Gerard Carruthers and Liam McIlvanney, 159–72. Cambridge: Cambridge University Press, 2012.

Finn, Daniel, with David Runciman, Neal Ascherson, James Butler, T. J. Clark, Jonathan Coe, Sionaidh Douglas-Scott, Dawn Foster, Jeremy Harding, Colin Kidd, Ross McKibbin, Philippe Marlière, James Meek, Pankaj Mishra, Jan-Werner Müller, Susan Pedersen, J. G. A. Pocock, Nick Richardson, Nicholas Spice, Wolfgang Streeck, and Daniel Trilling. "Where Are We Now? Responses to the Referendum." *London Review of Books* 38, no. 14 (2016): 8–15.

Fiske, Shanyn. "From Ritual to the Archaic in Modernism: Frazer, Harrison, Freud, and the Persistence of Myth." In *A Handbook of Modernism Studies*, edited by Jean-Michel Rabaté, 173–91. Chichester: John Wiley & Sons, 2013.

Fittler, James. *Scotia Depicta; or, The Antiquities, Castles, Public Buildings, Noblemen and Gentlemen's Seats, Cities, Towns, and Picturesque Scenery of Scotland*. London: W. Miller, 1804.

Fitzpatrick, Benedict. *Ireland and the Making of Great Britain*. New York: Funk & Wagnalls, 1922.

Flood, J. M. *Ireland: Its Saints and Scholars.* Dublin: The Talbot Press, 1917.

Fogarty, Anne, and Timothy Martin, eds. *Joyce on the Threshold.* Gainesville: University Press of Florida, 2005.

Fogelin, Robert J. "Hume's Skepticism." In *The Cambridge Companion to David Hume*, edited by David Fate Norton and Jacqueline Taylor, 209–37. Cambridge: Cambridge University Press, 2008.

Ford, Charles. "Dante's Other Brush: *Ulysses* and the Irish Revolution." *James Joyce Quarterly* 29, no. 4 (1992): 751–61.

Fordham, Finn. *Lots of Fun at Finnegans Wake: Unravelling Universals.* Oxford: Oxford University Press, 2007.

Foster, R. F. "Bribery, Corruption and Other Ways to Curb Celtic Nationalists." *Financial Times*, May 8, 2015.

———. *Modern Ireland, 1600–1972.* New York: Penguin, 1988.

Fraser, Robert. Introduction to *The Golden Bough*, by James George Frazer, ix–xliii. Abridged ed. Oxford: Oxford University Press, 2009.

Fraser, W. Hamish, and Irene Maver, eds. *Glasgow Volume II: 1830–1912.* Manchester: Manchester University Press, 1996.

Frazer, James George. *The Golden Bough.* Abridged ed. Oxford: Oxford University Press, 2009.

Freedman, Carl. "Beyond the Dialect of the Tribe: James Joyce, Hugh MacDiarmid, and World Language." In *Hugh MacDiarmid: Man and Poet*, edited by Nancy K. Gish, 253–73. Edinburgh: Edinburgh University Press / Orono, ME: National Poetry Foundation, 1992.

French, Marilyn. *The Book as World.* Cambridge, MA: Harvard University Press, 1976.

Friedman, Susan Stanford, ed. *Joyce: The Return of the Repressed.* Ithaca, NY: Cornell University Press, 1993.

Gallagher, Shaun. "The Theater of Personal Identity: From Hume to Derrida." Supplement: Studies in Personalist Philosophy, Proceedings of the Conference on Persons, *Personalist Forum* 8, no. 1 (Spring 1992): 21–30.

Gardiner, Michael, Graeme Macdonald, and Niall O'Gallagher, eds. *Scottish Literature and Postcolonial Literature: Comparative Texts and Critical Perspectives.* Edinburgh: Edinburgh University Press, 2011.

Garrow, Duncan, and Chris Gosden. *Technologies of Enchantment? Exploring Celtic Art, 400 BC to AD 100.* Oxford: Oxford University Press, 2012.

Garvin, John. *James Joyce's Disunited Kingdom.* Dublin: Gill and Macmillan, 1976.

Gaskill, Howard, ed. *The Reception of Ossian in Europe.* London: Thoemmes Continuum, 2004.

Gibbons, Luke. *Joyce's Ghosts: Ireland, Modernism, and Memory.* Chicago: University of Chicago Press, 2015.

———. *Transformations in Irish Culture.* Cork: Cork University Press, 1996.

Gibson, Andrew. *James Joyce.* London: Reaktion, 2006.

———. *Joyce's Revenge.* Oxford: Oxford University Press, 2002.

Gibson, Andrew, and Len Platt, eds. *Joyce, Ireland, Britain.* Gainesville: University Press of Florida, 2006.

Gibson, George Cinclair. *Wake Rites: The Ancient Irish Rituals of "Finnegans Wake."* Gainesville: University Press of Florida, 2005.

Gifford, Don, and Robert J. Seidman, eds. *Ulysses Annotated.* Rev. and exp. ed. Berkeley: University of California Press, 1988.

Gifford, Douglas, et al., eds. *Scottish Literature.* Edinburgh: Edinburgh University Press, 2002.

Gilbert, Stuart. *James Joyce's "Ulysses."* London: Faber and Faber, 1930.

Gish, Nancy K. "Jekyll and Hyde: The Psychology of Dissociation." *International Journal of Scottish Literature,* no. 2 (Spring/Summer 2007): 58–67.

Glasheen, Adaline. *A Census of "Finnegans Wake."* London: Faber and Faber, 1956.

Glen, Duncan. *Hugh MacDiarmid and the Scottish Renaissance.* Edinburgh: W. and R. Chambers, 1964.

Golden, Seán. "Post-Traditional English Literature: A Polemic." In *The Crane Bag Book of Irish Studies,* edited by M. Hederman and R. Kearney, 7–18. Dublin: Blackwater, 1982.

Gordon, John. *"Finnegans Wake": A Plot Summary.* Dublin: Gill & Macmillan, 1986.

———. "The Multiple Journeys of 'Oxen of the Sun.'" *ELH* 46, no. 1 (Spring 1979): 158–72.

———. "Obeying the Boss in 'Oxen of the Sun.'" *ELH* 58, no. 1 (Spring 1991): 233–59. Gorman, Herbert. *James Joyce.* London: Allen Lane, 1941.

Graham, Colin. "Ireland (Postcolonial) Scotland." In *Ireland (Ulster) Scotland: Concepts, Contexts, Comparisons,* edited by Edna Longley, Eamonn Hughes, and Des O'Rawe, 244–50. Belfast: Cló Ollscoil na Banríona, 2003.

Gray, Alasdair. "Alasdair Gray's Answers to Several Questionnaires." Interview by Kathy Acker, Institute of Contemporary Arts, London, 1986. Website of Alasdair Gray. http://www.alasdairgray.info/.

Gregory, "Lady." *Our Irish Theatre: A Chapter on Autobiography.* Gerrards Cross: Colin Smythe, 1972.

Groom, Nick. "Romanticism and Forgery." *Literature Compass* 4, no. 6 (2007): 1625–49.

Gwynn, Stephen. *The History of Ireland*. London: Macmillan and Co., 1923.

Hammond, J. R. *A Robert Louis Stevenson Companion*. Basingstoke: Macmillan, 1984.

Hart, Clive. *A Concordance to "Finnegans Wake."* Minneapolis: University of Minnesota Press, 1963.

———. *Structure and Motif in "Finnegans Wake."* London: Faber and Faber, 1962.

Hart, Matthew. "Nationalist Internationalism: A Diptych in Modernism and Revolution." *Journal of Modern Literature* 31, no. 1 (2007): 21–46.

Harvie, Christopher, and Peter Jones. *The Road to Home Rule: Images of Scottish Nationalism*. Edinburgh: Polygon at Edinburgh University Press, 1999.

Hassan, Gerry, and Eric Shaw. *The Strange Death of Scottish Labour*. Edinburgh: Edinburgh University Press, 2012.

Hassan, Ihab. *The Postmodern Turn*. Columbus: Ohio State University Press, 1987.

Hayes-McCoy, G. A. "Robert Louis Stevenson and the Irish Question." *Studies: An Irish Quarterly Review* 39, no. 154 (June 1950): 130–40.

Hayman, David. "Nodality and the Infra-Structure of *Finnegans Wake*." Structuralist / Reader Response Issue, *James Joyce Quarterly* 16, no. 1/2 (Fall 1978 / Winter 1979): 135–49.

———. *The "Wake" in Transit*. Ithaca, NY: Cornell University Press, 1990.

Heaney, Seamus. *The Redress of Poetry*. New York: Farrar, Straus and Giroux, 1995.

Hegglund, Jon. "Hard Facts and Fluid Spaces." In *Joyce, Imperialism, and Postcolonialism*, edited by Leonard Orr, 58–74. Syracuse, NY: Syracuse University Press, 2008.

Henkes, Robbert-Jan. "Before King Roderick Became Publican in Chapelizod: The Origins of the Origins of *Finnegans Wake*." *Genetic Joyce Studies*, no. 12 (Spring 2012): n.p.

Herbert, W. N. *To Circumjack MacDiarmid: The Poetry and Prose of Hugh MacDiarmid*. Oxford: Clarendon Press, 1992.

Herman, Arthur. *The Scottish Enlightenment: The Scots' Invention of the Modern World*. London: Harper Perennial, 2006.

Herr, Cheryl. "Ireland from the Outside." *James Joyce Quarterly* 28, no. 4 (1991): 777–89.

Herring, Phillip H. *Joyce's Uncertainty Principle*. Princeton: Princeton University Press, 1987.

Heslinga, Marcus Willem. *The Irish Border as Cultural Divide*. Assen: Van Gorcum, 1971.

Hodgart, Matthew J. C., and Mabel P. Worthington. *Song in the Works of James Joyce*. New York: Columbia University Press, 1959.

Hofheinz, Thomas C. *Joyce and the Invention of Irish History*. Cambridge: Cambridge University Press, 1995.

Hook, Andrew, ed. *The History of Scottish Literature*. Vol. 2, *1660–1800*. Aberdeen: Aberdeen University Press, 1987.

Howes, Marjorie. "Joyce, Colonialism, and Nationalism." In *The Cambridge Companion to James Joyce*, edited by Derek Attridge and Marjorie Howes, 254–71. 2nd ed. Cambridge: Cambridge University Press, 1994, 2004.

Huddard, David. *Homi K. Bhabha*. Abingdon: Routledge, 2006.

Jackson, John Wyse, and Peter Costello. *John Stanislaus Joyce: The Voluminous Life and Genius of James Joyce's Father*. London: HarperCollins, 1997.

Jameson, Fredric. "Modernism and Imperialism." In *Nationalism, Colonialism, and Literature*, edited by Terry Eagleton, Fredric Jameson, and Edward Said, 43–68. Minneapolis: University of Minnesota Press, 1990.

———. *The Modernist Papers*. London: Verso, 2007.

———. *The Political Unconscious*. London: Routledge, 2002.

———. *A Singular Modernity*. London: Verso, 2002.

Janusko, Robert. *The Sources and Structures of James Joyce's "Oxen."* Ann Arbor, MI: UMI Research Press, 1983.

Jolas, Maria. "'I write,' said Joyce." In *Joyce and Paris, 1902 . . . 1920–1940 . . . 1975: Papers from the Fifth International James Joyce Symposium*, edited by Jacques Aubert and Maria Jolas, 7–9. Lille: Editions du CNRS, 1979.

Jones, Peter. "David Hume." In *A Hotbed of Genius: The Scottish Enlightenment, 1730–90*, edited by David Daiches, 1–42. Edinburgh: Edinburgh University Press, 1986.

Kearney, Richard. *Poetics of Modernity: Toward a Hermeneutic Imagination*. Amherst, NY: Humanity Books, 1995.

Kee, Robert. *The Green Flag: A History of Irish Nationalism*. London: Penguin, 1972.

Kelleher, Margaret, and Philip O'Leary, eds. *The Cambridge History of Irish Literature*. Vol. 2. Cambridge: Cambridge University Press, 2006.

Kenner, Hugh. *Dublin's Joyce*. London: Chatto & Windus, 1956.

———. "The Joycean Present." Papers from the Joyce and History Conference at Yale University, October 1990, *James Joyce Quarterly* 28, no. 4 (Summer 1991): 853–56.

———. *Ulysses*. Rev. ed. Baltimore: Johns Hopkins University Press, 1987.

Kershner, R. B. *Joyce, Bakhtin and Popular Literature*. Chapel Hill: University of North Carolina Press, 1989.

Kiberd, Declan. *Inventing Ireland: The Literature of the Modern Nation*. London: Vintage, 1996.

———. "Joyce's Homer, Homer's Joyce." In *A Companion to James Joyce*, edited by Richard Brown, 241–53. Oxford: Blackwell, 2008.

———. "Postcolonial Modernism?" In *Modernism and Colonialism*, edited by Richard Begam and Michael Valdez Moses, 269–87. Durham, NC: Duke University Press, 2007.

———. *"Ulysses" and Us: The Art of Everyday Living in Joyce's Masterpiece*. New York: Norton, 2009.

———. "Writers in Quarantine? The Case for Irish Studies." The Question of Tradition, *Crane Bag* 3, no. 1 (1979): 9–21.

Kidd, Colin, with David Runciman, Neal Ascherson, James Butler, T. J. Clark, Jonathan Coe, Sionaidh Douglas-Scott, Daniel Finn, Dawn Foster, Jeremy Harding, Ross McKibbin, Philippe Marlière, James Meek, Pankaj Mishra, Jan-Werner Müller, Susan Pedersen, J. G. A. Pocock, Nick Richardson, Nicholas Spice, Wolfgang Streeck, and Daniel Trilling. "Where Are We Now? Responses to the Referendum." *London Review of Books* 38, no. 14 (2016): 8–15.

Killeen, Terence. *Ulysses Unbound*. Bray: Wordwell, 2004.

Kimball, Jean. *Odyssey of the Psyche: Jungian Patterns in Joyce's "Ulysses."* Carbondale: Southern Illinois University Press, 1997.

Kintzele, Paul. "'The Urb It Orbs': James Joyce and Internationalism." *Intertexts* 16, no. 2 (Fall 2012): 55–78.

Kirk, John M., and Dónal P. Ó Baoill, eds. *Language Links: The Languages of Scotland and Ireland*. Belfast: Cló Ollscoil na Banríona, 2001.

Kitcher, Philip. *Joyce's Kaleidoscope*. Oxford: Oxford University Press, 2007.

Klein, Scott W. "National Histories, National Fictions: Joyce's *A Portrait of the Artist as a Young Man* and Scott's *The Bride of Lammermoor*." *ELH* 65, no. 4 (1998): 1017–38.

Knowles, Sebastian. Foreword to *Joyce, Ireland, Britain*, edited by Andrew Gibson and Len Platt, i–viii. Gainesville: University Press of Florida, 2006.

Koch, Ronald J. "Giordano Bruno and *Finnegans Wake*: A New Look at Shaun's Objection to the 'Nolanus Theory.'" *Finnegans Wake* issue, *James Joyce Quarterly* 9, no. 2 (Winter 1972): 237–49.

Korg, Jacob. "Polyglotism in Rabelais and *Finnegans Wake*." Joycean Possibilities, *Journal of Modern Literature* 26, no. 1 (Autumn 2002): 58–65.

Lacan, Jacques. *Ecrits*. Translated by Alan Sheridan. London: Tavistock, 1977.

——— . *The Four Fundamental Concepts of Psychoanalysis*. Translated by Alan Sheridan. London: Karnac, 1977.

Laing, Lloyd, and Jenny Laing. *The Picts and the Scots*. Stroud: Alan Sutton Publishing Limited, 1993.

Latham, Sean, ed. *The Cambridge Companion to "Ulysses."* Cambridge: Cambridge University Press, 2014.

Lawrence, Karen. *The Odyssey of Style in Ulysses*. Princeton: Princeton University Press, 1981.

Leask, Nigel. "Robert Burns." In *The Cambridge Companion to Scottish Literature*, edited by Gerard Carruthers and Liam McIlvanney, 71–85. Cambridge: Cambridge University Press, 2012.

Lee, J. J. *Ireland, 1912–1985: Politics and Society*. Cambridge: Cambridge University Press, 1989.

Lehner, Stefanie. *Subaltern Ethics in Contemporary Scottish and Irish Literature*. Basingstoke: Palgrave, 2011.

Lernout, Geert. *Help My Unbelief: James Joyce and Religion*. London: Continuum, 2010.

Lernout, Geert, and Wim Van Mierlo, eds. *The Reception of James Joyce in Europe*. 2 vols. London: Thoemmes Continuum, 2004. Levin, Harry. *James Joyce: A Critical Introduction*. Rev. ed. London: Faber and Faber, 1960.

Levine, Jennifer Schiffer. "Originality and Repetition in *Finnegans Wake* and *Ulysses*." *PMLA* 94, no. 1 (1979): 106–20.

Lévi-Strauss, Claude. *The Savage Mind*. London: Weidenfeld and Nicolson, 1972.

Lincoln, Andrew. *Walter Scott and Modernity*. Edinburgh: Edinburgh University Press, 2006.

Litz, A. Walton. *Art of James Joyce: Method and Design in "Ulysses" and "Finnegans Wake."* Oxford: Oxford University Press, 1961.

Longley, Edna. "The Whereabouts of Literature." In *Beyond Scotland: New Contexts for Twentieth-Century Scottish Literature*, edited by Gerard Carruthers, David Goldie, and Alastair Renfrew, 151–65. Amsterdam: Rodopi, 2004.

Longmore, Murray, et al., eds. *Oxford Handbook of Clinical Medicine*. 8th ed. Oxford: Oxford University Press, 2010.

Lukács, Georg. *The Historical Novel*. London: Merlin, 1974.

Lyall, Scott. *Hugh MacDiarmid's Poetry and Politics of Place: Imagining a Scottish Republic*. Edinburgh: Edinburgh University Press, 2006.

——— . "'The Man Is a Menace': MacDiarmid and Military Intelligence." *International Journal of Scottish Literature* 8, no.1 (Spring 2007): 37–52.

Lynch, Michael, ed. *The Oxford Companion to Scottish History*. Oxford: Oxford University Press, 2001.

———. *Scotland: A New History*. London: Pimlico, 1992.

MacArthur, Ian. "Some Notes for 'Ulysses.'" *James Joyce Quarterly* 41, no. 3 (2004): 523–35.

MacCabe, Colin. "*Finnegans Wake* at Fifty." *Critical Quarterly* 31, no. 4 (1989): 3–5.

———. *James Joyce and the Revolution of the Word*. New York: Macmillan, 1978.

MacDonald, Catriona M. M. *Whaur Extremes Meet: Scotland's Twentieth Century*. Edinburgh: Birlinn, 2009.

MacDonagh, Thomas. *Literature in Ireland*. New York: Frederick A. Stokes, 1916.

MacDougall, Hugh A. *Racial Myth in English History*. Hanover, NH: University Press of New England, 1982.

Mackay, Marina. "Great Britain." In *The Cambridge Companion to European Modernism*, edited by Pericles Lewis, 94–112. Cambridge: Cambridge University Press, 2011.

MacLysaght, Edward. *Irish Families*. Blackrock: Irish Academic Press, 1991.

Maguire, Peter A. "*Finnegans Wake* and Irish Historical Memory." *Journal of Modern Literature* 22, no. 2 (1998–99): 293–327.

Maley, Willy. "Ireland, Versus, Scotland: Crossing the (English) Language Barrier." In *Across the Margins: Cultural Identity and Change in the Atlantic Archipelago*, edited by Glenda Norquay and Gerry Smyth. Manchester: Manchester University Press, 2002, 13–30.

———. "'Kilt by Kelt Shell Kithagain with Kinagain': Joyce and Scotland." In *Semicolonial Joyce*, edited by Derek Attridge and Marjorie Howes, 201–18. Cambridge: Cambridge University Press, 2000.

Maley, Willy, and Rory Loughnane, eds. *Celtic Shakespeare: The Bard and the Borderers*. Farnham: Ashgate, 2013.

Maley, Willy, and Kirsty Lusk, eds. *Scotland and the Easter Rising*. Edinburgh: Luath, 2016.

Maley, Willy, and Alison O'Malley-Younger, eds. *Celtic Connections: Irish–Scottish Relations and the Politics of Culture*. Reimagining Ireland 38. Oxford: Peter Lang, 2013.

Manganiello, Dominic. *Joyce's Politics*. London: Routledge and Kegan Paul, 1980.

Mark, Colin. *Am faclair Gàidhlig-Beurla*. London: Routledge, 2003.

Marx, John. "Empire, Imperialism, and Modernism." In *A Handbook of Modernism Studies*, edited by Jean-Michel Rabaté, 107–21. Chichester: John Wiley & Sons, 2013.

Marx, Karl. *Selected Writings*. Edited by David McLellan. Oxford: Oxford University Press, 1977.

Matthews, F. X. "Festy King in 'Finnegans Wake.'" *James Joyce Quarterly* 6, no. 2 (1969): 154–57.

Mautner, Thomas, ed. *Dictionary of Philosophy*. London: Penguin, 2005.

Mays, Michael. "*Finnegans Wake*, Colonial Nonsense, and Postcolonial History." *College Literature* 25, no. 3 (Fall 1998): 20–34.

McCarthy, Patrick A. *Critical Essays on James Joyce's "Finnegans Wake."* New York: Macmillan, 1992.

———. *The Riddles of "Finnegans Wake."* Rutherford, NJ: Fairleigh Dickinson University Press, 1980.

———. "Three Approaches to Life's Robulous Rebus in the Quiz Section of *Finnegans Wake*." *Journal of Modern Literature* 5, no. 3 (September 1976): 407–35.

McClure, J. Derrick. "What's Scots?" In "Talking Scots," supplement, *Fortnight*, no. 318 (1993): 3–5.

McCourt, John, ed. "The Last of the Bardic Poets': Joyce's Multiple Mangans." In *Essays on James Clarence Mangan*, edited by Sinéad Sturgeon, 124–39. Basingstoke: Palgrave Macmillan, 2014.

———. Review of *The Strong Spirit: History, Politics, and Aesthetics in the Writings of James Joyce, 1898–1915*, by Andrew Gibson. *James Joyce Quarterly* 50, no. 3 (2013): 890–97.

———. *Roll Away the Reel World: James Joyce and Cinema*. Cork: Cork University Press, 2010.

———. *The Years of Bloom: James Joyce in Trieste, 1904–1920*. Dublin: Lilliput, 2000.

McCrea, Barry. *In the Company of Strangers: Narrative and Family in Dickens, Conan Doyle, Joyce and Proust*. New York: Columbia University Press, 2011.

McCulloch, Margery Palmer, ed. *Modernism and Nationalism: Literature and Society in Scotland, 1918–1939; Source Documents for the Scottish Renaissance*. Glasgow: Association for Scottish Literary Studies, 2004.

———. "Scottish Modernism." In *The Oxford Handbook of Modernism*, edited by Brooker et al., 765–81. Oxford: Oxford University Press, 2010.

———. *Scottish Modernism and Its Contexts, 1918–1959*. Edinburgh: Edinburgh University Press, 2009.

McDonald, Michael Bruce. "'Circe' and the Uncanny, or Joyce from Freud to Marx." *James Joyce Quarterly* 33, no. 1 (Fall 1995): 49–68.

McGarry, Fearghal. *The Rising: Ireland, Easter 1916*. Oxford: Oxford University Press, 2010.

McGee, Patrick. *Joyce beyond Marx*. Gainesville: University Press of Florida, 2001.

———. *Paperspace*. Lincoln: University of Nebraska Press, 1988.

McGuirk, Carol. *Robert Burns and the Sentimental Era*. Athens: University of Georgia Press, 1985.

McHugh, Roland. *Annotations to "Finnegans Wake."* Rev. ed. Baltimore: Johns Hopkins University Press, 1991.

———. *The "Finnegans Wake" Experience*. 3rd ed. Baltimore: Johns Hopkins University Press, 2006.

McIlvanney, Liam. *Burns the Radical*. Phantassie, East Lothian: Tuckwell Press, 2002.

———. "Robert Burns and the Ulster-Scots Literary Revival of the 1790s." *Bullán: An Irish Studies Journal* 4, no. 2 (Winter 1999 / Spring 2000): 125–43.

McIlvanney, Liam, and Ray Ryan, eds. *Ireland and Scotland: Culture and Society, 1700–2000*. Dublin: Four Courts, 2005.

McNamee, Colm. *The Wars of the Bruces: Scotland, England and Ireland, 1306–1328*. East Linton: Tuckwell Press Ltd., 1997.

McNeill, F. Marian. *The Silver Bough*. Edinburgh: Canongate, 1989.

Melchiori, Giorgio. *The Tightrope Walkers: Studies of Mannerism in Modern English Literature*. Westport, CT: Greenwood Press, 1974.

Mercanton, Jacques, and Lloyd C. Parks. "The Hours of James Joyce, Part II." *Kenyon Review* 25, no. 1 (1963): 93–118.

Millican, Peter. "Hume's Skeptical Doubts concerning Induction." In *Reading Hume on Human Understanding*, edited by P. Millican, 107–73. Oxford: Clarendon Press, 2002.

Mink, Louis O. *A "Finnegans Wake" Gazetteer*. Bloomington: Indiana University Press, 1978.

Mossner, Ernest C. Introduction to *A Treatise of Human Nature*, by David Hume, 7–28. London: Penguin, 1969.

Muir, Edwin. *Scott and Scotland: The Predicament of the Scottish Writer*. Edinburgh: Polygon, 1982.

Mulholland, James. "James Macpherson's Ossian Poems, Oral Traditions, and the Invention of Voice." *Oral Tradition* 24, no. 2 (2009): 393–414.

Munich, Adrienne Auslander. "Form and Subtext in Joyce's 'The Dead.'" *Modern Philology* 82, no. 2 (1984): 173–84.

Murray, Alex. *Giorgio Agamben*. London: Routledge, 2010.

Nabokov, Vladimir. *Lectures on Literature*. San Diego: Harcourt, 1982.

Nairn, Tom. *The Break-Up of Britain*. 2nd, exp. ed. London: Verso, 1981.

Newman, Robert D., and Weldon Thornton, eds. *Joyce's "Ulysses": The Larger Perspective*. Newark: University of Delaware Press / London: Associated University Presses, 1987.

Nolan, Emer. *James Joyce and Nationalism*. London: Routledge, 1995.

———. "State of the Art." in *Semicolonial Joyce*, edited by Derek Attridge and Marjorie Howes, 78–95. Cambridge: Cambridge University Press, 2000.

Noon, William T. *Joyce and Aquinas*. New Haven: Yale University Press, 1957.

Norris, Christopher. *Deconstruction: Theory and Practice*. London: Routledge, 1982.

Norris, Margot. *The Decentred Universe of "Finnegans Wake."* Baltimore: Johns Hopkins University Press, 1974, 1976.

O'Brien, Flann [Myles na Gopaleen, pseud.]. *The Hair of the Dogma*. London: Hart-Davis, MacGibbon, 1977.

O Hehir, Brendan. *A Gaelic Lexicon for "Finnegans Wake."* Berkeley: University of California Press, 1967.

O Hehir, Brendan, and John M. Dillon. *A Classical Lexicon for "Finnegans Wake."* Berkeley: University of California Press, 1977.

Orr, Leonard. "From High-Modern to Postcolonial Subject: An Introduction to the Political Transformation of Joyce Studies." In *Joyce, Imperialism, and Postcolonialism*, edited by Leonard Orr, 1–11. Syracuse: Syracuse University Press, 2008.

O'Toole, Fintan. "The English Have Placed a Bomb under the Irish Peace Process." *Guardian*, June 24, 2016.

———. "Three-State Union May Be Answer to Brexit." *Irish Times*, July 26, 2016.

Ó Tuairisc, Eoghan. "The Psychic Partition (1975)." *Irish Pages* 1, no. 2 (Autumn 2002 / Winter 2003): 171–73.

Parr, Adrian. *The Deleuze Dictionary*. Rev. ed. Edinburgh: Edinburgh University Press, 2010.

Parrinder, Patrick. "Science and Knowledge at the Beginning of the Twentieth Century: Versions of the Modern Enlightenment." In *The Cambridge History of Twentieth-Century English Literature*, edited by Laura Marcus and Peter Nicholls, 9–29. Cambridge: Cambridge University Press, 2012.

Perryman, Mark, ed. *Breaking Up Britain: Four Nations after a Union*. London: Lawrence and Wishart, 2009.

Pittock, Murray. *Celtic Identity and the British Image*. Manchester: Manchester University Press, 1999.

———, ed. *The Edinburgh Companion to Scottish Romanticism*. Edinburgh: Edinburgh University Press, 2011.

———. "Enlightenment, Romanticism and the Scottish Canon: Cosmopolites or Narrow Nationalists?" In *The Cambridge Companion to Scottish Literature*, edited by Gerard Carruthers and Liam McIlvanney, 66–102. Cambridge: Cambridge University Press, 2012.

———. *Poetry and Jacobite Politics in Eighteenth-Century Britain and Ireland*. Cambridge: Cambridge University Press, 1994.

———. *The Road to Independence?* London: Reaktion, 2008.

———. *Scottish Nationality*. Basingstoke: Palgrave, 2001.

Platt, Len. *Joyce and the Anglo-Irish: A Study of Joyce and the Literary Revival*. Amsterdam: Rodopi, 1998.

———. *Joyce, Race and "Finnegans Wake."* Cambridge: Cambridge University Press, 2007.

———, ed. *Modernism and Race*. Cambridge: Cambridge University Press, 2011.

———. "'Unfallable Encyclicing': *Finnegans Wake* and the *Encyclopedia Britannica*." *James Joyce Quarterly* 47, no. 1 (2009): 107–18.

Plock, V. M. "'Knock knock. War's where!': History, *Macbeth* and *Finnegans Wake*." *Joyce Studies Annual* (2006): 212–23.

Pocock, J. G. A. *The Discovery of Islands: Essays in British History*. Cambridge: Cambridge University Press, 2015.

Popkin, Richard H. *The History of Pyrrhonism from Savonarola to Bayle*. New York: Oxford University Press, 2003.

Porter, James. "'Bring Me the Head of James Macpherson': The Execution of *Ossian* and the Wellsprings of Folkloristic Discourse." *Journal of American Folklore* 114, no. 454 (Fall 2001): 396–435.

Pound, Ezra. "The Renaissance: I—The Palette." *Poetry* 5, no. 5 (February 1915): 227–34.

Quigley, Megan. "Ireland." In *The Cambridge Companion to European Modernism*, edited by Pericles Lewis, 170–90. Cambridge: Cambridge University Press, 2011.

Quinones, Ricardo J. *Mapping Literary Modernism*. Princeton: Princeton University Press, 1985.

Rabaté, Jean-Michel. *Joyce upon the Void: The Genesis of Doubt*. London: Macmillan, 1991.

Radford, Fred. "James Joyce and the Question of Historicist Desire." *James Joyce Quarterly* 33, no. 2 (1996): 271–91.

Raynor, David. "Hume and Berkeley's *Three Dialogues*." In *Studies in the Philosophy of the Scottish Enlightenment*, edited by M. A. Stewart, 231–50. Oxford: Clarendon Press, 1990.

Reaney, P. H., and R. M. Wilson, eds. *The Oxford Dictionary of English Surnames*. Oxford: Oxford University Press, 2005.

Reichenberg, Peter J. "*Finnegans Wake*: The Dating Game." *James Joyce Quarterly* 6, no. 2 (2009): 362–65.

Renan, Ernest. "What Is a Nation?" In *Nation and Narration*, edited by Homi K. Bhabha, 8–22. London: Routledge, 1990.

Riach, Alan. "Was There Ever a 'British' Literature?" In *Association for Scottish Literary Studies*, Glasgow, 2007, http://asls.arts.gla.ac.uk/Was_There_Ever.html.

Richardson, Brian. "The Genealogies of 'Ulysses,' the Invention of Postmodernism, and the Narratives of Literary History." *ELH* 67, no. 4 (Winter 2000): 1035–54.

Rikard, John S. *Joyce's Book of Memory: The Mnemotechnic of "Ulysses."* Durham, NC: Duke University Press, 1999.

Robertson, Fiona. *Legitimate Histories: Scott, Gothic and the Authority of Fiction*. Oxford: Clarendon Press, 1995.

Robichaud, Paul. "Joyce, Vico, and National Narrative." Post-Industrial Joyce, *James Joyce Quarterly* 41, no. 1/2 (2003/2004): 185–96.

———. "MacDiarmid and Muir: Scottish Modernism and the Nation as Anthropological Site." *Journal of Modern Literature* 28, no. 4 (Summer 2005): 135–51.

Robinson, Mairi, ed. *Concise Scots Dictionary*. Edinburgh: Polygon at Edinburgh, 1999.

Rose, Danis. *The Textual Diaries of James Joyce*. Dublin: Lilliput, 1995.

Rose, Danis, and John O'Hanlon. *Understanding "Finnegans Wake."* New York: Garland Publishing, 1982.

Roughley, Alan. *James Joyce and Critical Theory: An Introduction*. Hemel Hempstead: Harvester Wheatsheaf, 1991.

Russell, Bertrand. *History of Western Philosophy*. London: Routledge, 2004.

Russell, Paul. "Hume on Religion." In *Stanford Encyclopedia of Philosophy*, edited by Edward N. Zalta, Winter 2014 ed., http://plato.stanford.edu/entries/hume-religion/.

Russell, Richard Rankin. "Irish Unionism, North of Ireland Protestantism, and the Home Rule Question in Joyce's *Dubliners*." *Joyce Studies Annual* (2013): 62–94.

Ryan, Catherine. "Leopold Bloom's Fine Eats: A Good Square Meal." *James Joyce Quarterly* 25, no. 3 (1988): 378–83.

Ryan, Ray. *Ireland and Scotland: Literature and Culture, State and Nation, 1966–2000*. Oxford: Oxford University Press, 2002.

Said, Edward. *Culture and Imperialism*. London: Vintage, 1994.

———. *Orientalism*. London: Penguin, 2003.

Salmond, Alex. "Way to Unleash the True Potential of Scotland." *Glasgow Herald*, April 23, 1997.

Sandison, Alan. *Robert Louis Stevenson and the Appearance of Modernism: A Future Feeling*. London: Macmillan, 1996.

Schultz, Matthew. "'Arise, Sir Ghostus!' Textual Spectrality and *Finnegans Wake*." *James Joyce Quarterly* 49, no. 2 (Winter 2012): 281–95.

Scott, Paul H. *Still in Bed with an Elephant*. Edinburgh: Saltire Society, 1998.

Scottish National Party. *Manifesto 2016*. Website of the Scottish National Party. 2016. http://www.snp.org/manifesto.

Senn, Fritz. *Inductive Scrutinies: Focus on Joyce*. Dublin: Lilliput, 1995.

———. *Joyce's Dislocutions: Essays on Reading as Translation*. Baltimore: Johns Hopkins University Press, 1984.

———. "Ossianic Echoes." *A Wake Newslitter*, n.s., 3, no. 2 (1966): 25–36.

Sidorsky, David. "The Historical Novel as the Denial of History: From 'Nestor' via the 'Vico Road' to the Commodius Vicus of Recirculation." Reexamining Critical Processing, *New Literary History* 32, no. 2 (Spring 2001): 301–26.

Smidt, Kristian. "'I'm Not Half Norawain for Nothing': Joyce and Norway." *James Joyce Quarterly* 26, no. 3 (Spring 1989): 333–50.

Smith, Anthony D. *Nationalism and Modernism*. London: Routledge, 1998.

Smith, G. Gregory. *Scottish Literature: Its Character and Influence*. London: Macmillan and Co., 1919.

Smith, Janet Adam. "Some 18th Century Ideas of Scotland." In *Scotland in the Age of Improvement*, edited by N. T. Phillipson and Rosalind Mitchison (Edinburgh: Edinburgh University Press, 1970), 108–13.

Sollers, Philippe. "Joyce and Co." Translated by Stephen Heath. *Tel Quel*, no. 64 (Winter 1975): 3–13.

Spufford, Francis. "Dialects." *London Review of Books* 9, no. 7 (1987): 23.

Stafford, Fiona. Introduction to *The Poems of Ossian and Related Works*, by James Macpherson, v–xix. Edited by Howard Gaskill. Edinburgh: Edinburgh University Press, 1996.

———. *The Sublime Savage: A Study of James Macpherson and the Poems of Ossian*. Edinburgh: Edinburgh University Press, 1988.

Stanistreet, Paul. *Hume's Scepticism and the Science of Human Nature*. Aldershot: Ashgate, 2002.

Stevenson, Randall. *Literature and the Great War*. Oxford: Oxford University Press, 2013.

———. "A Postmodern Scotland?" in *Beyond Scotland: New Contexts for Twentieth-Century Scottish Literature*, edited by Gerard Carruthers et al., 209–28. Amsterdam: Rodopi, 2004.

Stewart, A. T. Q. *The Narrow Ground: Aspects of Ulster, 1609–1969*. London: Faber and Faber, 1989.

Stone, Harry. "'Araby' and the Writings of James Joyce." *Antioch Review* 25, no. 3 (1965): 375–410.

Stroud, Barry. "Hume's Skepticism: Natural Instincts and Philosophical Reflection." *Philosophical Topics* 19 (1991): 271–91.

Sturgeon, Sinéad. "Night Singer: Mangan among the Birds." In *Essays on James Clarence Mangan*, edited by Sinéad Sturgeon, 102–23. Basingstoke: Palgrave Macmillan, 2014.

Swartzlander, Susan. "Multiple Meaning and Misunderstanding: The Mistrial of Festy King." *James Joyce Quarterly* 23, no. 4 (1986): 465–76.

Swinson, Ward. "Macpherson in *Finnegans Wake*." *A Wake Newslitter*, n.s., 9, no. 5 (1972): 89–95.

Syrotinski, Michael. *Deconstruction and the Postcolonial*. Liverpool: Liverpool University Press, 2007.

Thomas, Ronald R. "In the Company of Strangers: Absent Voices in Stevenson's *Dr. Jekyll and Mr. Hyde* and Beckett's *Company*." *Modern Fiction Studies* 32, no. 2 (Summer 1986): 157–73.

Thomson, Derick S. *The Gaelic Sources of Macpherson's Ossian*. Edinburgh: Oliver and Boyd, 1952.

Thurston, Luke. *James Joyce and the Problem of Psychoanalysis*. Cambridge: Cambridge University Press, 2004.

———. "Scotographia: Joyce and Psychoanalysis." In *A Companion to James Joyce*, edited by Richard Brown, 407–26. Oxford: Blackwell, 2008.

Tindall, William York. *A Reader's Guide to "Finnegans Wake."* Syracuse, NY: Syracuse University Press, 1969.

Tóibín, Colm. "After I Am Hanged My Portrait Will Be Interesting." *London Review of Books* 38, no. 7 (2016): 11–23.

———. "Joyce's Dublin: City of Dreamers and Chancers." *Guardian*, Friday, June 15, 2012.

Tymoczko, Maria. *The Irish Ulysses*. Berkeley: University of California Press, 1994.

Van Hulle, Dirk, ed. *James Joyce: The Study of Languages*. Brussels: Peter Lang, 2002.

———. "Modernism, Mind, and Manuscripts." In *A Handbook of Modernism Studies*, edited by Jean-Michel Rabaté, 225–38. Chichester: John Wiley & Sons, 2013.

Vickery, John B. "*Finnegans Wake* and Sexual Metamorphosis." *Contemporary Literature* 13, no. 2 (Spring 1972): 213–42.

———. *The Literary Impact of "The Golden Bough."* Princeton: Princeton University Press, 1973.

Voelker, Joseph. "The Beastly Incertitudes: Doubt, Difficulty, and Discomfiture in James Joyce's 'Exiles.'" *Journal of Modern Literature* 14, no. 4 (Spring 1988): 499–516.

Wallace, Gavin, and Randall Stevenson, eds. *The Scottish Novel since the Seventies: New Visions, Old Dreams.* Edinburgh: Edinburgh University Press, 1993.

Watson, George. "Aspects of Celticism." In *Ireland and Scotland: Culture and Society, 1700–2000*, edited by Liam McIlvanney and Ray Ryan, 129–43. Dublin: Four Courts, 2005.

———. "Scottish Culture and the Lost Past." *Irish Review*, no. 9 (Spring 1991): 35–44.

Watson, Roderick. *The Literature of Scotland.* Basingstoke: Macmillan, 1984.

Waxman, Wayne. *Hume's Theory of Consciousness.* Cambridge: Cambridge University Press, 1994.

Whelan, Kevin. "The Memories of 'The Dead.'" *Yale Journal of Criticism* 15, no. 1 (2002): 59–97.

Whyte, Christopher. *Modern Scottish Poetry.* Edinburgh: Edinburgh University Press, 2004.

Williams, Trevor L. *Reading Joyce Politically.* Gainesville: University Press of Florida, 1997.

Winkler, Kenneth. "Hume's Inductive Skepticism." In *The Empiricists: Critical Essays on Locke, Berkeley, and Hume*, edited by M. Atherton, 183–212. Lanham, MD: Rowman and Littlefield, 1999.

Winston, Greg. *Joyce and Militarism.* Gainesville: University Press of Florida, 2012.

Wittig, Kurt. *The Scottish Tradition in Literature.* Westport, CT: Greenwood Press, 1958.

Woolf, Alex. *From Pictland to Alba.* Edinburgh: Edinburgh University Press, 2007.

Worthington, Mabel P. "American Folk Songs in Joyce's *Finnegans Wake.*" *American Literature* 28, no. 2 (1956): 197–210.

Yenor, Scott. "Between Rationalism and Postmodernism: Hume's Political Science of Our 'Mixed Kind of Life.'" *Political Research Quarterly* 55, no. 2 (June 2002): 329–50.

Young, Robert J. C. *Postcolonialism.* Oxford: Blackwell, 2001.

Žižek, Slavoj. *Less Than Nothing: Hegel and the Shadow of Dialectical Materialism.* London: Verso, 2012.

INDEX

RICHARD BARLOW is an assistant professor of English at Nanyang Technological University, Singapore.

CPSIA information can be obtained
at www.ICGtesting.com
Printed in the USA
LVOW12*0318130217
523909LV00002BA/11/P